OUR TIMES
VOLUME VI

CALVIN COOLIDGE

FROM THE PAINTING BY PHILIP DE LASZLO

MARK SULLIVAN

OUR TIMES

1900-1925

Introduction by Dewey W. Grantham

VI
The Twenties

New York

CHARLES SCRIBNER'S SONS

A-2.72(MH)

Printed in the United States of America

SBN 684-12524-2

Library of Congress Catalog Card Number 70-138308

INTRODUCTION TO VOLUME VI
THE TWENTIES

This is the sixth and final volume of Mark Sullivan's popular history of the United States during the first quarter of the twentieth century.* It is the work of a discerning contemporary and an experienced journalist. Although entitled "The Twenties," it is largely concerned with the years 1919-1925. The political coverage, which forms the first part of the book, and the year-by-year chapters taken up with the listing of ephemeral events, which comprise the last section, are confined to that period. Only in the two long chapters on literature and popular songs do the later years of the 1920's receive much attention. As a narrative the volume is strongest in dealing with the immediate postwar years and with the Harding administration.

The first half of "The Twenties" is devoted to national politics—to the election of 1920, the emergence of Warren Gamaliel Harding, the Harding regime, the death of the President, the scandals and corruption that stained the administration's record, and the early presidency of Calvin Coolidge. Sullivan's intimate knowledge of national issues and personalities is evident in his treatment of the politics of normalcy. He uses the images of public figures as a means of recapturing popular views and emotions. As in other volumes of *Our Times*, he relies upon the testimony of participants and close observers. He illustrates his method by describing his handling of Harding's

---

* A more comprehensive discussion of Mark Sullivan and the writing of *Our Times* is contained in the general introduction to Volume I of this edition.

nomination, noting that many of the major influences and decisions in bringing that nomination about were never matters of written record. "The method of writing history which combines the formal records with the recollections of participants and eye-witnesses," Sullivan insisted, "results in greater accuracy than any other." This procedure, he believed, would enable the historian to screen out errors, to correct distortions, to destroy legends. He cited as an example his own discovery that, contrary to contemporary impression, Senator Boies Penrose of Pennsylvania had not played a dominant role in the nomination of Warren G. Harding. Although recent historians have probed much more deeply than Sullivan did into the inner recesses of the political culture of the early twenties, his accounts of such developments as the election of 1920 and the controversy over Teapot Dome are vivid, informative, and pervaded with the atmosphere of the time.

Sullivan's personal correspondence provides many illustrations of his penetrating evaluations of the events he later chronicled in *Our Times*. He wrote a friend in December, 1919, for example, that the feeling in Washington at that time was "rather strong that Harding will come out big in the last quarter." The Old Guard, continued the journalist, "want a neutral and easy-going personality in the White House, and Harding would suit them perfectly." Again, in early February, 1921, Sullivan revealed his misgivings about President-elect Harding and certain members of his Cabinet. "We will have to assume," he wrote, "that Harding is a man whose impulses are good and right, but so weak that he permits himself to be worried and argued out of those impulses by Old Guard politicians who have no impulses at all but know exactly what they want all the time." The selection of Harry M. Daugherty as the new Attorney General struck Sullivan as a "very bad" appointment, and he suspected that Albert B. Fall, the choice for Secretary of the Interior, was "a good deal of a bad egg, especially for that particular job in which he is supposed to be the custodian of the public property as against private interests who want to acquire it."

Nevertheless, Sullivan had supported Harding in 1920, and he approved of the back-to-normalcy movement. In reviewing an earlier volume of *Our Times*, the historian John D. Hicks expressed the opinion that, as his series unfolded, Sullivan might eventually become "the official apologist of Coolidge prosperity and Hoover adversity." This volume confirmed Hick's suspicions. "There is something immensely revealing," he wrote in his review of Volume VI, "in the fact that Mark Sullivan in his youth was the ardent champion of Roosevelt progressivism, but in his maturity cooled off to the point where the normalcy of Harding, the frigidity of Coolidge, and the stoicism of Hoover seemed to bring complete satisfaction to his soul." It is probably true that Sullivan became more conservative as he grew older, and at the time he wrote this concluding volume of his history, he was a vigorous critic of Franklin D. Roosevelt and the New Deal. Yet it can be argued, as Otis L. Graham does in his study of old progressives and the New Deal, *An Encore for Reform*, that Sullivan continued to believe in the principles and ideals of his youthful insurgency—in short, that he had changed far less than the times. In any case, Sullivan is not an apologist for the Harding administration. He tells the story of the Ohio Gang and of the sordid side of Harding's presidency. At the same time, he shows his respect for Harding and makes a case for the administration's constructive actions. In some respects his account of the

Harding era forecast the reappraisal recently made by Robert K. Murray in *The Harding Era: Warren G. Harding and His Administration.*

Sullivan's chronicle of politics during the days of Harding and Coolidge is readable, frequently dramatic, and sometimes original in interpretation. But it is sketchy in many places, and some important aspects of the political scene—such as the Muscle Shoals controversy—are dealt with in cursory fashion. There are some minor errors. For example, Harding was the sixth, not the fifth President to die in office; Alfred E. Smith was governor of New York four rather than three times; and woman suffrage was the nineteenth, not the twentieth amendment to the United States Constitution. Such mistakes are few, however, and they do not diminish the general reliability of this engrossing narrative.

The careful reader of *Our Times* will detect a subtle change in the author's outlook in the last two volumes of the series. That shift is most apparent in this concluding volume. Sullivan, it appears, is less at home in the postwar America than he was in the earlier period, and his aversion to some of the new directions in the national life occasionally manifests itself. It is more difficult for him to keep the changes he associates with progress in equilibrium with the elements of stability he associates with the traditional American values. "The decade was cordial to change," he observes wryly, and "at times seemed to prefer strangers to old friends."

Sullivan shared in the new sense of insecurity and disillusionment that many Americans experienced after 1918 —the "mood of exasperation, of expectations unfulfilled, of high emotion trickling out to disappointment." In the brief analysis of the postwar mentality with which "The Twenties" opens and in a later chapter on the tumultuous social scene in 1919 and 1920, Sullivan describes the shock of change that nourished the reaction of the period. He examines the "war books" of the 1920's for their reflection of the decade's disillusionment. But he discusses the "Younger Generation" as well as the "Lost Generation," and in his consideration of novels, plays, poetry, the Jazz Age, and the rebellion of youth he suggests many of the new points of view that were helping shape the postwar era. He also presents a long chapter on popular tunes as "a facet of the times."

The second half of this volume lacks the coherence of the first half and is interesting largely as a repository of songs, stories, books, plays, and crazes. Many social and cultural developments of the period are neglected, including the Ku Klux Klan and other manifestations of intolerance, the anti-evolution crusade, prohibition, behaviorism, and the radio as a new instrumentality for the diffusion of culture through modern society. Nor does Sullivan give much attention to the economic accomplishments and ideas of the New Era, even though they appeared to justify his faith in material progress. Yet despite their fragmentary nature and disordered structure, the social and cultural sections of this volume help make it an intriguing book, a shrewd and audacious attempt to bring history up to the present and to redefine it to include the fashions and fads, the songs and sensations of ordinary people.

The publication of this volume marked the successful completion of Sullivan's imaginative scheme "to follow an average American through this quarter-century of his country's history." "No other American historian who has written of these days," asserted William Allen White in a review of the first volume of *Our Times*, "has devoted himself so passionately to the thesis that history is the story of the changes in the hearts of the people; not the story of those who do the ornamental standing around, those who wear the gold braid." This was doubtless one reason for the warm reception *Our Times* received from Americans in the 1920's and 1930's. But the grandiose scale of the work, the panoramic sweep of its narrative, the catholicity and diversity of its content, and the apparent relevancy of its splendid evocation of the immediate past also contributed to the appeal the series had for this generation. For our own times, Mark Sullivan's sprawling history is important as a compilation of valuable raw materials and as a source for an understanding of the first quarter of the twentieth century in the United States. It is a mirror that reflects a fascinating and sharply-etched image of an earlier America.

Dewey W. Grantham
Vanderbilt University

CONTENTS

ILLUSTRATIONS

xv

ILLUSTRATIONS xix

The Twenties

1

THE WORLD IN 1920

Changes That Had Been Wrought by the War. And Other
Conditions That Had Been Wrought by the Peace Conference, Which Was in Some Respects as Damaging to Stability as the War Had Been. The Whole Being, Roughly, an
Outline of the World as It Was When the Twenties Began.

OF all the nostalgic longing for the past that man has
experienced since theology first taught him to look back
toward Eden, hardly any was greater than the homesickness with which much of the world of 1920 looked
back toward the world of 1914, in vain. That homesickness was responsible for many of the votes that Warren G. Harding got when he ran for President of the
United States in 1920; of all the speeches he made in
his campaign, the three words that most appealed to the
mood of the country, the one phrase for which he was
most applauded, was "back to normalcy."

Yet the wish, as the average man felt it, as it arose
from his particular circumstances, was not for the return of any specifically visualized time or scene; rather
it was a discontent with the post-war commotion, the
turbulence and unsettlement, that surrounded him and
fretted him; it was a wish for settled ways, for conditions that remained the same long enough to become
familiar and therefore dear, for routine that remained
set, for a world that "stayed put." It was a yearning
for "the time of peace wherein we trusted" — not meaning merely for peace in the sense of absence of war, but
for peace in the sense of serenity, for a state of things

in which it was possible to feel trust, to rely upon permanence.

As always, under the worst of circumstances, the average American kept some humor for the condition that beset him. He had a phrase for it. The phrase was used in a spirit of tolerant resignation; it denoted acceptance of conditions that were extraordinary, unreasonable and contrary to common sense — but which, nevertheless, were. Any one who found conditions taking some course that was unprecedented and inexplicable — and the occasions were many — conveyed his sense of disagreement, accompanied by enforced tolerance, in a phrase which was not so much a resentful epithet as a baffled acknowledgment of what could not be denied, a, so to speak, verbal shrug of the shoulders, a resigned shaking of the head, "the cock-eyed world."

Yet if we were to describe the state of the world after the Great War as frivolous slang described it, in terms of physical defect, we should be obliged to use terms implying greater infirmity than a mere congenital misdirection of one of the organs of vision. Hardly even was Shakespeare's phrase enough, "the time is out of joint." The world was, if we must use this kind of analogy, half-blind, half-deaf, and chronically dazed.

But if we are to picture the world of after the war in terms of similitude to a defective human being, we ought to use the terminology, not of congenital deformity, but of wound, for wound was mainly what had happened. To say, as cartoonists did, that the world walked on crutches, with its arm in a sling, and that it had besides several dislocated ribs and a fractured skull — all that would be a mild portrayal of the degree of temporary decrepitude in which the war left the world. We should add, that it was shell-shocked besides; that term, as an item in a description of the post-war world, would be no figure of speech, it would be literal, the condition was patent.

Even that was not the whole of it. "Wounds" may be a convenient expedient with which to describe what had happened to the world. But to imply that the world was merely suffering from injuries, which could be restored, would be to mislead, seriously. Some were wounds, curable by the beneficent processes of nature or by the intelligence of man, if that should happily be present, in sufficient quantity and in the right places. But some of what had occurred was fundamental alteration, from which we would never go back.

To assemble an adequate account of the world as it was about 1920, we should have to talk with Atlas. That venerable figure must have had an anxious time from about 1914 on. Not that his burden weighed any more, but it had become subject to extremely fitful departures from equilibrium. Up to 1914, Atlas, one supposes, by taking care to spread his legs well apart, and perhaps steadying himself with his hand against a pillar, could safely have dozed on his feet. The world was heavy, but it stayed still. Beginning about 1914, however, the world developed what must have struck Atlas as an alarming susceptibility to going off-balance, a tendency to sudden starts and plunges and tremors. Lack of equilibrium was the largest single cause of the world's confusion.

But let us be literal. Let us list, partially, the changes that had taken place in the world during some seven years prior to March 4, 1921, when Harding became head of its leading country. The process of identifying the changes might be conceived as an exercise in arithmetic: Take the world as it was in 1921, and subtract

from it the world as it was in 1914 — the difference
would be the changes that had occurred between. But
perhaps it should be the other way 'round; it may be
that of the two the world of 1914 was the larger, or at
least the more amply satisfactory; hence the process
should consist in subtracting 1921 from 1914. In any
event, let us set the two side by side and observe the differences; the operation, supplemented with the benefit
of hind-sight, will enable us to see what were the conditions facing the statesmen of the world at the time
Harding became head of its most powerful nation. It is
not enough to say merely that the world had endured the
greatest war of all time; that statement resounds oratorically to the ear, but does not help us to know what statesmen were called upon to take account of, or ought to
have taken account of had they been more nearly om-
niscient than any of them turned out to be. We must
identify the respects in which the world had changed,
at least the more important of them:

II

A World Out of Balance

Of all the changes there was one that went deepest,
and included many of the others. Preceding the Great
War, the world had had a status, an equilibrium. Fundamental in that status — and fundamental in the status
of the world during almost every period — was the
existence of one nation more powerful than any of the
others. For more than a century this position had been
occupied by Britain, latest in a long and colorful line
of dominating nations that went back through France
and Spain and Holland all the way to Tyre.

The rôle of a dominating nation includes giving stability to the status quo; the status quo may be desirable or not, relative to past periods or succeeding ones; whatever the status quo is, the mere fact of the existence of one dominating nation tends to give it balance, and preserve it.

Britain had filled the rôle in a larger variety of ways than most of its predecessors. For upward of a hundred years Britain, to an increasing degree, had provided the world with most of its fabric of international trade; had supplied the unit of currency, the pound or the gold sovereign, in which most international transactions were carried on; had been the richest nation and the greatest lending nation, source and storehouse of most of the accumulated capital with which development of the world was carried on; had possessed the largest number of mercantile ships, and accompanying them, the most powerful navy; had kept order in many parts of the world; had been the source of international law, and the final authority under it — at all times, international law, in practice, consists of such concessions of power to enlightenment as the nation having the most powerful navy is willing to make. Britain had been the source of most of the ideas that the rest of the world was increasingly accepting — the English language and the Anglo-Saxon conception of jurisprudence were constantly spreading; spreading also was the British conception of government, maximum of liberty for the individual, minimum of power of government over the individual. In sum, Britain, measured by power of arms, power of wealth and power of ideas, was the center about which the world, in most respects, revolved.

This position, Germany envied. Germany called it the "place in the sun," coveted it and tried to take it. She had not succeeded, but she had weakened Britain seriously. In 1920 (and up to the year in which this history is written) it was uncertain whether there was any one leading nation. To that lack was due much of the chaos that the world suffered. When a leadership long held by one nation ceases, and there is failure of any other nation to step into the succession, a period of chaos appears historically to be the rule. This accounts for the frequency with which scholars and statesmen apprehensively compared the period following the Great War to the period following the fall of Rome — predictions of a new Dark Ages, a prolonged interruption of civilization, were common during the 1920's, and came from exalted sources.

In the course of nature, America should have stepped into Britain's vacated dominance. We emerged from the war by far the world's richest and most powerful nation. By analogy to what had happened in past eras, we should have become the most important mercantile nation, become the greatest lender, put the dollar in the place of the pound in international trade, built the largest navy, and accepted the rôle that fate thrust toward us. But America did not care for the power, or did not know how to use it; she did not take the responsibility.

For a time, the world considered a proposal that no longer should there be any dominant nation, no longer should the world be organized on a basis of, so to speak, national individualism; that instead we should have a federated world, a League of Nations. That, too, America rejected.

The result was two fundamental, world-embracing uncertainties. We did not know whether the world was to go forward on the basis of federation, or on the old basis of national individualism. And if the latter, we did not know which was the dominating nation, did not indeed know if there was to be a dominating nation. Any status, long preserved, gives sense of security. Any abrupt change to a different status brings sense of insecurity. When the change is from a long stable status to no status at all, the sense of insecurity is greater, and tends to increase.

Out of this condition, more than any other, arose the confusion, and the apprehensions of worse, that bedeviled the world in 1920 and for at least fifteen years following.

III

New Concepts of Government

Associated with this cause of insecurity was another. There had come into the world a new conception of society and government. In Russia, some aggressive exponents of new thought about society, taking advantage of chaos arising out of collapse of the old régime, imposed on that country a conception of government that not only was novel but ran counter to every pattern of society the world had ever experienced. The new ideal of society denied most of the things which governments are founded to secure; it denied the right of the individual to own property; it denied practically every right of the individual — the individual had no privilege or right that the state was bound to respect; it denied the validity of many of the social and family relationships that in other countries were sanctified; it denied religion, it not merely denied the right of the individual to practice religion according to his conscience or tradition, it actually barred the existence of religion, extirpated it.

The nation in which this new conception of society was set up had some 170 million people; measured by man-power and resources it was the most potentially powerful unified nation in the world. If this nation should choose to arm, it could be a formidable contender for the position Britain had lost, which America put aside, and which now was vacant. To this, actually, the leaders of Russia aspired; they began energetic efforts to cause the rest of the world to accept their theory of society.

Additional causes, or details, of the confusion that beset the world in 1920 included:

Every great trade-route in the world had been interrupted; many completely paralyzed. Some would never recover, at least not within any foreseeable future, for the nations which were the termini of them had been so reduced in commercial power that the trade of the world would have to beat new paths, determined by the new relations of the nations to each other. It was as if the whole web of international trade, patiently woven through centuries, composed of sea-lanes intricately criss-crossing, had sunk beneath the water, and must be re-woven. By another figure of speech, these trade-routes were the links which bound the world together, and now many of them had been broken.

The currencies of the principal nations of the world were either in process of devaluation or were destined to be devalued, even the currency of the United States. Among other effects, these changes in the values of currencies, taking place in differing ratios in different countries, made international commerce difficult, accentuated the disruption of trade-routes.

The wealth of the world had been destroyed to a degree almost immeasurable. For periods of eighteen months to four years, in most cases the latter, all the great nations had concentrated their energies upon the destruction of the wealth of the others. Much tangible wealth had been ruined, and that part of wealth which consisted of goods in motion, goods in transit and in process — civilization as a "going concern" — had been ruined to an even greater extent.[1]

Every great nation had borrowed enormous amounts. The money had been borrowed not for the normal, fruitful purpose of creating more wealth; not even had it been borrowed for purposes of mere waste; it had been borrowed for the direct, affirmative purpose of destruction, of bringing it about that there should be less wealth in the world. The borrowings were beyond any possible capacity of the borrowers to repay.[2]

Three great nations,[3] and some smaller ones, had passed through revolutions in their forms of government.

One great nation, Austria-Hungary, had been disrupted. Parts of it had been set up as political entities which did not have the economic basis to make their political autonomy possible.

Elsewhere throughout Europe, new nations, and new autonomies and hegemonies, had been set up, with new economic structures which, in many cases, had not the basis to endure. The number of separate nations in Europe when the World War began was 17; at the end the number was 26.

---

[1] The cost of the World War was set at $337,946,179,657 in a book published by the Carnegie Endowment for International Peace, containing the results of an investigation made by Professor E. L. Bogert of the Department of Economics of the University of Illinois. Loss of life from all causes was set at 9,998,771, which was more than twice the loss of all the wars of the nineteenth century from Napoleon down to 1914. Direct costs were set at 186 billions and indirect ones at 151 billions. "The very breakdown of modern economic society" was given as a still further price that the war might exact.

[2] As it turned out, none did repay in full. If it be objected that the United States did not default on its war-time borrowings (in this case from its own people) the answer is that the United States did default. For its war-time borrowings the United States gave promises to repay "in gold dollars of the present standard." That is, in gold dollars weighing 25.8 grains. In 1933, the United States reduced its dollar to $15\frac{5}{21}$ grains and compelled its citizens to accept the smaller dollars in payment of the billions of war-time (Liberty) bonds still outstanding.

A few small nations, conspicuously Finland, met their obligations in full.

[3] Russia, Germany, Austria.

A wholly new conception of government had secured
a foothold in the world, Communism in Russia. And the
condition was such that yet another new conception,
Fascism, was destined to emerge[4] in Italy, to be followed, after ten years, by Nazism[5] in Germany.

In all the leading nations, ancient moral concepts had
been shattered. Youths who in home and Sunday school
had been taught that murder is sin, had now been re-
taught that murder is virtuous if done by sanction of the
state. This was merely the most vivid of many examples
of ancient moral standards for individuals coming into
conflict with different moral standards for the state.
Everywhere the tendency was for the state standards of
morals to supplant the individual ones.

By the years of war-strain, the peoples of every great
nation (especially the European ones) had been made
spiritually and intellectually abnormal. (I use the word
"abnormal" as meaning different from what had been,
under previous conditions, normal.) The effect of the
strain was greatest on growing children; consequently it
would affect the peoples for many years to come. In one
nation, Germany, the war-strain was intensified, and the
effect on children increased, by malnutrition, by lack of
sufficient food, or of the right kinds of food. The two,
emotional war-strain and physical malnutrition, would
make the nations suffering from them, so soon as the
war-time children should be adults, likely to be in some
degree neurotic.

IV

The altered conditions came not only as a direct consequence of the war. After the war had come the peace

[4] In 1922.   [5] In 1932.

treaty, as after death comes judgment. The peace treaty had sought to put a strait jacket on the changed world, had sought to "freeze" it as it was, and had thereby made impossible whatever might have been the healing courses that nature would have taken. The peace treaty had fixed national boundaries that did not conform to nature; had imposed on the principal loser in the war, Germany, reparations she could not possibly pay, and had forbidden the exchanges of goods with which any large degree of payment could be made.

Using the hypothetical reparations as a base, the victorious nations fixed, among themselves, intergovernment obligations which must be defaulted so soon as Germany should default.

v

Changes in America

Some of the changes were peculiar to America. We were affected, of course, by the universal changes, more affected than we were intelligent enough to see, or flexible enough to admit. But some of the changes had greater application to us than others, and some were local to us.

America, like other nations, had gone deep into debt. In 1914 our national debt was $1,188,235,400; in 1921 it was $23,976,250,608.

Our economic structure had been seriously warped (though for the time being made seemingly more powerful). We had greatly enlarged and speeded up our factory capacity, first to supply the war needs of Europe, and later our own; as a result our capacity to produce was greatly beyond our peace-time capacity to consume, and greater than we could find markets for abroad, so soon as the other nations should return to normal production.

Similarly our agricultural production had been stimulated and greatly expanded to feed the peoples of warring nations who previously had been supported by their own fields, and now would again turn to their home acres. In the process (and for other causes associated with the war) prices of farm products and farm land, especially the latter, had risen to fantastic heights. This had been attended by much buying of land at prices the land would not be able to support so soon as prices for crops should descend to normal. In the speculative buying, great quantities of mortgages had been given, which would be impossible to pay so soon as prices of crops should fall.

America had ceased to be a debtor nation and become a creditor one, had paid off some three billions which before the war it had owed to Europe, and assumed a creditor relation in which Europe owed America some ten billions. That reversal of position rendered it necessary that other changes, far-reaching ones, should be made in our relations with the world, and in our domestic economy, changes which required reversals in many of our ways of thinking about trade. The reversals of thought, it turned out, were difficult to make, and were not made soon enough.

Every male in America between 18 and 45 had been registered for the army; some four millions had actually been taken into military camps and nearly half sent abroad. The psychological effect of this experience varied, of course, with the temperaments of the men. Large numbers who previously had accepted and practised, each according to his limitation, the American ideal of self-help and reliance upon individual initiative, had learned, through their army experience, to prefer a status in which decision is made for them, their routine of life prescribed for them, their needs provided for; they had learned to like immunity from responsibility, to prefer regimentation.

The war had accelerated the economic and social ferment that is always at work in America; had wrought a change in the status of large numbers of persons, whole groups and classes of them. There was a "new rich" side by side with a "new poor." By war-time inflation the purchasing power of the dollar sunk from a normal 100 to 45. Those who had fixed incomes, who lived upon the returns from bonds, mortgages and rents — and these had been a large portion of the wealthy — had become the "new poor." Their fate was shared by those who lived on fixed salaries, government employees, school teachers, college professors — all these were reduced in economic status. The "new rich" were those whose wealth was in lands, goods, shares in corporations, and who therefore profited by the rise in prices. To a degree not very significant the "new rich" included labor, whose wages rose greatly. This dislocation of groups from former economic and social positions was, as always happens with changes in the value of money, a cause of much discontent. The former rich, those of them who lived on income from bonds, had been, to some degree, the custodians of culture, and of standards of manners. With their lapse from economic elevation, their standards came to have less authority. Reduction in the real income of college teachers — who continued to receive the same salaries but found themselves unable to live as amply, who found in many cases artisans able to live better — was one of the causes of a questioning of the American form of society which became common among intellectuals during the 1920's.

VI

I have been speaking of changes that had accompanied the Great War, changes that had occurred during some seven years preceding 1921. These were accentuated and made more difficult to meet by another group of changes. The latter group were the advanced stages of developments that had been under way, with cumulative force, for decades preceding. We can conveniently suggest them by the device of making a partial list of the innovations and inventions, mainly scientific and mechanical ones, that had come into the world during the life-time of the man who became President of the United States in 1921. Harding had been born in 1865. In the year in which he became President he was 55 years old. During that half-century and a little more, greater changes had come into the world than in all recorded time previously. The things which in the year of Harding's birth did not exist, but which in the year of his inauguration were as commonplace as the weather, make a list which is the picture of more than a changed world, almost a new one.

Within Harding's life-time had come electric power, with electric light and all its other manifestations. In the year of his birth, the only sources of power available to man (other than his own muscles and beasts of burden) had been the wind, falling water, and steam — and the steam engine was still crude. When Harding was born, there had been no gas power or oil power — the first oil well was only six years old. During Harding's life-time had come all the devices for transmission of the human voice — the telephone had been invented in 1875 and by 1921 was universal in America; Harding during his Presidency would participate in a ceremony initiating the first under-sea telephone. The radio, in 1921, was being developed to the stage of practicability — Harding's successor in the Presidency would deliver his inaugural speech direct to the whole nation. Within Harding's life-time had come the motion-picture, fruitful agency for the rapid dissemination of information and ideas. At the time of Harding's birth there had been no transcontinental railroad; had Harding as a child been taken from Ohio overland to California, part of the journey would have been by covered wagon. Within Harding's life-time had come the automobile and the airplane. Harding had been seven years old when, in 1872, Jules Verne entertained Europe and America with a fantasy of the impossible, "Around the World in Eighty Days"; by 1921, with the airplane, it was possible to circle the globe in less than ten days.

These innovations in the material world had many effects. The one appropriate to point out here is the increased rapidity of communication as respects both goods and ideas. The world had been made smaller, peoples and nations brought closer together. A result, one of the many important ones, was that dislocation at any point would more quickly and more surely bring repercussions elsewhere. Whoever was head of the United States would be obliged to take account of, and be to some degree at the mercy of, developments in the state of the world outside the United States. The area of what could be called purely domestic affairs was narrowed; domestic affairs and foreign relations tended almost to merge with each other.

2

HARDING AND DAUGHERTY

Being an Account of a Meeting between Two Men, Which
Took Place About the Turn of the Century. And the Con-
sequences, Personally Dramatic and Publicly Important,
Which Resulted from This Chance Encounter. The Am-
bition Which Arose in One of the Two, for the Other and for
Himself. The Persistence, Audacity and Resourcefulness
with Which One of the Men Promoted the Political Fortunes
of the Other. Harding Rises to Comfortable Affluence as a
Small-town Newspaper Publisher, and Later Goes to the
United States Senate. Daugherty Pursues an Adventurous
Career in the Twilight Zone Between Politics and Law.
Daugherty Pushes Harding "Off His Log" and "Makes
Him Swim, first to the Senate, then Farther."

THE place was a little town in Ohio, its small population enlarged for the day by a Republican campaign
meeting. The bustle of the event centred about the
town's hotel. This, like most small-town hotels of the
time and section, had a tiny back yard, a few square yards
of grassless earth. To the eye, the clutter of it was distasteful; its dankness offended the nostrils. As deposi-
tory of the débris of hotel operation, crates of empty
bottles and cans of refuse from the table sprawled on
the back porch and along the decaying wooden fence.
As the arena for the less public functions of caravansary
life, it was not, in the days before modern plumbing, a
place where men would choose to go, or linger, except
for the conveniences it housed.

On a morning about the turn of the century, two men
were present. (There was also the bootblack, but the
bootblack and his stand figure in this history merely as

the place where the two principals became acquainted.)
One of the two was already receiving his morning shine.
The other, awaiting his turn, observed, from the corner
of his eye, the occupant of the chair.

He was worth looking at. He was at this time about
35 years old. His head, features, shoulders and torso
had a size that attracted attention; their proportions to
each other made an effect which in any male at any
place would justify more than the term handsome — in
later years, when he came to be known beyond his local
world, the word "Roman" was occasionally used in descriptions of him. As he stepped down from the stand,
his legs bore out the striking and agreeable proportions
of his body; and his lightness on his feet, his erectness,
his easy bearing, added to the impression of physical
grace and virility. His suppleness, combined with his
bigness of frame, and his large, wide-set, rather glowing eyes, heavy black hair, and markedly bronze complexion gave him some of the handsomeness of an Indian. His courtesy as he surrendered his seat to the other
customer suggested genuine friendliness toward all mankind. His voice was noticeably resonant, masculine,
warm. His pleasure in the attentions of the bootblack's
whisk reflected a consciousness about clothes unusual in
a small-town man. His manner as he bestowed a tip suggested generous good-nature, a wish to give pleasure,
based on physical well-being and sincere kindliness of
heart.

All this the other customer observed. He was inspired
to an extraordinary reflection, "Gee, what a President
he'd make!"

With easy geniality the two men scraped acquaintance.
The handsome one was a small-town editor and publisher named Warren G. Harding; his paper was the

Marion *Star*, leading journal and Republican organ in a town of some ten thousand and a county of some thirty thousand. The other introduced himself as a lawyer from the state capital, Harry M. Daugherty, and at once was recognized by reputation — the reputation being not

From a photograph by Brown Brothers.

Warren G. Harding about 1900 when he was beginning his political career.

so much that of lawyer as of rising Republican politician. In token of acquaintance made and sealed, the two went through a ceremonial of polite manners common at the time and place; the editor held out, and the politician accepted, a plug of tobacco; the politician bit off his chew and handed the plug back; the editor took his chew and restored the plug to his pocket.

The two parted, remembering each other agreeably. Of the two, it was the politician who, in moments of reflection, most often recalled the meeting; he thought of Harding as a man having potentialities.[1]

Had the bootblack's occupation permitted him to concentrate his mind on men's faces instead of on their feet, and had he had insight into men's natures, he would have observed that his two customers of the morning were opposites in temperament and personality; that the handsome Harding was easy-going, placid, took things much as they came, while Daugherty was physically energetic, mentally active, had a restless vigor of personality which would not take things as they come but rather would cause things to become what he wanted them to be. And the bootblack might have concluded that in any future coming together of the men's orbits, it would be Daugherty who would emanate initiative, who would influence the destiny of the other; always Harding would be the bigger man, but always Daugherty, by his greater adventurousness, would be creating the conditions that would influence the fate of both.

II

Daugherty

Harry[2] (not Henry) Daugherty was born at Washington Court House, a small county-seat some thirty-five

---

[1] This legend about the first meeting of Warren G. Harding and Harry M. Daugherty was told the author of this history by Jess Smith. Smith said he had heard it many times from Daugherty, who regarded it as a romantic and historic episode, as indeed it was. The place was Richwood, Union County, Ohio.

In 1935, I spent some days at Columbus, Ohio, going over proofs of this book with Daugherty. He confirmed the story as told above, except as to one or two immaterial details. His recollection, at this time, was that he had gone to the back yard to get a drink at the pump, and that Harding was already there. Other versions of the story have been current among Ohio politicians and newspaper men. All agree about the time and place, and in the main about the circumstances, the differences being largely about just which of the back yard's facilities the two men were making use of when they struck up an acquaintance.

[2] His middle name, as if to take the curse of colloquiality off "Harry," was Micajah. This echo of the Old Testament, strong in the time and section in which the two men were reared, was duplicated in Harding's middle name, Gamaliel.

miles southwest of Columbus. His background, similar
to that of Harding, was supposed, in the American tradition of the day, to be the ideal starting-point for story-
book success. He went through the local high school,
got a law degree from the University of Michigan,
opened an office in his home town, and practised there
twelve years. He and his brother "Mal," the local
banker, were the town's most promising young men, on
their way to be its leading citizens.

Daugherty was elected to the legislature. At the end
of two terms[3] he remained at the capital, Columbus,
opening a law office there.

Daugherty's practice, when later it became a subject
of newspaper discussion, was described as having been
less law than lobbying. While it is true the sum of
Daugherty's appearances before higher courts would
hardly make the record of a leader of the bar, yet to call
him merely a lobbyist would be to demean his intellectual quality and the spirit in which he undertook and
carried on the affairs entrusted to him. He was a competent lawyer and had the mentality to be an outstanding one. A restlessness of temperament, a zest for action,
led him to prefer that part of the lawyer's function
which did not confine him to poring over books. When
something that needed to be done was in the borderland where law overlaps upon politics, when the talent
required for carrying on to success was resourcefulness
and momentum of personality rather than minute acquaintance with legal precedent, Daugherty was the man
to engage.[4] It was a time when small, local telephone,

---

[3] 1890–94.

[4] A case of the type with which Daugherty was associated was that of Charles
W. Morse. Morse was a promoter who, making himself head of a New York
bank, violated regulations and was sentenced to a long term in Atlanta penitentiary. There he began to manœuvre for a pardon. Among other agencies he

gas, and electric plants were being merged into larger systems; the operation in many cases called for new charters from legislatures, consents from regulatory bodies, negotiations with minority groups of stockholders, suits in the courts, suits in which the main consideration was compromise, or other quick and definite conclusion, to be attained either by appeasement or by resoluteness. In all this, Daugherty became adept; he almost never appeared himself in court nor before a legislative committee or public utility commission; but always he knew who could make the appearance with

---

employed Daugherty, and Daugherty was also employed by some interests who wished Morse out of jail so that they could use his testimony in law suits.

The pardon could only be granted by President Taft. That Taft was a Republican, and from Ohio, may have suggested to Daugherty's client that Daugherty could reach Taft's ear. But if Daugherty's client thought Daugherty could have exceptional weight with Taft, Daugherty knew that Taft was perfectly high-minded. Actually, Daugherty, in acting as attorney for Morse, never spoke to Taft, but only to Taft's Attorney-General, George W. Wickersham. In that, Daugherty did no more than any attorney asking for a pardon would have done.

But Daugherty did not stop with making formal application to the Attorney-General — perfunctorily laying his application before the appropriate official would neither have satisfied Daugherty's instinct for success nor have surely brought the pardon. With Daugherty, practising law meant getting results. Having gone through the motions of the prescribed official formula, he looked about for a leverage outside the official hierarchy. It occurred to him to work through a powerful politician and newspaper publisher, John R. McLean, owner of the Cincinnati *Inquirer* and the Washington *Post,* with whom he had friendly relations, and who, as a publisher of important newspapers, could reach Taft's ear.

McLean sent one of his reporters to Atlanta; the reporter found Morse showing evidence of extreme ill-health. With this information to justify him, McLean sent one of his editors to President Taft to ask for a pardon for Morse. Taft ordered that a physical examination be made of Morse. The physicians reported that Morse was very ill. Taft pardoned him. (Meeting McLean later, Taft asked him humorously if he had any more friends in prison for whom he wanted pardons.)

Morse, released, lived comfortably for some ten years, during which a cloud of stories arose about how the physicians who examined Morse had come to believe he was *in extremis*. Probably the stories were inventions; Morse may have been ill, and his recovery could have been due to the treatment which freedom enabled him to take, including a course of baths in Europe. But the stories were whispered widely. One tale said that Morse had swallowed a substance which would give his excretions the symptoms of disease. All the yarns were probably untrue; it is likely Morse's lawyers may have been as misled about his health as the doctors and Taft. But circulation of the stories reflected the common appreciation of Harry Daugherty's ingenuity, his habit of achieving his goal under difficulty. There is much about Daugherty's connection with the Morse case in the Senate debates in the *Congressional Record* for May, 1922.

the best advantage; always he knew what wire to pull; always he kept a web of wires running from his office out to all sorts of men who occupied places of leverage; always he knew how to get results.

With success at Columbus, Daugherty's reputation spread; he was in demand at other state capitals, in New York, at Washington. In time, in the circles in which he moved, he became known as the man to handle situations at once difficult and dangerous. This Daugherty liked. He cared more for the game than for the fee; he liked the clash of personalities; he liked the thrill of climactic success, of putting something over. He liked difficulty, he liked danger, and he liked to be on the move. Always he had a dozen irons in the fire, always he was rushing from one to the other. He lived dangerously; always he was leaping, just in time, from one ice-floe to another, in a stream that was forever turbulent. By 1920 he had an immense acquaintance all over the country, an acquaintance which included many types of men, for Daugherty could entertain a President with shrewd views about public affairs as capably as he could play poker and drink whiskey with minor politicians in hotel bedrooms. The heart of his range of acquaintance was with men who had in other states the position that Daugherty had in Ohio, a position which kept one foot steadily in politics, the other in law, or in law combined with business, men in whom high talent was united with low tastes, men whose equipment for success lay largely in shrewd judgment about other men, including their weaknesses.

Daugherty's insight into men, and his application of it in practice, amounted to an art. One of his eyes was imperfect, and the other, at the beginning of an acquaintance, seemed to circle round a man rather than focus on him, as if he was getting his impression, not from the physical man, but from some psychic aura about him, not visible to an ordinary eye. By whatever talent, Daugherty had the stranger "sized up," and mentally classified; knew how to get his good-will, or in the alternative how to bluff him; knew whether he was

Harry M. Daugherty as he looked in the early years of his association with Warren Harding.

pliable, amenable to blustering, or susceptible to flattery. Whatever was called for, Daugherty could do. In the wide spectrum of attitude that can arise when man meets man, Daugherty could adopt whatever manner was called for. Once he wished to make a political alliance with a rich Oklahoma oil man and politician, "Jake" Hamon. Through a mutual acquaintance Daugherty sent an invitation for Hamon to come and take break- fast with him. Hamon came. Daugherty sized Hamon up as the kind of man who prides himself on being a "he-man" — in truth Hamon was a male of the commonest sort, an unusual combination of fat and force, gross as a pig and vain as a peacock. Daugherty bowed his guest to the table. A waiter hovered. Daugherty waved a hand of courtesy toward his guest. Hamon gave his order, "three fried eggs and plenty of ham" — loudly emphasizing the "three," as if experience had taught him that waiters, unless instruction is impressed upon them, universally bring the conventional two.

The waiter expressed understanding, wrote the order on his pad and turned to Daugherty, who — much to the astonishment of his stomach undoubtedly — echoed firmly, "I'll take three fried eggs and plenty of ham."

Accompanying Daugherty wherever he went, after he was well on in his career, was a curious character named "Jess" Smith. He was a large, loose-framed, rather stout man in his late thirties or early forties, with pink, loose-hanging cheeks, a black mustache and large brown eyes. He was naïve, crude, and friendly; quite unread except as to newspapers, and in them, only as to the political and sports news, perhaps also the "funnies" — a country-come-to-town. Smith had been born and brought up in Washington Court House. When he was three years old, his father had died. Daugherty, with a genuine benevolence that was strong in him, took an interest in the boy, advised him and, when he grew up, helped him get started in a business which became an important small-town department store. Smith, grateful and loyal, became to Daugherty a combination of son, secretary, valet, nurse and intimate friend. He accompanied Daugherty on his journeys; one would see the two of them walking up to a hotel desk, Daugherty with the quiet of assured success, Smith following with the bustling manner of vicarious importance. Daugherty came to have a curious dependence upon Smith. In the hotel suites in which they spent much of their hurrying, restless life, Daugherty never liked to sleep with his bedroom door shut, always the door to "Jess" Smith's room

From a photograph by Wide World.

Jess Smith.

was kept open. Day-times, while Daugherty transacted affairs in the local court house or state capital, or in the back rooms of law offices or big business establishments, Smith would sit in the hotel lobby, swaying pleasurably in a big rocker facing the window, a cigar in his mouth. If he could find an old acquaintance or make a new one — he was a friendly and gregarious soul — he would enjoy telling, again, how Harry Daugherty was the greatest man in the world.

The two, returning from forays to Washington, to

New York, to Chicago, to state capitals all over the country, would go for rest to a little, isolated bachelor "shack" they had along a stream, Deer Creek, in the country. There, in early summer mornings, Daugherty in pajamas would walk bare-footed in the dewy grass, chewing his before-breakfast quid of tobacco and musing luxuriously on the dream that had become permanent with him, muttering half to himself and half to the faithful Smith, "Gee, but he'd make a great-looking President; we'll put it over sometime, Jess!" [4a]

III

Harding

Harding meanwhile made an increasing success of his Marion *Star*. As a natural development of his editorial career he was active in Republican politics. He served two terms in the Ohio State Senate; was Lieutenant-Governor from 1904 to 1906; and was the Republican nominee for Governor in 1910. At the Republican National Convention at Chicago in 1916 he served as chairman, and did it well — his performance there, under the eyes of Republican leaders from all over the country, was destined to be an asset to him on an important future occasion. Many of the delegates in that 1916 convention who observed his handsome figure and his dignified poise as chairman, and who listened to his exceptionally well-handled keynote speech, were favorably impressed. Many of them, perhaps more than half

[4a] This sylvan picture, as it is told here, was given me by Jess Smith. Daugherty, when he read the proofs of this chapter, took strong exception to some details, declaring that he never chewed tobacco before breakfast, and averring, vehemently, that he was not addicted to walking bare-foot in the dewy grass, or any other kind of grass, neither in the early morning nor at any other time. The historian is obliged to leave the issue of verity where it is, between the two men who participated.

of them, would be delegates to the next convention in 1920, and would remember him.[4b]

In 1914, one of Ohio's seats in the Senate at Wash-

From a photograph by Brown Brothers.

Harding at his desk in the office of his newspaper, the Marion *Star*.

ington was about to be vacant. Daugherty, keeping always a careful eye on the politics of the State, thought

[4b] Will Hays, in a letter, says I should emphasize "the effect of Harding's speech in the 1916 national convention — it was an important item in developing a national acquaintance among those who go to conventions, the organization men, etc. There is no doubt about the impression that speech of Harding's made on every one who was in that convention. I never forgot that speech."

Harding could be elected. Harding was in Florida for the season. Daugherty sent him a telegram saying he would like to see him. Harding at once went to Columbus. Daugherty told him how the Senatorial situation lay, told him there was a chance he might win, and urged him to run. Harding demurred, but went back to Florida, packed up, returned to Ohio, announced himself a candidate, and began a stump-speaking tour of the State. After some two weeks, Daugherty, arriving at his office one morning, found Harding there. Harding was discouraged; the weather had been bad, the stump-speaking and travel had been wearying. Harding declared he was through, he would quit the race. Daugherty listened and said; "Oh, go out and get your shoes shined, get your clothes pressed, get a good meal, and take a little rest."[4c] Harding did so, resumed his campaigning, and won.

In the Senate, Harding looked the part as adequately as any man who ever sat in the body. "He was superbly handsome; his face and carriage had a Washingtonian nobility and dignity, his eyes were benign."[5] Perhaps his looks did him a dis-service — no one could be as great a Senator as Harding looked. While he was not conspicuous intellectually, yet he hardly deserved the cynical characterization that a New York editor[6] put upon him, "an undistinguished and undistinguishable unit in the ruck of Republican Senators." He took adequate part in the debates, made an occasional formal speech, and bore his share in the committee work. To a much greater degree than is usual in a body where jealousy is not uncommon, Harding had the esteem and affection of his fellows. But his public record was mediocre; no one

[4c] Told the author by Daugherty, June, 1935.
[5] "Only Yesterday," Frederick Lewis Allen.
[6] Charles R. Miller, of the New York *Times*.

ever heard of a "Harding bill," [6a] hardly even a "Harding Amendment"; had his career stopped with the Senate

From a photograph by Brown Brothers.

Harding and Mrs. Harding. The photograph was taken on the lawn of their private residence in Washington while Harding was Senator.

he would have been only an obscure and forgotten name preserved like a thousand others in old Congressional Directories.

[6a] Some friends of Harding who have read the proofs of this chapter think that Harding's unimportance in the Senate is here over-emphasized. They say that if there was never a "Harding bill" the reason was that the Democrats were

Once[7] he attracted some attention, by criticizing the war-time campaign to make citizens buy Liberty Bonds. The steam-up propaganda, the strong-arm personal pressure, amounting sometimes to physical violence,[8] was, Harding declared, "hysterical and unseemly." The charge was true, the words were well chosen, and the sentiment was characteristic of Harding, one of whose qualities was a sense of taste about simple matters. The word "becoming,"[9] used in an old-fashioned sense, as applied to conduct or manners, was frequent in Harding's vocabulary, and he lived up to it. If his standards were unsophisticated, "small-town," that was the fruit of his background. And if his standards sometimes emphasized regard for appearances as distinguished from substance, that was as much a characteristic of the time as it was of Harding. His loathing of compulsion was not a matter of superficial manners; instinctively and strongly he prized fair-dealing and tolerance, whether between man and man or in public affairs. His protest against the methods used to sell Liberty Bonds came from deep within him, and reflected the best in him.

That one burst of feeling from Harding as a Senator led, vicariously, in a boomerang sort of way, to a kind of inverted distinction. It stirred into pungency of phrase a political opponent whose customary gift of words was quite as ordinary as Harding's own. William G. McAdoo, Secretary of the Treasury in President

in control of the Senate, and that a Republican could not well initiate a bill. They say that Harding led the attempt to have the Senate direct President Wilson to permit Theodore Roosevelt to go to France as head of a division of the army; and they claim that some of Harding's formal speeches, especially one he made on the eve of America's entrance into the war, were worthy.

[7] June 8, 1917.

[8] For an account of the Liberty Bond "drives" during the Great War, see "Our Times," Vol. IV.

[9] "His acid test for everything that was proposed to him, involving his participation, was to ask himself if it would be becoming." — Boyden Sparkes, N. Y. Tribune, August 2, 1923.

Wilson's war-time cabinet, irritated by Harding's criticism of McAdoo's methods of selling Liberty Bonds, was inspired to say that Harding

was a speechmaker; he spoke in a big bow-wow style of oratory. His speeches left the impression of an army of pompous phrases moving over the landscape in search of an idea; sometimes these meandering words would actually capture a straggling thought and bear it triumphantly, a prisoner in their midst, until it died of servitude and overwork.

IV

Harding Is "Pushed into the Water"

Had Harding been left free to follow his own wish, he probably would never have left the Senate. The honor of it was as much as he ever wanted, more than he had ever hoped. The work of it was largely what he chose to make it. He could look forward to days of ease and honor, nights of peace. He was completely happy.

But fate, and Harry Daugherty, had another use for him. Daugherty, ever since the two had met, had carried in the back of his mind the idea that Harding would make a "great President" — sometimes, unconsciously, Daugherty expressed it with more fidelity to exactness, "a great-*looking* President." (Probably what Daugherty meant was that Harding would make a good candidate, a good man for the purpose of leading the public to make him President; or that Harding, in looks and manner, would live up to the popular conception of a President.) And to Daugherty — since he was in the political game and was by nature a player for the highest stakes — making a President would be the apotheosis of his career. Yet it was only as a remote possibility that Daugherty carried his dream. He never mentioned it to

Harding seriously, and when he mentioned it facetiously or tentatively, Harding turned it aside. It was — in the early days of the vision certainly — just a thing that might conceivably come about, as one chance in a thousand, only possible to happen through some extraordinary contribution of accident to other favoring conditions.

In the early winter of 1920, accident contributed the conditions that turned Daugherty's dream into the possibility of reality. It was a situation, and a sequence of developments, of the sort that make politics fascinating. The Republican State organization in Ohio was in the control of Harding and Daugherty, Harding remote and titular, Daugherty active. They were threatened by a rival group. The rival group, taking advantage of the fact that it happened to be a Presidential year, was backing General Leonard Wood for the Republican Presidential nomination. Since Wood had much popularity in Ohio, the rival group were likely to be able to elect delegates pledged to Wood. And if they did, they would acquire for themselves control of the Ohio Republican organization. The menace was especially serious, because Harding, later in the year, would come up for renomination to his seat in the Senate; if he and Daugherty should lose control of the organization, Harding might not get the re-nomination to the Senate.

Briskly Daugherty described the situation to Harding; resourcefully he suggested a counter-move. They must put forward an Ohio candidate for the Presidential nomination, a "favorite son." The gesture was one familiar in politics. The "favorite son" candidacy would be, not so much in hope of getting the Presidential nomination as merely to garner the Ohio delegates and enable Harding and Daugherty to keep their Ohio leadership. For the rôle, Harding himself was the obvious man.

Harding shrank from it. He did not like the turmoil of it, he cherished his ease, the leisure for whist and poker, and golf, and long sojourns in Florida. "I found him," said Daugherty, "sunning himself, like a turtle on a log, and I pushed him into the water." [10] The water, Harding understood, would not be deep, nor the pool big. Harding was not actually to try seriously for the Presidential nomination; he was merely to run for the purpose, mainly, of getting the Ohio delegates.

Even so, Harding was reluctant. But he realized the force of Daugherty's suggestion. To seem to try for the Presidential nomination was the best way of actually assuring his return to the Senate. Perfunctorily Harding permitted his candidacy to be announced and began to make speeches, the first one at a dinner of the Ohio Society of New York City, followed by others in Ohio.

But Ohio was suspicious of the good-faith of the Harding candidacy; much of Ohio really wanted General Wood and set about electing delegates for him. In this situation, Daugherty explained to Harding that as a matter of strategy Harding must seem to show good faith by running in some states outside Ohio — not many states, just enough to seem to be a bona fide candidate on a nation-wide basis. Harding consented, though reluctantly. Without dreaming there was much real likelihood of the nomination descending on him, thinking he was only serving Daugherty's and his own desire to keep their hold on the Ohio state machine, Harding extended his speech-making to a few other states.

[10] This sentence, like many that sparkled from Daugherty's flashing mind, became familiar wherever politicians gossiped, and later crept into books. Historically, though not importantly, there is some doubt whether the incident occurred on this occasion, or at the earlier time when Daugherty was urging Harding to run for the Senate.

V

But Daugherty's adventurous, far-ranging mind had foreseen something which, as yet, he kept to himself. He foresaw — but he did not yet tell Harding — that Harding might really get the nomination, might get it, not by effort on Harding's part, for Harding would not make the effort, but by the fall of the cards in the convention.

There were two principal candidates, General Leonard Wood[11] and Frank O. Lowden. Daugherty's shrewd mind foresaw a typical situation arising: The followings of the two principal candidates would be roughly equal. As the battle progressed, each following would come to hate the candidate of the other more than it would hate any third candidate — the two principal candidates would, as Daugherty put it, "fight each other to a frazzle";[12] they would, in the political phrase, "kill each other off." The prize would go to some third candidate, to some one who had not been conspicuous enough or aggressive enough to arouse antagonisms.

Quietly, subtly, Daugherty arranged his cards. The essence of his subtlety was that he did not, as yet, let Harding fully know; if Harding really thought there was any chance — "any danger" Harding would have called it — of his getting the Presidential nomination, he might back out of the situation into which Daugherty had manœuvred him.

Daugherty, with a carefully assumed manner of casualness, began to "gumshoe" up and down the county;

11 Some account of General Wood and ex-Governor Lowden will be found later in this chapter.

12 This and some of the other quotations from Daugherty in this chapter are taken from a book he wrote (in collaboration with Thomas Dixon) twelve years later, in 1932, "The Inside Story of the Harding Administration."

everywhere he got in touch with Republican leaders, not to suggest that they support Harding, not at all, but merely to refresh old acquaintance and to recall Harding to local Republican leaders who had seen him when he presided at the Republican National Convention at Chicago four years before. Most of the leaders were already committed to one or the other of the major candidates, or they had favorite sons of their own; Daugherty's plan was merely to establish such friendly relations as might qualify him, and Harding, as heirs, as "second choice," when and if the leaders should be obliged to see that they could not nominate the candidates to whom they were primarily committed.

In two rooms of a dingy old hotel in Washington, Daugherty set up Harding headquarters. (The Wood and Lowden candidacies had whole floors and immense staffs in the leading hotels of Chicago and New York.) To a newspaper man[13] who called at the Harding headquarters, Daugherty explained his strategy. With a candor that was part of his intellectual armory, to be used where his instinct told him candor would serve him best, and with a pictorial vividness of speech that was part of his rich endowment of imagination, he said: "I won't try to fool you; you can see what we've got here, it's only a shoestring. I'll tell you, in confidence, what's in my mind. All I'm doing is getting in touch with the leaders and delegates who are for Wood and Lowden, being friendly with them. When the convention comes, those two armies will battle each other to a standstill. When both realize they can't win, when they're tired and hot and sweaty and discouraged, both the armies will remember me and this little headquarters. They'll be like soldiers after a battle, who recall a shady spring[14]

---

13 Mark Sullivan.

14 Daugherty's salty pungency of speech, his vividness of phrase, was one of his salient characteristics. That, with his richness of imagination, his shrewd judg-

along a country road, where they got a drink as they marched to the front. When they remember me that way, maybe both sides will turn to Harding — I don't know — it's just a chance."

Toward the newspapers generally, and the public, Daugherty practised a finesse that was the ultimate refinement in subtlety. For the sake of Ohio looking on, he had to seem to be pushing the Harding candidacy seriously. But if he actually pushed it seriously, he would destroy the only chance he had, by antagonizing the major candidates and their delegates. However, to be between the devil and the deep sea was a familiar experience with Daugherty. He enjoyed it and spent most of his life in that exhilarating strand, or in pulling clients out of it. His present dilemma was no great tax on his resourcefulness.

Toward newspaper men who surmised the Harding candidacy was merely for the purpose of strategy within Ohio, and whose surmise was borne out by the slightness of Daugherty's headquarters and organization compared with those of the major candidates — toward newspaper men thus skeptical, Daugherty practised an art which told the truth but, in the sight of his questioners, cast

---

ment and comment about men, and his sense of humor, caused me to like him much, though I had no illusions about his political morals or his tastes. I do not wish to seem Pecksniffian. Throughout my life I have fought, mainly, for the principles of the reformers, but for entertainment, have usually preferred the politicians.

A story Daugherty told, one of many, remained in my mind for years. He told it on the occasion of our first scraping acquaintance with each other — it was in the smoking room of a Pullman car between Washington and Columbus. Daugherty, groping for common interests on which to build acquaintance, asked me if I knew Colonel Ed Greene of Texas. I said I did not. "Ed's a great fellow," said Daugherty. "You ought to know him. Ed has a wooden leg. One day, Ed and I were sitting in the back of a bar-room down in Texas. A fellow from the North came in who knew me. I introduced him to Ed. This fellow asked us to come up to the bar and have a drink. As we walked over, the fellow from the North noticed Ed's wooden leg. He was a brash fellow, had fresh manners, and he said to Ed, 'Colonel,' he said, 'where'd you lose your leg?' Ed never took his eyes off his drink, kept on drawing his glass across the bar, and said, 'I ain't lost it, I know just where it is.' "

over the truth the manner of openly throwing a bluff. He told them exactly what he was relying on — but told it in such a way as to let them think he didn't believe it himself.

"Well," he said, in answer to skeptical questions, "there will be no nomination on the early ballots. After the other candidates have failed, after they have gone their limit, the leaders, worn out and wishing to do the very best thing, will get together in some hotel room about 2:11 in the morning. Some fifteen men, bleary-eyed with lack of sleep, and perspiring profusely with the excessive heat, will sit down around a big table. I will be with them and present the name of Senator Harding. When that time comes, Harding will be selected, because he fits in perfectly with every need of the party and nation. He is the logical choice, and the leaders will determine to throw their support to him." [15]

[15] This statement by Daugherty, as reprinted here, is combined and paraphrased from quotations in the New York *Times* of June 13, 1920, and the Washington *Post* of February 27, 1921.

It was printed, in varying forms, in — I feel safe in saying — practically every newspaper in America, and many times. It struck the popular imagination, was repeated, and talked about, and smiled at cynically, by innumerable persons. A little later, after it turned out to be, roughly, a correct prediction, it was again reprinted and again discussed and re-discussed. It became a "famous saying" — a part of America's contemporary folk-lore. A condensed and slightly paraphrased version — "fifteen men in a smoke-filled room" — became, throughout the English tongue, certainly in America, an accepted and universally familiar *cliche,* the newspaper and conversational symbol for political manipulation of a somewhat sordid sort.

So far as the purpose of this narrative is concerned, I might conclude this allusion to a "famous saying" at this point; books of history do not ordinarily go deeper, nor indeed as deep. Daugherty said it, or something sufficiently like it; and it correctly expressed Daugherty's thought, and described his political philosophy and methods.

But it occurs to me to append an authentic account of how the phrase arose — for the sake of the bearing it has on the authenticity of many "famous sayings," sententious sentences, "last words," and the like. The account is given by Charles D. Hilles of New York, who was present at, so to speak, the obstetrical bedside of this verbal birth. Mr. Hilles writes me:

"Daugherty was hastily packing his bag in a Waldorf Astoria Hotel room when two reporters called. He expressed regret that he had not time for an interview. One of the reporters persisted in asking questions. Daugherty indifferently uttered a few laconic sentences and started for the elevator. The reporter, try-

The newspapermen, generally, didn't believe it. They didn't believe Daugherty believed it. Almost no one expected Harding to get the nomination. Least of all did Harding expect it.

Daugherty's "2:11 a.m." statement drew more attention to Harding than he and his candidacy had yet received. The statement became the subject of austere editorials and cynical jests; it became universally familiar. But the discussion was all about the statement, not about Harding. Newspapers solemnly condemned the statement as an abstract picture of political manipulation. The association of the statement with Harding was forgotten. Harding as a candidate was ignored, he was too unimportant.

To Daugherty almost alone (among important persons) did it seem possible Harding might be nominated.

---

ing to provoke Daugherty into talk, followed. He said that he presumed that as Daugherty could not support by an authentic table of delegates his boast that Harding would be the nominee, it followed that Daugherty must expect to win by manipulation — probably in some back room of a hotel with a small group of political managers reduced to pulp by the inevitable vigil and travail. The reporter went on to say to Daugherty that he presumed the conferees would be expected to surrender at 2 A.M. in a smoke-filled room. Daugherty, unaffected by the taunt retorted carelessly, 'Make it 2:11.' "

From which one may infer that many "famous sayings" were not truly, or at least not wholly, the expressions of those to whom they are attributed, but were in many cases the inventions, partly or wholly, of a bystander, a reporter or chronicler, whose sense of the dramatic knew better what the hero ought to say than the hero — being under strain of one kind or another, sometimes indeed being in apprehension of death — could possibly know himself.

Whence I take it to be a pity, and a detriment to history, that some contemporary Hilles was not present when Marie Antoinette was said to have said, "Let them eat cake," and Louis XVI "After me the deluge!" Patrick Henry's "Give me liberty or give me death" was in a formal public address, and therefore authentic. Captain Lawrence's "Don't give up the ship!" always struck me as being, under the circumstances, a simple and natural thing to say, and therefore probably authentic. So also Grant's "I will fight it out on this line if it takes all summer." But I doubt whether that earthy and salty Vermonter, Ethan Allen, at his capture of Fort Ticonderoga, ever put his demand on the British commander in any such ten-dollar words as "Surrender this fort instantly . . . in the name of the great Jehovah and the Continental Congress!" And I knew a man who was familiar with the circumstances in which a Vanderbilt did *not* say, "The public be damned!"

Upon Daugherty, almost alone, rested the promotion of the Harding candidacy. For a brief time, early in Daugherty's promotion of Harding, he had some encouragement, tentative and rather furtive, from some powerful Republican Senators, "elder statesmen," so to speak, of the party. But it was friendly blessing rather than active help, or even serious expectation. Their principal motive was that Harding was their Senate crony, they liked the idea of putting a colleague in the White House, especially one with Harding's amiability and amenability. Once a group of them, with Harding, gathered in the Washington home of ex-Senator Jonathan Bourne of Oregon for an evening of cards. While awaiting late comers Harding fell into a doze, his head resting on the back of the chair. Bourne looked at the napping Senator and then looked at the others with a manner of questioning, as if asking, "Do you really intend to try to put that man in the White House?" One of the others, with a manner of replying to an accusation, said, "Anyhow, you could talk to him, he would 'go along.' "

Whatever slight notion the Senators ever had of backing Harding for the nomination, they abandoned when he made little progress in getting delegates, especially when he did not get all the delegates from his own state, and when his manager, Harry Daugherty, was defeated as a candidate for delegate. Promotion of Harding rested almost alone on Daugherty and his scanty organization.

VI

Republican Aspirants in 1920

As the 1920 Republican National Convention approached, the leading candidate was General Wood. He was, by any fair estimate, one of the half-dozen most distinguished Americans of the time, perhaps better equipped than any other individual to provide America with leadership in the difficult post-war and reconstruction years ahead. As a young man he had entered the Army as a medical officer during the 80's, when Indian troubles, while they had ceased to be common and had diminished in formidableness, were still occasional; he had become an officer of the line, had served as superior in command to Theodore Roosevelt in the Rough Riders during the Spanish War, had become Governor-General of Cuba and had been Chief of Staff of the Army. Though without professional training at West Point, he became the best type of Army-man. Just before the Great War, and during the early part of it, he had been leader of the movement, later well justified, for preparedness.[16] That service, as well as his other distinctions, had commended him for a corresponding part in America's participation; refusal by President Wilson to let him serve in France had increased Wood's standing among Republicans, made him appropriate as the man to lead the Republicans in the election which would choose a successor to Wilson. Wood, because of his association with Theodore Roosevelt in the Rough Riders and in the fight for preparedness, had the support of most of the conservatives among Roosevelt's followers. At the same time, the fact that he was a soldier was a handicap to him. The country had just gone through the Great War, had not liked the experience, and to some degree disliked military men. As the shrewd Harry Daugherty put it, "There's not enough money in the world to buy the nomination for a man with epaulettes on his shoulders in 1920." This handicap to Wood was increased by his advocacy, during his campaign, of universal military service for America. Wood had a strong

16 See "Our Times," Vol. V.

claim on the country's esteem; the main concern of his life was America, a highminded, calm, steady-burning zeal that the country should be well-managed, that strong ideals should be held before it, and that the people should be at once stimulated and disciplined to follow

From a photograph by Underwood & Underwood.

Senator Harding, on the reader's right. General Leonard Wood on the left, during the Chicago Convention.

the ideals. Though his career had been mainly military (except during the years' he was Governor-General of Cuba), his interests and abilities were so broad as to entitle him to the rank of statesman, a statesman of the best type of Victorian England.

Next to Wood, the principal candidate was Frank O. Lowden. He had been a poor boy in Minnesota and Iowa, had become a successful lawyer in Chicago; had married a daughter of one of the powerful rich of the day, George Pullman; had been a long-time member of the Republican National Committee, and had recently made a striking record as Governor of Illinois. He had served five years in Congress, and had been distinguished

From a photograph by Brown Brothers.

Frank O. Lowden, former Governor of Illinois; a leading candidate for the Republican Presidential nomination in 1920.

in that body at a time, 1906 to 1911, when the quality of Congress was exceptionally high. In mind, he was able; in temperament hearty and forceful; in personality agreeable. He was of the best of the type from which the United States had been accustomed to choose its Presidents.

Third, in numerical strength, was Hiram Johnson. He had first come to the country's attention by his conduct of a famous criminal prosecution in San Francisco,[17] had been Governor of California, had been the candidate for Vice-president on the ticket with Theodore Roosevelt when the latter started the Progressive party in 1912, and had been, since 1917, United States Senator from California. His support included the more progressive part of the old Theodore Roosevelt following. Another large area of support accrued to him from strong opponents of America's joining the League of Nations; Johnson, with some ten others in the Senate, had composed the group whose unceasing opposition to the League had brought them various designations of implacability, the "bitter-enders," the "battalion of death," the "last-ditchers."

Others among the candidates included a Governor of Massachusetts, named Calvin Coolidge, who had arrested nation-wide attention by his attitude toward a strike of Boston policemen; Coolidge had sent to the head of the American Federation of Labor, Samuel Gompers, a telegram as notable for its laconic force of style as for the principle it declared: "There is no right to strike against the public safety by anybody, anywhere, any time." [17a]

Others included Herbert Hoover, then fresh from his exalted services to America during and just after the war, and to Belgium before the war; Senator Robert M. LaFollette (the elder) of Wisconsin — he was always a candidate, though he rarely received more than the votes of his own state; Nicholas Murray Butler, President of Columbia University, New York — he had little more than the votes of his own state, and of his own state not all — his rank that of perfunctory favorite son.

[17] See "Our Times," Vol. III, p. 458.
[17a] For an account of the Boston police strike see Ch. 9.

There were some ten other favorite sons, or otherwise negligible candidates.

And there was Harding — his rank, as subsequently measured by strength on the first ballot, was sixth, below Wood, Lowden, Johnson, Butler, and Governor Sproul of Pennsylvania. He was identified with no conspicuous group or cause; the country knew no more of him than it knows of any inconspicuous Senator.

VII

As the convention neared, the time came when Daugherty had to take Harding completely into his confidence, had to tell him that, in Daugherty's judgment, there was really a chance of his being nominated for President, and that Daugherty intended to push the chance to the limit.

The tensity of opposition between the two foremost contenders which Daugherty had been hoping for, upon which he had built all his own plans, had developed as Daugherty had foreseen. Beginning with the earliest primaries for the election of delegates, there had been strong rivalry between the camps of Wood and Lowden — rivalry which had soon turned to bad feeling and to over-eagerness, expressing itself in competitively lavish organizations. This grew into large expenditures of money, to which the country's attention was called by one of the other candidates, Johnson of California, and his Senate colleague, Borah of Idaho. Promptly the outcry was taken up by other Republican leaders and by press and public. Borah in the Senate charged that a "plot" was afoot to "buy the Presidency," that the use of money by Wood and Lowden constituted a "saturnalia of corruption." [17b] Promptly a committee was ap-

17b New York *Times,* March 27, 1920.

pointed to investigate. At the hearings it developed that Lowden had spent about half a million dollars and that contributions had been made to Wood, by wealthy friends and believers in him, totalling $1,200,000. The disclosures were damaging to both. Lowden was hurt most, because $5,000 of his money had been sent by his campaign managers to two minor Republican leaders in Missouri; the money was sent for legitimate campaign purposes, but the two recipients themselves ran for delegate and were elected, which without intention of bribe gave the incident that color.[17c]

The lavish expenditures of Wood and Lowden in their effort to head each off, and the scandal ensuing, increased the likelihood that their mutual feud would have its natural result, and that some other candidate would win.

For Daugherty, nursing along Harding's candidacy with consummate care, the turn events had taken was tremendously heartening; he recognized, though hardly any one else did, that now there was a real chance for Harding to win. Harding's term in the Senate was ending; and there was a crucial date ahead, when, under the Ohio law, Harding would be obliged to say whether or not he would be a candidate for another term in the Senate. Harding had taken it for granted that before that date came, his *pro forma* candidacy for the Presidential nomination would be over, and he would be free to run for the Senate seat which he loved and knew he could get again. Now Daugherty told him he would have to take his chance on the Presidential candidacy and forego the Senatorial one. He must, Daugherty told him, "go into the big circus."

Harding had one of his rare bursts of anger. Pro-

[17c] In June, 1935, Daugherty told me that but for this misadventure to Lowden, it was doubtful if he, Daugherty, could have nominated Harding.

fanely he swore he would do no such thing. The incident occured in Harding's Senate office. Daugherty, unable alone to compel Harding, sent for Mrs. Harding. She was an alert, sharp-voiced compound of energy and a kind of nagging ambition for her husband. "The two of us," said Daugherty[18] later, "backed him against the wall and made him stick."

The day of decision for Harding, when he must file for the Ohio Senatorial nomination — or by not filing put the Senate away from him — came while the Republican Presidential nominating convention was in session; it was Friday of the week in which Saturday would see the Presidential nomination made. It was, to Harding and to Daugherty, in different ways, a major crisis, not only in their present enterprise, but in their careers.

Decision was beset by bedevilling contradictory considerations. If there was any real chance that Harding

---

[18] To Mark Sullivan.

The account here given of Harding's candidacy for the Republican Presidential nomination is based, as respects parts of it, on my own contact with events. Some of the more intimate details were told me at the time by Daugherty and by Jess Smith. These differ, in some cases, from an account written by Daugherty (in collaboration with Thomas Dixon) twelve years later, in 1932, "The Inside Story of the Harding Tragedy." Among other variations, all relatively immaterial, Daugherty in his book pictures Mrs. Harding as continuously opposed to her husband trying for the nomination, or lukewarm about it. I suspect that Daugherty in his book was unconsciously intent on defending Mrs. Harding from a charge, not very serious at the worst, that her ambition, through being the cause of her husband's elevation, became the cause of his tragedy. Daugherty's book as a whole is, in the nature of things, a defense of Harding, of himself and of Mrs. Harding. Having so much to defend, he fell into a state of mind in which he defended where he did not need to. Also, by the time Daugherty wrote his book he was an old man, had had personal sorrows and had suffered with his friends in many public tragedies, including accusations of crime. Aside from these possible impairments to accuracy of memory, he had much to explain, about himself and others. The making of the picture he wished to make necessarily included some silences. Altogether, I have no hesitation in preferring what he, and his intimate, Jess Smith, said in private conversations in 1920, over what he wrote for the world in 1932.

might get the Presidential nomination, then by all means he must not file for the Senate in Ohio. To do so would instantly be exploited by his opponents, and be seen by all as an act of defeatism. Such an act would be taken by enemies of Harding in his own Ohio delegation as release from any obligation to continue to support him for the Presidential nomination. It would be used by rival candidates for the nomination as a reason to seduce his support from him.

On the other hand, if Harding did not file for the Senate in Ohio, and then should fail to get the Presidential nomination at Chicago, he would be without anything, would be obliged to sink, probably for the rest of his life, to the status of an ex-Senator editing a small-town newspaper. Some other Republican, probably one antagonistic to the Harding and Daugherty control, might be elected to the Senate from Ohio, and Harding and Daugherty might lose their leadership of the state organization.

In the effort to decide, friends made confusion of counsel by advising in different directions. There were days of painful pulling and hauling.

In all the discussing and the doubt, the starting-point fact was that, by every sign, the Presidential nomination was remote from Harding. He did not even have all the delegates from his own state, only 39 of them, the other 9 were for Wood; other than his Ohio delegates he had only some 26, scattering ones from here and there, in all only 65[19] in a total of 984, in a situation in which it took 493 to win.

Nevertheless Daugherty was determined to play his

---

[19] This was Harding's nominal strength on the first ballot. Actually he had more, perhaps as many as a hundred in all. In the strategy Daugherty practised, he held some of his delegates back, others he "threw," on the early ballots, to Lowden, in order to bring it about that Lowden should "kill off" Wood. Also, Harding had many "second-choice" delegates.

shoestring out, was determined that Harding should not file for the Senatorship. Daugherty would have made that decision for himself, had he been in Harding's shoes, as readily as he urged it on Harding. Always Daugherty was one to play for the highest stakes, "put everything on the red." To carry insurance against total loss, to think about salvaging a lesser prize when he was playing for the first, was not in Daugherty's nature.

In the end, however, the decision was to file for the Senatorial nomination; an agent was sent on to the state capitol at Columbus, and at 11:58 P.M., Friday night, two minutes before the deadline, he filed Harding's name.

To Harding the whole episode had been acutely displeasing. He had felt from the beginning of the discussion about whether he should file for the Senatorship or not, that to be running for two offices at once would be unsportsmanlike, "unbecoming," the thing his inner spirit most disliked to be. That it "wouldn't seem right" had been, in all the discussions, his argument against running for both Presidency and the Senate at the same time.

Throughout the whole week his manner, as he walked about the hotel corridors, was noticeably dejected. To Nicholas Murray Butler, visiting him in his headquarters, he said, "I can't afford to keep these rooms any longer, I have sent word downstairs that I am giving them up this evening; this convention will never nominate me, I am going to quit politics."[20] Some of the time he spent alone in a hotel suite with a young friend. To the young man he talked much about his early days in rural Ohio, the loveliness of the country roads in spring, the charm of the old-time one-room schools. Whenever he mentioned the battle for the Presidential

[20] Letter from Nicholas Murray Butler to the author.

nomination raging a stone-throw away, it was to express a hope that he would not get it.

While Harding waited, aloof and gloomy, Daugherty was a dynamo of nervous force. For him, it was an occasion that comes only once in a life-time, and to many, never — an occasion that all important politicians live for, and ninety-nine out of a hundred never see.

3

HARDING NOMINATED

Daugherty Plans Shrewdly and Manœuvres Skilfully for His Candidate. The Game of Games — Winning a Presidential Nomination — and the Rules Which Govern Its Play. The Leaders, Wood and Lowden, Kill Each Other Off and thus Make Possible the Victory of Harding. Aid Is Received from the "Elder Statesmen" Who Reach a Decision, as Forecast, in a "Smoke-filled Room at 2:11 A.M."

FROM the opening day of the convention, Daugherty drew his talents tense. Emanations from his personality penetrated into every hotel where delegations stopped, almost into every convention seat. By intuition and experience, by the information he had acquired during the weeks before, and through scores of scouts who now served him, he knew the mind of every leader, almost of every delegate. Better than many of them knew themselves — for it is the way of leaders and delegates passionately devoted to a candidate to think their choice must win and to give no thought to any alternative — Daugherty knew what leaders and delegates would do so soon as it should be apparent that their candidates could not win. He knew not only their probable second choices but their third and their fourth.[1] Most useful of all, he knew what they would do when all their choices had lost, when they were disappointed, tired, disgusted, and had no wish other than to nominate somebody, anybody, and go home.

While the delegates were Daugherty's main concern,

[1] "We put . . . Harding lookouts in every hotel in town and got one or more of our representatives into the headquarters of every rival. We ordered a roll made of every delegate from every state, got their addresses and the number of each room they occupied. . . . We had, I believe, the most complete poll of delegates from first choice to fourth." — H. M. Daugherty, "The Inside Story of the Harding Tragedy."

he gave shrewd and subtle thought to all the aspects of his project. Throughout, his aim was to make the convention have a friendly feeling about Harding, to create what Daugherty called a "sweet atmosphere." With a major contender that would be impossible, for a major contender inevitably inspires rivalries, enemies, partisan resentment. But for a candidate who had few delegates, whom no one expected to win, Daugherty could make friends everywhere. He brought from Columbus a glee club of 75 voices. Ordinarily the function of such a club would have been to parade up and down the streets, and push through the crowded hotel lobbies, singing and shouting, truculently and raucously, something like, "We want Harding!" Not so with Daugherty's singers. His instructions to them were to visit the headquarters of all the other candidates and serenade them.

The Political Value of a Musical Voice

To make the speech putting Harding in nomination, Daugherty picked an Ohio Congressman named Frank B. Willis. Willis had the kind of personality delegates understood, made the type of speech that pleased political gatherings. He had one of the most orotund voices in contemporary America; in a crude way he understood the emotion-stirring qualities of certain sounds, knew the value of the long "o," especially when combined with "r," as in "glory." To Willis's art, the fact that national conventions are held quadrennially, lent opportunity. In all his convention speeches, as in this one, he managed to get in, fairly early, the words "four years ago" — to hear Willis roll that out was to get the combined enjoyments of oratory, grand opera, and hog-calling. Another art he introduced into his speech nominating Harding. He realized that this was the first convention — I think the first[2] — containing women delegates. Taking advantage of that, Willis interrupted his rotund periods to lean over the platform railing and say with colloquial intimacy, "Say, boys — and girls too — why not name . . ." There was spontaneous laughter and applause, and pleased response by delegates who rose and cheered and began to march in the aisles, saying, "That's right, we are all boys and girls, the girls are in politics now, too." It made friendliness for Harding, the agreeable friendliness everybody can afford to have toward one not expected to win.

II

The Game of Games

It was a thrilling game that Daugherty was now about to begin. If tiger-hunting is the sport of kings, how shall we describe the sport of making kings, of making Presidents? Good practitioners at it are as rare as the opportunities for playing it; and these occur only once every four years, in two arenas, in the Democratic National Convention and in the Republican one.[3] Not as often as that, for more than once out of every two occasions, the Presidential nomination is a foregone conclusion; either a President in office is renominated, or for other reasons there is no contest.

[2] Certainly it was the first national convention in which women had a conspicuous part. The Twentieth Amendment to the Constitution, giving national suffrage to women, had just been passed, and party leaders hurried to recognize the innovation with gestures compounded as much of self-interest as of chivalry. Five of the candidates for the Presidential nomination felt it advantageous to have women make seconding speeches: General Leonard Wood's name was seconded by Mrs. Corinne Roosevelt Robinson (sister of Theodore Roosevelt). Governor Calvin Coolidge was seconded by Mrs. Alexandria Carlisle Pfeiffer. Governor Frank O. Lowden was seconded by Mrs. Fletcher Dobyns. Senator Hiram Johnson was seconded by Mrs. Katherine Philip Edson. Nicholas Murray Butler was seconded by Miss Helen Varick Boswell.

[3] A "bush league" diminutive of the game is, of course, played in state conventions, and even city and county ones.

As often as it arises, it is the game of games, a sport of supermen; one can describe it only by analogy of parts of it to other games and sports. Yet it has characteristics that no other sport has.

That part of it which is played on the convention floor has some rules, or conditions, of a kind not duplicated in any other game. Once the play begins, the player must keep his candidate's tally of delegates growing on each successive ballot; at least it must remain as high as on the preceding ballot. To this, there is an exception if the candidate is a dark-horse; so long as he is obscure and unnoticed, it is no damage if he slips back a little on an early ballot. But a candidate who is in the front line of contenders, who is being watched by all the delegates, must make some gain, great or slight, on each ballot — to slip back is fatal. With this rule goes a second: a candidate in the lead must keep in the lead. Once he is passed by another, on any ballot, he is out. A bandwagon must keep the bandwagon's position, continuously.

I do not know clearly why this should be so in this one game, and not in any other. In baseball, a team may lead in the early innings, be behind in the middle ones, and still end a winner. Perhaps the distinction lies in the difference between a baseball and a human being. A baseball has no human attributes; a delegate in a convention has hopes, fears, self-interest, and capacity for treachery. A baseball does the things that make the score — but it cannot watch the scoreboard, and therefore cannot be psychologically influenced by it. In national conventions, a delegate does the things that make the score — but also he watches the score, is aware of it and moved by it. Playing the political game is like playing chess with bishops and knights who are flesh-and-blood, who have emotions and impulses, who occasionally dart about the board on their own initiative, or even desert to the enemy. In the convention game, you have a few men whom you can put where you want them, and who you know will stay where you put them — but as to most of the pawns, the art of the game consists in knowing where they will go of their own initiative, when they yield to self-interest, or are moved by panic or other emotion. And, essentially, this is what the political game is. The skilled player lets the delegate, or leads him to, do what he thinks is in his own self-interest or desire; lets him act on individual hope or fright. But the master-player so manœuvres as to cause most of the delegates to defeat their individual desires. He causes the mass as a whole to do what more than half of them never intended to do. A skilled player can cause a thousand men in a room to do what nine hundred never thought they would do.

On the board as it lay when the balloting was about to begin, Wood had about a third of the delegates and Lowden about a third. For Harding, Daugherty had somewhat less than a tenth. The rest were scattered among some fifteen minor candidates and favorite sons. As between Wood and Lowden, Wood had a few more, hence Wood would be in the lead in the early ballots.

With the board standing thus, Daugherty arranged his little army of Harding delegates with a skill composed of alertness and patience. Most of them, of course, he must vote[4] for Harding on the first ballot, and continuously. But others he would save, concealing them, spreading them about among other candidates, so as to be able to add them to Harding's tally little by little on later ballots, and thus make that impression of steady

---

[4] "Vote" as a transitive verb, in the sense of a manager "voting" his delegates, is not recognized by the dictionary but is familiar in the terminology of conventions.

growth which operates powerfully on convention psychology.

Yet others of his Harding delegates Daugherty reserved for another purpose. He knew his first task must be to "kill off" Wood. For killing off Wood, he knew the best instrumentality, indeed the only one, was Lowden. So Daugherty went to Lowden's manager and

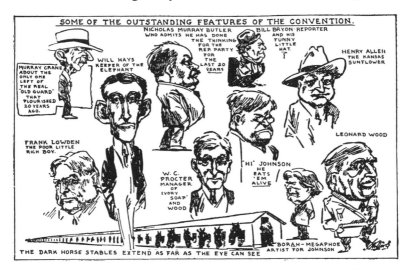

Caricatures from the New York *Tribune* of important figures at the Republican National Convention of 1920. Bryan was present as a reporter.

made an alliance, a carefully qualified alliance. Daugherty would, he told the Lowden manager, help Lowden beat down Wood, would devote to that purpose as many of his Harding delegates as he could spare. "We can't allow," Daugherty said, "Harding's vote to be too small, but we'll loan you every vote we can until you pass Wood." [5] Daugherty was explicit about the strictly limited duration of the alliance. He carefully told the Lowden manager that "the minute you pass Wood, the minute Wood is out of the race, all friendship between

[5] "The Inside Story of the Harding Tragedy," H. M. Daugherty.

us on the floor of this convention ceases — you understand that." [6] The Lowden manager said, "Certainly, you couldn't make a fairer proposition." The two shook hands and Daugherty went off to deploy his delegates.

The balloting, when it began, took the course that Daugherty had sensed it would. The two principal candidates, Wood and Lowden, had each about the same number of delegates. On the first ballot, there was material difference; Wood having 287½, Lowden only 211½. But from the beginning, Lowden grew more rapidly than Wood. (Partly with the aid of the delegates temporarily "loaned" to him by Daugherty.)

By the fourth ballot, Wood was still in the lead, with 314½, but Lowden had come up close behind, with 289. And it was apparent to persons who were experienced in such battles and knew the present conditions, that on the next ballot, Lowden would pass Wood. Yet it was equally apparent, to the elder statesmen paternally watching the scene, if not to the candidates or delegates, that Lowden could not win. The law of human nature that Daugherty had counted on would now work. Each of the two major candidates would prevent the nomination of the other. First, Lowden would keep Wood from success. Thereafter, many of the Wood delegates would vote for anybody rather than Lowden. Similarly the Lowden delegates, so soon as they should realize their own candidate could not win, would blame his defeat on Wood and would vote for anybody rather than Wood. Neither Wood nor Lowden could win. This was not yet, however, apparent to the delegates, nor to any except those experienced with conventions.

The time when this became apparent was about five

[6] "The Inside Story of the Harding Tragedy," by H. M. Daugherty.

o'clock of the first day's balloting, Friday afternoon, with the convention only one day to go. The condition constituted a considerable concern to the party elders. Two of them acted.

Senators Reed Smoot of Utah and Henry Cabot Lodge of Massachusetts — the latter was the presiding officer — whispered together on the platform. Smoot stepped forward to the edge of the platform. "I move," he said, "that the convention do now stand adjourned until ten o'clock to-morrow morning." In the silence of a surprised convention, Lodge put the motion, put it with characteristic Harvard precision — always Lodge preserved the manner of the scholar in politics. "Those in favor of the motion to adjourn will signify it by saying 'Aye.' " There were a few scattering "Ayes." Again Lodge intoned, "Those opposed 'No.' " There was a roar of "Nos." The delegates, especially those of Wood and Lowden who composed the majority of the convention, were still in fighting heat, still expected their respective candidates to win, were still eager to be at each other and were in no mood for adjournment. But Lodge, with complete insouciance, ceasing to be the scholar in politics and becoming the practised political manipulator — Lodge announced, turning boredly from his desk before he completed the sentence, "The 'Ayes' have it and the convention is adjourned until to-morrow morning at ten o'clock." Every delegate knew the "Nos" had far outnumbered the "Ayes," but accepted the chairman's decision calmly, rather smilingly. Assuming that the party gods must have some good reason, the delegates accepted the palpably false decision in the spirit of "father knows best." [7] Both the Wood dele-

---

[7] The account of this in the stenographic report published by the Republican National Committee, differs from what I have here said. The official report says there was "a mighty chorus of Ayes" and "Quite a number of Noes." I think the stenographic reporter was practising good manners. Since the chairman of the

gates and the Lowden delegates, and their leaders, continued to think their respective candidates would win the next day.

As Senator Smoot left, I went with him. We rode downtown together. I asked him, "Why did you and Lodge force that adjournment?" He replied, "Oh, there's going to be a deadlock and we'll have to work out some solution; we wanted the night to think it over." [8]

III

Smoot and Lodge had acted spontaneously, without consultation with any one except each other. Their intervention was much in the spirit of a couple of faculty members observing a freshman football game likely to become dangerously rough, and finding some excuse for

---

convention, the exalted Senator Lodge of Massachusetts, had stated officially that there were more Ayes, the stenographic report could hardly say there were less. What Smoot and Lodge did was evident to every one. I was on the platform at the time. A few minutes before, following the third ballot, there had been a motion to adjourn which had come from the floor, not from the elders; on that earlier motion there was a roll call, of which the result was, Noes 701½, Ayes 275½. No one had any great objection to the action of Smoot and Lodge. Every one assumed they had some good reason; no one charged at any time that the adjournment was forced in the interest of any candidate or against the interest of any. The delegates, a great majority of them, wanted to go on balloting. The wish to adjourn came from the elders of the party who foresaw, as the delegates did not yet, a prolonged deadlock between the Wood forces and the Lowden forces, which the elders wished to avert.

[8] Leaving Smoot at his hotel I went to the room of Wood's manager, Frank H. Hitchcock. "Frank," I asked, "do you expect Wood to gain on the first ballot to-morrow?" He said he did. I questioned him in detail as to where he expected to get his additional delegates for the next ballot and the next and the next. To all my questions he gave answers which seemed to reflect genuine confidence on his part that Wood could continue to grow. By the time I had ended my questioning his lieutenants began to arrive for conference. Feeling that I might get involved in betrayal of confidence, I merely said, "Well, good luck to you, Frank," and took myself off.

I was obliged to decide between the judgment of Smoot that Wood could not win, and the judgment of Hitchcock that Wood would. I chose to rely on Smoot, and wrote a despatch for the next day's papers saying that Wood would be beaten.

calling "time out." By their action, the two Senators had achieved a breathing-spell over night, during which the elders could consider what to do. But neither they nor any of the other elders knew what to do. They knew that the convention, if left to itself, would go first into a deadlock, and then into unorganized confusion, and that in the confusion anybody might be nominated, perhaps some one undesirable. Moreover, that kind of ending of the convention would leave scars and hates, which might be damaging in the ensuing campaign against the Democrats. The elders realized it would be well for them to take hold of the situation, to have a plan, and a candidate.

In speaking of the "party elders" I use the term merely as a convenient description for some twelve or fifteen individuals. They were not a body having any formal place or function in the party hierarchy. They were not a body at all. They were not conscious of any obligation for collective action. They were merely men who as individuals had held, at one time or another over a long period, high positions in the party, or held high public office as Republicans; men who through attendance at many conventions had come to know and understand each other, and who had a sense of responsibility for the fortunes of the party as a whole, as distinguished from concern' with candidates or factions. Most of them were Senators. Others had served long periods as members of the Republican National Committee; others had long had command of the party organizations in their respective states; still others had various titles to be regarded as elders.

That night four of them dined together, Senator Charles W. Curtis of Kansas (later Vice-President), Senator Frank Brandegee of Connecticut, Senator Henry Cabot Lodge of Massachusetts, and George Harvey.

Harvey was not really a Republican elder; he was not a delegate to the convention, he was hardly indeed a Republican. So far as he was a Republican at all, he was a recent apostate from the Democrats, and his apostasy had been caused by the failure of the Democratic President, Woodrow Wilson, to appreciate Harvey at what Harvey regarded as his true worth. Harvey's present position in the inner circles of the Republicans gathered at Chicago had been achieved largely by self-election. He was an ambitious person and he managed to secure for himself a larger hand in affairs than the real party elders would have voluntarily given him, and a larger amount of publicity than any of the real Republican elders would have sought — and a larger amount of credit for what now took place than was justified by the facts. The dinner of the four was in Harvey's suite at the Blackstone Hotel; Harvey managed to make his rooms, during the night, a kind of informal headquarters for all the elders, and to make himself a kind of self-selected master of ceremonies.

The four agreed that Wood and Lowden would deadlock each other next morning, and that thereafter the nomination would be likely to go to whoever among the other candidates should have the first "pick-up," that is, whoever should show strength in the first ballot after the deadlock and the ensuing "break." They agreed that it was desirable not to leave the outcome to chance, and they decided that the elders should have a candidate and should see to it that their man had the first "pick-up." But whom should they take? They discussed several possibilities: Charles E. Hughes, whose name had not figured in the convention; Senator Philander C. Knox of Pennsylvania, Governor Sproul of Pennsylvania, Will Hays, who as chairman of the Republican National Committee had made a record of energetic efficiency (he

was particularly the choice of George Harvey). Finally,
and dubiously, they discussed Harding. Unable to be enthusiastic about any of the possibilities, they gave thought
to adjourning the convention over Sunday. Giving up
that recourse to procrastination, they again reviewed the
possible nominees. Finally, and reluctantly, some of
them, though not all, decided Harding was the most
available.

Of the four, Curtis was the most confident they had
best take Harding. Energetic and competent, Curtis
started out to call on state leaders and arrange to have
delegates vote for Harding in the morning, so that Harding should be the one to have the first "pick-up." The
others remained in Harvey's suite. From time to time
during the night, Curtis came back to the room; he
brought other leaders with him; yet other leaders
dropped in. On each, as he came, the Harding suggestion was tried out. Some opposed the notion; none had
any enthusiasm or conviction for it. From time to time
they renewed their discussion of other possibilities. Harvey suggested Will Hays, but the suggestion did not take
hold. Discussion of one suggestion after another was succeeded by intervals of moody silence. "It was," wrote
Senator Wadsworth reminiscently years later,[9] "a sort
of continuous performance. I was in and out of that
room several times that night. They were like a lot of
chickens with their heads off. They had no program
and no definite affirmative decision was reached. If they
came to any decision at all it was a decision to let the
Harding suggestion go through, the fact being that they
did not have any one else to propose."

The room became, so far as there was any such thing,
the "smoke-filled room" that Daugherty had anticipated. Daugherty, however, was not in it — but his

[9] In a letter to the author, March 5, 1935.

logic was, and his logic was as effective as his presence. From time to time, procrastination was discussed, to adjourn the convention over Sunday. But Daugherty had taken that, too, into account. From long experience and insight into human nature, especially delegate nature, Daugherty knew that the next day, Saturday, the delegates would be tired, that they would be coming to the end of the funds they had brought to Chicago with them, that two-thirds of them would have become disgusted by realization that their candidates could not win, and that in their emotional exhaustion they would make some nomination before Saturday night. Daugherty was in a position to sit tight, and he did. In the end, the "fifteen men" came to a kind of indifferent, tired unanimity — more a negation of other candidates than an affirmative agreement on Harding.[10]

About two o'clock in the morning — near enough to 2:11 to be sufficiently dramatic — Harvey sent for Harding. Harding came, heavy-eyed, heaving from time to time the sighs of strain and anxiety. Harvey received him alone, in another room.

Harvey addressed him, solemnly — and George Harvey could be very solemn indeed. He wore heavy horn-rimmed spectacles — he had acquired some of his fame years before, had caused people to notice him and re-

[10] Once the elders decided to let Harding have it, they concluded that that was what they had wished and intended from the begining. One of them unbosomed his wisdom, and prescience, to a newspaper man, Mark Sullivan, who printed it on June 14. The despatch, here condensed and paraphrased, said:

"The theory behind the nomination of Senator Harding is that the man in the White House must not think he is bigger than the Senators. They wanted a man who was by nature disposed to seek counsel rather than act independently. They wanted a man in the White House who would more or less defer to the leaders of his party in the Senate. They think that the President should not send legislation to Congress to be passed, but that Congress should send legislation to the President to be signed."

Actually, Harding, when in the White House, did not defer particularly to the Senate.

member him, when he was a comparatively young man, during the 1890's, by being the first person to wear shell-rimmed spectacles in an America which, up to that

From a photograph © by Harris & Ewing. From Globe.

Harding and Colonel George Harvey, at the time Harvey was made ambassador to Great Britain.

time, knew only gold or other metal. Behind the heavy spectacles were eyes solemnly slumbrous; the impression was borne out by heavy, immobile features, slow and impressive speech, and extreme seriousness of manner. "We think," Harvey said to Harding, "you may be nominated to-morrow; before acting finally, we think you should tell us, on your conscience and before God, whether there is anything that might be brought up against you that would embarrass the party, any impediment that might disqualify you or make you inexpedient, either as candidate or as President."

Harding, rather stunned, said he would like to have a little time. Harvey showed him into a vacant room of the suite.

The ten minutes that Harding spent alone in that room were fateful. It would be interesting to know what went on in Harding's mind. Some years later, a story[11] about Harding emerged sensationally, a story which if based on facts would have constituted an impediment to Harding as candidate and as President. It was what politicians call a "woman story," precisely the kind covered by the question Harvey had asked. Did Harding think about this? Conjecture is made difficult, and Harding's personal situation at the time was made complex, by the fact that in his heart he had not wanted the nomination; had tried, in his too easy-going way, to escape it. Was this story one of his reasons for not having wanted the nomination? Did he now give consideration to finally renouncing the nomination by telling Harvey there was an impediment?

Harding, after some ten minutes alone, opened the door into the room where Harvey was waiting. He told Harvey there was no impediment. Harvey went back to the smoke-filled room where the others were still in conference.[12]

---

[11] The story is told in Chapter 15 of this history.

[12] It was not really a conference but a shifting group made up of some twelve or fifteen men who from time to time came into Harvey's room and went and returned. Because it was dramatic and important, and because it seemed to con-

IV

At ten o'clock the next morning, when the convention came together, the elders took hold of the situation. Not too firmly or too openly. They did not need to do that. All they needed, as respects the early ballots of the day, was to let events take the course which the experienced elders knew to be pre-destined. It would be a mistake, a detriment to their later purpose and a possible damage to the party, for them to seem to be responsible for eliminating Wood and Lowden. They must let Wood and Lowden mutually eliminate each other, as was bound to happen. Happening that way, there would be no resentment on the part of the third of the convention who were for Wood or the third who were for Lowden. That is, of course, no resentment except as against each other; there would be no resentment against the party leaders nor against the candidate who must ultimately be chosen. And so there were several ballots which were partly the natural development of the situation and partly the shrewd directing of the elders, designed for window-dressing, face-saving and other desirable effects.

The elders, partly to let Lowden and his delegates save face, conducted one ballot, the fifth of the convention, in which Lowden took the lead, registering 303 to Wood's 299. That gave pleasure to Lowden and his delegates; it was to be a kind of consolation prize.

Then there were three ballots in which Wood and Lowden were exactly even or practically so: 311½ to

---

form to the phrase Daugherty had made famous, "fifteen men in a smoke-filled room," much talk arose about it, and much print. Many versions were told. The incident of George Harvey's talk with Harding was told me on Sunday morning, June 13, within 36 hours after the conference took place, and in the same room, by Harvey.

311½ in the sixth ballot; 312 for Wood to 311½ for
Lowden in the seventh; and 299 for Wood to 307 for
Lowden in the eighth. Those three ballots, with the
two major candidates seesawing within a margin of eight
delegates, was notice to both that neither could win. It
left each, and the friends of each, with no grievance, nor
any reason to sulk in the coming campaign against the
Democrats.

By the ninth ballot all the amenities and anticipatory
prudences had been taken care of. It was late Saturday
afternoon, 46 minutes past 4; it was time to conclude.
On this ballot Harding was given 374½ votes — his
highest preceding had been 133½. That ballot was
notice to all that Harding was the man; notice to all who
desired to ride on the bandwagon that the wheels were
about to roll. The delegates rushed for it.[13] On the
tenth ballot, Harding's total was 692⅕ and he was nominated.

It was late on a Saturday afternoon, 6:23 p. m. Harding, sought by every reporter at the convention, focus-
point now of all the country's instrumentalities of light,
the whole country awaiting what he should say —
Harding, flustered, not at his best, not even at *his* modest
best, but very accurate, put his comment in words that
reflected his background and habit of mind: "We drew

---

[13] That is, all rushed for the bandwagon who preferred thrift over loyalty.
There was one sizable group that preferred loyalty. They numbered 156, and
they voted for General Wood on the last ballot as they had on the first. It was a
tribute to Wood, to his character, his personality, his leadership, his ability to
inspire loyalty.

"Of all the candidates [wrote Mark Sullivan in the New York *Evening Post,*
June 15, 1920] Wood was the more gallant figure in defeat. He met defeat standing squarely in his solid military boots in the middle of the entrance to his headquarters, giving to every comer smiles of almost jovial composure in return for
condolences. That is what duty and taste call for at such a time, and that is
what Wood would always do. He is one of the most completely self-disciplined
of living men."

to a pair of deuces,[14] and filled." He said it with more
ruefulness than elation.

Daugherty, during the afternoon when the strain was
tensest, had come up behind Mrs. Harding, seated in a
box, and leaned over to whisper to her that on the next
ballot her husband would be nominated. Mrs. Harding,
by the sudden start she gave, drove two hat-pins into
Daugherty's side. He felt the pain, felt what seemed
the trickling of blood down his side, and was a little
alarmed. Characteristically he said nothing to Mrs.
Harding. Characteristically he did nothing — the next
ballot would be the crisis and climax of his career. As he
hurried about he felt the queer swish of liquid in his
shoe. After all was over, late that night, he tottered
to his room, took off his shoe and found it full of perspiration.[15]

[14] The metaphor is from the American game called poker. The expression was
not characteristic of Harding — it violated his canon of seemliness. He may
have said it because he was "off balance" from excitement. Or he may never
have said it — it may have been some reporter's conception of what he ought to
say.

[15] This naïvely vivid story about Daugherty's strain during the climax of his
long effort is told by him in his book, "The Inside Story of the Harding
Tragedy."

About Daugherty's mood after the strain was over, and victory won, there
was another incident characteristic of the degree in which temperament entered
into his complex make-up :

The following day Daugherty, after a hurried cleaning-up of the débris of
victory at Chicago, returned to his home town, Columbus. Arriving at the station, he told the chauffeur to drive past the office of the Columbus *Evening Despatch,* whose owner, editor, and cartoonist had been conspicuous opponents of
Harding's nomination, conspicuous scoffers at the notion that Daugherty could
"put Harding over." Passing the *Despatch* office, Daugherty leaned out the taxi-
cab to fling a jeering shout and a jeering gesture at the cartoonist, William Ireland, who was at work by an open window. When Daugherty arrived at his own
office, his first act was to tell his secretary to go out and buy a small alarm clock,
to set the hands at 2:11, and to deliver the clock to cartoonist Ireland at precisely 2:11. Then Daugherty called up several of the leading citizens of Columbus, friends of his and of Ireland's, and told them to call Ireland on the
'phone immediately after 2:11 and ask Ireland what time it was.

4

A FOOTNOTE

Concerning the Writing of Contemporary History; and the
Situations, Sometimes Painful but Salutary for Accuracy,
in Which the Historian Occasionally Becomes Involved.

I HAVE given much space to this story of the nomination of Warren Harding for the Presidency, and of the 1920 Republican National Convention, partly of course because it was an important event in the history of our times, and partly because it seemed to me worth while to have on record a detailed and authentic account of how a candidacy was promoted. I was moved, too, by an apprehension, felt faintly and reluctantly yet palpably in the year in which this history was written, 1935, that this method of choosing the head of the nation might in time be displaced by another; and that a description of the process by an eye-witness, checked by the recollection of living participants, might come, in time, to have the interest and value of a contemporary account of an obsolete institution.

The process, though an important part of the mechanism of government in the United States, is understood by few except a quite small group of leaders in each of the two great parties. Nowhere, so far as I know — and I am familiar with most of the literature of American politics — is there an account as complete and detaiied as the one I have here written. There is in Volume IV of "Our Times" a narrative of the struggle between Theodore Roosevelt and William H. Taft at the Republican National Convention of 1912; but that describes the duel between two candidates, rather than, as in the present case, the moves by which one candidate was made to win. There is an excellent detailed account of the Republican National Convention that nominated Lincoln in 1860 — it is in Mr. George Fort Milton's "Age of Hate" — but inasmuch as Mr. Milton wrote in 1930 he was obliged to rely wholly on written records. And a national convention, the process of nominating a Presidential candidate, is to an exceptional degree a thing about which the formal record fails to tell the whole story. In that process, the informal understandings of men with men, agreements achieved sometimes by a look from one man and a nod from another, the reactions of men to sudden and unexpected crises on the convention floor, the play of human psychology, individual and mass — these form, in many cases, the major part, a part which the stenographic reports of the convention, and the statistics of balloting, cannot even faintly reveal.

In the writing of this narrative of the nomination of Harding (as in the writing of all of "Our Times") the process began with composing a first draft. In making this, the ordinary sources were searched, the official proceedings of the Republican National Convention at Chicago in 1920, newspaper files covering the months of the pre-nomination campaign and during the week of the convention, the reports of certain Senate investigations and parts of the *Congressional Record* containing relevant material, the biographies, autobiographies, and other books that deal with or allude to the convention and the nomination. The material thus garnered was united with material of my own, notes I had made at the time, correspondence I had had, newspaper despatches I had written. Out of all this the first draft was made.

This early draft I sent to a job printer, with instructions to set it up and make fifty copies. These I sent to all those who had had any part in the events described and were still living, with requests that they read the drafts carefully and make notes of anything which, according to their recollections and records, was in error — any mistakes of fact, any omissions, anything which in their opinion was an error of judgment or an incorrectness of characterization. As a result of these requests I received some fifty letters, practically all painstaking and voluminous — it is my experience that men are generous about this sort of enterprise.

Examination of these letters, comparison of each with each and of all with my own early draft, sifting out what was corrective, or new, or otherwise relevant and important; and weaving the additions and modifications into my own text — that constituted, in large part, the final writing of the chapter.

This is not an easy method of writing history, but it is very much worth while; indeed, I think it is a superior method. By no possibility could a complete or fully accurate account of the events covered by this chapter be achieved, if the writer were confined to the documents and other printed records. Much of the most important, the most decisive, of what happened was never put on record. Not that there was, in the present case, any great reason for concealment; it was merely that decisive episodes occurred in word-of-mouth conversations, which there was no occasion to put on record.

The method of writing history which combines the formal records with the recollections of participants and eye-witnesses results in greater accuracy than any other. But it is a method which on occasion causes the historian's person to become, so to speak, a bloody battleground, upon which contending witnesses struggle to make their varying versions "stick." Mere dissonances of memories are comparatively easy to reconcile. But it sometimes happens that a participant in events has urgent reason to try to have his version accepted. The place of a man in history, the esteem of posterity for him — in some cases his escape from obloquy — may depend on his persuading history to accept his account of what he did and why. With almost equal frequency, it happens that another participant has equally urgent reasons to have a contrary version accepted. Such contradictions of assertion, accompanied by almost passionate insistence of each upon his own version, have led to strong argument, with the historian in the rôle of at once, umpire and arena. About handling such situations, there can be no standard technique. Most of them present no insuperable difficulty, for almost always one version or the other is so supported by evidence from other sources that the historian, who alone has brought all the facts before him, is able to say which is correct. When the facts of any situation are completely assembled, they usually compose a pattern, a picture, in which it is as difficult for an inexactness to find a place as for an alien piece to be fitted into a jig-saw puzzle.

II

In this account of the nomination of Harding, the differences of the participants, with me and with each other, grouped themselves mainly into some four.

One was a question about an easily verifiable fact: Some asserted that Harding did not file for the Senate, others that he did. As it happened, what should be the final authority, the records at the State House in Columbus, Ohio, failed to show. But indisputable evidence came from the man, still living, who acted as Harding's agent.[1] Harding did file.

Another group of differences were in a field where overt fact is inextricably mingled with invert motive — and the motive of any man in any situation is, of all matters, one of the most difficult to be exact about; in the nature of things, any assertion about it by any man involves knowing what went on in another man's mind. To speak of "knowing" in that connection is a misuse of the word. At best, one can only make inferences from the man's words and actions, and in many cases a man's words, and even more his actions, are not a complete sign of his motives; often a man is himself unaware of the motives that inspired him to a given action.

Some questioned my assertion that Harding did not want the Presidential nomination. The much greater weight of evidence and opinion, however, agrees with my own observation at the time, that Harding did not want to run, that he longed to stay in the Senate. In the situation in which Harding was placed, he was obliged, as part of the dissimulation forced upon him, to seem to want the nomination. To strangers, to the audiences he was addressing, to casual acquaintances, and particularly to party leaders, he was obliged to seem to be striving for the prize. Only to the most intimate of his friends could he relax and be frank. One of these was Harry S. New, later Postmaster-General under Harding, and Mr. New wrote me: "What you say of Harding's lack of desire

[1] Extract from a letter from Geo. B. Harris, of Cleveland, Ohio, dated August 7, 1935:

"On Thursday evening of the week of the Chicago Convention in 1920, at the request of Senator Harding, I left [Chicago] for Ohio, bringing with me a declaration of candidacy for the office of United States Senator. My instructions from him were to go to the Deshler Hotel, be there the evening of Friday, which was the last day for filing such declaration, and await instructions from him. He called me between eight and nine o'clock and directed me to file the declaration. I did before midnight. At the same time I paid the filing fee. Why this does not appear in the records of the Secretary of State I am of course unable to state, but the information above set forth is correct."

to be President is absolutely true. I know well that he
did *not* want to be President." Charles Curtis, Senator from Kansas, later Vice-President, said: "I was on
the train with Mr. and Mrs. Harding (together with
Speaker and Mrs. Nicholas Longworth, future Justice
of the Supreme Court George H. Sutherland, and Senator Frank Brandegee) when they went from Washington to the convention at Chicago; Harding said he had
no show for the nomination, was extremely reluctant to
be in it; said he felt like withdrawing even if his withdrawal left Daugherty out on a limb." [2]

As one group of differences had to do with Harding's
mind, so another had to do with Mrs. Harding's. A few
questioned my assertion that Mrs. Harding urged her
husband toward the Presidency. But about this, also,
there can be no doubt. Ralph V. Sollitt, who was
active in Republican politics at the time, writes: "I remember one incident. Harding was out in Indiana making some speeches. He determined that the fight was not
worth the effort, and he decided he would withdraw his

[2] ". . . He did not *want* to be President, but as you point out, would have
much preferred to remain in the Senate. But his friends having prevailed upon
him to permit the use of his name, he most reluctantly withheld *withdrawing it*,
thereby leaving in the lurch the friends who had really maneuvered him into a
position from which he feared he might be nominated. Of course, toward the
culmination of it all he did stand up and fight a little, because he was goaded
into doing so." — Harry S. New, Postmaster-General in Harding's cabinet. In
a letter to the author, March, 1935.

"*Prior to the convention he [Harding] really had no expectation of being nominated. A month before the convention he and I went to Boston together, occupying the same drawing room in the parlor car to attend the annual dinner of the
Home Market Club, where Harding and I were speakers. Harding had partially
lost his own state and had just lost Indiana; and on our trip he told me that he
considered himself entirely out of the race and was glad of it. In his speech at
Boston he conveyed the same thought, venturing the prediction that Coolidge,
then Governor of Massachusetts, might receive the nomination, but that he himself had no expectation of receiving it.*" — Irvine L. Lenroot, former Senator
from Wisconsin, Judge of the United States Court of Customs and Patent Appeals. In a letter to the author, March, 1935.

"*He [Harding] stated to me that he did not desire it; that he had rather be
Senator from Ohio than anything else in the world, in which I know he was
sincere.*" — Joseph I. France, former Senator from Maryland. In a letter to the
author, March, 1935.

candidacy. Mrs. Harding consulted a crystal-gazer. The crystal-gazer gave Mrs. Harding the answer that Mrs. Harding desired, and Mrs. Harding got Harding on the long-distance phone, raising Cain with him because he had any notion of quitting, and telling him he had to keep on."

Some questioned the largeness of the part played by Harry Daugherty in making Harding President. The thesis of these was mainly that Wood and Lowden were certain to cancel each other, and that in the ensuing stalemate Harding would have been chosen even had there never been a Daugherty. But I doubt whether a nomination for the Presidency (or anything else) ever merely "happens," always it must be brought about and always somebody must play the part of bringer about. And no one except Daugherty had ever taken upon himself the business of bringing about the nomination of Harding. Indeed, I never knew any one[3] else who was on record as having said seriously, before the convention, that Harding would be the nominee. On the Thursday of convention week, about fifty hours before the nomination was made, a New York banker, Fred W. Allen, gave a luncheon in the Blackstone Hotel. The guests included men who should have known who the nominee would be, if knowing were possible at all. Allen proposed that we each write our guess about the nomination and deposit it, with a $5 bill, in a pool, to be given, afterward, to some worthy institution. (There was some badinage as to whether the pool should go to

[3] There is one exception. Colonel George Harvey told me — this was after the event but I think the story was true — that at a house-party on Long Island in the early Spring of 1920, some four months before the Republican National Convention, talk arose about who would be named for President. Harvey said he would write the name, put it in an envelope, seal the envelope, and leave it with his host. The name Harvey wrote was Harding. But Harvey was merely making a guess in the dark. At the convention, Harvey was promoting Will Hays for the nomination — and Harvey was not the man to be promoting one candidate if he felt sure another was to win.

Yale, which was Allen's university, or to Harvard, which was mine.) I wrote the name of General Wood, and forgot the incident. Some weeks later I received a letter from Allen, enclosing my $5, and saying that no one of the twelve or fourteen guests, all supposed to be wise in politics, had named Harding.

III

The method of writing history followed in this volume screens out error. Contemporaneous stories which if left unexamined would presently get a place in history as accepted legends, evaporate under the checking of persons who took part in the events. Any history of the nomination of Harding which should depend on current newspaper accounts would say that a large part, even a dominant part, was taken by Senator Boies Penrose of Pennsylvania. Newspaper stories, and talk of the day that echoed newspaper stories, assigned to Penrose a rôle at once dramatic, mysterious and supreme. Even in a Senate investigation held some years later, witnesses declared or implied that Penrose had dominated the convention, had dictated the nomination of Harding. But I was interested to observe that neither in my own early draft, nor in any of the some fifty letters that gave me information about the convention, did the name "Penrose" appear. The nomination of Harding was no better than one Penrose might have made, but it happened that Penrose did not make it.

The legends that arose at the time were based on one fact, a fact much too dramatic to escape enlargement of its significance. Penrose during convention week was ill at his home in Philadelphia, much of the time in coma. From his sick room two wires, a telephone one and a telegraph one, were routed into a room in the

Auditorium Hotel at Chicago. They were installed at the instance of a Republican politician from Connecticut, an inferior henchman to Penrose, named John T. King. King's purpose was the double one of pleasing and flattering the sick Penrose, and giving himself an appearance of importance. From time to time King took Republican leaders, old acquaintances of Penrose, into the room to send messages and gossip to the latter. But none of the messages had any bearing on the vital part of what the convention was doing. Penrose did not on this occasion control the Pennsylvania delegation, it was controlled by Governor William C. Sproul; and even if Penrose had had control, he was too sick to exercise it. In truth, Penrose was a burnt-out man, shorn of his power and destined soon to die. He would not need to be alluded to in this history except as an illustration of that virtue of contemporary historical writing which consists of the disinfection of romantic legend.

IV

Yet one other virtue contemporary writing of history has; it is published during the life-time of thousands who had some information or contact, faint or large, with the events dealt with. If a book of contemporary history contains mistakes, as it is likely to — no amount of pains can completely exclude error — they are certain to be caught and corrected. The volumes of "Our Times," read by millions of people who lived through the period they cover, of whom many took the pains to write the author letters of comment or criticism or recollections of their own, became, after revision, rather more faithful to truth, I think, than any history written from records after all who could check it had passed away.

5

POSTSCRIPT TO THE NOMINATION
OF HARDING

The Nomination for Vice-President, Done in the Spirit of
an Afterthought, Which, Acted upon in Haste and Taking
an Unintended Direction, Resulted, after the Passage of
Some Three Years, in Happenings of Much Moment.

IT was a sign of the tautness of the convention that little
thought had been given to the nomination for Vice-
President.[1] The party elders had been too deeply concerned about the deadlock between Wood and Lowden;
besides, the party elders could do nothing about the Vice-
Presidency until after they knew, or could safely estimate, who would be the candidate for President — by
unwritten law and common-sense the candidate for
President must be consulted, should indeed have a deciding voice, in the selection of his running-mate.

[1] A legend about the Vice-Presidential nomination that arose during the convention was for years afterward told by word of mouth and in print. It said that
when Senator Knox of Pennsylvania was under consideration for the Presidential nomination, backers of him suggested an ingenious yet convincing pairing:
Knox for President and Hiram Johnson for Vice-President. The combination
was geographically appealing. Pennsylvania on the Atlantic Coast, California
on the Pacific — for that and other reasons it could have commanded, on paper,
enough delegates to win. The proposers of the idea, hot with the fervor of invention, hurried to Johnson. As an allurement, they told him, in strict confidence,
that Knox had heart disease and, if nominated and elected, would probably not
live out the four-year term. Johnson blew up, emitted an indignant sentence:
"You would put a heart-beat between me and the White House!" He was, he
told them sternly, a candidate for the Presidential nomination, and would take
no less.

Later, when the nomination of Harding was assured, his backers — so the legend said — seeking a running-mate, approached Johnson, as one who would help
carry the West, and the progressive part of the Republican party. Again Johnson
blew up. Again he declared that if he could not have first place, he would take
nothing.

Within four years, both Knox and Harding died. Had Johnson either made the
arrangement that Knox's friends suggested, or consented to be the running-mate
of Harding, he would have become President, would have stepped into the shoes
that actually were filled by Calvin Coolidge.

Thus it was not until about midway of the tenth and final ballot, when for the first time it was certain that Harding would win, and within an hour of his nomination, that several of the party elders bethought them of the Vice-Presidential nomination. Hastily they beckoned each other into a little arcanum beneath the stage, not a room, just a space, hardly lighted at all, concealed among the timbers supporting the platform. In a huddle there they discussed what to do. After a few excited minutes they agreed that the best man for Vice-President would be Irvine Lenroot,[2] Senator from Wisconsin — mainly on the theory that Lenroot, a progressive, would give balance to a ticket headed by the conservative Harding. Hurriedly the elders laid out their improvised plan: Senator Medill McCormick of Illinois would go up on the platform and make the speech putting Lenroot in nomination. In picking seconders they took account of the fact that Arkansas begins with "A" and therefore votes early on the roll-calls. Head of the Arkansas delegation was H. L. Remmel, a stout oldguardsman, well known to the delegates from all the states as a spokesman and agent for the elder statesmen — seconding by Remmel of Lenroot would have a bell-wether effect, would be notice to all the delegations, especially the Southern ones, of what the elders wanted done.

Hastily the huddle dissolved, Senator McCormick to go up on the platform and make his nominating speech, others of the elders going out on the floor to notify the three selected as seconders and to whisper the word among the delegations, "It's Lenroot."

The program went according to schedule — up to a certain point. McCormick made his speech putting Len-

[2] A messenger, Will Hays, despatched to notify Lenroot, found him reluctant, even unwilling. After urgent pressing by Hays, Lenroot, still unwilling, said he would consult his wife. She agreed with her husband in his unwillingness. Lenroot hurried to tell the Senators that he would not take the nomination; but by the time he could reach them the stampede for Coolidge was on.

root in nomination. Remmel and the others made their speeches seconding him.

But before there was time for a motion that the nominations be closed, a wiry, active delegate from Oregon, Wallace McCamant,[3] climbed on his chair, demanded and got the attention of the presiding officer, and put in nomination "for the exalted office of Vice-President, Governor Calvin Coolidge of Massachusetts."

At once there arose what the stenographer at the convention described as "an outburst of applause of short duration but of great power." That meant that the convention was going to take the bit in its teeth and run away, the plan of the elders was "in the soup," the beans were spilled, the applecart upset, the nomination of Lenroot was "out." Earliest to recognize it and act was Remmel of Arkansas. Promptly he executed one of the quickest "about-faces" in the history of deliberative bodies, and proceeded to do his bell-wethering in another direction, the direction in which, he saw, the bandwagon was going to go. Rising for the second time in ten minutes, Remmel got the attention of the chair and announced, after a sentence or two of awkward explanation: ". . . I now wish to withdraw my second of the nomination of Senator Lenroot and to second the nomination of Governor Coolidge." The arrant apostasy, far from being reproved, was greeted with applause.

Even before the outburst of applause that attended first mention of Coolidge's name, most of the elders had

[3] Mr. McCamant wrote me in 1935: "A notice to the effect that Lenroot was the program choice for Vice-President was handed to the chairman of the Oregon delegation, Honorable John L. Rand, by, I presume, one of the scouts from the group of party elders who had so decided. Mr. Rand passed the notice around to the other seven delegates then remaining in the convention. No one of the delegates was pleased by the Lenroot suggestion. The suggestion that Coolidge's name be put before the convention was made by Honorable Charles H. Carey of Portland. He also suggested that I speak for the delegation in so doing. I asked the others whether the suggestion met with their approval. They nodded yes."

realized their plan of nominating Lenroot was in danger. One of the seconders of Lenroot had been interrupted by a voice from the floor crying "Not on your life." It was noticeable that this affirmation of negation came not after the name of Senator Lenroot, but after the words, "of Wisconsin." The delegates had nothing against Lenroot — but much against Wisconsin. Not really against Wisconsin either, but against Wisconsin's most conspicuous citizen, Senator Robert M. LaFollette the elder. Daily they had seen LaFollette's Wisconsin delegates come dourly into the convention, holding themselves self-righteously apart. Daily they had seen the little Wisconsin group take an "off" position on practically every question that came up, a recalcitrant little minority, holier-than-thou. On every ballot they had seen the Wisconsin delegates vote for LaFollette — and no one else vote for him; when all was done and the customary motion was made "that the nomination of Senator Harding be made unanimous," they had seen Wisconsin alone say surlily "No," to a chorus of hisses from the more sportsmanlike remainder of the convention. The delegates had seen that; and most of them, habitual attendants at conventions, had seen LaFollette and his Wisconsin delegates perform similarly in every convention for twelve years past. The convention was sore at LaFollette; because LaFollette meant Wisconsin, they were sore at Wisconsin; and because Lenroot came from Wisconsin, they would not have him for Vice-Presidential nominee.

The rejection of Lenroot was as misdirected as spite frequently is, and as any vicarious revenge is always sure to be. Lenroot was not a LaFollette man. He had been, during his earlier years in politics, a lieutenant of La-Follette; but as he grew more mature he had been repelled by the stridency and extremeness of LaFollette's dogmatism, and had begun to go his own way, not by any means to stand-pat conservatism, but to a reasonable liberalism of his own.

It was not alone distaste for Wisconsin that caused the convention to reject Lenroot. The delegates, in the hour that had followed Harding's nomination for President, had become irritable. They were hot and tired — it was late Saturday evening; those of them who had been for Wood and Lowden and other unsuccessful candidates felt "grouchy"; many of them had begun to be resentful about the "elder statesmen," mainly Senators, who were in charge of the convention. Now, when they saw the Senators try to give the Vice-Presidential nomination to one of their own body, Lenroot, the delegates took a kind of bitter pleasure in frustrating the programme.

II

For the spontaneity with which the convention turned to Coolidge, there was solid reason. The convention and the country thought well of him.

Coolidge had come to the attention of the country in a striking way nine months before. He was governor of Massachusetts. A large part of the police force of Boston had formed a union and affiliated with the American Federation of Labor. 1117 patrolmen, practically 90 per cent of the body, had gone on strike, leaving the city practically defenseless against crime and riot. The incident had startled the whole nation. Governor Coolidge had called out the entire State Guard. The national head of the American Federation of Labor, Samuel Gompers, had proposed an arbitration "to honorably adjust a mutually unsatisfactory situation. . . ." Coolidge had sent a reply in which one terse sentence stood out: "There is no right to strike against the public safety, by anybody, anywhere, any time." [3a]

That sentence had made Coolidge known to the country. Some friends and admirers, mainly fellow-gradu-

From a photograph by Brown Brothers.

Governor Calvin Coolidge at his desk in the State House, Boston.

ates of Amherst, had started a movement to get him the Presidential nomination. Some of Coolidge's speeches had been collected into a volume,[3b] which was sent to political leaders throughout the country. Coolidge had disavowed the movement, had written a public letter in which he said it was his duty to administer the office of Governor for the benefit of the people of Massachusetts, and not use it as a means to attain a higher office. "It is

[3a] For an account of the Boston police strike see Ch. 9.
[3b] Entitled "Have Faith in Massachusetts."

always well for men to walk humbly," he added. But his admirers kept the movement up. A great Boston merchant, Frank W. Stearns, set up modest Coolidge headquarters at the convention and personally put a copy of "Have Faith in Massachusetts" into the hands of the delegates. Coolidge's name, as a candidate for the Presidential nomination, had been placed before the convention in two especially felicitous speeches, one by Frederick H. Gillett who said that Coolidge's action in the police strike had rejoiced "every lover of order"; another by a woman who had been a talented actress, Alexandra Carlisle Pfeiffer — her dramatic recital of a series of epigrammatic sentences praising Coolidge proved that charm is as potent an accessory to women in politics as in any other sphere, and was a refreshing oasis in the desert of turgid nominating speeches the delegates had sat under.

All this, and what else they knew of Coolidge, had impressed the delegates — if the Coolidge candidacy for the Presidential nomination had been pressed with half the astuteness that had been behind Harding's, Coolidge would have been the nominee. Now the convention leaped to the opportunity to give him the Vice-Presidential place.

The vote, 674½ out of a total of 984, was recorded "with tumultuous applause and cheers" — it was the one spontaneous thing the convention had had a chance to do. A spectator, a quite important spectator — he was by this time 86 years old and a kind of grandfather to the whole Republican party, Chauncey M. Depew, wired to Coolidge in Boston: "I have been present at every Republican convention beginning with 1856, and I have never seen such a spontaneous and enthusiastic tribute to a man as the vote for you for Vice-President." [4]

---

[4] The telegram is here quoted as it was remembered by Frank W. Stearns.

Coolidge in Boston — it was about eight o'clock of a Saturday night when he would have finished his evening walk from the State House along the Common, past the dry goods store of his friend Frank W. Stearns, to his hermit-like two-room apartment in the old Adams House — Coolidge was visibly unexcited.

In the room with Coolidge was his wife — she used to come in occasionally from their home at Northampton. The telephone rang. Coolidge listened. Putting down the receiver he said: "I have been nominated for Vice-President." Mrs. Coolidge said: "You are not going to accept it, are you?" The expression on Coolidge's face did not change; he replied: "I suppose I shall have to." [5]

[5] This account of Coolidge's receipt of the information that he had been nominated for Vice-President is from a letter of Mrs. Coolidge to the author, June 8, 1935.

6

HARDING ON HIS FRONT PORCH

*The Environment, Background, and Antecedents of a Man
Who Was Nominated for President of the United States.
His Personal Traits, Which Included Kindliness and Gener-
osity. And Likewise Tolerance — Perhaps Too Much of
That. And Loyalty — Too Much of That Also. And Easy-
goingness about His Friends — Clearly Too Much of That.*

HARDING, nominated, told the Republican managers
he would make the campaign from his home at Marion;
he would — in the phrase made familiar by the practice
of an Ohio Republican candidate of a quarter-century
before, William McKinley — "conduct a front-porch
campaign." Some[1] advisers and Republican managers
demurred; times had changed, they told Harding; the
Presidency, like other goals of ambition, must be gone
after; it must be sought in the modern manner and
tempo, by "go-getter" methods. The people, they told
Harding, might resent a front-porch campaign, might
think it "high-hat," "snooty." But just because the
front-porch method was more dignified, Harding clung
to it. It appealed to a trait that was strong in him, his
regard for seemliness, becomingness.[1a] He made few
speech-making trips, and those reluctantly.

The front-porch method brought the ends of telegraph wires to the house next door to Harding's, and a
swarm of newspaper men to Marion. These learned, and

[1] Not all of them. Several of the Republican Senators strongly favored the
front-porch type of campaign. The principal Republican manager, Will H.
Hays, Chairman of the Republican National Committee, favored it emphatically,
felt that "Harding's dignity and hominess" made him an ideal front-porch candidate.
[1a] "[Harding] has . . . two pet words that he uses constantly. They are 'becoming' and 'seemly.' "—Edward G. Lowry, "Washington Close-Ups."

through them the country, the personality, antecedents and background of the little-known man who was proposed as head of a nation of a hundred and twenty million people.

II

Marion was, to the average American taste, a lovely town. Though it had grown rapidly during the two decades preceding, from eleven thousand in 1900 to twenty-eight thousand in 1920; though it had ceased to be wholly a leisurely place of stores and shops accommodating the nearby farming territory, and had acquired a great steam-shovel factory and other manufactures, nevertheless it had still the characteristics of a small, simple rural community, a maple-shaded little town of the kind that many Americans, exiled in cities, looked back to with homesick affection. With some imagination, and making allowance for the difference in size, and for the difference between the old world and the new, one could think of Marion, in those lush August days of 1920, as having been, a while before, "Sweet Auburn, loveliest village of the plain." Level, rich fields of corn and alfalfa came up to its borders, and pastures dotted with fat Holsteins. The countryside, the fertile farms with their big barns and well-kept houses, made an effect of plenty, comfort, a material abundance widely diffused and accessible to all.

Framed in that background, the town made an impression of simple living, easily acquired; with little difference in wealth, and none in pride and self-respect, between its richest and its poorest — if indeed "rich" or "poor," or any differentiation of economic or social standing, could be applied to any one living in Marion. Harding's house was next-door to that of his secretary — a supernumerary acquired, somewhat reluctantly, when Harding was elected to the Senate — and none could tell the difference in simplicity between the two homes. The people were friendly and had the leisure to practise friendliness. When a large delegation of Republican editors from all over the country came to make a front-porch call on Harding, the lunch they were

Birthplace of Warren G. Harding; it had disappeared before he was nominated for the Presidency.

given in Masonic Hall was served by the wives and daughters of Marion. Twenty-seven church bells summoned its people to Sunday services, and to several weekday evening prayer-meetings; its children trooped to fifteen schools. Deep-graven in the portal over the gray stone courthouse was the admonition, prophetic in its implication, "fiat justitia, ruat coelum" — *Let Justice Be Done Though the Heavens Fall.*

The nearby countryside when the newspaper correspondents searched it for details of Harding's ancestry and boyhood, yielded a galaxy of alluring place-names:

Blooming Grove, where, a century before, the first
Harding settler, Amos Harding, and his sons, had begun
to clear the forest, and where the old one-room school-

From a photograph by Brown Brothers.

Warren G. Harding and his two sisters as children.

house, now abandoned and ivy-covered to the peak of its
silent belfry, had been built by Harding's brick-mason
grandfather; Corsica, where Harding had been born, the
son of a country doctor — by 1920, every trace of the
house had disappeared, the place was now a wheat-field;
Canaan township, where Harding had spent some of his
youth on a farm; Whetstone Creek, in which was his
boyhood swimming hole; Caledonia, where he had

learned to set type in the *Weekly Argus* office, and had played the cornet in the village band; Iberia, where he had gone to a little college, Ohio Central, now extinct, and where he had helped to pay his way by odd jobs, among them painting the local churches — "I was a

Old-time country school in which Harding as a young man taught for a term.

good grainer,"[2] Harding said, when the newspaper men recalled the boyhood experience to him. It all seemed homely, simple, and very American, like the sweet-briar and black-eyed Susans along the country roads, where almost every third or fourth farm housed some degree of cousinship to the Harding clan — "We're all real proud of Warren" they shyly said to visitors.

III

These, and a thousand eager residents of Marion who "knew him when —" volunteered details of Harding's career. In the early 1880's his father, the country doc-

[2] "Grainer" — a word now almost obsolete, meaning one who paints in imitation of the grain of wood or of marble.

tor, had moved to Marion, bringing his family with him. Young Warren worked on a local newspaper, primarily as a typesetter, but also — since specialization of labor was rare on the small newspapers of that day — as writer of "locals," meaning that the young compositor brought to the office, and put in type from his head, items of news that he had picked up, information about visitors from out of town, Marion citizens who had taken a trip to Cleveland or Columbus; news of births, deaths, and sickness that accrued to the young printer from his doctor-father's practice.

Separation from this first job was caused, so one legend said, by an incident of forgetfulness on Harding's part, and a lack of tact that was unusual with him. Having taken part in a Republican parade one afternoon during the late Fall of 1884, he neglected to strip himself of all the paraphernalia and appeared at the office wearing a hat-band glorifying the name of James G. Blaine, to the grieved embarrassment of his editor-employer who, as a good Democrat, was supporting Grover Cleveland. After the ensuing deluge of harsh remarks, Harding, with a printer-chum, bought with a shoestring a decrepit daily newspaper, a five-column four-page sheet which had been founded and conducted, unsuccessfully, by — this detail is a verity — a former peanut vendor. On November 26, 1884, the Marion *Star* printed an announcement; its somewhat truculent affirmation of permanence suggested the new owners' consciousness of the degree of dubiety in which the sheet had formerly been held:

> "*We Have Purchased the Star and Will Stay.*
> "STAR PUBLISHING COMPANY."

The legends of Harding's upward climb, as retailed by old Marion residents to metropolitan newspaper men who now sought information about the early career of a candidate for President, were mainly of struggles to make ends meet — or devices adopted when no exertion

Harding in his early 20's, when he was beginning his career as owner and editor of the Marion *Star*.

or ingenuity could make the ends touch; explanations and importunities to employees when the ghost did not walk[3] on Saturday night; payment of employees with due-bills on advertisers — a printer could thus collect his pay, or part of it, in groceries and other necessities;

[3] An Americanism of the time, especially common in newspaper offices, meaning inability of the employer to pay the week's wages.

Harding borrowing small sums to pay the express charges
on paper and plate matter which the vendors had cau-
tiously sent C.O.D.; Harding buying out his partner's[4]
interest because Harding thought a telephone was desirable while the partner thought the novelty to be of
dubious value and certainly an extravagance; Harding
acting as both "make-up"[5] man and editor — transition
from the mechanical occupation to the literary one being accomplished with no more ceremony than a brief
wiping of ink-stained hands on the office towel.

About Harding as a man, all the stories emphasized
kindliness, a kindliness that expressed itself in generous
responsiveness to any appealing situation. It included
kindness to animals. The stories that were recalled by
old residents for newspaper men seeking copy included
Harding's giving a boy ten cents to find a home for a
kitten. Meeting a farmer coming to market with a crate
of pigeons, he had bought the crate and, after the farmer
was out of sight, released the pigeons. Once he and
George Christian, sitting on Harding's porch, observed a
line of ants climbing up the railing. Christian, alert to
safeguard the house against a nuisance, began to brush
the ants off and stamp on them. "Don't do that," Harding called to him. "Don't kill them; just brush them
away."

At the *Star* office the stories about him were all about
his good-nature, his tolerance. Observing, one morning,
that one of the old compositors[6] was not on the case,[7] he

---

[4] The partner was "Jack" Warwick, later a well-known paragrapher on big-
city newspapers, among others the Toledo *Blade*. Harding's long-time secretary,
George R. Christian, thinks that Warwick's terminating of his partnership with
a man destined to be President was due in part to sheer fatigue and impatience
with trying to keep the feeble Marion *Star* alive.

[5] Newspaper term for lifting the galleys of set type into the iron frames on
the stone table and arranging them in page-forms.

[6] Newspaper term for a type-setter.

[7] Newspaper term for the high wooden stand that contained the fonts of type.

was told that Lew[7a] had fallen behind in his dues to the union and was not allowed to work. "We must fix that up," he said, and did it; "we can't spare Lew, the place wouldn't seem right without Lew around." There were countless stories of his ready assurances to wastrels,

From a photograph by Underwood & Underwood.

Harding working on the "stone" in the composing room of the Marion *Star*. While this is a posed photograph taken during the 1920 campaign, Harding frequently worked in the composing room for his own pleasure.

weaklings, or the blamelessly unlucky who, caught in some jam or other, begged him "not to put it in the paper — if the old mother saw it it would kill her." Many repetitions of such incidents, and publisher Harding's frequent exercise of the charity of silence even when not requested, made the editors and reporters of the *Star* familiar with his point-of-view and the paper's policy. After Harding became a candidate for the Presi-

[7a] Common American abbreviation for Lewis, Louis, and Luther; in this case it was Luther.

dency, one of the *Star* editors compressed the unspoken and informal office rules into a code which, for campaign purposes, was given out as having been formally written out and signed by Harding and as having hung for years on the office wall. The exaggeration was harmless and did not violate essential truth. The code was printed and talked about all over the country; as late as 1934 part of it was quoted[8] in a discussion of newspaper ethics:

If it can be avoided, never bring ignominy on an innocent man or child, in telling of the misdeeds or misfortunes of a relative. Don't wait to be asked, but do it without the asking. . . .

Never needlessly hurt the feelings of anybody.

Be decent; be fair; be generous.

I want this paper to be so conducted that it can go into any home without destroying the innocence of any child. . . .

IV

He was the town's leading citizen, and one of the most well-to-do, but was no more pretentious than when he used to carry a pail of newsboys' pennies to the bank. He still, on frequent occasions, took off his coat and "made up" the paper, or set some type, doing it merely for the pleasure of recalling his younger years, mingling with the men, and enjoying the agreeably acrid smell of printer's ink. At the Marion Club of evenings he played whist and poker with old friends and cronies. For thirty years his morning walk from home to office had been a refrain of "Hello, Jim!" "G'mornin', Bill!" He was utterly modest, wholly without egotism, incapable of making the faintest effort to create an impression.

In the strong light that now beat upon him, this native unpretentiousness did not evaporate. Rather it was increased, became a quiet humility. He had a task — he

8 In "City Editor," by Stanley Walker.

set his face to it and he would go through with it; he would work at it with earnestness because being earnest is part of the task; but he would not pretend to be more than he was.[9] Outwardly, Marion saw no change in him.

Marion thought of him as one of them, and liked him, extravagantly. By every superficial appearance he was one of them. Yet some of the newspaper correspondents and others, who had had wide experience with men, and who now focussed their minds intently upon understanding a man who might be President of the United States, felt that Marion did not fully know Harding. He was baffling to classify; he did not conform to any familiar pattern.

Physically he was a distinguished person; that was the most patent fact about him. Probably he was aware of his advantage of appearance — he was aware of most things about himself — but he showed no faintest disposition to parade his distinction of appearance, or capitalize it, nor any other consciousness except perhaps some quiet care about his clothes. The physical distinction was not — not on first acquaintance, certainly — borne out by his mind. In off-hand talk he was commonplace, often crude, sometimes banal. Yet, observing him among his friends and neighbors, one was aware that they, after a lifetime of acquaintance, had a regard for his mind and his judgment. In any Marion group, Harding's word weighed more than that of any other. The atmosphere would be one of completely relaxed camaraderie, but there would be unconscious deference to one.

v

The most available measure of his personality was the institution that was his reflection; rarely has any relation

---

[9] "He was a much abler man than he thought himself."—Harry New.

between man and work so fully lived up to Emerson's rule that every institution is the elongated shadow of one man. The Marion *Star* was Warren Harding. It had been Warren Harding from the time of his taking hold of it as a derelict infant to its present very considerable eminence as a prosperous property covering its field as few newspapers do, its circulation in proportion to the population of the town hardly exceeded by any other paper in the country.

Stories sent out from Marion during the campaign, inspired more by zest for the dramatic than regard for the literal, said that much of the *Star's* success, and of Harding's, was due to his wife. She was pictured as the vibrant dynamo who kept an inert husband going. There was little to that. It is true that for fourteen years after their marriage she had gone daily to the *Star* office, at a time, beginning in the early 1890's, when a woman in an office was novel. It was this conspicuousness, perhaps, that gave rise to the legend that the active and aggressive and talkative woman who bustled about the *Star* office was the source of much of its growth, and of Harding's. Passers-by on the street had seen, on a thousand hot summer afternoons, Harding's outstretched feet reposing on the window-sill of the editorial sanctum on the second floor, and an equal number of times had seen Mrs. Harding chattering at the newsboys whom she managed in the first-floor office. From the contrast, some had deduced incorrect conclusions. The repose of Harding's personality, the reflective quality of his mind, his easy-goingness of spirit, coupled with his common sense and his touch with the common man, were precisely what had enabled the *Star* to become what it was. A thousand acts of quiet, off-hand judgment, a thousand refrainings from actions urged by the impetuous, a thousand waivings of what seemed immediate self-interest,

had entered into the institution Harding had built, and
the place he had made for himself in the community.
Marion was a growing town, the *Star* needed only to
grow with it; its guiding spirit needed little more than

From a photograph by Brown Brothers.

Home of Harding's newspaper, the Marion *Star*.

to have calm judgment, avoid mistakes and keep the
common touch.

The too hecticly active-minded Mrs. Harding, had
she had charge of the *Star*, would have made, many a
time, precisely the kind of mistake which, in that kind
of community and that situation, would have been
serious. Her coming to the *Star* office daily was due to a
busying quality she had, coupled with a desire to be
always where her husband was, always showing to the
public, and to herself, her possession[8a] of her handsome

[8a] An intimate of the Hardings who read the proofs of this chapter wrote, in
June, 1935: "She was at all times jealous and at most time suspicious of Hard-

mate. It had, too, the motive of safeguarding her possession; her presence near him was a "No Trespassing"
sign, not unneeded. She had been, when she married
him, a divorcee eight years older than he. She was the
daughter of the town's richest citizen, and all Marion
knew her father had bitterly opposed the match. The
marriage had been childless. As a wife, she had that
particular kind of eagerness to make good which, in a
personality that is at once superficial and unsure of itself,
sometimes manifests itself in a too strenuous activity, a
too steady staying on the job. Daytimes she bustled,
sparrow-like, in and out of Harding's office with pert
chatter to him and his friends. Evenings at home she sat
in at the games of bridge and poker, or, if she was unneeded as player, kept the glasses filled, always brightly
jabbering. In appearance she was a little too mechanically marcelled, too shinily rouged and lipsticked, too
trimly tailored. Towards her, Harding was always
gravely deferential, and his men friends learned to be
the same. They, and he, always addressed her as "Duch-
ess" and gave her a deference and eminence appropriate
to the fantastic title. Harding's habitual manner of
grave respect toward her may have been the atonement
a husband sometimes unconsciously pays for having let
his inner heart admit to itself that his marriage entails
living up to a bargain that might have been better. A
good many exercises of quiet patience must have entered
into the induration that enabled him to endure the harsh,
catarrhal r's of her half commanding, half archly play-
ful "Now Warren —" From other women, bemused by
his vital maleness and handsome figure, he had heard
tones more seductive.

---

ing, who, with his placid disposition and reluctance to face unpleasant situations,
let her have her own way, or appear to have it, oftener than most men would
have. . . ."

VI

We were puzzled by a contradiction between Harding's physical energy and his emotional calm, his spiritual disinterestedness. Seeing him as he sat upon his front

From a © photograph by Harris & Ewing from Globe.

Harding playing golf.

porch, one would have said he was inert, even indolent. But for years he had played hard tennis nearly every day with men younger than himself, at a time and in a place where tennis was not the usual thing, under circumstances in which it took effort to achieve the daily game. He had bought one of the first ping-pong tables ever sold in America, had set it up on the lawn between his house and his secretary's, and for months the two had spent an hour or so a day in an exercise which, if Marion

misjudged the strenuousness of it to be in proportion to
the size of the ball, was known to the adept to be no
small exertion. A friend much younger than Harding,
Albert Lasker, accompanied him on a trip through
Florida, which turned out to include visits to all the
golf-links Harding could find within automobile distance, with Harding at each links putting Lasker under
friendly conscription to play with him; at the end of a
day which to Harding had been a fair average of enjoy-
able exercise, Lasker, dropping limply into bed, sighed,
"Gosh, I'm glad Harding doesn't skip rope!"

The contrast between Harding's zest for physical exercise and his almost torpor when in repose, between
his trenchant vigor of body and his poise of spirit, was
but one of his many puzzling qualities. Marion thought
Harding's kindliness was undiscriminating, a little soft,
one with his unwillingness to see an ant stepped upon,
almost a fault and certainly a weakness. To the more
experienced persons who now put Harding under close
observation, his kindliness seemed one facet of a personal
philosophy which had generated within himself, by
which he guided himself — and which he kept to himself. He seemed to have an inner life, which he did not
permit to extrude upon his Marion surface. It was as if
his daily touch with his neighbors had planed and
smoothed his exterior to slide smoothly along his Marion
contacts, while within himself, and to himself, he kept
judgments and standards and points-of-view that were
individual to himself; and as if, beneath the smooth and
placid surface, a considerable intensity of emotional life
might go on.

In most respects he was as much a part of Marion as
Main Street, and the dry-goods store, and the courthouse
steeple, and the crowd at the post-office Sunday morn-

ings. In other respects he seemed like something exotic, something slightly Buddhic dropped into this commonplace American community. What in other men might have been natural casualness seemed in Harding an innately developed philosophy. When his friends warned

From a photograph © by Edmonston.

At the residence of President Harding, Marion, Ohio, August 12, 1920.

Harding in a characteristic pose and action on his front porch at Marion during his campaign for the Presidency. The little girl to whom Harding has given a piece of chewing gum is Narcissa Sullivan; the larger girl is Sydney Sullivan. The woman looking on from the steps is Mrs. Harding. The man to the left is Mark Sullivan.

him against some who had hitched themselves to his rising public fortunes, and who had so manœuvred as to put Harding under a seeming obligation to accept association with them, Harding's reply was, "They won't cheat me." The head-shaking friends thought it was fatuous weakness, and in the outcome it led to tragedy, but I felt it was a conscious philosophy about human nature that Harding had worked out for himself and taken for his guide. When a Marion wise-cracker asked him, "Do you know the difference between you and George Washington? George Washington couldn't tell a lie and you can't tell a liar" — I felt that maybe Harding could tell the liars, but chose not to tell them. In politics, the liars and frauds sometimes have other characteristics which make them, as wholes, more trenchant in personality, more able for many purposes, or more amusing and engaging, or more generous and tolerant, and better companions for hours of ease, than some whose virtue is their only, and somewhat chill, appeal. And some who in politics are frauds and liars, are in other relations of life completely dependable, and — this would have appealed to Harding — generous and likable.

However we might explain and understand Harding's tolerance, we wondered uneasily if a trait that was harmless and even laudable in a small town's leading citizen might become a handicap and danger in a nation's President. One of the legends about him quoted the remark made to him by a friend sterner than himself, "Warren, your weakness is that you always treat everybody as good 'til you find them bad." A President of the United States, if Harding should become that, would need to be more hard-boiled. We were troubled, too, by his emphasis on loyalty.[10] "God," he was quoted as having exclaimed, when he was urged not to yield too much to an unworthy friend, "God, I can't be an ingrate!" A sense of fraternity, of standing by one's own gang, may be harmless in the politics of a small community, but may be deadly in the White House. We knew that some who had helped Harding toward the Presidential nomination, who had put him under what his code felt to be

---

[10] "He liked politicians for the reason that he loved dogs, because they were usually loyal to their friends. And if ever he was disloyal to a friend, I am sure the action never ceased to trouble his conscience."—Boyden Sparkes.

an obligation, were men who might be dangerous, if Harding should, through fear of seeming ungrateful to them, do what they asked. They were "raw propositions," some of them. Harding would never ask any man what the man need fear to grant — but some around Harding would not hesitate to ask him for things it would be dangerous for a President to grant.

Though he had a reticence which, we recognized, kept some of his personality hidden from the world, there was no dissimulation in him; indeed, some deep inchoate sense of taste, coupled with a natural honesty, led him to shun forms of pose which, in politicians and other public men, are taken for granted. When a currently well-known writer arrived in Marion on a Sunday morning, sent by the Republican campaign managers to go to the Baptist Church with Harding and describe the candidate as a worshipper, Harding vetoed the exploitation, explaining gently that he was not really as religious a man as this kind of publicity would make him seem to be; that this was Communion Sunday, and that, while he was a member, he doubted whether he was good enough to take part in the communion. His refusing caused him some pain, for it wounded one of his other qualities, his wish to be accommodating. The incident disturbed him, he spent much of a valuable day in being friendly to the writer; he did not like the fellow, felt an inner disdain for one who would exploit religion, but he had made the man's errand fruitless, and felt he owed him something.

One of the town stories about him did not seriously impress us at the time; we felt it was a fiction, having the nature of a cartoon; one of those synthetic stories which, like an artist's drawing, is invented as frank exaggeration, not meant to be taken as fact. The story purported to be about the last occasion when Harding's father punished him corporally. The old gentleman was still alive, still vigorously moving about Marion to call

From a photograph by Underwood & Underwood.

Harding on his front porch addressing one of the gatherings of visitors that were almost daily, and sometimes more than daily, incidents of the front porch campaign.

on his patients. Our acquaintance with the father, the flavor of him, his strong common sense, the respect we had for him, all added to the piquancy of the story about

him and his son. When the incident occurred, the boy
had been about fifteen. The trouble he had got into and
that had made his father angry with him was some boy-
ish escapade, not any real fault of his own, but due to
his "going along" with his gang, boys of greater initiative and daring than himself. In the ensuing rendez-
vous with his father in the woodshed, the physical
punishment was accompanied, as is usual on such occasions, with verbal reproach. Between descents of the
strap, old Doctor Harding remarked, "I suppose I ought
to be thankful for one thing, that you're a boy; if you'd
been a girl, by this time every boy in town would have
had his way with you."

VII

The first chance of the country to judge him directly[11]
came when he made his acceptance speech.[12] For the
ceremony, a wooden platform had been improvised in
the Marion park; upon it in a semi-circle sat the members of the Republican National Committee assembled
from the 48 states; in front sat delegations from all over
the country; back of these sat, or informally stood, as
many people of the town and nearby country as cared to
come. They were many, for the affection of the community for Harding was united with a solemn pride in
the distinction he had brought to them, and with a genuine reverence which they — simple, old-fashioned
Americans — felt for the office toward which their
townsman was started. It was this audience and these

[11] Directly, that is, in the sense of reading the acceptance speech in the newspapers. There was no radio on July 22, 1920. Four years later, the acceptance
speeches of Coolidge and Davis were the first ever heard by radio.

[12] In the ceremonial of Presidential nominations, a committee of the convention
that made the nomination goes, some six weeks later, to the candidate's home,
where the chairman makes a "notification speech" and the candidate an "acceptance speech."

sentiments, rather than the worldly National Committee or Senator Lodge with his erudite notification speech, who determined the occasion's emotional flavor. It was Harding's neighbors — their generous affection personified and concentrated in the local Catholic priest, proud and thrilled to invoke a blessing on a ceremony that brought extraordinary distinction to his friend — it was these who made the keynote of the ceremony.

"The Harding notification," wrote one of the newspaper observers,[13] "was an exalted and moving ceremony. . . . Your correspondent was conscious of a distinct surprise when he found himself acutely sensitive to an atmosphere usually associated with churches and with ceremonies that have to do with eternity. Much of the solemnity came from the audience, one was quite sure, but also much from Harding himself. Not that he consciously created it. He has almost nothing of the dramatic in him. But he was obviously moved and moved in a way that was perfectly in tune with the occasion. Throughout his speech, both in substance and manner, the dominant note was one of reverent approach to high responsibilities. In no part of his speech did he speak slightingly of the opposition party or of its leaders. Senator Lodge's speech of notification had been full of ironic allusions to Wilson, waspy malice against the man then occupying the White House. But the whole spirit of Harding's speech contained nothing aspersive nor even disputatious.

"You felt sure, from his speech and from his bearing, that he had determined there should be no false pretenses. He had the air of a man who is going to do his best and is going to make sure that the public shall not expect from him any more than he was able to give. He

---

[13] Mark Sullivan, in the New York *Evening Post* and other newspapers, July 23, 1920, here partly paraphrased.

was the picture of a diffident, almost a shy, man, called upon to accept a high responsibility, sincerely wishing to be sure that the country understood his limitations,

From a photograph by Brown Brothers.

The first photograph taken of Harding and Coolidge together, soon after they were nominted for President and Vice-President. Mrs. Harding stands between. The man on the left is Will Hays, Republican National Chairman during the campaign.

earnestly determined to make clear exactly what were his ideas for the administration of the office to which he was being invited; almost more concerned, you felt, with giving voters reasons why they might properly prefer another rather than soliciting the office for himself.

"His final note of solemn and earnest dedication to high service dominated every gesture of his arm, every expression of his countenance, every tone of his voice and every word of his speech:

Mr. Chairman, members of the committee, my countrymen all: I would not be my natural self if I did not utter my consciousness of my limited ability to meet your full expectations, or to realize the aspirations within my own breast, but I will gladly give all that is in me, all of heart, soul and mind and abiding love of country, to service in our common cause. I can only pray to the Omnipotent God that I may be as worthy in service as I know myself to be faithful in thought and purpose. One can not give more. Mindful of the vast responsibilities I must be frankly humble, but I have that confidence in the consideration and support of all true Americans which makes me wholly unafraid. With an unalterable faith and in a hopeful spirit, with a hymn of service in my heart, I pledge fidelity to our country and to God"

The necessity of the occasion, the fact that this was a notification ceremony and that he must give formal notice of acceptance, caused the last few words of his speech to have, unconsciously, the nature of anti-climax:

— and accept the nomination of the Republican party for the Presidency of the United States.

7

THE 1920 CAMPAIGN

In Which the Republican Candidate Was Harding and the
Candidate to Whom the Democrats Had Given Their Nomi-
nation Was James M. Cox — But in Which the Man Upon
Whom the People Were Really Voting Was Woodrow Wil-
son. Those Who Liked Wilson, Voting for Cox, Those Who
Disliked Wilson, Voting for Harding — and There Were
Many More of the Latter. The Post-War Mood of the
American People, Which Determined the 1920 Election —
and Accounted for Much Else that Occurred in America
During 1920, and for Years After. The Passing of Three
Political Gods Who Had Dominated the Scene for a Quarter-
Century, and the Failure of New Gods, Even Demi-Gods, to
Emerge. The "Great and Solemn Referendum" on the
League of Nations, Which Wilson Asked for— and Got.

To run against Harding, the Democrats nominated[1] a
man having much the same background (though quite
different qualities of mind), a small-city editor and publisher, James M. Cox, who had spent two terms in Congress and was now Governor of Ohio.

Cox, when he was nominated, was at his home in
Dayton, Ohio. As his first act in the rôle of candidate,
with the country watching intently to learn about his
views and personality, he made a journey to Washington to call on President Wilson in the White House. It
was, for Cox, a fateful journey; the atmosphere of the
time gave to it the color of a pious pilgrimage, an act

[1] July 5, 1920, at San Francisco. The leading candidates, besides Cox, were A.
Mitchell Palmer, Attorney-General in Woodrow Wilson's Cabinet, and William
G. McAdoo, Wilson's son-in-law. This relation of McAdoo to Wilson was a
handicap; opponents slew him with jeers, "heir apparent," "crown prince," the
latter epithet particularly poisonous, because of still fresh memories of the
odium which newspapers during the war had put upon the Crown Prince of
Germany.

of devotion and dedication. That, to the public mind, identified Cox with Wilson, and with Wilson's ideals. And Wilson's ideals, to much more than half of Amer-

From a photograph © by Keystone View Co.

The Democratic nominees in 1920, James M. Cox (on the reader's right) for President, and Franklin D. Roosevelt for Vice-President. The photograph was taken on the grounds of the White House on the occasion of Cox's visit to President Woodrow Wilson.

ica, had come to the stage in which early popular fervor was succeeded by disillusion, bitterness.

Wilson had presented the war to us as a fine spiritual adventure — and the four million Americans who participated had found it, most of them, disillusioning. Wilson had told us it was a "war to make the world

safe for democracy" — and America had already begun
to sense the decline of democracy that had begun with
Communism in Russia in 1918, and was destined to put
democracy on the defensive everywhere. Wilson had
told us it was a "war to end all wars" — and America
had begun to feel that that promise, too, would fail.
Wilson had committed America to membership in a
League of Nations — and America had become suspicious that that meant commitment of America to send
troops abroad on future occasions, repetitions of the experience that was already, and recently, dust and ashes
in our mouths. Wilson, in short, was the symbol both
of the war we had begun to think of with disillusion,
and of the peace we had come to think of with cynicism.
And Cox, by identifying himself with Wilson, took
on Wilson's liabilities.[2]

II

Rarely has any national mood been so definite or so
nearly universal as the American one which followed
on the heels of the Great War. A word-of-mouth story
of the day — one of that type of narrative that never
happened but spontaneously generated as the epitome of
a condition, a story whose essential truth lay in the delighted recognition with which hearers received it,
rather than in fidelity to any actual event — was about
a negro soldier returning from Europe on a transport.
As the ship reached that nearness to home shores where

[2] "The people of the United States . . . did not vote for Harding; nor did
they vote against Cox; in 1920 they did not vote for anybody; they voted against
somebody; and the somebody they voted against was not a candidate; it was
Woodrow Wilson." — Charles Willis Thompson, "Presidents I Have Known."

"Cox will be defeated not by those who dislike him but by those who dislike
Wilson. . . . This seems mighty unjust. Cox, I think, has made a gallant fight;
he is to be beaten because Wilson is as unpopular as he once was popular." —
Franklin K. Lane, "Letters." Lane was a Democrat, a Wilson man, and had been
Secretary of the Interior in Wilson's Cabinet.

it permitted the soldier to see the Statue of Liberty in New York harbor, her face looking out toward Europe, he gazed rapturously at that first outpost of home shores, and solemnly vowed, to the statue and to the world, "Lady, once I gets behind you, I promise I never will look at yo' face again."

That was not merely the returning soldier's homesickness for his familiar America; it was repugnance for his recent experience. That his repugnance was not very vocal, that he put his occasional expressions of it sometimes in terms of humor, was a characteristic American trait, and did not lessen the disrelish which the returning veteran felt.

He had gone to France thinking war romantic, glorious. That notion had come to him through the toys he played with and the ditties he had learned as a child; it had come to him from the stories and poems and orations about war and patriotism in his school "Readers": "The Sword of Bunker Hill," "The Old Continentals," "Marco Bozzaris," "The Battle of Waterloo," "The Lord of Hosts Shall Arm the Right." It had been made fresh and personal to him, when, as a child about the turn of the century, he had thrilled at the sight of soldiers marching off to the Spanish War or to the Filipino Insurrection, the bands playing "Good-bye Dolly Gray," and the home folks singing,

> Don't you hear the tramp of feet, Dolly Gray,
> Sounding through the village street, Dolly Gray?
> 'Tis the tramp of soldiers true, in their uniforms of blue . . .

War as a romantic adventure had been impressed upon him by the Memorial Day parades of the Grand Army of the Republic in the North or the Confederate Veterans in the South; by the tales he had heard from his father and grandfather about the Civil War. That war was fine and glorious had been impregnated into his spirit by the Civil War songs that were familiar in every family, sung at every gathering, songs of sentiment and glamour, and of war as a nostalgic memory: "Tenting Tonight on the Old Camp Ground," "When I Fit Fur Gineral Grant," "The Bonnie Blue Flag," "John Brown's Body," "Marching Through Georgia," "The Battle Hymn of the Republic," "Rally Round the Flag, Boys" — those airs, familiar to him throughout his boyhood, had been repeated by the bands that played him off to France. Plays about the Civil War, such as "Shenandoah" and "Secret Service" and "The Drummer Boy of Shiloh," had made war seem glamorous, and only sufficiently dangerous to give the zest of adventure. Practically all the literature about war that was familiar during the boyhood of those who grew up to cross the ocean with the American Expeditionary Force, had pictured war as an adventure, as sentimental, as not-to-be-missed, as falling in love.

Exalted by that sentiment about the wars in which his older brothers and his father and grandfather had fought, and by the whole literature that war had produced since writing about war began, the young American had gone to France and to the front — but had found something very different from the skirmish which his school reader had called the Battle of Lexington, and nothing to remind him of Henry the Fourth's leading his soldiers "Once more unto the breach, dear friends." This was not a war of gallant dashes and cavalry charges, there was nothing like Sheridan galloping up from Winchester twenty miles away. This war was a thing of machinery and poison gas, of trenches, dug-outs, mud.

Many conditions contributed to the young American's disillusion. The glow of high emotion about saving

France had dulled upon acquaintance with Frenchmen en masse and in person — it was a common saying that American soldiers who after the Armistice occupied German territory had found the order and kindliness of the Germans, their *ordnung* and *gemüthlichkeit*, more appealing than any qualities they found in the French. A story that went up and down the lines in France and trickled back to America was to the effect that the French charged the Americans rent for the land upon which the Americans dug trenches to defend France against the enemy. The story was not true,[3] but, like many inventions, it reflected a prevailing mood.

The mood of exasperation, of expectations unfulfilled, of high emotion trickling out to disappointment, was accentuated by the manner of the war's ending. The inconclusive outcome did not conform to human nature. It was not a clean fight to a finish. About the time the Americans had got into the full heat of fighting spirit, the Germans quit. The Germans did not have the emotion of being beaten, the Americans did not have the emotion of winning — and that lack of the normal end for a fight was bad for both, led in both nations to distortion of nature's course. The fighting mood of the Americans, frustrated, deprived of its natural fulfilment, turned sour. Then after the fighting ended with the armistice of November 11, 1918, most of the Amer-

[3] The facts, so far as there were any, were supplied to the author of this history by the Historical Section of the Army War College, June 8, 1935, in the form of a letter that had been written in 1919 by the Commanding General of the American Expeditionary Force:

"There is no foundation for the statement that America has 'paid rent or taxes for the use of the trenches in France.' I understand that this unjustified and hurtful rumor, which for a while had some circulation in France, has gained some credence in the United States, and it is believed that the minds of our people should be disabused on the subject in some appropriate way."

Probably the story arose from the arrangements made by the American forces for the occupation and use of the privately owned land of French citizens, held under lease or requisition, on which American installations — barracks, camps, hospitals, warehouses, machine shops, docks, railroad yards, etc. — were located.

icans were kept in Europe throughout nearly all the tedious length of the Peace Conference. By the time they could get back to America, their mood about their recent experience, and about Europe altogether, was "Never Again!" So also felt, as a rule, the young veteran's sister and his mother and his aunt, and his brother and his father.

Not much was said of it yet; we still felt obliged to pretend to ourselves that the war had been a fine experience; the returned soldier hated to forego one of war's rewards, the thought of tales he would tell his children,[3a] like those his grandfather had told him about the Civil War. This subconscious unwillingness to acknowledge disillusionment, even to ourselves, did not rob the mood of its force; rather the unconsciously enforced self-repression gave the country a kind of fretful sullenness. It is to be observed that after the Great War we set up

[3a] Foreseeing this, in 1919, Franklin P. Adams, poet and wit, wrote a parody of Southey's "It Was a Famous Victory," picturing the melancholy fate awaiting the veterans of the World War in their old age:

"IT WAS A FAMOUS VICTORY"
(1944)

It was a summer evening,
  Old Kaspar was at home,
Sitting before his cottage door—
  Like in the Southey pome—
And near him with a magazine
Idled his grandchild, Geraldine.

"Why don't you ask me," Kaspar said
  to the child upon the floor,
"Why don't you ask me what I did
  when I was in the war?
"They told me that each little kid
Would surely ask me what I did."

"I've had my story ready
  For thirty years or more."
"Don't bother, Grandpa," said the
  child;
  "I find such things a bore.
Pray leave me to my magazine,"
Asserted little Geraldine.

Then entered little Peterkin,
  To whom his gaffer said:
"You'd like to hear about the war?
  How I was left for dead?"
"No. And besides" declared the youth,
"How do I know you speak the truth?"

Arose that wan embittered man,
  The hero of this pome,
And walked, with not unsprightly step,
  Down to the soldiers' home,
Where he with seven other men,
Sat swapping lies till half past ten.

no heroes, no equivalent of Grant or Sheridan or Sherman or Lee or Jackson. And when books and plays about the Great War began to emerge, such as "What Price Glory," and the bitterly sardonic "Plumes," they emphasized not war's glamour but its grimness.[4] The postwar literature, the "war books," not only reflected and expressed American disillusionment about the war, they had a far-reaching effect on our national thought in many respects.[5]

III

Of this American mood about the recent war, Wilson was the unhappy victim, symbol of the exaltation that had turned sour, personification of the rapture that had now become gall, sacrificial whipping-boy for the present bitterness.

This the Republicans sensed, and reflected — and took advantage of. "Mr. Wilson," said Republican keynote orator Senator Henry Cabot Lodge of Massachusetts at the National Convention of 1920 — "Mr. Wilson and his dynasty, his heirs and assigns, or anybody that is his, anybody who with bent knee has served his purposes, must be driven from all control, from all influence upon the government of the United States."

Perforce the Democrats could not disavow Wilson, nor the war Wilson had fought. Sincerely or by semblance they had to be proud of it. Indignantly candidate Cox exclaimed in his acceptance speech: "There

---

[4] Writing on July 1, 1935, I think it is accurate to say that no book, play, or motion-picture, in any language, about the Great War, glorified it. The books, plays, and motion-pictures which made the war grim, repellent, hideous, were many. They included "All Quiet on the Western Front," Erich Remarque; "Paths of Glory," Humphrey Cobb; "Under Fire," Henri Barbusse; "The Open Room," E. E. Cummings; "The Return of the Beast," Liam O'Flaherty; "Three Soldiers," John R. Dos Passos; "Farewell to Arms," Ernest Hemingway.

[5] For an account of the "war books" and their effect on national thought, see Ch. 16.

is not a line in the Republican platform that breathes an emotion of pride or recites our national achievement [the winning of the war]; in fact, if a man from Mars were to depend upon the Republican platform or its spoken interpretation by the candidate of that party, he would not find a syllable telling him that the war had been won and that America had saved the world."

If to the people, a large majority of them, the war was merely distasteful, the peace, the League of Nations, was odious, a menace. Wilson, after the Senate had wrangled for months over the treaty and the League, and after he had become bitter and sick, had said[6] the election of 1920 should be "a great and solemn referendum." This declaration by Wilson, Cox endorsed. He made the issue clear, declared unequivocally what he would do if elected. "The first duty of the new administration," Cox said, "will be the ratification of the treaty. . . . The League of Nations is in operation. The question is whether we shall or shall not join. As the Democratic candidate I favor going in."

To which the Republican answer, if translated into the slang of the day, would have been, "Oh boy! Go to it!" The Republicans were sure a majority of the voters opposed our adhering to the League, and disliked Wilson. In addition to the general disapproval of Wilson, specific groups of voters disliked him for specific reasons, all associated with the war or with the peace: German-Americans disliked Wilson because he had made promises to the German people which the Peace Conference did not keep; Italian-Americans disliked him because at the Peace Conference he had prevented Italy from getting Fiume and other territory to which Italy thought she was entitled; Austro-American voters

[6] At the Jackson Day dinner of Democrats at Washington in January, 1920.

disliked him because of the dismemberment to which the Peace Conference had subjected their unhappy homeland. Irish-American voters disliked him because of an episode at the Peace Conference; he had refused to give audience to an Irish delegation which wished to present claims to that "self-determination of small peoples" which Wilson had proclaimed for all — but which it was inexpedient to give to a dependency of Great Britain at a time when the British Lloyd-George was Wilson's associate in the Peace Conference. Nearly every racial group of alien-born voters (except the Poles) had some such reason for disliking Wilson, something Wilson had done at the Peace Conference, some shifting of a national boundary in Europe, some denial of racial aspirations. And all this the Republicans capitalized.

To the Republicans, the situation had that sum of perfect advantages that is called a "natural"; they had only to take the goods that the gods provided. There was just one faint flaw in the picture, not so much a handicap as a slight embarrassment.

Some Republicans, not many in number but high in station, believed that America should adhere to the League of Nations. These Republicans, as individuals, had publicly endorsed the League in the beginning; when the fight over it arose they had tried to achieve some workable compromise, in the shape of reservations, which would permit ratification; in the recent Republican National Convention, this group had tried to get into the platform some kind of qualified endorsement of the League, but their timorous effort had been swamped by the truculent die-hard opposition of the anti-League irreconcilables, Senators Borah, Johnson, McCormick, Brandegee, and others.

The group of pro-League Republicans — they included ex-President Taft, Charles E. Hughes, Elihu Root, George W. Wickersham — these Harding felt it prudent to placate. They were eminent in the party and in the country; some of them had personal followings. There was, besides, a measurable number of voters, mainly idealists, who would normally vote the Republican ticket, but who felt the Republican party ought not to set its face against such a noble purpose as the prevention of future wars, either by the League or by some equivalent association of nations.

Of all this, Harding took notice. In his acceptance speech[7] he said little about the League of Nations, and what little he did say was, so to speak, clearly vague. His first task if elected, he declared, would be to sign peace treaties with the Central Powers — America was still technically at war because of the Senate's refusal to assent to the Versailles Treaty:

Then we may . . . proceed deliberately and reflectively to that hoped-for world-relationship which shall satisfy both conscience and aspirations and still hold us free from menacing involvement. With a Senate advising as the Constitution contemplates, I would hopefully approach the nations of Europe and of the earth, proposing that understanding which makes us a willing participant in the consecration of nations to a new relationship, to commit the moral forces of the world, America included, to peace and international justice, still leaving America free, independent, and self-reliant, but offering friendship to all the world.

To the pro-League Republicans, Harding's weak and vague, if high-sounding, promise was not satisfactory. They felt that Harding's tortuous words masked a complete surrender by him to the extreme anti-League irreconcilables; they were disturbed and unhappy. An influential newspaper having pro-League views, The New

[7] July 22, 1920.

York *Evening Post,* commented acidly that Harding's "program is nothing less than a repudiation." "Harding Scuttles the League," read a caption in the pro-League New York *Times.*

There was no real danger that the anger of pro-League

Democratic satire on the position of the Republicans about the League of Nations during the 1920 campaign. Pro-League Republicans interpreted the platform one way, anti-League Republicans the other way. Knott in the Dallas *News.*

Republicans might cost Harding the election — that he would win was as certain as anything could be in politics. But Harding's love of harmony and concord was perturbed over the possibility of a breach in his party, with a small body of pro-League Republicans deserting to the Democrats. Such an eventuality would not only be "unbecoming," and therefore displeasing to his feeling for order, decorum, but it would also raise obstacles to the domestic programme he had in mind, which was much closer to his heart than any point in international relations. Moved by his own instinct for keeping things regular, his temperamental shrinking from anything like a breach, and urged by campaign managers anxious for party solidarity, Harding set about finding some common ground on which both pro- and anti-League Republicans could meet. The problem was hardly to get the pro-League Republicans to vote for him — most of them would do that anyhow. It was rather to give them a bridge, to enable them to save their faces.

Harding, with the aid of party leaders[8] and friendly newspaper men, worked out a formula. It was now late in August, midway of the campaign. He chose, as the occasion for putting out his straddle, a visit to Marion of Republicans from Indiana and Minnesota. To this gathering, Harding, standing on the front porch of his house, read a long and very carefully worded speech — carefully worded, indeed, for the precise purpose of achieving obscurity — a declaration which, he hoped, might win, if not the support of pro-League Republicans, at least their silence and their abstention from making a fight against him. The speech was so spun out that to quote from it would be tedious; in substance it amounted to:

1. Immediately upon being inaugurated, Harding would call into conference either a committee of the Senate or "the most experienced minds of this country from whatever walks of life they may be derived and without regard to party affiliation" to formulate "a defi-

---

[8] Two who helped Harding steer his difficult intellectual straddle were George Harvey and Richard Washburn Child. Harding was extravagantly grateful — the two had enabled him to achieve a subtlety in words of which Harding, unaided, was utterly incapable. After he was elected he made his two literary aides ambassadors. Harvey to Great Britain, Child to Italy.

nite practical plan" for a world court "with teeth in it" to be submitted to the consideration "of the controlling foreign powers."

2. The League of Nations to be reconstructed by those entrusted with the formulation of the new plan for preserving peace.

3. The foundation of the reconstruction to be "a World Court of Justice supplemented by a world association for conference," which would be "a society of free nations . . . so organized as to make attainment of peace a reasonable possibility."

4. The use by this world association of such machinery of the League of Nations as the world tribunal "can use properly and advantageously."

To sincere advocates of the League, especially Democratic ones, Harding's suggestion of an alternative was more infuriating than placating. Cox ridiculed it. The Democratic and pro-League Richmond, Virginia, *Journal* emitted a jeering pun, "Harding's False-Teeth Proposal." [9] An important pro-League newspaper, the New York *Evening Post*, satirically translated Harding's polysyllabic vagueness into what *The Post* called "the language of every-day":

The paramount issue in this campaign being Republican victory; such victory being threatened in the first place by Hiram Johnson's [anti-League] club; . . . such victory being threatened from an opposite quarter by discontent among Republicans who are convinced that national honor and duty call for the League; now, therefore, I, Warren G. Harding, feel it necessary to declare that provided I am allowed to keep Hiram Johnson quiet till election day, and provided that I am allowed to reject the League of Nations formulated under a

[9] The pungency of this pun may not be grasped by present readers as fully as by newspaper readers of 1920. The force of it lay in the fact that advocates of the true League of Nations insisted there must be "teeth" in it, that is, an authority which would enable the League to discipline by force any nation attempting an act of war. "Teeth" had become a familiar word in the American debate over the League; and the clause of the League covenant which provided the teeth, Article X, had been the principal issue in the controversy.

Democratic Administration, I will, when elected President, be perfectly open to reason on this subject of the League.

Harding's proposal came to be known as "The Association of Nations," in distinction from the "League of

"A Banner With a Strange Device."

Pro-League of Nations newspapers satirized Republican failure to join. The cartoonist took his inspiration from a phrase attributed to General Pershing when he visited LaFayette's tomb while in France at the head of the American Army "Lafayette we are here." Harding in the Brooklyn *Eagle*.

Nations." Nothing much came of it; it was not expected that much would. But, in the campaign, it did the work intended. It provided a ladder upon which pro-League Republicans could climb upon the band wagon of their party.

But all this manœuvering about the League of Nations was for the high-brows. For appealing to the

masses and winning the election, the Republicans depended upon jeering at Wilson and picturing the League
of Nations as a monster. Hundreds of Republican spell-
binders, and minor speakers carefully instructed, went
up and down the country appealing to prejudice against
Wilson, reminding communities of alien voters that Wilson at the Peace Conference had treated their homelands
badly. One speech, repeated over and over, pictured the
Peace Conference as a poker game: " 'I'll bet you
Fiume,' says Lloyd-George; 'I'll raise you Alsace,'
says Wilson." The spirit, the keynote of the Republican
campaign, was contained in a speech the venerable but
still humorous Chauncey M. Depew had made to the
Republican National Convention, a speech describing
Wilson at the Peace Conference, in which he was pictured as at once innocent-minded and stubborn, vain and
shut-minded, fatuous and gullible, and altogether a victim of foreign statesmen shrewder than he. It was this
sort of speech, deriding Wilson, that won the campaign
for the Republicans:

He was dealing with the ablest men in the political game, in
the diplomatic game, in the international game, there are in
the world. And he was a babe confident of himself. And what
happened? Why, those great gamblers in international politics said to him: "What do you want, Mr. President? You
are the greatest man in the world; what do you want? You
represent the greatest nation in the world, and you speak for
every one of your people; what do you want?" He said:" I
want a League of Nations which will put us like a heaven on
earth, reproduced on this round globe, of which I will be the
recording angel." Those astute old players said to him: "All
right, Mr. President, that is the most magnificent proposition
ever offered since Calvary two thousand years ago." Said
Lloyd George: "I would like to have the German possessions
in Africa, just to settle the negro question there." "All right,"
said the President. It was larger than all Europe. And that
little Irishman from Australia, Hughes, said: "Mr. President,
it is a luxury for a man from the Antipodes, way the other
side of the world, to meet such a great man as you. That

scheme of yours for a League of Nations is simply magnificent. But Australia wants Guinea, belonging to Germany, but close to us." And Wilson said: "Take it." And then came forward Clemenceau and he said: "We need coal; we need iron; we need the Saar Valley and we need the Ruhr Valley." The President said: "Take them." And then came Sonnino, and he said: "We want Fiume." Precisely what there was in the mentality of the Chief Executive of the United States that made him object I do not know, but he said: "You can never have Fiume." It so happened that nobody there had ever heard of Fiume. Nobody knew where Fiume was, whether one of the Sandwich Islands or a fixed star. (Laughter and applause long continued.)

IV

The campaign was extraordinarily unexciting. After it was three-quarters over a Minnesota great-grandfather among politicians of the day[10] wrote, "I haven't heard of anybody getting mad and punching somebody else on the nose over a political argument this year yet." The editor of *Collier's* asked a journalist[11] of the time to answer the question, "Why is it that at this late day, with only four or five weeks left to go, nobody is taking much interest in the election?"

One reason lay in the recent passing of a group of great personalities from American politics. Reversing Emerson's[12] formula, the gods had gone, and, compared to them, those who took their places, the present Presidential candidates, were hardly even half-gods, barely quarter-gods. For more than a generation, three great personalities, Wilson, Bryan, and Theodore Roosevelt, had dominated the American political scene. That all three were immense personalities every one would con-

[10] Ed Smith.   [11] Mark Sullivan.

[12] Heartily know,
When half-gods go,
The gods arrive.

cede; as to any one of them, a partisan might like or not like the kind of personality — but could hardly fail to concede the quantity of it. In every Presidential election for twenty-four years, since 1896, one of these had been a candidate, and sometimes two;[13] and when any of them was not a candidate, he was active, sometimes overtowering the candidate. Now all three had passed to one kind or another of desuetude. Theodore Roosevelt lay in a hillside grave at Oyster Bay. Wilson was broken physically and politically — in the Democratic convention of 1920 his name had figured in one ballot of the 44, and he received the votes of two delegates out of a total of 1094 — he who less than two years before had truly bestrode the world.

Bryan, with his extraordinary vitality, though he had come to the front of American politics earlier than the other two, was still active, still had much prestige, still exercised some power. At the Democratic convention of 1920 he had been the most impressive figure, had made by far the most stirring speech, a plea for a "dry" plank in the platform. The convention listened respectfully, paid him complete deference — but did not adopt his plank, and Bryan, leaving the convention and taking a train for the North, bade a poignant farewell, "My heart is in the grave." The words were regret over the failure of the Democrats to be as "dry" as Bryan thought the party should be; but also, I think, he really felt old, and was giving expression to a mood deeper than the public knew. "My memory went back to the slender, black-haired, gallant, flashing, vital, resonant Bryan of 1896, and I had a somber feeling of the inexorableness of

[13] 1896 Bryan ran for President
1900 Bryan ran for President, Roosevelt for Vice-President
1904 Roosevelt ran for President
1908 Bryan ran for President
1912 Wilson and Roosevelt ran for President
1916 Wilson ran for President

Underwood & Underwood.

Wide World.   *United Newspictures.*

"The Titans Had Gone."

Top: Roosevelt's grave at Oyster Bay. *Bottom left:* Wilson, in his broken old age. *Bottom right:* Bryan, at the Dayton, Tenn., trial of John Scopes; a few weeks after this photograph was taken, Bryan died.

time.[14] One thought of Bryan at that 1920 convention as an elderly uncle who comes to visit us, wearing his black alpaca coat and his starched white shirt and his narrow black tie. He read us the Bible every night, he said grace at every meal, he quoted a good deal from Isaiah and the prophets, and he exhorted us to morality and virtue. We were all glad to see him; we listened to him very respectfully; we paid him the greatest deference; we treated him altogether with genuine and unstudied affection; but when he got around to telling us what we should do about our business, we gently and kindly, but firmly, elbowed him aside."

The Titans had gone; and a generation that had known the strong wine of Bryan, Wilson, and Theodore Roosevelt could hardly be stirred by Harding and Cox. It was put succinctly by Senator Brandegee when explaining on the evening of Harding's nomination the reason why Harding had been chosen — Brandegee was one of the most cultivated men in public life, a graduate of Yale, but he chose to be colloquial: "There ain't any first raters this year. This ain't 1880 or any 1904; we haven't any John Shermans or Theodore Roosevelts; we've got a lot of second raters and Warren Harding is the best of the second raters." Neither was Cox, it may be added, a Wilson or a Grover Cleveland.

v

Into the lukewarmness of the national mood, Cox tried hard to inject ginger. While Harding remained almost continuously on his front porch, Cox travelled incessantly — one of his campaign trips was the longest on record, a swing through 18 states west of the Mississippi which consumed 29 days (from which he was

14 Mark Sullivan in *Collier's,* October 9, 1920; here partly paraphrased.

destined to reap not one electoral vote). He had an active personality; he was emotionally shocked by the country's attitude toward the League of Nations, did not believe it could be so. He had made his way in politics so far

From a photo. © by Baker Art Gallery by Brown Brothers.

James M. Cox, former Governor of Ohio, Democratic candidate for President in 1920.

by being aggressive and progressive[15]; he thought the country was still as progressive and idealistic as it had been during and before the war (in differing ways); and so, in addition to advocating the League, he charged the Republicans with standpattism.

[15] "Unqualified credit should be given Cox for being a progressive. He has the record to prove it. His administration as Governor of Ohio was conspicuously and consistently progressive. When Cox became governor of Ohio there were some 50,000 law-suits pending between injured employees and their employers. Fifty thousand law-suits between two classes of the community comes close to being a kind of suppressed civil war. Today, Governor Cox tells me, there are not five such law-suits. The difference is due to progressive legislation about accidents to workmen which Cox put through, the 'Workmen's Compensation' law." — Mark Sullivan in *Collier's,* October 9, 1920.

But the war had made so much mess in the world that many Americans who had been ardent about progressing a few years before were now disposed to take kindly to the idea of standpatting a while. Against that mood Cox could make no headway. In his indignation and earnestness, Cox fell into a manner of campaigning that did less than justice to himself. Provoked by the calm self-assurance, the taking-it-all-for-granted attitude of the Republicans, and by the even more discouraging taking-it-for-granted attitude of much of the public; realizing that the force of inertia was on the side of Harding; feeling that he was unknown, that he had to make the people look at him and that he had only a few weeks to do it — in that state of emotion Cox practised an aggressiveness[16] which did not move the country but merely jarred it, made it lean farther toward Harding. Cox's campaign was gallant, and sincere — but it was not in tune with the times.

It got no rise out of Harding when Cox called him a standpatter. Harding was a standpatter, a genuine one, his temperament made him one. Harding loved an orderly world, a neat world, a world of carefully gravelled paths and nicely clipped hedges — above all, a world that stays the same from day to day. Harding

---

[16] "Cox has made the public think of him as a little like a frontier 'bad man' shooting up the meeting. . . . In his eagerness to start something, he has put himself in something like the rôle of the brigand in the comic opera, who gallops up just as the wedding is about to take place and tries to kidnap the bride. He is like Lochinvar at the wedding; only he isn't at all so soft-spoken and knightly a person as Lochinvar. He doesn't doff his hat and ask for just one glass of wine and one turn of the dance. Not at all like that is Cox. 'Give up that bride,' says Cox, 'and give her up quick, or I'll shoot you full of holes.' 'Get off that front porch,' says Cox, 'and cut out that pink tea — I'm here with the rough stuff.' Cox would have done better for himself if he had made his entire campaign on his record — if he had merely gone up and down the country and told everybody just what he had done as Governor of Ohio, and what the results have been, and how well satisfied everybody in Ohio is, employers as well as employees and courts and business men — if Cox had told that story, and told it quietly and persuasively, he would have made a better campaign." — Mark Sullivan in *Collier's,* October 9, 1920.

hated to see things torn up by the roots and moved above, hated the messy debris that goes with change. Harding loved a world that stayed put. He winced at all the mess the war had made in the world, and he wanted to get

From a photograph by International News Photos, Inc.

Franklin D. Roosevelt and members of his family when he was Democratic Vice-Presidential candidate in 1920. Next to Roosevelt is his mother and next to her his wife. The others are his four sons and daughter.

it cleaned up and out of the way, and get back to normalcy. The country felt the same, sensed the desire for order and normalcy in Harding — and voted for him.

VI

The one sensation of the campaign, a story that Harding had negro blood, exploded during the last few days before the election. It emerged first in whispered word of mouth. Then circulars appeared, anonymous of course, directly stating that Harding had negro blood and supporting the assertion with a pseudo-genealogical table. Two hundred and fifty thousand of the circulars were discovered in the mails at San Francisco — the Post Office Department at Washington, under Democratic President Wilson, ordered them destroyed and forbade postmasters to receive more. No one charged the national Democratic campaign management with giving any countenance to the thing. One minor Democratic worker in Pennsylvania, charged with distributing some of the circulars, was arrested for libel. An attempt to distribute the circulars on suburban trains running into Chicago resulted in a small riot. Tens of thousands were slipped under doorways at night.

The Republican party management, consisting mainly of one man, probably the most vigilant and energetic national chairman either party ever had, Will H. Hays, had received information that this charge might be made, and had prepared for it. Promptly Chairman Hays issued an authentic family tree, compiled in part by the historical society of Wyoming, Pa., where a generation of the Hardings had stopped on their way westward to Ohio, from which it appeared that Harding's blood was composed of the best strains from Pennsylvania, New York, New Jersey, and Connecticut. Harding's personal manager, Harry M. Daugherty, declared, with some pontifical pomposity, that, "No family in the state [Ohio] has a clearer or more honorable record than the Hardings, a blue-eyed stock from New England and Pennsylvania, the finest pioneer blood, Anglo-Saxon, German, Scotch-Irish, and Dutch."

While some might smile at the inclusiveness of Daugherty's assertion, might say he was practising the familiar political device of claiming everything, and might humorously suggest that had he thought of the electorate in Minnesota he would have added Swedish

and Norwegian strains to Harding's lineage, yet no one
gave serious credence to the charge that Harding had
negro blood; it was with humor, mainly, that the charge
was received — though Republican Mr. Frank Munsey,
then owner of the New York *Herald*, screamed in his
paper phrases about "dastardly conspiracy," "insidious
assertion," "villainous undertaking," "foul eleventh-
hour attack."

The charge, in its most concrete form, appeared in a
circular calling itself "An Open Letter" addressed

TO THE MEN AND WOMEN OF AMERICA

and containing what purported to be five affidavits. The
principal affidavit had at the bottom the facsimile signature, "W. E. Chancellor." (Doctor Chancellor told
me in 1935 that he never signed the affidavit, nor knew
of it.)[17] A man bearing this name was at the time a
member of the faculty of Wooster College, located not
far from Marion. The affidavit represented that the
man whose name was attached to it had authoritative
qualifications: "I have studied ethnology in America
and in Europe . . . I have measured the heads and
carefully observed the other physical features of many
thousands of persons. In Washington, where I was city

[17] Just how and to what degree Doctor William E. Chancellor was associated
with the story of Harding having negro blood was not, in 1935, easy to determine,
nor did it seem important. Immediately after the purported affidavit came to
public attention, Doctor Chancellor's connection with Wooster College was terminated by the Board of Trustees, with an announcement which in part said (as
reproduced in the Cincinnati *Enquirer,* October 30, 1920) :
"It having come to the knowledge of the Board that circular letters are being
scattered broadcast throughout the country with reference to Senator Warren G.
Harding, Republican nominee for the Presidency, which letters are attributed to
Professor William E. Chancellor, and part of which he admits to having been
written by him. . . . Therefore, be it Resolved by the Board that the College of
Wooster indignantly disclaims all connection with, knowledge of, or authority
for making and issuing of any such circular letters."
After Harding's election, but before his inauguration, Doctor Chancellor went
to Canada and remained there until the end of the Harding administration.

school superintendent for several years, I had the opportunity of dealing with the largest colored population of any American city."

Basing its authority on these qualifications, the affidavit asserted that "Warren Gamaliel Harding is not a white man." With scientific precision, the affidavit particularized: "he is not a creole, he is not a mulatto, he is a mestizo." For which reason, the affidavit prayed "May God save America from international shame and from domestic ruin."

Attached to the principal affidavits were four supporting ones purporting to be signed by elderly persons who had spent their lives in the countryside where Harding's family and ancestors had lived. All the affidavits of these ancients were in terms of "has been told," "it has been stated," "it was common talk that," "it was the accepted belief that," "it had repeatedly been reported that," "the Harding family has never, to my knowledge, denied that." The one phrase that was uniform in all the affidavits was "colored blood in his veins" — why not in his arteries also was not explained.

The purported affidavits, and the accompanying alleged genealogical tree, averred too much, the proofs stumbled over each other. Not only one of Harding's lines of ancestors, but four, four separate ones, had been colored. His great-great-grandfather, Amos Harding, had been colored; his great-great-grandmother (wife of Amos Harding) had introduced a second line of colored blood; the wife of Harding's great-grandfather had been a third separate source of colored blood; the wife of Harding's grandfather had been of that degree of color which the alleged ethnologist in his refined expertness about such matters, called "pass-for-white." (Modern genetics knows that if Harding had really had that many strains of negro blood, some members of his fam-

Harding's grandmother, Mary Ann
Crawford Harding. Died 1896.

Harding's grandfather, Charles
Harding.

Harding's mother, Mrs. George
Tryon Harding.

Doctor George Harding, father of
President Harding.

To the Men and Women of America

AN OPEN LETTER

When one citizen knows beyond the peradventure of doubt what concerns all other citizens but is not generally known, duty compels publication.

The father of Warren Gamaliel Harding is George Tryon Harding, second, now resident of Marion, Ohio, said to be seventy-six years of age, who practices medicine as a one-time student of the art in the office of Doctor McCuen, then resident in Blooming Grove, Morrow County, Ohio, and who has never been accepted by the people of Crawford, Morrow and Marion Counties as a white man.

ily would have been completely black.) The affidavits proved the charge by alleging that the original Ohio ancestor of Harding had been of West Indian negro and French stock; proved it again by saying that Blooming Grove (where the early Hardings lived) had been a station on the "underground railroad" for fugitive slaves from the South; proved it yet once more by saying Harding's sister had in 1908 "taught in colored schools at Washington, D. C.; was also missionary in Murmah" (*sic;* did it mean Burmah?). Yet again the affidavit proved it by alleging that Ohio Central College, to which Warren Harding had gone, had had some negro students. The proof was, as Artemus Ward used to say, "2 mutch."

Such tangible origin as the story had was run down by newspaper correspondents at Marion. It went back some seventy years to a school-yard quarrel of children, one side of which, after exhausting the effectiveness of tongue stuck out and thumb to the nose, and after using up the more familiar epithets of "scum" and "trash," had the happy inventiveness to think of "nigger." As it happened, this particular quarrel did not have the fortunate evanescence of most school-yard flare-ups. An incident of physical violence attended it and this led to a neighborhood feud that included grown-ups. "Nigger" became an epithet which one side hurled at the other; for generations the epithet remained alive; whenever Harding had run for office, the innuendo was whispered; persons who for any reason hated Harding used the epithet.

VII

Election night Harding spent in his Marion home, a few friends with him. From his secretary's home next door (which had been used throughout the summer as a campaign headquarters) newspaper correspondents came in and out. It happened to be Harding's birthday, as well as election day, and he was a sentimental person. "On the dining room table was a cake covered with candles and decorated with pink icing. A small group of people straggled up the front walk and onto the porch. One of the women in the party stepped over to the bell, hesitated a moment and then rang it. There was a brief exchange of words with the negro who opened the door and then Mr. Harding appeared, his table napkin still in his hand.

"One of the group stumbled through a carefully prepared presentation speech and then — it was old Luther Miller, a long-bearded printer, oldest employee of the Marion *Star* — fairly poked a gift into the editor's hand. It was a printer's rule, made of gold. Then the old printer delivered the last line of his speech. He said that everybody on *The Star* knew that the country was going to have a good President.

"It was the editor of *The Star* who tried to speak then. His face twitched. The lines beside his nose and mouth deepened and then tears streamed from his eyes. He tried again to make some kind of reply and then he just began to shake hands with all of them." [18]

[18] Quoted from a description by Boyden Sparkes, in the New York *Tribune*.

8

HARDING CONFERS SOME APPOINTMENTS

Of Which Many Were Adequate, Some Excellent, Others Very Bad. He Names a Cabinet Which Included at One Extreme Three of the Best Public Servants America Has Ever Had — Hughes, Hoover, and Mellon; but Which at the Other Extreme Included Fall, Who Was Destined to Go to Jail, and Daugherty, Destined to be Indicted. The Part that Old Associations and Personal Affection Had in Some of Harding's Appointments, Both to the Cabinet and to Lesser Offices. A Human Trait of Harding Which, Working Cinderella Miracles, Brought It about that Obscure Persons, Long-time Friends of the President, Found Themselves Suddenly Elevated to High and Responsible Office.

HARDING was elected President of the United States. Some of his emotions were those that would come to any man, some were the fruit of Harding's particular temperament, up-bringing, and environment. None were unworthy. Among the earliest was a sense of personal romance. It was not grandiose self-complacency — that Harding never had. But he would now be able to confer on old friends such elevations as they had never dreamed.

To a crony of his early days in Ohio, "Ed" Scobey, all of whose experience as an executive had been gained while holding small political offices — his most important job had been sheriff of Pickaway County — and who some years before had had to go to San Antonio on account of his lungs — to him Harding gave the technically and legally exacting post of Director of the Mint.

For secretary to the President, he retained his next-door neighbor in Marion, already his secretary, George Christian — and that was a victory for friendship in a choice which to Harding must have been difficult, a choice between personal friendship and party loyalty — for Christian was a Democrat.

From a photograph © by Underwood & Underwood.

Ora M. Baldinger. He had been a newsboy on the Marion *Star* when Mrs. Harding was circulation manager for the paper. He had gone to Washington with Harding when the latter was Senator, and had been made a page. Entering the Army, he became a flyer in the Air Service, and when Harding became President he was made White House military aide.

To a former newsboy on the Marion *Star*, now a major in the Army Air Service, "Orrie" Baldinger, Harding gave a White House post as aide to the President. When the President and Mrs. Harding made their first trip back to Marion and appeared in a box at the county fair, the town "whooped and yelled in vain efforts to express their pride, but when they saw with the President a glittering figure in blue and gold, whose white-gloved hands were primly folded on the hilt of a shining sabre and whom they recognized as the red-headed former newsboy, their enthusiasm became hysterical; they had a picture of democracy that the rest of the world seldom sees."[1]

He appointed a Marion homeopathic physician, Doc-

Doctor — and, through appointment by Harding, Brigadier-General — Sawyer, mounted on the horse "Turco" that was one of his official perquisites.

tor Charles E. Sawyer, to be physician to the President, and, to clothe him with dignity appropriate to the function, made him a brigadier-general in the Medical Reserve Corps of the United States Army. The perquisites of the rank included a horse, a cavalry horse, a big horse; since Doctor Sawyer was diminutive, and unaccustomed to any seat higher or less secure than that of an automobile, the sight of him in his new military uniform, bobbing about in a too ample army saddle, his epaulettes[1a]

[1] The quotation is from Boyden Sparkes, New York *Tribune,* August 2, 1923.
[1a] Certain military persons who have read the proof of this chapter point out that generals, when riding horse-back, do not wear dress uniforms, but only

flapping on his thin shoulders like the leaden wings of a dead bird, accented the irony with which Washington now universally addressed him as "General." Harding's appointment of Sawyer was an act of consideration for Mrs. Harding. "She was subject to a stoppage in the functioning of her kidneys; on such occasions, her life depended upon keeping her in a profuse perspiration to eliminate the poisons from her system until the kidneys resumed functioning; only the watchful care of Doctor Sawyer kept her from death on a number of occasions; and it was the idea of her protection which influenced Harding to make this appointment." [2] (Though much of Washington smiled about Doctor Sawyer, he was a keen, perfectly honest, loyal person with independent means, whose coming to Washington was an act of service to Harding and his wife. The service was more than medical — Sawyer was faithful and shrewd for Harding in some important public matters.)

To his sister's husband, a missionary of the Seventh Day Adventist Church, Heber Votaw, Harding gave the post of Superintendent of Federal Prisons.

Most of these appointees chosen on the basis of old association were adequate, did not differ in ability and equipment from the average Harding would have got had he selected men coming to him through the ordinary channels, without regard to personal association with himself. But some turned out to be, in differing ways, unfortunate.

To a Marion pal, a small-town lawyer whose experience in finance was limited to a few months as head of a

---

khaki, and therefore do not wear epaulettes. I accept the correction, as I must. It must have been when Doctor Sawyer was riding in an official automobile that one observed his epaulettes bob up and down. But I decided to let the passage stand as it is, in this case sacrificing literal exactness to the larger accuracy of a true artistic portrayal of "General" Sawyer.

[2] The quoted words are from one close to the Harding family.

local bank, Daniel R. Crissinger, Harding gave the post of Comptroller of the Currency, and subsequently promoted him to the highest banking office in the country,

From a photograph by Underwood & Underwood.

Two of Harding's old Ohio friends who were given high posts in the government, Edward F. Scobey (*left*) and Daniel R. Crissinger (*right*).

Governor of the Federal Reserve System, an office comparable to head of the Bank of England. "One always had the feeling that when the blinds of the White House were down, Harding would be smiling to himself at the thought of Dick Crissinger, barefooted Dick, with whom he used to steal watermelons, as Governor of the

Federal Reserve Board."[3] (That was one of the triumphs of affection over judgment that did not turn out well. After Harding died, his successor, Coolidge, who did not like to make changes, kept Crissinger in office; thus it happened that Crissinger was head of the Federal Reserve System during a period[4] in which was made a mistake of Federal Reserve policy that was the largest single cause of the depression of 1929, so far as the causes arose in America.[5])

To an acquaintance he had made on a vacation in Honolulu, Colonel Charles R. Forbes,[6] Harding gave a post that would disburse some 450 million dollars a year, head of the Veterans Bureau. This act appealed powerfully to the melodramatically romantic and generous that was strong in Harding's nature — a stranger who had made acquaintance with a Senator on a vacation trip would by that incident'become, a few years later, a high government official. Harding — indeed everybody who made contact with the breezy, joke-cracking, hustling, red-headed Forbes — was impressed by him. He was of a familiar American type, the go-getter. He had a kind of genius for the sort of enterprise, compound of animal

[3] The quotation is from Boyden Sparkes, New York *Tribune,* August 2, 1923.

[4] From May 1, 1923, to September 15, 1927.

[5] I refer to the failure to raise rediscount rates at the end of the rising market that should have come to a normal end about 1925. As a consequence of the failure to raise discount rates, a second rising market was piled on top of the first, inviting the collapse of 1929. The motive for keeping discount rates low was laudable — to present no temptation to European gold and capital to come to the United States, and thereby to enable Britain, France, and Germany to get back on a normal fiscal basis. The story, too long to tell here and not within the period this volume covers, when adequately written, will compose perhaps the most important American chapter in the causes of the great depression.

[6] See Ch. 15. Because the post to which Harding appointed Forbes, head of the Veterans Bureau, had a relation to the army, Forbes's military record was material. An inquiry about it was made at the War Department. The Department merely verified what Harding already knew, that Forbes had enlisted in the Great War as a private, had risen to be a colonel, and had won the Distinguished Service Medal and the Croix de Guerre. Years later, when Forbes turned out badly, and was put on trial for crime, it was discovered that he had had a prior military record; he had been in the Army and had deserted.

energy and a shrewd workaday knowledge of applied psychology, which a decade later came to be known as "muscling in." Forbes was a superb "muscler-in" — to his skill at that art he owed his lone-handed capture of one of the best jobs Harding had to bestow. Also, Mrs. Harding liked him and had confidence in him, and that fact had weight in the President's decision. Probably the conferring of this distinction on Forbes gave Harding as much pleasure as any appointment he made. But probably it gave equal pleasure, of a different kind, to the gods of tragedy who had begun to take Harding's fate in hand.

II

It was in a similar mood, though of course with much more justification — indeed in most cases with complete justification — that Harding, as he began to choose his cabinet, turned to his old associates in the Senate. Harding's selections for his cabinet from that body were, with one exception, adequate — but Harding's reason for picking them was as much a sentiment as a reason, the pleasure he took in conferring honors on old associates in political life. His selection for Secretary of War, former Senator John W. Weeks of Massachusetts, was excellent, above the average of cabinets in any Administration. His selection from his old Senate friends to be Post-master-General (after Harding had been in office two years), Harry S. New, was an exceptionally competent official who had once been head of the Republican National Committee, and by that service had acquired, as custom goes, a kind of title to the Post-Office portfolio.

Harding's one other cabinet selection from his Senate friends, Albert B. Fall of New Mexico, was destined to

bring him the worst of his griefs. Habitually Harding
went further than merely thinking that his friends could
do no wrong; to his expansive generosity of temperament, a friend was, by the fact of being a friend, suffused

From Globe. Copyright Harris & Ewing.

Three members of Harding's cabinet, photographed on their way to the White
House in 1922. On the reader's left, Edwin Denby, Secretary of the Navy;
in the middle, Charles E. Hughes, Secretary of State; on the right, John
W. Weeks, Secretary of War.

with a glowing glamour. He wanted to give Fall the
highest cabinet post, Secretary of State. He persuaded
himself — generosity inventing reasons to justify itself
— that our relations with Mexico would be the State
Department's principal concern during his Presidency,
and that the command Fall had acquired of the Spanish
tongue — as spoken in New Mexico — made him the

best possible man for Secretary of State.[7] That impulse
was checked by protests made privately to Harding by

Senator Lodge, Secretary of the Interior Albert Fall, and President Harding.

Republican party leaders. Expressing embarrassment to
Fall for not giving him the highest post, apologetically
suggesting that later on some vacancy occurring on the Supreme Court might enable him to more fully honor his

[7] "On the occasion of my visit to Harding, November 5, 1920, at Marion, he
asked me, 'What do you think the New York newspapers would say if I appointed Albert Fall Secretary of State?' I remember the incident very well because of the surprise it gave me. I knew something of Fall's reputation as a
Western Senator with a good deal of the out-doors around him, but that reputation contained not one element of anything that pointed to him as a Secretary of
State, and I told Harding that I thought the New York newspapers would cer-

friend, Harding made Fall Secretary of the Interior. At this, the demons who had taken Harding as their subject for a fantastic tragedy must have laughed aloud.

III

It was twenty years since Harding and Harry Daugherty had met in the back yard of the hotel in a small Ohio town. Largely through the efforts of the one, the other had become President of the United States. In the personal contacts between the two no change had taken place; always they had respected each other, treated each other with dignity. They were close, but the relation between them never had the relaxation of camaraderie; they were not so much pals as two friends who had serious matters in hand.

That Harding, when in a position to do so, should confer honor on a friend, was a first instinct of his nature. That a President should give a cabinet post to the author and manager of his campaign, is a first law of politics. When intimate friend and political manager

tainly so value him."—A member of Harding's cabinet, in a letter to the author, June, 1935.

Senator George H. Moses of New Hampshire, Senator Medill McCormick of Illinois, and Senator Philander C. Knox of Pennsylvania "raised such a row that Harding abandoned it."—From a letter of ex-Senator Moses to the author, June 27, 1933.

Harding's disposition to make Fall Secretary of State was not publicly known. When he made Fall Secretary of the Interior, there was no protest, private or public, except that some strong partisans of the policy of conservation doubted whether Fall, having the point-of-view of a Western owner of ranches and cattle, would be loyal to the policy. Fall as Secretary of the Interior was regarded as a fit appointment, both by his fellow-Senators and by the public.

After Harding delivered his inaugural address at the Capitol March 4, 1921, he went to the Senate and in person read the list of his cabinet selections. When he came to Fall's name the Senate interrupted with a spontaneous burst of applause. After Harding had finished and left the chamber, Fall rose and presented his resignation as Senator to Vice-President Coolidge. Thereupon occurred an incident unique in the Senate's history. On the motion of Lodge of Massachusetts, the Senate confirmed Fall's appointment as Secretary of the Interior without the formality of referring it to a committee. Lodge's motion was carried, unanimously, to the accompaniment of a thunder of applause. On that day Democrats as well as Republicans were his friends and well-wishers.

are one, the compulsion is doubly binding. Failure of Harding to put Daugherty in his cabinet would have been a pointed exception to political practice, a pointed personal rebuff — and Harding was not the man to violate either the code of politics or that of friendship.

Had Daugherty happened not to be a lawyer, the situation would have been simpler; in that case Harding could have made him Postmaster-General, with fidelity to the rule that this post commonly goes to a political manager, and without offense to a public opinion that condones the rule. But Daugherty was a lawyer. Under the circumstances, to give him less than a legal post would have been only a little less pointed than to give him none. And the only legal post in the cabinet was an exalted and exacting one, Attorney-General. The appointment ought to go to a lawyer of the highest standing — and Daugherty, far from that, was, so to speak, outstanding in the dubiety of his standing. The situation was one to make a headache for Harding; and for Daugherty, too — if Daugherty had not been immune to headaches from that kind of cause.

Harding went through much turmoil about it, but always his mind moved farther and farther in the direction in which it was headed from the beginning. Protest by newspapers and by Republican leaders made Harding defiant, increased his sense of obligation for what Daugherty had done for him, stiffened his conception of human relations — in Harding's case having the force of a conviction of righteousness — that a man, and more so a President, should live up to the obligations of friendship and past services.

As for Daugherty, he was of several minds about it. Undoubtedly he would have felt hurt had Harding passed him by. Yet characteristically he cared more for getting the post than for having it; and he had already won, so to speak, the right to the office by his success in nominating Harding for the Presidency.

Daugherty declared at the time, and repeated in the book he and another wrote twelve years later,[8] that he did not want to be Attorney-General, that he urged Harding not to appoint him, that at all times he tried to persuade Harding to give the office to one who as man and lawyer was of the highest type, the Honorable George Sutherland of Utah (formerly a United States Senator from Utah, later a Justice of the Supreme Court). Daugherty doubted whether his experience had qualified him for the difficult and intricate legal work of the Attorney-General's office; I think also he shrank from the irksomeness of the job; the mental habits he had acquired in a lifetime of dashing here and there made the prospect of onerous plodding in the Attorney-General's office a little unwelcome to him.

At the same time, Daugherty was beset by complex emotions. I think that for one reason he wanted the office, or at least the public tender of it — it would take away some of the curse of the dubiety of his career as a lawyer, would give him, so to speak, sanctified standing in his profession. It would be vindication for him, or at least an officially refulgent veneer over his past reputation. In politics also, as well as in his profession, the office would be a vindication. To Ohio friends he used to say there was one reason he wanted to be Attorney-General, so he could walk down Broad Street in Columbus and tell "Bob" Wolfe to go to hell — Wolfe was an Ohio banker, business man, and newspaper owner who for a lifetime had fought Daugherty.

Of one thing I am confident: Daugherty did not want the office of Attorney-General nor any other relation to Harding for any purpose of corrupt advantage to

[8] "The Inside Story of the Harding Tragedy."

himself.[9] About Harding, Daugherty was high-minded
— though he could be realistic about nearly every
other man or thing. It was not merely that Daugherty
would not himself deliberately do anything that might
reflect on Harding. His regard for Harding went farther. He knew better than any one else Harding's mind
and soul, knew Harding's easy-going tolerance, Harding's lack of that insight into men which Daugherty
himself supremely had. Knowing these qualities of
Harding, Daugherty knew he would be in constant danger from political and other adventurers. Daugherty
told me at the time that his chief concern was to protect
Harding: "I know Harding and I know who the crooks
are and I want to stand between Harding and them."
Daugherty's attitude was somewhat like that of a
worldly, hard-boiled father toward a daughter — a
daughter whose easy-going generosity makes her exceptionally subject to the dangers attending excessive amiability.

The situation was the more trying because it was as
plain to the newspapers as to Harding and Daugherty
— their relations for several months were carried on in
a goldfish bowl. From the time public discussion of
cabinet possibilities began, newspapers watched and
wrote of what Harding would do about Daugherty, the
discussion being almost universally to the effect that
Daugherty was not, either as man or as lawyer, a fit
selection for Attorney-General. One journalist[10] of the
day wrote pointedly and strongly about Daugherty's un-

[9] This was my judgment at the time, and continued to be my judgment fifteen
years later, when I wrote this book. I was confirmed in my judgment by the man
who in 1920 had been Daugherty's principal newspaper critic and pursuer, Louis
Seibold, who in 1935, after reading a proof of this chapter, wrote me. "I have
always believed," Seibold wrote, "that Daugherty really wanted to protect Harding but that he was unable to stand off the other fellows who were also demanding rewards which Harding felt he could not refuse."
[10] Mark Sullivan.

fitness; suggested that Harding's sense of obligation might lead him to tender the office to Daugherty — but that if Daugherty was as good a friend as he claimed to be, he would decline the proffer. The New York *World* carried on a campaign against Daugherty, called him a lobbyist, unfit for that or any other high office; published sustained attacks on him, printed accounts of his career which laid emphasis on his lobbying. To Daugherty, *The World's* assaults were as water on a duck's back, his integument had long been indurated to that sort of thing; to be the centre of a swirling whirlpool of controversy was, for Daugherty, to be in his habitual habitat. To Harding, however, *The World's* campaign against Daugherty was infuriating, he felt Daugherty was being crucified by a Democratic paper because of loyalty to him.

Finally, at a conference[11] with the newspaper correspondents, Harding noticed *The World* correspondent[12] who had written many of the attacks on Daugherty. Harding, growing red, let his anger force his own hand. He broke out — even in anger there was about Harding's words an aura of old-fashioned formality: "I am ready to-day to invite Mr. Daugherty into the cabinet as my Attorney-General; when he is ready there will be an announcement, if he can persuade himself to make the sacrifice; . . . if I can persuade him to accept the post. And" — pointing his finger at *The World* correspondent and recalling from his own experience a technical newspaper term — "you can set that up in a block on your first page."[13]

A few minutes later, Daugherty coming down the steps, saw at the foot the other of his two principal news-

11 At St. Augustine, Florida, a few days before Harding was to be inaugurated.
12 Louis Seibold.
13 A "block" or "box" is a newspaper term for an announcement or other item made conspicuous by surrounding it with a border of rules.

paper critics, the author of this history. As he came face to face with me I assumed, I suppose, what manner of smile a man can summon up for such an occasion, and held out a congratulatory hand, saying: "Well, you're

From a photograph by Globe.

Harding's cabinet as first appointed. Seated from left to right: Secretary of War, John W. Weeks; Secretary of the Treasury, Andrew W. Mellon; Secretary of State, Charles E. Hughes; President Harding; Vice-President Coolidge; Secretary of the Navy, Edwin Denby. Standing: left to right, Secretary of the Interior, Albert B. Fall; Postmaster-General, Will Hays; Attorney-General, Harry M. Daugherty; Secretary of Agriculture, Henry C. Wallace; Secretary of Commerce, Herbert Hoover; Secretary of Labor, James J. Davis.

going to be Attorney-General!" Daugherty, with a manner that was one of his assets as a politician, the ability to preserve friendly relations with opponents and critics — Daugherty said, with complete good humor, "Yes, no thanks to you, goddam you." [13a]

[13a] To Seibold, Daugherty, with characteristically humorous irony, said: "You did me a good turn by showing up today; you know Harding sometimes doesn't know how to make up his mind and needs a little pushing."

IV

About the time Harding had completed roughly half his cabinet selections, he passed through one of those sudden emotional elevations that brought out the best in him — some of his friends used to think of them as "camp-meeting conversions," though in fact they came to Harding when he was most alone. To an acquaintance who saw him in his Marion home early in January, 1921, he said, with a manner which to a sensitive observer seemed poignant, "You know, before I was elected President, I thought the chief pleasure of it would be to give honors and offices to old friends — I thought that was the one big personal satisfaction a President would get. But you know — " here Harding put his hand on his heart and ·his features took on a kind of solemn grief — "you can't do that when you're President of the United States; you have to get the best men."

And in that altered mood Harding, combing the country for talent, appointed three of the best men ever in any cabinet, men who had no personal relation to Harding at all: Charles E. Hughes to be Secretary of State, Andrew W. Mellon to be Secretary of the Treasury, and Herbert Hoover to be Secretary of Commerce.[14]

But the demons boiling the brew that was to be Harding's destiny knew they did not need to feel disturbed. One of the commonest contributions to tragedy is a moral decision, made too late.

[14] The reader will understand that this chapter does not discuss all Harding's appointments, but only those that illustrate a trait of Harding's character. Elsewhere in this volume there are allusions to several, and characterizations of a few. The great majority of his appointments were up to the average of other administrations. It fell to him to appoint 70 Federal judges of various ranks; these as a whole were felt by lawyers to be of strikingly high quality.

9

THE UNITED STATES, WHEN HARDING BECAME PRESIDENT

A Period of Frazzled Nerves, Caused by the End of War-time Strain; of Disunity Caused by the End of the More or Less Artificially Built-up Unity of the War Period; of Strikes Caused by Continuation of War-time's High Cost of Living; of Business Depression Which Came when War-time Prices Began to Fall; and of Other Disturbances Due in Part to Economic Dislocations Brought by the War and Its Aftermath. From All of Which Arose Emotions of In-security and Fear, Which Expressed Themselves in Turbul-ence and Strife. The Boston Police Strike, the Steel Strike, the "Buyers' Strike" and the "Rent Strike." The "Red Scare." The Bomb Plots. A Dynamite Explosion in the New York Financial District. Deportation of Radicals. Demand for Reduction of Immigration. The I. W. W. and the "One Big Union." Sacco and Vanzetti. Race Riots Between Whites and Negroes. The Whole Reflecting an Unhappy Country when Harding Became Its President.

THE America in which Harding became President suffered from not only the world-wide dislocations and distresses caused by the war,[1] but also from domestic turbulence and rancor, mainly the outgrowth of the war, domestic expressions of the world-wide condition. In America, the coming to an end of war-time emotion and of the spirit of national unity (partly fomented artificially) that had accompanied the war,[2] was succeeded by a swing to the other extreme. The lifting of war-time controls over industry, the ending of war-achieved compactness, together with the cessation of war-time

[1] For an outline of the world as it was when the Twenties began, see Chapter 1.
[2] For an account of post-war emotion, largely disillusionment, see Chapter 7.

demand, followed by descent from war-time prices of food and other goods, led to severe economic dislocations which increased the harsh and discordant mood of the people. The resulting phenomena conformed, roughly, to a cycle. War-time prices[3] continued to rise for two years after the war ended — the peak was almost exactly November, 1920. Consequently, the years 1919 and 1920 were a period of strikes, not only strikes to get increased wages, but also strikes against high costs of living, "buyers' strikes," "rent strikes." About November 1, 1920, began descent in the prices of goods (rising value of money[4]) which led to different but equally disturbing phenomena — failures in business, foreclosures of mortgages, distress on farm, reduction in wages, unemployment.

The two sets of clashing phenomena, with the many expressions of them in emotions of rancor, met and overlapped during the two years preceding the inauguration of Harding, and the ensuing swirling of untoward forces was at its worst when Harding became President. The sum of them composed the background in which he took responsibility for the country's well-being. The nation of which Harding became President was not happy, and forces were under way which seemed likely, unless arrested, to bring more serious unhappiness.

[3] The index of retail food prices for war and post-war years, taking 1913 as 100, was:

1918—168.3	1919—185.9	1920—203.4
1921—153.3	1922—141.6	

[4] "Of all the causes that give rise to discontent, which undermine the good faith and comity of man in relation to man, and class in relation to class, the greatest is fluctuation in the purchasing value of the unit of the currency. When the value of the dollar goes downward, as happens during a war, one portion of the people is distressed and feels it has a grievance toward the other portion. When the value rises, as after a war, the other portion is distressed and has a corresponding sense of grievance. Lecky said of such changes in the basis of currency that it 'beyond all others affects most deeply and universally the material well-being of man.' " — Mark Sullivan, "Our Times," Vol. I, "The Turn of the Century."

II

Post-War Labor Disturbances

A long series of strikes and lockouts began January 9, 1919, with a strike of harbor workers in New York. . . . January 21, 35,000 dress and waist makers in New York, mostly young women, struck for a 44-hour week and a 15 per cent increase in pay. . . . February 6, the country was shocked by the calling of a "general strike" — always an ominous thing — in Seattle, in support of striking shipbuilders. . . . February 17, a threatened strike by 86,000 packers' employees was called off when the packers agreed to a wage increase amounting to $13,-000,000 for the year. . . . March 12, every car of the Public Service Railway Co., which ran through 141 New Jersey cities and towns, ceased operation at 6 P.M.; company officials explained that they preferred to give up service for the night rather than risk violence from their employees, who, 4500 strong, had walked out at 4 A.M. . . . April 11, demands of railroad workers for higher pay were conceded by Director General Hines (the railroads were still under Government control), who ordered advances amounting in their sum to $65,000,000 a year. . . . July 17, 30,000 cigar makers struck in New York City. . . . July 18, 30,000 construction workers were locked out in Chicago. . . . August 1, 70,000 railroad shopmen in the Chicago district quit work; a strike of street-car, elevated, and subway workers in Boston and Chicago partially paralyzed transportation in those cities. . . . Letter carriers appealed, August 3, to President Wilson for wage increases. . . . August 4, 4500 railroad shopmen at Washington, D. C., and vicinity quit work. . . . August 6, Brooklyn's surface, subway, and "L" lines shut down at 10 P.M. because of violence at-

From a photograph © by Western Newspaper Union through Underwood & Underwood.

Left: A strike on the Brooklyn Rapid Transit lines led to use of bicycles.
Right: A strike scene in Chicago.

From a photograph by International News Photos, Inc.

Chicago Race Riots of 1919. — Negro residence after a crowd of whites
had attacked it.

tending a strike; during the day flying squadrons of strikers had halted cars, beat motormen, conductors, and policemen, and fled in automobile trucks. . . . August 7, actors walked out in New York, closing most of the city's theatres; on the same day a walk-out of New England railroad shopmen caused the suspension of 102 passenger trains. . . . September 5, a strike of engineers and firemen forced tenants of the Metropolitan Building in New York to walk up forty-five flights of stairs. . . . September 19, at Chicago, 15,000 carpenters who had been on strike since July 18, forcing 80,000 other workers out, won their strike for $1 an hour, the highest wages paid carpenters in the United States. . . . September 30, a lockout of pressmen by printing shops started a strike which spread until more than sixty periodicals which normally were printed in New York had transferred to other cities. . . . A strike beginning October 31, which closed every bituminous coal mine in the country, causing everywhere a crippling of industry and transportation, was sustained until December 6, when President Wilson effected a compromise settlement.[5]

III

The Steel Strike

The coming of the greatest strike of the year was foreshadowed August 27 when Judge Elbert H. Gary, head of the United States Steel Corporation, refused to deal with leaders of a newly formed union of steel workers organized by the radical wing of the American Fed-

---

[5] This picture of American conditions in 1919 and 1920, composed of a large number of mentions of separate events, is made up largely from newspaper accounts at the time, from summaries in the weekly issues of the *Literary Digest* during 1919–21, from the contemporary annual issues of the "World Almanac," and from similar sources. While there is no doubt of the accuracy of the items, they have not been checked and investigated to the original sources as have most of the other contents of this volume.

From a photograph by Underwood & Underwood.

Children of the lower East Side doing picket duty during the rent strike
in New York.

From a photograph by Underwood & Underwood.

An incident of the actors' strike in New York.

eration of Labor. September 10, the mill employees of the Steel Corporation set September 22 for a general strike. September 17, Judge Gary reiterated his determination to stick to the open shop policy at whatever cost; in the Chicago district strike signs were posted on the walls of mills. September 18, a request by President Wilson that the strike be postponed was rejected by the leaders of the union. September 22, the great steel strike began. At the end of the first day union leaders claimed that 279,000 out of 350,000 workmen had quit. The companies said that not more than 20 per cent of the men had left their jobs. At Pittsburgh the bulk of the workers remained at work, but in Chicago most of them walked out. Trouble occurred between strikers and mill guards at Homestead, Pa., and at New Castle five men were shot. September 23, at a Buffalo plant, two strikers were killed and fifty wounded by mill guards. At Farrell, Pa., two were killed and several wounded. At Chicago and Youngstown the strike spread. September 29, the Bethlehem Steel Company having rejected the demands of the union, a strike was called and about a quarter of the workers walked out. At Chicago the Jones and Laughlin plants were forced to close, and 4000 men quit at Clarksburg and Weirton, W. Va. October 6, General Leonard Wood and Federal troops took charge at Gary, Ind. The strike dragged to its end January 8, 1920, when the American Federation of Labor conceded defeat. William Z. Foster, radical leader of the strike, was compelled to resign his post with the union.

IV

The Boston Police Strike

In the excited state of mind that had been induced among American workers one item of news about a labor development abroad found a favoring ambient. August 2, 1919, a cable from London recited that 1000 police at London and 929 at Liverpool had gone on strike. Among American police the idea of organizing into unions, though long discussed, had never taken hold. In 1919, of all wage-earners the police had most cause for complaint. During the war their salaries had increased little if at all and the greatly higher prices for food, clothing, and housing had made it increasingly difficult for them to make ends meet. From the reports they read about the police strikes in England, they took hope that by organizing unions they could improve their condition. Several police unions were formed, among them one in the city of Boston.

The Boston union, chartered on August 15, 1919, and affiliated from the start with the American Federation of Labor, quickly ran into difficulties with the city officials. August 26, nineteen patrolmen, leaders in the union movement, were summoned before a trial board charged with disobeying a ruling by the Commissioner of Police, Edwin U. Curtis, forbidding organization. Meantime a "Committee of 34" appointed by Mayor Andrew Peters, conducted an investigation and presented a conciliatory report suggesting that the men be permitted to retain their union provided it be divorced from any connection with the American Federation of Labor. This solution Police Commissioner Curtis refused to accept. Thereupon the union officials called a strike for 5 P.M. Tuesday, September 9. At that hour 1117 patrolmen out of a total force of 1544 walked out. For the first time a great American city was left without protection, completely at the mercy of the lawless. Merchants, frightened, closed and locked their shops and prepared to make armed defense of their property. At 11 P. M., with not a policeman on the streets anywhere, looting began; all night long, Boston witnessed such scenes as had never before occurred in an American city in peace-time. "In the morning a sight not beautiful

From a photograph by International News Photos, Inc.

The Boston police strike, 1919.

met the eye; lawlessness continued; license ran wild; daylight robbery, . . . the voluntary police were assaulted." [6]

On September 10, Mayor Peters called on the militia for police duty, and the soldiers, trying to put down lawlessness, became involved in fights with rioters which resulted in the killing of two persons and the wounding of many more. Next day, with the strike still on but with disorder diminishing, Governor Coolidge took

[6] Much of the detail about the Boston police strike is taken from Horace Green's painstaking book, "The Life of Calvin Coolidge."

command and issued an edict calling on the citizenry of
the State to uphold the forces of the law. That was the
turning-point. September 12, the places of the striking
police were filled by new men, including a number of
war veterans, and the trouble was over.

But though Boston was again serene there was still to
happen an event both dramatic and historic. A plea by
President Gompers of the American Federation of Labor
that the defeated strikers be allowed to return to their
jobs was denied by Governor Coolidge, who replied in a
telegram which, when printed in the newspapers,
brought him a message of congratulation from President
Wilson and applause from the public:

There is no right to strike against the public safety by anybody, anywhere, any time.

v

The Buyers' Strike

During the two years following the war, prices of
food and other goods had continued to rise. Sugar went
to 30 cents a pound; shoes, which before the war had
been priced at $3, now sold for $10 and $12. Wages
and incomes had not increased in proportion. The public, resentful, demanded that the government stop the
"profiteering." Government, national and local, sought
by persuasion and threat and otherwise to bring prices
down. Great quantities of foodstuffs that had been
bought during the war for the army and navy were taken
from government warehouses and put on sale to the
public. By action of government maximum prices were
fixed for bread, coal, milk. In Washington, D. C., Congress took steps to prevent increases in rent; in other
parts of the country, state and city governments did the
same.

Despite all that government could do, prices remained high. There followed, by a kind of spontaneous generality, a "buyers' strike." Men who normally bought one or two suits a year and two or three pairs of shoes,

A cartoon by Harding in the Brooklyn "Eagle."

The humpty-dumpty of 1920 did not fall easily.

determined to wear their old suits longer and to have their old shoes re-soled. Women, defying the mandates of style, appeared on the streets wearing their last year's hats and last year's dresses; since everybody was doing it, the wearing of old clothes became itself a vogue. The "rent strike" took the simple form of not paying;

when landlords turned off the heat, the courts took harsh notice of them.

The country went about it all in a spirit of gaiety; innumerable stories were told of ways devised by ingenious persons to beat the high cost of living. The newspapers, sensing the public mood, gave prominence to dispatches telling of housewives who fed their families on half a dollar a day. Propaganda, spontaneous in origin and ingenious in method, spread the movement. William G. McAdoo, former Secretary of the Treasury, son-in-law of President Wilson, financially well able to buy a new suit, and ordinarily meticulous about his raiment, appeared on the streets and had his photograph taken with patches on his trousers, patches of a newness which suggested that they were not really necessary and of a conspicuousness which implied that the purpose was to make a vogue of thrift.[7]

One facet of the "buyers' strike" was a movement to substitute cotton overalls for men's woollen suits. Beginning about April, 1920, when the movement got its start in the South, newspaper readers everywhere were able to follow day by day the spread of the overalls movement northward and westward, its jump across the ocean to England, and its appearance not long afterward in

[7] About the time when prolongation of use of clothes was a civic virtue, I, with Senator Medill McCormick of Illinois, discovered in New York, a little tailor who could "turn" a suit of clothes. He remembered the art from his early training in London, at a time, some forty years before, when economy had been more prized than style. The process was difficult; to turn a suit inside out and have the button holes and other details come right was an art. The result was a suit with a fresh surface in place of a shiny one, at a cost of $13 instead of $100 for a new suit. Senator McCormick and I had several suits turned. Soon after, visiting Edward Beck, managing editor of the Chicago *Tribune,* I exhibited the achievement in economy. He, having a newspaper man's sense of the passing waves that engage public interest, printed a column about my "turned suit." At any other time it would not have been news, but only an obscure example of eccentric parsimony. Now the story was printed far and wide; from a clipping bureau I received reprints from London and from Shanghai. The little tailor was overwhelmed with orders; one who patronized him was a New York financier, Frank Vanderlip, whose ample capacity to buy new suits was eclipsed by desire to give public encouragement to thrift.

Argentina. Overalls invaded the offices and homes of clerks, school-teachers, brokers, bankers; they even penetrated the Capitol, draped upon the thin shoulders and spindly legs of eccentric "Willie" Upshaw, Con-

Cover for the *American Legion Weekly* of October, 1920, expressing the resentment of veterans over inability to get jobs. By this time the business depression of 1920–21 had set in and millions were out of work.

gressman from Georgia. Sympathetic reception was given to accounts of a movement starting in Spain for the substitution of sandals for shoes and the complete dispensing with hats.

Partly, but only slightly, on account of the buyers' strike, and more because of economic forces that always operated, prices began to decline. The peak of the rise came in early November, 1920; soon after, retail clothing stores reduced prices 20 per cent, and other merchants made similar reductions. "How cheerful it is," remarked the Buffalo *News*, "to see a $4 pair of shoes marked down from $20 to $17.98." That was when prices first began their fall; later the $4 shoes could be bought for $4.

Accompanying the decline of prices, and equally and inevitably a characteristic of the course of the business cycle, came failures in business, closing of factories, or part time operation of them. With that came unemployment, until it was estimated that between 5 and 6 millions of people were without work.[8] "We were," said Secretary of Labor Davis, a year later, "in the throes of one of the greatest industrial depressions we had ever known." Now the strikes of 1919 and early 1920 were succeeded by disorders arising out of unemployment.

VI

The "Reds"

Some of the strikes and other violences connected with labor had their origin in the I. W. W. and other radical and socialistic organizations. The radicals, always regarded with repugnance by the average American, were, in 1919, because of their trouble-making, looked upon with more than ordinary dislike. Violence on their part, whether of act or word, provoked immediate counter violence, sometimes by individuals, often by such organizations as the American Legion and, later, the Ku Klux Klan. The government also on occasion harried them.

February 4, following a declaration by Senator King of Utah that the Russian Bolsheviks were conducting

[8] The estimate was by Secretary of Labor James J. Davis, in the Department of Labor's annual report for 1922.

propaganda for the overthrow of the American and other capitalistic governments, a Senate committee was appointed to investigate Bolshevik activities in the United

© *George Matthew Adams.*

The wholesale deportation of alien agitators from the United States in 1919 and 1920, and the presumably not very comfortable lot of the deportees after their return to Russia, supplied the inspiration for this cartoon.

States. . . . February 11, the Department of Justice brought fifty-three Reds from the far West to Ellis Island for deportation. . . . A month before, on January 8, Representative Victor L. Berger and other socialists and radicals, including the Reverend Irving St. John Tucker, Episcopal rector and Red propagandist and pacifist leader, had been convicted by a Federal jury at Chicago of sedition and disloyalty under the Espionage Act. . . . February 20, a jury at Hammond, Ind., after deliberating two minutes, acquitted Frank Petroni, naturalized citizen whose patriotic emotion had led him

From a photograph by Underwood & Underwood.

One of the many bombs addressed to public men in a nation-wide dynamite conspiracy during 1919. The paper in which the bombs were wrapped had either been stolen from or was a counterfeit of paper in which packages were sent out by a well-known New York department store.

to shoot and kill Frank Petrich, alien, for yelling: "To hell with the United States!" . . . March 10, the United States Supreme Court unanimously sustained the conviction of Eugene V. Debs, four times Socialist candidate for President, found guilty of violating the Espionage Act through statements made in a speech at Canton, Ohio, in June, 1918, and sentenced him to ten years imprisonment. Debs, two days later, in a farewell public address at Cleveland, upheld the Bolshevist rule in Russia and referred to Lenin and Trotzky as the "foremost statesmen of the age." Debs said the judges of the Supreme Court were "begowned, bewhiskered, bepowdered old fossils who have never decided anything." Entering Moundsville (W. Va.) prison, April 13, 1919, to begin serving his sentence, Debs was made clerk in the hospital. . . . April 14, a group of I. W. W., attempting to hold a meeting at Farrell, Pa., were driven out of town. . . . April 30, what was asserted to be a nation-wide plot by Reds to celebrate May Day with wholesale assassinations of jurists, Cabinet members, and other public officials was thwarted by the discovery of sixteen packages in the General Post Office in New York containing dynamite bombs. Throughout the country a total of thirty-four infernal machines, addressed to public officials, all of the same make, were seized in the mails or after delivery. Among those who received bomb-packages, or were marked for death in some other way, were: Justice Oliver W. Holmes of the Supreme Court; Postmaster-General Burleson, Federal Judge K. M. Landis, Governor Sproul of Pennsylvania, Secretary of Labor Wilson, Attorney-General A. Mitchell Palmer, Mayor Hylan of New York. . . . May 1, upward of 400 soldiers, sailors, and marines, including some Victory Loan workers, raided the office of the New York *Call*, Socialist newspaper, beat several editors, and damaged the plant. . . . May 5, the I. W. W., holding a convention in Chicago, were denounced by the Board of Aldermen. . . . May 7, Governor Alfred E. Smith of New York signed a bill forbidding a display of red flags in New York State. . . . June 2, a bomb wrecked the residence of Attorney-General Palmer, arch-foe of the Reds, in Washington; a man thought to be the bearer of the bomb was blown to pieces. The homes of Mayor

Davis of Cleveland, and Justice Albert F. Hayden of
Roxbury, Mass., were dynamited at about the same

From a photograph by Western Newspaper Union.

The R Street Washington home of A. Mitchell Palmer, Attorney-General in
Wilson's cabinet. The house was wrecked by a bomb thrown by an
unknown person who was killed by the explosion.

hour. A bomb partially destroyed the residence of Judge
C. C. Nott in New York City. . . . June 17, the
American Federation of Labor convention at Atlantic
City rejected the I. W. W. plan for one big union, and
passed a resolution condemning Bolshevism. . . . Oc-

tober 7, 118 foreigners, steel strikers belonging to the I. W. W., were forced to kiss the American flag by police at Weirton, W. Va. . . . November 7, the Department of Justice, alleging a revolutionary plot had been uncovered, began a nation-wide raid on Reds, arresting more than 200 in New York City alone. . . . November 10, the House of Representatives, by 309 votes to 1, unseated Socialist Representative Victor L. Berger of Milwaukee. . . . November 11, at Centralia, Wash., three ex-service men, members of the American Legion, attempting to raid I. W. W. headquarters during an Armistice Day parade, were shot to death. One of the shooters was lynched. . . . December 2, President Wilson in a message to Congress urged action for the curbing of Reds. . . . December 29, Red headquarters at Buffalo, Rochester, and Utica, N. Y., were raided. . . . December 21, the United States transport *Buford*, with 249 Reds, among them three women, marked for deportation, sailed for Russia. January 7, 1920, the New York State Legislature refused to permit the seating of five Socialists elected to the Assembly from New York City. Alfred E. Smith, Governor of New York, protested: "Although I am unalterably opposed to the fundamental principles of the Socialist party, it is inconceivable that a minority party, duly constituted and legally organized, should be deprived of its right to expression so long as it has honestly, by lawful methods of education and propaganda, succeeded in securing representation, unless the chosen representatives are unfit as individuals."

VII

Sacco and Vanzetti

On April 15, 1920, carrying $15,000, the payroll of the shoe factory for which they worked, Frank Parmenter and Alexander Berardelli, paymaster and guard, were shot and killed on a street in South Braintree, Mass. They had gone to Boston at noon to get the payroll and had returned on the train reaching South Braintree at 3 P.M. Leaving the station, they were almost at their

From a photograph by International News Photos, Inc.

Nicola Sacco and Bartolomeo Vanzetti.

destination when an automobile drew swiftly up beside them and two of five men riding in it, according to stories told by eye-witnesses, started shooting with re-volvers. Parmenter and Berardelli slumped to the ground, killed instantly. The murderers, brandishing their weapons, leaped to the sidewalk, seized the pay-roll, and sprang back into their car, which dashed around a corner and disappeared. Numerous persons who saw the crime told the police that the murderers and their companions were swarthy of complexion and appeared to be Italians.

Three weeks after the murders, two Italian workmen, Nicola Sacco and Bartolomeo Vanzetti, were arrested at Brockton and charged with the crime. In the trial, presided over by Judge Webster Thayer, the men protested their innocence. Both furnished alibis. A clerk

From a photograph by International News Photos, Inc.

Funeral of Sacco and Vanzetti in Boston, following their execution in the Charlestown Prison, August 23, 1927.

in the Italian Consulate at Boston testified that Sacco had been in his office on April 15 at about the time the crime was committed. Vanzetti, according to several witnesses, had spent the day selling fish in Plymouth, 35 miles from South Braintree. Evidence against the men was largely circumstantial. Judge Thayer, when charging the jury, said, "There is a most strenuous dispute as to the identity of the murderers; the real issue you must determine is" their identification. The jury brought in a verdict of guilty and Judge Thayer sentenced the two men to death.

Before their arrest neither Sacco nor Vanzetti had been convicted of a crime. Sacco was a shoe worker and watchman, and one employer testified to his honesty. Vanzetti had done menial work. For some months prior

From a photograph by Underwood & Underwood.

A demonstration in Union Square, New York, by radicals and other sympathizers with Sacco and Vanzetti, against the execution of the two men. 12,000 persons were in the crowd.

to his arrest he had made a living peddling fish in the Italian colonies near Boston.

Both men were radicals. Shortly before their arrest they had been leaders in arranging a mass meeting of protest against the alleged brutality of Department of Justice agents towards a fellow radical, who had leaped to his death from the New York offices of the Department of Justice while undergoing questioning. Both Sacco and Vanzetti were active in strikes, though not as paid organizers.

With the arrest of the two Italians, friends and sympathizers formed a "Save Sacco and Vanzetti" committee, which raised a defense fund and for years after the trial agitated for the release of the prisoners. Radicals everywhere in the world affiliated themselves with the cause. Joined with the radicals were numerous other persons of high standing who believed that the two Italians had been "convicted by atmosphere, not evidence." [9]

VIII

Dynamite Explosion in the New York Financial District

A few minutes before noon September 16, 1920, a horse-drawn wagon pulled up to the curb before the United States Sub-treasury and Assay Office, and opposite the granite building of the J. P. Morgan Co., at the corner of Wall and Broad Streets in New York City. The intersection of Broad and Wall, in the heart of New York's financial district, is on week-days dense with people. On this day the sidewalks were as usual thronged with stock-exchange traders, brokers, clerks, bank messengers, stenographers — all hurrying about their business, jostling each other as they sought to make headway. Though the wagon, with its driver and horse, were in the view of hundreds, seemingly nobody gave it more than a cursory glance — afterwards no one came forward with a trustworthy description. The wagon had seemed just a wagon, no different from hundreds of others on the streets of down-town New York. The driver was vari-

[9] They were executed August 23, 1927, at the Charlestown, Mass., State Prison.

ously pictured as swarthy and fair, tall and short, heavy and slight, foreigner and American. How long the equipage stood in front of the Assay Office is also in doubt, but probably it was there not longer than five minutes.

Suddenly the wagon seemed to disintegrate with a crashing roar that reached for miles about. Up from the street swept a wall of flame which thrust fiery tongues into windows lining both sides of Wall Street, setting desks afire and burning the hair from the heads of office workers; people at windows six stories from the ground were badly burned. Even more destructive than the flames were the thousands of fragments of iron, later found to be parts of sash-weights, which the explosion drove in a deadly rain in all directions. The immediate dead, for the most part passers-by in the street, numbered thirty-eight. Hundreds were injured, fifty-seven badly enough to require hospital treatment. The damage to property was estimated at between half a million and two millions and a half. For several blocks plate glass windows in stores were shattered and the façades of buildings were badly pitted. Several fine hand-wrought bronze doors were warped and broken.

Police made their appearance quickly. Of the mysterious wagon they found broken splinters and pieces of wheels, but nothing that would give a hint as to its ownership. The horse had been blown to pieces, but one of its shoes was found, which police took to blacksmiths around New York for identification, without success. One theory was that the explosion was not intentional but an accident. Excavations for new buildings were being made in the neighborhood and it was suggested that the wagon contained dynamite destined for some building job. The explanation did not fare very well in the subsequent investigation. Transportation of explosives through New York City streets was hedged about by precautions. It had to be done at certain times when few people were about and always with a guard. Besides, examination of the books of explosive sellers failed to reveal the despatch of any shipment which could have been the one causing the explosion.

Large rewards for information leading to the arrest of the perpetrators of the crime have gone unclaimed. For months, even years, the police of New York, agents of the United States Secret Service, and private detectives have worked to solve the mystery. Scores of suspects have been arrested. But as this is written, fifteen years after the event, as little is known as at the moment the blast occurred.

An opinion held by the police, which seems logical, is that the explosion was an act of terrorism by radicals. Also it has been suggested that it was the work of a criminal maniac.

IX

Riots Between Negroes and Whites

When on February 17, 1919, a large body of colored soldiers, returning from France, marched up Fifth Avenue in New York, they were given as fine an ovation as any white troops had received. That was the last time returning negro soldiers were cheered, by white people. Colored troops returning to their homes after demobilization, carried themselves with a jauntiness which the whites did not like. Trouble between the races broke out in several places. At Washington, D. C., in late June, 1919, for several days the nation's capital witnessed street fighting between blacks and whites almost on the scale of a small civil war. At Chicago a racial clash occurred July 28 and lasted for three days, during which

36 persons were killed. Equally serious trouble occured in Arkansas and St. Louis. Throughout the South racial feeling ran high, though not attended by much violence. The feeling, continuing, stimulated the growth of the Ku Klux Klan and added one more to the rancors and class conflicts that beset the country.

x

"The government," said the periodical *The New Republic*,[10] "during the next four years will have to deal with a group of political and economic problems of altogether exceptional stubbornness and difficulty. Only once before in the history of the nation, in the years immediately preceding the election of Washington, has the American people been confronted with the necessity for an equally grave and complicated group of decisions. In reaching these decisions the next President must for good or ill play the leading part. The government and public opinion can obtain leadership from no other source."

For meeting these tasks and responsibilities, Harding had a method — not so much a consciously worked-out method as a simple expression of his personality. Its spontaneousness, its naturalness, as an emanation of Harding's personality, was not altered by the artificiality of the phrases in which his editorial training had led him to put it, in a speech at Boston in May, 1920:

America's present need is not heroics, but healing; not nostrums but normalcy; not revolution but restoration . . . not surgery but serenity.

[10] June 23, 1920.

THE PRESIDENCY OF HARDING

For meeting the problems, domestic and foreign, that faced America, Harding had qualifications that were unique and, for those conditions and that time, very valuable. Much of what troubled the world was rancor, rancor between nation and nation abroad, between class and class at home. For the assuaging of rancor, Harding was an ideal statesman, well adapted, had he lived and things gone well, to make America a gradually spreading area of calm in the storm-tossed waters that the world was. Toward rancor directed at himself, Harding's reaction was always patience. As a mediator of anger between others, he had a personality that induced quiet. As the clamant quarrellers grew more and more excited, Harding's spirit flowered into greater and greater poise; in the end the storming contenders were infected by his calm. It cost him no effort, did not exhaust him, for his tolerance, his charity, his good-will were not policies with him, nor arts improvised to meet emergency; they were natural emanations from his personality. While he had quiet, simple convictions, he was utterly without pride of opinion, and he was completely free from any disposition to generate plans for the management of the world, or the wish to impose them. Distinctly, his spirit radiated a definite quality of healing, a technique of remedy that permitted and encour-

From a photograph by International News Photos, Inc.

A photograph that brought out some of Harding's stronger and better qualities.

aged the curative processes of time and nature to work their beneficence.

"The most notable quality of Harding," said one of the wisest commentators[1] of the day, "was the sweetness of his nature. His friendliness was not a matter of poli-

[1] Edward S. Martin. The tribute, written after Harding's death, appeared in *Life,* August 16, 1923. Martin differed strongly from Harding in his viewpoints, felt almost bitter about Harding's refusal to lead America into the League of Nations — but he recognized Harding's good qualities and the usefulness of these qualities in a President of the United States at a time when the world was in one of its most turbulent moods. The passage as printed here is condensed.

tics but something born in him. He came to office at a
time of extraordinary public irritation. Everybody was
cross, there had been a deadlock in government for
months and the main occupation of the articulate was in
fixing the blame for it on the man or the group that they
did not like. To that condition of affairs Harding was
a Godsend. He had modesty, humility, and a desire to
do right. There was a definite limit to what he could
accomplish as a statesman. It was a time of waiting
until men's minds found new positions, and for such a
period he was remarkably well suited. He liked his fellow man and didn't seem to mind being jostled by him.
There are people in the world who have a place and a
recognized value that nothing can touch. They sweeten
life. Come to analyze them and it is discovered that they
give out love, and then one realizes anew that love is
the greatest thing in the world, and why. That is what
Harding seemed to do; he gave out love, and that is a
service that is far from common and never will be cheap.
In just so far as it can be furnished, civilization is safe,
and peace in the world assured."

II

Destiny Invites America; America Declines

For the management of the changed world, only one
comprehensive device had been proposed, the League of
Nations. (There were many others, as many as there
were inventive-minded altruists, but the League was the
one that got world-wide attention.) This, America had
declined to subscribe to. From that approach to the new
world, Harding was held back, even had he wished to
take it, which he did not.

The League of Nations, as ardent advocate H. G.

Wells stated it, and italicized it, was "*a world law under a world government.*" It was an attempt to make corporeal what a poet had dreamed half a century before, a "parliament of nations" — that phrase of Tennyson's was seriously overworked by fervid altruists during the pitch of discussion about the League.

The League contemplated a federated world. If that was not to be, the opposite alternative must be to continue with a world organized on the pattern of individualism, each nation independent and having power and standing in proportion to its wealth, its strength, and its other attributes of force and prestige. If that path were to be resumed, there was a plain destiny for America. We should have stepped into the position of leading nation which until that time, and for a century and a half past, had been held by Britain. What had happened — a succinct summary of the Great War would say in a few sentences — was that Britain had been the leading nation; that Germany coveted the position — her "place in the sun," Germany had called it; that Germany set out to seize the place of dominance; that she failed; and that in the attempt she fatally weakened — fatally for purposes of primacy — both herself and the nation which she had chosen, somewhat too cocksurely, to challenge. Now the position of primacy was vacant; for a tenant, it called to one who in the contest of ambitions had been an innocent bystander, America. So slight had our interest and ambition been that when events called us to the place of leadership we were reluctant, unprepared. The opportunity, with the accompanying responsibility, had we been willing to take it, would have included international aggressiveness in trade, substituting the dollar for the pound in world finance, taking Britain's place in world trade. Toward that we made some half-hearted gestures. It would have included also

building the strongest navy in the world — possession of
the strongest navy, dominance on the sea, has been the
attribute of every nation that has had leadership in the
world ever since the long succession began with Tyre.
Toward that, too, we made some gestures.

In the end, however, we concluded — not "concluded," for it was not a thought-out cerebration — we
stumbled into a middle course between a federated world
and an individualist one. So far as we did it consciously,
we took it as the easier way. We entered into an arrangement — this step we took on our own initiative — by
which naval dominance, instead of being the possession
of ourselves or any other one nation, was, so to speak,
allotted among several nations and put in trust.

This action was taken at the Washington Conference
for the Limitation of Armaments.

III

America's Relations with Japan

Among the scintillant phrases that flashed from
Woodrow Wilson's pen when he was summoning America to take up arms against Germany, was "war to end
war." As a stimulant to crusading militancy in the
Great War, the phrase was extraordinarily effective.
Millions of Americans, and more millions in the countries fighting Germany — for the phrase travelled far
— took the slogan on faith, put trust in the promise it
held out, and believed that any sacrifice would not be too
great to pay for the attainment of permanent peace for
the world.

But as with other alluring phrases and the high hopes
they inspired, so with this. Even while the peace com-
missioners were bickering at Paris after the Great War,

the people of the United States became aware of a rising threat to their peace, in the Pacific.

Japan, when the Great War broke out, lost no time coming to the aid of England, to whom she was bound by an Anglo-Japanese treaty. Japan's principal aim as a belligerent, she announced, would be to protect England's interests in the Far East, and also, as a direct war effort, to expel Germany from her foot-hold in China at Kiao-chau. Japan invested Kiao-chau, took it, kept it.

Japan's war tasks, consisting mainly of nominal police duty with her navy and the loan of a few cruisers to convoy Allied troop-ships, left her free to advance her own commercial, industrial, and political interests. Exports from the great maritime nations had been stopped by the war; the trade and shipping of the Orient was anybody's for the taking. Japan took them. Eagerly she expanded her industry, enlarged her merchant marine. Soon she achieved a practical monopoly of China's foreign trade, out of which she drew enormous profits. At the beginning of the war she had been financially weak, as a result of fighting Russia in 1904; by the end of the war she was relatively rich. She had money; she had a strong army; she had a splendid navy; she had a population that was virile, ambitious, patriotic. Also she had need to expand; since the turn of the century she had grown so fast that there was not room on her small islands for her millions — new outlets must be found for the overflow. In a word, the materials were all present for a career of adventure, expansion, and colonization of the sort which Western nations had engaged in since the time of Rome.

Japan took her first step along the road to a place in the sun while the Great War was still in its early stage. In 1915, in a note to China, she made "twenty-one de-

mands" — for years that phrase was familiar in headline and editorial — which had the purpose of achieving for Japan a favored status in Chinese affairs. From
that time on she took advantage of every opportunity to
strengthen her position as a great power. She took over
Shantung, and, after the war, laid claim to permanent
possession of the islands in the western Pacific formerly
held by Germany. By arrangement with several Latin-
American countries she established settlements of Japanese in the New World. She laid claim to the Island of
Yap in the far Pacific. Here for the first time she came
into sharp collision with American interests, for we
wished the island internationalized so that an American
cable to the Orient could have a relay-station there.

Meanwhile, and partly as a result of the aggressiveness shown by Japan immediately after the war, the
anti-Japanese sentiment that had long smouldered in the
Pacific Coast States of the United States blazed into
fresh flame. There were acts of violence against Japanese farm laborers in California; State legislatures
passed laws prohibiting the owning of land by Japanese;
a barrage of anti-Japanese agitation was kept up by
jingo newspapers. For months the newspapers of California fulminated against the custom of Japanese in
America of selecting wives, "picture brides," in Japan
from photographs, and having them brought to the
United States.

The feeling against Japan on the West Coast of the
United States was more than matched by the animosity
towards the United States that grew up in Japan. One
long-standing cause of this feeling was the provision in
America's immigration laws excluding Asiatics. With
much justification the Japanese regarded this as gratui-
tously insulting to them — they objected naturally to
being lumped with all the backward peoples of Asia in a

classification which marked them as inferior to the white races. To aggravate still further the growing bad feeling between the two peoples, some Japanese politicians and a part of the Japanese press made capital for themselves by exaggerating every incident of friction and misunderstanding.

America's anxiety was increased by apprehension over the safety of her possessions in the Orient, the Philippine Islands, 1200 miles to the south of Japan. It was feared that in the event of a crisis in Japanese-American affairs resulting in war, the Japanese navy would swoop down on the Philippines and capture them.

The United States had acquired the Philippines in 1898 as an incident to the war with Spain. The wish to take them had not been among our war aims, and after we had them we were not very comfortable with them. The task of governing the islands had for two decades been expensive and occasionally unsatisfactory. The Filipinos felt no gratitude toward us; many of their leaders were at all times shrilly insistent that we set them free. However, our Army and Navy wanted them kept, and also some American business interests; the wishes of these, in the main, coupled with reluctance to let go what we had once possessed, determined our national policy.

Keeping the Philippines meant that we must have a navy large enough to protect them. For this reason and others, Congress was willing to provide funds for a large building programme. Japan had been building since the beginning of the war; now she increased her efforts. In December, 1920, a great new battleship, the *Mutsu*, largest and most modern in the world, paid for with small coins contributed by Japanese laborers and school children, was being rushed to completion on the ways at Tokio.

The situation was made the more trying by the treaty between Japan and Great Britain; the same treaty that had caused Japan to support England in the Great War would put some degree of obligation on England to support Japan, or at least not embarrass her, in case of war with the United States.

At Washington, following President Harding's induction into office, sober thought was given to the threatening situation in the Pacific. Among those apprehensive about the situation was Senator William E. Borah, a member of the Foreign Relations Committee of the United States Senate. Borah felt that the incipient naval race between Japan and the United States, if permitted to get fully under way, would sooner or later end as such rivalries everywhere had in the past. He wanted it stopped. The best way to stop it, he decided, was to have the United States and Japan (and England also, for England was building to hold her supremacy) declare a naval holiday during which no ships of war would be built. Borah took his idea to Harding. Harding approved, and added the suggestion that land forces be reduced too. Hughes was consulted; he, too, approved.

IV

The Washington Conference for the Limitation of Armament

Invitations were sent to the four nations which, with the United States, were dominant in world affairs following the war, Japan, England, France, Italy, and also to five secondary powers having trade or other interests in the Orient, to meet at Washington on November 12, 1921; to confer on joint limitation of armament.

The delegations included the leading statesmen from

the respective nations: from Britain, Balfour; from France, Briand; from Japan, Ito. Present also was the largest group of journalists that had ever assembled in Washington, including representatives from practically

From a photograph by Brown Brothers.

American delegates to the Washington Conference for the Limitation of Armament, 1921. From left to right, Elihu Root, Henry Cabot Lodge, Charles E. Hughes, Oscar W. Underwood.

every important country and from many minor ones; they came from Britain and from China, from France and from Japan, from Italy and from Korea.

Harding at the Washington Conference

The conference opened. Upon the President of the United States devolved the function of making the opening address.

Harding,[3] as he rose, had his habitual air of disarming and ingratiating modesty. He bowed very formally and, for an American, deeply, and began. The most earnest and moving part of his speech was the passage in which he spoke of the emotions that had come to him the day before at the burial of the unknown soldier in Arlington Memorial Cemetery:

Here in the United States we are but freshly turned from the burial of an unknown American soldier, when a nation sorrowed while paying him tribute. Whether it was spoken or not, a hundred millions of our people were summarizing the inexcusable causes, the incalculable cost, the unspeakable sacrifices, and the unutterable sorrows; and there was the ever-impelling question: How can humanity justify or God forgive? Human hate demands no such toll; ambition and greed must be denied it. If misunderstanding must take the blame, then let us banish it.

As Harding ended his address, he again took on his habitual manner of self-effacing modesty. He tried to satisfy the clamoring audience with a smile of appreciation and gratitude as he began to move away toward the door. But Hughes grasped his hand and shook it glowingly. That caused the applause to rise again. Harding, still smiling and bowing shyly, kept trying to edge toward the door. But Balfour also grasped his hand, and then Briand and Viviani and all the others who could reach him as he made his way toward the door with as much speed as he could manage without seeming to lack courtesy to the applauding audience and to the delegates who were reaching out to congratulate him. Finally, he succeeded in edging his way beneath the gallery, and with a last diffident wave of his arm to the audience, stepped rapidly through the door.

[3] This description of Harding at the Washington Conference is taken from "The Great Adventure at Washington," Mark Sullivan, 1922.

Hughes at the Washington Conference

Now Hughes spoke. His words, in their effect upon the delegates and upon the watching multitudes throughout the world, might be likened to an immense lightning stroke flashing cleanly through an atmosphere of murk. Hughes proposed that the navies of the great powers should be "frozen" in their then ratio of strength

HUGHES PROPOSES TO NATIONS A 10-YEAR NAVAL HOLIDAY; WANTS 66 CAPITAL SHIPS SCRAPPED, 30 OF THEM BY AMERICA; BOLD CONFERENCE PLAN IMPRESSES BRITISH AND JAPANESE

Headline reflecting interest in the opening of the Washington Conference for the Limitation of Armament.

each to the other. The British and American navies in 1921 were about of a size, while that of Japan was about two-fifths smaller. Hughes's suggestion called for a permanent relationship for the three navies of, stated numerically, 5, 5, and 3. Not only that. Japan, England, and the United States all had ships on the ways, in one stage or another of completion, and had prepared blue-prints for hundreds of thousands of tons of new construction. All these Hughes proposed should be junked. More even than that. Hughes's plan proposed that some ships of the three navies already built and sailing the seas should be taken out of commission and destroyed.[4]

In making his proposal Hughes first named the ships of the American fleet which, he proposed, should be

---

[4] A shrewd and epigrammatic English observer at the Conference, Colonel Repington, remarked: "Secretary Hughes sunk in 35 minutes more ships than all the admirals of the world have sunk in a cycle of centuries."

scrapped. Then he went boldly on to deal in the same way with the British and Japanese fleets.

> It is proposed that Great Britain:
> (1) Shall stop further construction of the four new *Hoods* —

As[5] Hughes mentioned this name, sacred to the British navy, and as he went on to name the *King George the Fifth,* and others yet, Admiral Beatty, one of the British delegates, came forward in his chair. His eyes first widened and then narrowed; he looked at Hughes with an expression nothing less than the astonished but instantly combative dignity with which the head of the British navy, standing tranquilly on the bridge of his flag-ship in a peaceful sea, might receive an unanticipated and wholly uncalled-for shot across his bow; and who most decidedly and pointedly wants to know what it's all about. He might have said, if he had spoken, "Here, you — who are you? Does Britannia rule the waves, or doesn't she?" That the shot came from a whiskered person who most obviously had never trod a quarterdeck, nor even "polished up the handle of the big front door" of any Admiralty office, might be an element either of extenuation or of deepened offense, so far as you could gather from Admiral Beatty's slightly staggered and deeply disturbed expression. Lord Beatty was the head of the British navy — and the British navy was being treated impiously. Lord Beatty was the custodian in his generation of a tradition that had lasted for over two hundred years, and that tradition was being menaced — so it appeared at the moment, certainly — by an alien, a whiskered person with a loud voice and an utterly unrepentant manner. Lord Beatty, by a coincidence that

[5] This description of the speech of Charles E. Hughes at the Washington Conference is quoted, slightly paraphrased, from "The Great Adventure at Washington," Mark Sullivan, 1922.

is more often broken than kept, happened to have a good deal of that bulldog appearance which is traditionally associated with the headship of the British navy. When Hughes began to enumerate British ships to be sunk — ships whose very names are milestones in the history of

From a photograph by Underwood & Underwood.

Admiral Beatty of the British delegation to the Washington Conference for the Limitation of Armament.

British sea-power — Lord Beatty came forward in his chair with the manner of a bulldog sleeping on a sunny doorstep who has been poked in the stomach by the impudent foot of an itinerant soap-canvasser seriously lacking in any sense of the most ordinary proprieties or considerations of personal safety.

After Hughes had finished, but before the stunned delegates could gather their faculties together to make objection or criticism or other comment, the session was adjourned — it was Saturday — until the following Monday. This was a manœuvre planned in advance by the American delegates so that Hughes's bold message should get for two days the undivided attention of the world. On Saturday afternoon and Sunday despatches from three hundred newspaper correspondents, published in newspapers from London to Pekin, rallied world public opinion in support of Hughes.

For twelve weeks the Conference deliberated.[6] At all times the delegates of every nation co-operated earnestly, except those from France. The attitude of the Frenchmen was recalcitrant; much of the time they were sullen or truculent. They refused to permit a real limitation on submarine-building, though this weapon had never been used successfully by France and the likelihood was apparent that some day France might repent her attitude. The French delegates refused to consent that reduction of land armaments should be considered. France wanted the United States and Britain to sign a pact guaranteeing aid to her in the event of a future attack by Germany, and was recalcitrant because neither country would agree to make such a pact.

Results of the Washington Conference

The Conference produced seven treaties, of which the two most important were:

Five Power Navy Treaty (United States, Great Britain, Japan, France, Italy). This specifically designated the capital ships each power should retain and fixed the ratio of replacement for each. The allotments were: United States and Great Britain, 525,000 tons each;

[6] The Conference adjourned February 6, 1922.

Japan, 315,000 tons; France and Italy, 175,000 tons each. The capital ships of all were to be limited in size to 35,000 tons and their rifles to 16 inch bore. The treaty was to run for 15 years. It was ratified and went into effect August 17, 1923.[7]

Four Power Treaty (United States, Great Britain, France, and Japan). This treaty pledged each power to respect the rights of the others in relation to their Pacific possessions. It was to run ten years. Upon its ratification, the existing Anglo-Japanese Alliance was to be automatically terminated. This getting rid of the Anglo-Japanese Alliance was, to America, a very great advantage. The Four Power Treaty was proclaimed ratified August 17, 1923.

To settle the dispute between Japan and the United States over Yap, a treaty was arranged giving the United States free access to the island and equality with Japan in all that related to cable and radio communications.

v

The Proposal to Adhere to the World Court

In addition to the successful and beneficent Washington Conference, Harding made one other important effort toward world co-operation, this one futile. The League of Nations had set up a Permanent Court of International Justice, called, in American discussion, the World Court. The Court was so organized that America could adhere to it without joining the League. Harding, in February, 1922, sent a message to the Senate recommending that we adhere to the Court. At once

---

[7] This treaty was denounced by Japan in 1934. In the month this chapter was completed, July 1935, Great Britain announced that with the termination of the treaty she would begin on a great ship-building programme.

his proposal encountered the acrimony that had been generated by the long debate over adherence to the League of Nations. The anti-League "battalion of death"[8] mobilized once more, the "bitter-enders," the "last-ditchers" re-sharpened their swords. The same epithets, the same incitements to emotion filled the air again. It was more than four years before the Senate acted — and then voted to adhere only with reservations that other adherents to the Court were unwilling to accept. After thirteen years of intermittent argument and acrimony, the matter of America's adherence to the World Court was still open in the year this history was written, 1935.

VI

Other Steps in the Field of Foreign Relations

To tie up the loose ends left by the ending of the war, and by our refusal to unite with our Allies in the treaty of peace with our recent enemies, separate treaties were arranged restoring friendly relations with Austria,[9] Germany,[10] Hungary.[11] The treaty with Germany was followed by an agreement for the determination of the amount of American claims against Germany by a mixed commission.

Attempts by Russia to bring about resumption of commerce with the United States were rebuffed on March 25, 1921, by Secretary of State Hughes, who informed the head of the Russian Soviet Government in an official note that "this government is unable to perceive that there is any proper basis for considering trade relations." During the Russian revolution of 1917

---

[8] For the application of this terminology of combat, see account of the fight over the League of Nations in "Our Times," Vol. V.

[9] August 23, 1921.   [10] August 25, 1921.   [11] August 29, 1921.

American property and money in Russia had been confiscated by the Bolsheviks; they had also repudiated the large loans for war purposes floated in the United States by the Czarist Government. The Harding administration adopted the attitude of withholding diplomatic recognition until and unless the Soviet authorities should

From a photograph by Underwood & Underwood.

Americans who participated in the settlement of German reparations. From left to right: Owen D. Young, Charles G. Dawes, Henry M. Robinson.

agree to settle the American claims. Russia declined and a deadlock resulted which lasted until 1933.

Resentment on the part of the people of the Republic of Colombia against the United States because of the part the United States had taken in the uprising of the Colombian province of Panama in 1902 and the setting up of the independent Republic of Panama was placated by a treaty signed at Bogotá March 1, 1922, providing compensation to Colombia for the loss she had sustained.

Long-standing friction between the South American

republics of Chile and Peru over ownership of a strip of coastland lying between the two, and which periodically threatened the peace of all of lower South America, provided the United States with an occasion for offering its good offices in bringing about a settlement of the dispute. July 20, 1922, an agreement was signed by plenipotentiaries of Chile and Peru to submit the question to arbitration by President Harding. The President appointed a commission, headed at first by General Pershing, which after passing through many crises was successful in bringing about a peaceful settlement.

VII

The War Debts

During the War, we had loaned large amounts to the Allies. These were official transactions, loans by our government, as a government, to the Allied governments, as governments. To arrange terms for the repayment of these obligations, Congress[12] passed an act

to refund or convert, and to extend time of payment of the principal or the interest, or both, of any obligation of any foreign government now held by the United States, or any obligation of any foreign government hereafter received by the United States arising out of the World War.

There followed a parade of distinguished foreign officials to Washington commissioned by their governments to reach agreements with the United States.[13]

[12] February 9, 1922.

[13] Newspaper accounts of the meetings between the negotiators frequently mentioned the phrase "capacity to pay," which was the yardstick put forward by the American Commission as the proper measure for rates of interest and other terms of payment or compromise. The phrase became, for the time, colloquial English and served as a witticism in situations remote from intergovernment debts. While the Belgian Commission was in Washington conferring with the American negotiators, one of the Belgians, hearing that Senator Smoot was

They met with the commission appointed by President
Harding to represent the United States.[14] Negotiations
were concluded with our largest debtor, Great Britain,

The Yanks Are Coming.

A cartoon inspired by France's laggardliness in reaching an agreement with the
United States for the payment of the French four-billion war debt. "The
Yanks Are Coming" was a phrase from an immensely popular marching song
of American soldiers in the Great War. *Fitzpatrick in the St. Louis "Post
Dispatch."*

on the basis of annual installments spread over 62 years,
with interest at 3 per cent for a short period and 3½
per cent thereafter. Agreements varying in terms were

a Mormon, and being curious about the attitude of the Mormon Church toward
polygamy, asked Smoot how many wives a Mormon was permitted to have.
The solemn-visaged Utahan replied, "according to capacity to pay."

14 Members of the American Commission were: Chairman, Andrew W. Mel-
lon, Secretary of the Treasury; Charles E. Hughes, Secretary of State; Herbert
Hoover, Secretary of Commerce; Reed Smoot, Senator from Utah; Theodore
E. Burton, Congressman from Ohio; Charles R. Crisp, Congressman from
Georgia; and Richard Olney.

concluded with 12 other nations. The amounts,[15] and dates upon which agreements were reached, were:

Belgium	Aug. 18, 1925	$417,780,000
Czechoslovakia	Oct. 13, 1925	115,000,000
Esthonia	Oct. 28, 1925	13,830,000
Finland	May 1, 1923	9,000,000
France	Apr. 29, 1926	4,025,000,000
Great Britain	June 19, 1923	4,600,000,000
Hungary	Apr. 25, 1924	1,939,000
Italy	Nov. 14, 1925	2,042,000,000
Latvia	Sep. 24, 1925	5,775,000
Lithuania	Sep. 22, 1924	6,030,000
Poland	Nov. 14, 1924	178,560,000
Roumania	Dec. 4, 1925	44,590,000
Jugo-Slavia	May 3, 1926	62,850,000

Total $11,522,354,000

By the aggregate of these agreements, 13 European governments promised to pay to the government of the United States a principal sum of $11,522,354,000, and a further amount in interest, the whole payable in instalments, varying with each nation, during more than 60 years into the future.[16]

VIII

The Tariff, Under Changed Conditions

One of the conditions of the changed world, and America's changed relation to it, which we were called upon to take account of, was the reversal of our fiscal relation to Europe. From having been a borrowing nation we had become a lending one.

[15] The amounts here given include the principal of the original debt plus accrued interest to the time the agreements were made.

[16] Cuba alone of all the Allied countries receiving war loans from the United States Government, paid its debt in full. The loan to Cuba, $15,000,000, was paid off within two years after the war ended. By 1935, all the debtor nations which funded their debts had defaulted, except one. Finland alone continued to pay the instalments in full on the dates due.

From the time of the earliest colonial settlement in America until the war years 1914–1918, America had been borrowing capital from Europe to develop our native industries — agriculture, mining, manufacturing, transportation. Interest on these borrowings had been paid for the most part by means of exports of cotton from the South and farm products from the West — an arrangement advantageous to the United States and satisfactory to Europe. This condition, during the Great War, was abruptly and radically changed. Under the stress of war all the countries of Europe, belligerent and neutral alike, had imperative need for funds, either for the purchase of foodstuffs and munitions or to protect currencies threatened with depreciation. To obtain funds they offered for sale the billions of dollars of American securities they owned, for whatever price American investors cared to pay. Thus America bought, that is, liquidated the debts we owed in Europe, at discounts running as high as forty cents on the dollar. Not only that. With the vast profits accruing from the status America had between 1914 and 1917, as the only great mercantile nation able to trade with the world, we began shipping capital abroad. In South America and elsewhere, mines, electric power systems, street railways, steamship lines, which formerly had belonged to European interests, were transferred to American ownership. In addition, the American Government after we entered the war loaned to the governments of Allied powers amounts totalling just short of ten billions of dollars. Thus with the war's ending America found herself free of her old debt to Europe, owner of former European properties scattered about the world, and lender to Europe in the amount of approximately ten billions of dollars.

This change in our relation to the world, from debtor

to creditor, was a fact. That the change would have a bearing on our international trade, no one could dispute. As to just what the bearing would be, there could be refined variations of theory. It was clear, however, that the change should be taken into account when we considered our tariff policy. And the fact is, we did not take it into account. The Republicans, following the party's traditional tariff policy, proceeded to write a protective tariff, higher than the one that had been in existence at the time our changed relation to the world occurred. In 1921, an "emergency" act was passed raising the rates on a number of commodities, chiefly agricultural. In 1922, a broad upward revision was made, the Fordney-McCumber Act. The day it became law, the London *Daily Chronicle* published a brief elementary lesson about international trade. America, *The Chronicle* said, could not be a lending nation and at the same time a high-tariff nation: "It is only in goods that the foreigner can pay [interest on the debts owed to America] — and in proportion as you keep his goods out, you will make his payments impossible."

The complex that composed America's changed relation to international trade included the following factors:

1. The retaining of our position as a high-tariff nation.

2. Our insistence that our Allies in the recent war repay the loans we had made them.

3. The efforts of these nations to pay in gold when our high tariff made it difficult for them to pay in goods.

4. Our continued wish and effort to export cotton, other farm crops, and some manufactured goods, which would increase the amounts of payments necessary for Europe to make to us.

5. The wish of our bankers to lend further large amounts abroad, thus again increasing the amounts of payments necessary for the rest of the world to make to us.

The intricate reactions of each of these factors to the others, their permutations and combinations, determined much of the economic and fiscal history of America during the 1920's. After the Twenties had ended, an American occupying a high position in the leadership of national thought, Owen D. Young, aided by the benefit of hindsight, told us (in a speech at Philadelphia, May 16, 1933) what, from his point of view, we had attempted to do:

We insisted that our Allies sign the bond to return money which we had advanced. . . . They could only repay that debt by sending us their goods. To the extent that we would not accept sufficiently of their goods, they could only pay by sending us their gold. So, having refused their goods, we took their gold until we ruined the currency and banking systems of the world, including our own, until international exchanges and trade were paralyzed.[17]

IX

Prosecuting the War Frauds

During and just after the war Republican stump-speakers, Republican leaders in Congress, and Republican newspapers made charges that corruption had been widespread in the prosecution of the war by the Wilson Administration. Mainly the charges were directed at contracts for building ships, airplanes, army cantonments, and for the purchase of munitions and war sup-

---

[17] I should not wish to be understood as assenting completely to Young's way of putting it. In his phrases, the extremely complex condition is reduced to too great simplicity. But there is not space, within the scope of the present volume, to tell the economic and fiscal history of the United States, in its relation to other countries, from 1920 on. Many books have been written about it. More will be. The later ones, having longer perspective. will be more accurate.

plies. The Republicans, in making their charges, were not merely partisan; they believed the charges and much of the public believed them. The amount of money expended on the war by the United States, exclusive of the nearly ten billions loaned to the Allies, was $22,625,-252,842.[18] Income-tax returns for the war years showed the addition of 18,000 names to the country's list of millionaires. It seemed likely that the spending of such vast sums, and the creation of so many new millionaires, had not been unattended by dishonesty.

"Just how much thievery was there under the Democratic Administration during the war?" asked Republican Representative Frank Mondell.[19] "There is a good deal of hilarity on the Democratic side," he added, when Democratic confidence in their own virtue expressed itself in laughter, "but there may not be so much when by the steady grinding of the mills of justice the amount of fraud under their Administration has been developed." "Those are some of the things we propose to investigate," said Republican Congressman Nicholas Longworth.

Against these charges, one Republican protested. He was Charles G. Dawes and he had been in the war, as head of the supply procurement division in France. "Sure we paid," he roared to a select committee investigating expenditures by the War Department, in response to charges that excessive prices had been paid. "We didn't dicker. Why, man alive, we had to win the war. We would have paid horse prices for sheep if sheep could have pulled artillery to the front. Oh, it's all right now to say we bought too much vinegar and too many cold chisels, but we saved the civilization of the world. Damn it all, the business of an army is to win the war,

[18] Estimate made by Prof. E. L. Bogart of the University of Illinois for the Carnegie Endowment for International Peace.
[19] Of Wyoming. *Congressional Record,* May 9, 1922.

not to quibble around with a lot of cheap buying. Hell and Maria, we weren't trying to keep a set of books, we were trying to win the war!"

Dawes's "Hell and Maria" became famous; newspapers carried on etymological discussion as to whether

From a photograph by Wide World.

Charles G. Dawes.

it was "Hell and Maria" or, more ladylikely, "Helen Maria!" — the general public preferred the version that included a mild profaneness. The author of the cryptic expletive became better known as "Hell and Maria" Dawes than by either of the official titles he subsequently held, Vice-President of the United States and Ambassador to Great Britain.

But if Dawes's robust indignation disinfected the war fraud charges in the minds of much of the public, he did not check his fellow Republicans in Congress. They directed Attorney-General Daugherty to set up, in the

Department of Justice, a "Bureau of War Transactions," provided him with funds aggregating $3,200,-000, and ordered him to "institute investigations . . . for the purpose of indicting and prosecuting such persons as are guilty of criminal conduct and to institute civil suits for the recovery of any government funds which have been fraudulently or illegally paid."

Daugherty, led by some streak of common sense or fair dealing in his strange make-up, was dilatory. When Congress reproached him, he put twenty-five lawyers at work, investigated 800 cases — the papers in one case filled fifty filing cabinets — and reported[20] that "the investigations in a number of cases . . . are rapidly nearing completion."

Such evidence as could be distilled from rumor into sworn testimony, turned out to be petty. A time-keeper at Fort Sherman had seen "plumbers loaf on the job, they were shooting craps and playing poker." There were a few till-tapping trivialities, a few crates of shoes stolen, substitution of second-grade lumber for first, some padding of pay-rolls by subordinates. "After thorough investigation," wrote Daugherty later, "I found no reason to bring indictments against a single one whom I was urged to prosecute."[21]

There were a few attempted prosecutions. Of these the only important victims were a man who had been Assistant Secretary of War and a distinguished architect and builder who had been in charge of emergency construction during the war. Both were completely innocent; in both cases the attempted prosecutions were grossly unjustified, explainable only on the theory that hysteria had to find some one to crucify. Both men were

---

[20] May 9, 1922.
[21] There were some civil suits which recovered about $8,500,000, about one-tenth of one per cent of the total expenditure for war supplies.

exonerated by the' courts; for years men with a sense of fairness went out of their way to honor them.

The end was recorded in newspapers of the day before Thanksgiving, 1926, in an Associated Press despatch of 257 words, beginning: "The last of the war fraud indictments was wiped off the criminal records of the Supreme Court of the District of Columbia today when United States Attorney Gordon . . . entered a *nolle pros.*"

That outcome, the exoneration of a Democratic Administration on charges of corruption brought against it by Republicans, was to be made ironical by the position the Republicans soon found themselves in. Even while the war-fraud cases were floundering in the courts, treated with scant sympathy by judges and juries, scandals began to come to light which involved four Republicans who had been appointed to high office by Republican President Harding, three of whom were to be convicted of serious crimes and sentenced to fines and imprisonment.

x

*Harding's Policy of Economy.
The Budget*

Harding was convinced that one of the greatest services he could perform would be to get government spending back to a peace-time basis, with the national balance sheet showing healthy annual surpluses. Repeatedly during his 28 months in office he preached to the public on economy, lectured Congress on economy, admonished the personnel of the government on economy.

For years a drive had been carried on by public-spirited individuals for the establishment of a government budget. To this Harding gave his support. Shortly after his inauguration, he included among his recommendations to Congress "enactment of legislation providing for the national budget system . . . so that it may be employed in establishing economies and business methods so essential to the minimum of expenditure." [22] Congress acquiesced, passed the Budget and Accountancy

From a photograph by Brown Brothers.

Andrew W. Mellon when Secretary of the Treasury.

Act.[23] This provided for the creation of the Budget Bureau in the Treasury Department empowered to revise, reduce, or increase the estimates of the several departments prepared by the budget officer of each department. The purposes of the act included putting the several departments and bureaus of the government on a business basis and, quite as important, putting compulsion on Congress to keep its appropriations within the limits set by the budget officers. Congress was not to be bound by the budget estimates, but Harding hoped that

[22] Message. April 11, 1921.   [23] Signed by the President June 20, 1921.

a carefully prepared schedule made up by the experts of
the Budget Bureau would have an effect of moral restraint on Congress' tendency to lavishness in the expenditure of public funds.

For the post of Budget Director Harding chose a
colorful, dramatic, and highly competent man, a Chicago banker, who had served as a brigadier-general during the war, Charles Gates Dawes of Chicago, who had
a brilliant faculty for publicizing any cause with which
he became associated. Then Harding called a meeting
of Cabinet officers, their assistants, and the bureau and
division chiefs of all the Federal departments, to the
number of about 500. It was the first time in the history of the United States that the government's business
executives had ever been assembled for any purpose.
With Dawes beside him on the speakers' platform,
Harding told the gathering:

> The present administration . . . is committed to a period of
> economy in government. This statement is made not with any
> thought of criticizing what has gone before. It is made in a
> new realization of the necessity of driving out the loose, un-
> scientific expenditures of government. There is not a menace
> in the world today like that of growing public indebtedness and
> mounting public expenditures. There has seemingly grown up
> an impression that the public treasuries are inexhaustible
> things, and with it a conviction that no efficiency and no econ-
> omy are ever to be thought of in public expense. We want to
> reverse things.

Not entirely — but certainly in part — as a result of
Harding's insistence on economy, the fiscal condition of
the government showed steady improvement almost
from the day Harding took office. For the fiscal year
ending June 30, 1923, government expenditures
amounted to $3,697,000,000 — they had been $5,538,-
000,000 for the year ending June 30, 1921. In the fall
of 1921, Congress, acting on the recommendation of

Secretary of the Treasury Andrew W. Mellon, reduced
taxes by approximately $1,000,000,000 annually. De-
spite this reduction in revenue, the Treasury during
Harding's Presidency was able to make payments in reduction of the public debt at the rate of almost one hundred million dollars monthly.

Halladay in the Providence "Journal."

Cartoon published during the early stages of the demand of veterans for a bonus.

XI

The Soldiers' Bonus

The first of the measures making grants to ex-soldiers
passed by Congress in the years following the Great
War was introduced in the House of Representatives in
1920 by Joseph W. Fordney of Michigan. Because the
sponsors of the measure described the payments to be
made to the veterans by the frank word "bonus," dis-
satisfaction was expressed by the act's prospective bene-

ficiaries, who objected that this word carried a stigma, suggested a "tip," "gratuity." This fault was promptly corrected. The act's name was changed to the more virtuous-sounding "adjusted compensation" and again, in 1921, it was dropped into the Congressional hopper. By using his influence with Congressional leaders, President Harding succeeded in having action delayed on it for a year, but finally, in the summer of 1922 it again passed the House 333 to 70 and the Senate 47 to 22. The President found himself under the necessity of approving the act, which would win him the favor of the veterans, or vetoing it, which would satisfy his conscience. Courageously he vetoed the act[24] in a message which for logic, candor, and dignity deserves a place with the better of Presidential state papers:

With the avowed purpose of the bill to give expression of a nation's gratitude to those who served in its defense in the World War, I am in accord. . . . The United States never will cease to be grateful; it cannot and never will cease giving expression to that gratitude. In legislating for what is called adjusted compensation Congress fails, first of all, to provide the revenue from which the bestowal is to be paid. Moreover, it establishes the very dangerous precedent of creating a Treasury covenant to pay which puts a burden variously estimated between four and five billions upon the American people, not to discharge an obligation which the government always must pay, but to bestow a bonus which the soldiers themselves while serving in the World War did not expect. . . .

It is worth remembering that public credit is founded on the popular belief in the defensibility of public expenditure as well as the government's ability to pay. Our heavy tax burdens reach, directly or indirectly, every element in our citizenship. To add one-sixth of the total sum of our public debt for a distribution among less than 5,000,000 out of 110,000,000, whether inspired by grateful sentiment or political expediency, would undermine the confidence on which our credit is builded and establish the precedent of distributing public funds whenever the proposal and the numbers affected make it seem politically appealing to do so.

[24] September 19, 1922. The House overrode the President's veto but the Senate sustained it.

XII

Prohibition Enforcement

When Harding became President the Eighteenth Amendment had been for eight months a part of the Constitution. An enforcement law, the Volstead Act,

From a photograph by Acme Newspictures, Inc.

Wayne B. Wheeler, outstanding leader of the "drys" during the long fight to get national Prohibition, and the almost equally long fight to keep it.

had been passed by Congress in 1919, vetoed by President Wilson, re-passed over the President's veto. It went into effect at midnight, January 16, 1920.

Harding, though not himself a dry, and little interested in prohibition apart from regarding the Eighteenth Amendment a mandate from the people which he was duty-bound to enforce, accepted guidance in such acts as he took about prohibition from professional prohibitionists, chiefly Wayne B. Wheeler, counsel of the Anti-

Saloon League. In organizing an enforcement bureau and assembling the personnel for it, Harding acted on Wheeler's counsel. Things did not turn out well. There

Copyright by F. R. Publishing Corporation.   Courtesy of "The New Yorker."

"Don't you know you can't leave your car on Forty-ninth Street?"

A satirical drawing by O. F. Howard in *The New Yorker* which pictures, with a little exaggeration, the complacency with which the police of large cities looked upon violations of the prohibition law.

was confusion and uncertainty about policy, and many of the appointees, men who had been recommended by the professional drys, proved unsatisfactory. Enforcement, from the beginning, was generally inefficient, undignified, very costly, in some cases violent, in others corrupt. As a result of the fiasco of enforcement and for other reasons people who at the beginning had approved prohibition and wished earnestly that it might succeed, became antagonistic towards it. This angered the professional drys and they, having the President's ear, were able to force the adoption of more ruthless and extreme methods by the enforcement agents. The frequency with which violence now attended enforcement — bootleggers and prohibition agents killing each other in pitched battles on city streets and country roads, and occasionally killing an innocent bystander — still further alienated public support from prohibition and made it possible for opponents of the Eighteenth Amendment for the first time to make progress.

Outstanding among the early enemies of prohibition was Governor Alfred E. Smith of New York. On May 4, 1923, the New York Legislature, by a narrow majority, repealed the State's prohibition enforcement act. Before Governor Smith had made known whether he would sign the bill, President Harding, at the urging of professional drys, issued a public statement[25] making what was regarded as a warning to Smith not to approve the repeal bill:

The nation has deliberately, after many years of consideration, adopted the present policy, which is written into the Eighteenth Amendment. It is the law of the land and of every State within the Union. So long as it remains the national policy, there can be only one course for the national Government to pursue. That is to use every means to make effective the law passed in compliance with this constitutional mandate. To do this will be the unquestioning policy of the present Administration; and I may add that I am firmly convinced that it must be the policy of other Administrations that shall come hereafter. The Executive of the nation and equally the Executives of the States are sworn to enforce the Constitution. It is difficult to believe that public approval will ever be given to any other than a policy of fully and literally discharging this duty. . . . I venture that if by reason of the refusal or failure of any State to discharge its proper duty in such connection, the Federal Government is at length compelled to enter upon the territory and jurisdiction of the State and to set up those police and judicial authorities which would be required, the most difficult and trying situations would inevitably arise.

[25] May 16, 1923.

Resentment by the people of New York at what they regarded as a dictatorial attitude on the part of the national government and an unwarranted intervention in

From a photograph by Globe Photos.

President Harding bound for a round of golf at the Chevy Chase Club, Washington, D. C., with Grantland Rice, sports writer; Ring Lardner, author; and Henry P. Fletcher, Under-Secretary of State.

the State's affairs, strengthened Smith's determination. He signed the bill June 1.[26]

XIII

Harding as President and as Man

It is not only by his purely official acts that a President can be judged; indeed, his official acts are in many

[26] This event marked the beginning of the decline of Prohibition which was to culminate in 1933 in repeal of the Eighteenth Amendment.

ways a confused index, for in this area he is limited by
conditions outside himself, by how far his Congress is
willing to go with him, by the state of public feeling,
by the attitude of foreign governments with which he
must deal, by the need of observing precedent, by constitutional limitations on his prerogative. Use of the
official record of an administration to interpret a President is made further confusing by the fact that in every
administration many of the most important events arise
outside the White House; with some of them the President has only casual or perfunctory association, or none
at all.

There is, however, a field in which a President is
practically free to be himself; actions in which his official position merges with his private personality, cases
in which he takes initiative upon impulses that arise
within himself, in which he makes use of his power to
do what his nature suggests. These compose a true reflection of his personality.

Eugene Debs, long head of the Socialist party in
America, was in a federal penitentiary serving a ten-
year sentence for having "obstructed the conduct of the
war." Arrested during the summer of 1918, he had
been quickly convicted and sentenced. From jail he had
directed an appeal, which dragged its way through the
courts until finally, six months after the war had ended,
the United States Supreme Court held that the conviction must stand, Debs must serve his sentence. In
March, 1921, when Harding became President, Debs
had been for almost two years an inmate of the penitentiary at Atlanta, Ga.

At Atlanta, Debs had made a quite extraordinary
record — his presence, wrote one commentator, was

"like a breath of fresh air on the men with whom he came in contact." Everybody loved him: officials, guards, convicts. The warden felt under obligation to him because of the restraining effect Debs's gentle and kindly spirit had on the other prisoners, making easier

From a photograph by Underwood & Underwood.

Eugene V. Debs, while in prison, receiving notification of his nomination to be Socialist candidate for President.

the task of maintaining discipline and morale in a walled city of criminals, some desperate and dangerous.

To Harding, who shared the deep compassion which Debs had for the under-dog, the thought of the frail and aged Debs eking out his last years behind the sombre walls of a prison was distressing. For Debs's political beliefs Harding had no sympathy whatever; to his pragmatic Republicanism, Socialism seemed the most fatuous of all possible follies. But Debs had gone to jail because of his hatred and loathing of war, which was something more than, and different from, a mere detail of the Socialist creed. Harding himself hated war, as intensely as Debs if less violently. It seemed to him wrong, out of tune with the spirit of America, that Debs should endure further punishment. This was a reason personal to Harding why Debs should be set free. In addition, Harding saw a practical advantage to the country to be gained by releasing Debs. An after-effect of the Great War had been irritation on the part of some labor groups which, fostered by a few radical leaders, seemed pointed towards serious social unrest. These leaders were making skilful use of Debs's incarceration. Debs, they declared, was the victim of persecution by the same profit-greedy men who had manœuvred America into the war and made labor do the fighting while they amassed riches. Release of Debs, Harding felt, would checkmate this propaganda.

Harding might have released Debs on his first day in the Presidency, but that would have seemed to flaunt the somewhat rigid conception of justice of millions of Americans, that the breaker of law, any law, must pay the penalty for his act. That course not seeming feasible, Harding decided on action more in conformity with official routine. Two weeks before his inauguration he sent for his future Attorney-General, Harry Daugherty, told him he wished to have Debs released.

Daugherty on becoming Attorney-General went through the formalities requisite to the issuance of a pardon. Investigation of Debs's conduct in prison brought to light that Debs's "personality was a benediction to the criminals with whom he came in contact; he soothed their troubled spirits and healed more than one disordered mind." Daugherty ordered Debs released from Atlanta to go to Washington. Debs came, spent a day with Daugherty in the Attorney-General's office. During the interview, Daugherty recounts:[27]

We talked freely for several hours. He unfolded frankly his ideas on government, his ideas on religion, his own case, the cause of Socialism, his beliefs and disbeliefs. A more eloquent and fascinating recital I never heard. . . . I found him a charming personality with a deep love for his fellow man.

In the end, Daugherty wrote the President "that as Debs was 64 years old and had suffered three years imprisonment, the ends of justice had been met," and recommended that Debs's sentence be commuted to expire December 31, 1921. When the order was presented to the President for his signature, he changed the date to December 24, saying, "I want him to eat his Christmas dinner with his wife."

Harding, by Persuasion, Brings the Eight-Hour Day to the Steel Industry

In the steel industry, when Harding became President, the twelve-hour day was in effect, with a "stretch-out," every two weeks, of 24 hours' continuous duty. Some occupations in the steel mills called for a daily stint of 14 hours, week-days and Sundays, with almost never a day off. Harding in a way characteristic of his distaste for dissension, set about bringing the heads of the steel industry to his way of thinking. He did not emit barrages of denunciation from the White House, as two other recent Presidents did, one before Harding and one after him, both named Roosevelt — one, Theodore, Republican, the other, Franklin D., Democrat. Harding made no move to have Congress intimidate the industry with threats of an investigation or punitive legislation. Nor did he assail the heads of the industry for

[27] "The Inside Story of the Harding Tragedy."

having inhuman working conditions in their plants. Harding's way began with inviting 41 outstanding leaders of the industry to a dinner at the White House.[28] After the dinner, Harding set forth the case for a reduction in hours. To some of the individualistic-minded old timers, the incident was not pleasing. In the end the President's good-natured insistence won; after the meeting the industrialists joined in a public statement saying that the abolition of the 12-hour day was desirable "if, and when, practicable," and they promised to appoint a committee to see what could be done. Harding continued putting pressure on the steel men, and the following year, on August 2, 1923, Judge E. H. Gary, head of the United States Steel Corporation and president of the American Iron and Steel Institute, announced that elimination of the 12-hour day would begin at once. On August 13, the United States Steel plant at Gary, Ind., was put on an 8-hour day; soon the entire industry followed.

[28] May 18, 1922.

11

TRAGEDY BEGINS

Two Suicides, and Another Disquieting Episode, Cause
Harding to Know — Though the Public Was not yet
Aware — that there Was Scandal in the Administration.

AT all times, when a new President comes into office,
many classes of persons seek to find out who is close to
him, with whom does he spend his intimate hours, who
has his ear, with whom does he relax, who knows his
inner mind. The good seek to learn in order that they
may know through whom they may most advantageously
present the divers plans of bettering the world that the
good wish to promote. Newspaper men seek to learn
in order that, by association with the President's intimate,
they may find out the President's thoughts. Politicians
seek to learn in order that, by dropping suggestions to the
President's friend, they may hope the suggestions will
later reach the President. Office hunters and sponsors of
office hunters seek to learn in order that commendation
poured into the ear of the intimate may find ultimate
lodgment in the ear of the President.

To one class, knowing who is close to the President
— who is "next," this class would put it — is a career, a
business. The more elevated among them are lobbyists
in the familiar sense, the more sordid are an inferior caste.
Lobbyists in many instances have places in clubs, are met
at dinners; the objects for which they pursue acquaintance and influence are, while selfish, nevertheless legitimate; their work in many cases is helpful to Congress and
the government departments, and useful to the country.

The more sordid agents have purposes which are on the borderland of the sinister, attainable as a rule only by the evasion of law or the perversion of authority. Their pursuit of their objectives has some similarity to the stalking of prey. Lynx-eyed, they sit in hotel dining-rooms to observe who lunches with whom. Ingratiatingly they inject themselves into the semi-public conversations of hotel lobbies. Casually, but sharp-eyed, they stroll the streets in the neighborhood of the White House and the Cabinet departments. Obsequiously they make acquaintance with any one who seems to have a place in the hierarchy of power. Within a few months after a new administration is in office, they know the lines of friendship and acquaintance that lead up to the President, know the relations of minor satellite to major in the orbit of which the White House is the sun; know who is the friend of the President, who is the friend of the friend, who the friend of the friend of the friend, to the nth degree of consanguinity of power. Not always, indeed only rarely, can they get direct advantage from their knowledge — but often they can use it to impress the dubious seekers for illicit advantage, or the scared seekers of safety who are their clients.

For the services this gentry vended, the market had recently expanded. The government had made crimes of several kinds of action not morally odious, and this is at all times a cause of corruption, since more men will pay money to circumvent a mere regulation of government than will practice bribery to promote a purpose generally recognized as morally wrong.

National prohibition had just been adopted. The sale of liquor, even the ownership of it, under circumstances previously proper, was now a crime. Men made criminals by statue, under circumstances not convincing to their consciences, not convincing indeed to much of the community, were ready to pay intermediaries who would undertake to get immunity for them. In the legal machinery set up for enforcement, a distinction was made between drinkable alcohol and what was called com-

From a photograph by Underwood & Underwood.

Prohibition agents unearth a 1000-gallon barrel of whiskey buried beneath the floor of a garage of a private home.

mercial alcohol, alcohol denatured for use in industry. Permits to make commercial alcohol, issuable by the government, became valuable — the more valuable in the cases where the intent was to turn the commercial alcohol into drinkable — the re-naturing of de-natured alcohol was a highly profitable enterprise. A similar distinction was made between wine for the purpose of ordinary elation, and wine for communion in churches, sacramental wine — permits for the religious purpose were fraudulently sought by persons whose interest was strictly laic, and much wine intended for sacraments went down throats that never sang a hymn.

The income tax law had been in existence since 1913 but had only become important when the rates were enormously raised during the war. The machinery for collecting it was new and loose; distinctions were inexact between what was taxable and what not, between exemptions permitted and exemptions not allowed. To many the taxes seemed — as indeed taxes are — a seizure of the individual's property by force majeure exercised by the government. The ethics that would be recognized and lived up to in private transactions between man and man, voluntary on both sides, did not seem compelling in transactions in which the government demanded arbitrarily, and the citizen paid involuntarily. Men were willing to evade, in situations in which the risk attending evasion — while serious, being fine or imprisonment — nevertheless did not include any wound to the evader's conscience. The amounts involved were large. Taxpayers were willing to give corresponding remuneration to persons who could facilitate compromise, or plausibly promise to.

Congress had passed, ten years before, a law forbidding interstate transportation of motion picture films showing prize-fights; the occasion had been the defeat in 1910 of a white pugilist "Jim" Jeffries, by a colored one, Jack Johnson; and the purpose had been mainly to prevent exhibition in Southern states of a picture of a black man defeating a white one. The statute, however, had been made general — it banned from interstate shipment all films of all prize-fights. The law had caused no serious inconvenience until 1921 when a prize-fight at Hoboken, N. J., between an American, Jack Dempsey, and a Frenchman, Georges Carpentier, attracting much attention, stirred alert promoters with the notion that the motion picture of the fight would allure large audiences everywhere, and yield much money. The situation was a typical case of a law that has no relation to the average man's conception of

From a photograph by Underwood & Underwood.

Carpentier–Dempsey prize fight.

morals. To show the picture was perfectly legal in New York and many other States; only the act of transporting it across an invisible State boundary was illicit. Some lawyers devised a plan of having in each State a dummy consignee, an individual who would merely accept the film from the express company and then turn it over to the exhibitors. The dummy would, for a consideration, amiably submit to arrest and take his chance of punishment, the penalty imposed being in most cases merely a fine, which the promoters provided, and which was only a negligible fraction of the receipts from the exhibition. Carrying out of this ingenious arrangement necessitated understanding with the Federal prosecuting authorities that only a fine would be imposed, that not in any case would the dummy consignee be subjected to a prison term.

The government, during the war, had seized the property of German citizens and corporations. In the haste with which it was done, and in the spirit of war-time, not too much care was taken to make sure that the property seized was surely the property of Germans. Some that was seized belonged to citizens of other countries. Some belonged in part to Germans, in part to non-Germans. In all cases the seizure by the government was arbitrary — the practice of the government was to seize, and let the owners show they were non-German if they could. The practice was legal, and martial, but not moral. The true owners of the property felt justified in using any means that would facilitate their repossession of their own.

These and similar conditions, many arising out of the recent war, created, when Harding was in office, an exceptional market for intermediaries and fixers, many legitimate and some sinister, who, by methods in some cases regular and in other cases furtive, could get the government to grant some privilege that an honest citizen desired and had a right to, or some immunity that a corrupt person had no right to but ardently wished.

To everybody, the knowledge was universal that in the Harding Administration, Harry Daugherty was closest to the President, and Jess Smith was the satellite of Daugherty. All, all varieties, every shade in the spectrum, from altruists seeking action by Harding that would bring the millennium and pacifists wishing to lay before Harding the plan that would infallibly bring permanent peace, down through rich men seeking to be made ambassadors or ministers and politicians promoting appointment of a friend to office, and still further down to the lobbyists for great interests, and yet further down to the fixers for small and sometimes corrupt interests — all these gradations of suppliants for good causes and promoters of bad ones knew that Daugherty, more than any other man, had the ear of Harding, and presumed that Jess Smith had the ear of Daugherty.

II

When Harding was elected President, when that long journey of ambition was ended that had begun in the backyard of a small-town Ohio hotel a score of years before,[1] Daugherty, and with him Jess Smith, had reason to feel they were sitting at the top of the world. In the words of a familiar American saying they had "the world by the tail and a down-hill pull."

Not so much did Daugherty feel it; more accurately, Daugherty felt it, but did not exult excessively in it. Daugherty had known triumph, of a sort, before, and knew its impermanence. Daugherty had lived longer and ranged farther, he had observed men and read books, had seen many an experience of *sic transit gloria*. He knew that the top of the world is a narrow path along the peak of a mountain range, the foothold slippery, every step a new adventure into danger, on both sides deep descent. In a lifetime of politics he had had frequent occasion to observe that "the higher they go, the harder they fall." Daugherty's career had made him cold, and hard-boiled — not cold, either, but realistic.

[1] See Chapter 2.

Though he had too much imagination, too much sense of adventure, not to be aware of the height to which he had climbed; though there was too much of the dramatic in him not to have moments of exultation, yet his

From a photograph by Underwood & Underwood.
Harry M. Daugherty, while Attorney-General.

more continuous preoccupation was not the glory of his present elevation but the danger that he knew was inseparable from it, the care and caution that are the price of a foothold on the slippery steeps of power.

Not only was Daugherty cautious for himself, he was cautious for Harding. Daugherty's chief present aim in life was to stand between Harding and those he thought might do Harding harm. "The main reason I want to be in Washington," Daugherty had said when it was suggested he should be in the Cabinet, "is to protect Harding from the crooks; I know how trustful Harding is and I know who all the crooks are, and I want to protect Harding from them." Not only could Daugherty recognize the crooks and abruptly turn them off; with equal accuracy he knew the gradations of good-faith and worth among the highly-placed; with equal confidence in his judgment and his position he could discriminate among the exalted in politics and business; and could dismiss or "stand off" the pompous as readily as he could tell the crooks to be on their way.

That necessity for watchfulness, together with the weight of his office as Attorney-General, and his experience of life, saved Daugherty from too fatuous gloating over his position as a man who had made a President and was the closest to the White House. He went about Washington quietly alert-eyed, too busy to think much about himself, and with a modesty that was more than modesty, an insight which told him the danger of lack of modesty.

III

With Smith, however, it was sheer exultation. Within a few months, he had risen from obscurity in Washington Court House, Ohio, to conspicuousness in Washington, D. C. Senators called him "Mr. Smith," men of power liked to be seen in his company. It was complete joy. That there could be any peril in it never occurred to Smith; when Daugherty warned him to watch his step, Smith's reflection was that Daugherty had brought him to where he was, and Daugherty could hold him safe there — Daugherty was Allah, and Allah could make no mistake, suffer no misadventure. "God's in his Heaven, all's right with the world."

Smith would stand on the curb of what was then one of the great crossroads of Washington, the corner of Fifteenth and H Streets, location of the old Shoreham Hotel; two blocks to the South the White House, with Harding in it; one block to the North the Department of Justice, with Harry Daugherty presiding. Smith would stand on the Shoreham corner, his head up, his features eager and happy, his coat lapels spread back, his thumbs in the arm-holes of his vest. To an acquaintance across the street he would call, "Hey there, come on over." Always his greeting was the same, "What d' you know?" That had been the conventional opening for gossip in Washington Court House and neither in that respect nor any other did Smith change. To him, Washington, the nation, the world, was just another Fayette County, Ohio. The politics he liked to talk was, as Smith talked it, the same politics he had talked on the court house steps at home, wholly the politics of men, of personal relations, of alliances, loyalties and treasons: Were those guys in the Senate going to do right by Harding — Harding would use the club on 'em if they didn't. Y'oughta heard Harry Daugherty climb Lodge's neck the other night. Will Beveridge beat New for the senatorial nomination in Indiana? What's this World Court thing they're talkin' about; some of the boys over on the hill tell me it's not so good. What d' you hear about the Democrats? "Daugherty was over at the White House last night; Harding was awful sweet to him; Harry was awful happy when he came home." "The railroad strike? Aw, shucks, Harding'll fix that."

That was Smith's world, Harding at the head of it, Daugherty prime minister to Harding, and Smith — not prime minister to Daugherty — that would have implied an intellectual elevation which Smith would have been the last to claim — but Smith as the faithful retainer, combination of friend and valet and younger brother. Smith was to Daugherty at once the object of his affections, the source of his solace. Daugherty's wife was an invalid, in Columbus, his children away; in the midst of his power he was lonely. Daugherty had Smith live with him, his only companion, first in a house on H Street, later in an apartment at Wardman Park Hotel; Smith acted as housekeeper and factotum. In the Department of Justice, Smith had an office close by Daugherty's own.[2]

IV

A man of Smith's nature was sure to be liked, and one having his position was sure to be flattered and favored. Persons having no immediate ulterior motive paid attentions to him — the de luxe suite in a hotel for a nominal price or none, a free trip on a steamship, his check for services returned to him with a receipted bill and the compliments of the management.

Among it all he was sure to be sought by the fixers and lobbyists, and so naïve a person as Jess was sure to fall for them. Presently he was besought to get a pardon for this one, a liquor permit for that one, a release from the alien custodian's office for the other one. Presently tender of compensation was made to him, at first perhaps a case of pre-Prohibition whiskey, a tip on the stock market, but later, compensation more substantial. Smith became an occasional visitor to a greenstone house on K Street with a magnolia bush in the small front yard;

[2] The fact that Smith had an office close by Daugherty's in the Department of Justice, that Smith used the services of a Department stenographer and for a time had Department credentials, became, later, important as evidence that Smith had power to influence official matters in the Department. In 1935 Daugherty told me he never assigned the office to Smith and never knew Smith had it. This seems tenable; it would be natural for minor officials of the Department, knowing Smith's intimacy with Daugherty, to give Smith more perquisites than either Smith or Daugherty would have asked. But the point is immaterial; the closeness of Smith to Daugherty was and is indisputable.

it had been leased by an Ohio politician come to Washington as a lobbyist, and it became known (when subsequently commotion arose) as the "little green house on K Street." Here and elsewhere Jess became associated with persons expediting deals for large fees. He began to introduce lawyers having cases before government departments to the officials in charge of the cases — and to such lawyers, an introduction from a person having Smith's position was a valuable commodity.

v

Soon Jess learned that if he had thought the ordinary politics of Washington, D. C., to be much the same as the ordinary politics of Washington Court House, the sinister politics of Washington was much more intricate and formidable. Smith found himself beyond his simple depth. In his progress in sophistication, he was carrying large margin accounts in stock brokerage offices, and they went the way that the stock speculations of the inexperienced often do. Losses in this quarter led to desire for more money. A small fee taken for questionable services "just this once" became a precedent for larger fees taken for services more questionable. He was obliged to hold somber secrets, about himself, and this was corroding to his expansive nature. Smith became uncertain, nervous, dazed, then frightened. His mental condition was aggravated by illness; he had diabetes, and when he had an appendicitis operation, the diabetes prevented the wound from healing. Between physical illness and mental distress, Smith became a desperately unhappy man.

Jess was scared, a brooding terror settled down about him. A simple person, a country-come-to-town, he had become involved in conditions that only stout nerves could stand up to. For solace he turned to his divorced wife of ten years before, at Washington Court House, Roxy Stimson; he had never re-married her, but he saw her often and was friendly with her — she was the only woman friend he had. Now he turned to her as to a mother. He would call her up from Washington or go to Columbus to see her:

The last time he came home, I came to Columbus and he grabbed me there in the hotel, in the Deshler, and he threw his arms around me, and he said: "I never was so glad to see any one in my life." He seemed to have forgotten that he was doing something more or less embarrassing — it was not; it was sweet, and he meant it, just in his direct manner. . . . It was like that all the time. He was in fear, he was in mortal fear. He said: "They are going to get me." I said: "No they won't, Jess." And he said: "They passed it to me." And I knew what he meant. I didn't ask. He was in mortal fear. And I said: "Oh, don't Jess; you are all right; you are all right." He said: "Let's go home before dark." And I said all right. We took the two o'clock train home. Opposite me was a gentleman apparently asleep, and Jess said: "Don't talk so loud, he will hear you." I said to him I wasn't saying anything of any consequence. Jess said: "I don't like the looks of that fellow." I said: "Oh, stop looking at him." He said again: "I don't like the looks of that fellow"; and I said: "Yes, but stop looking at him." He walked down the middle of the street at night. He asked different people if they would stay all night with him. I said: "Tell me what the trouble is, Jess, you can trust me; tell me." "No, no, no," he said; "just cheer me up, just brace me up." And I said to him different times: "Now, hold your head up, Jess, straighten up — that is right." And I said to him: "Stand up; straighten up." He said: "Don't you talk cross to me; if you do I'll jump right out of this window." He always used to comfort me if I had troubles, and I tried to do the same thing for him. He had his house absolutely in order. He asked me to destroy his papers. I said: "Tell me all about it, Jess; I know so much." "No, no, no," he said, "just cheer me up, just cheer me up." It was pitiful. And he would say: "Do you miss me when I am gone?" — and I knew what he was going to do.[3]

[3] Quoted from passages of the testimony of Roxy Stimson; on pages 504 to 558 of Vols. 1 to 4, U. S. Senate Hearings, Investigation of the Attorney-General, 1924. The passages are here condensed and slightly paraphrased.

VI

Daugherty, too, for different reasons, was under strain; but he was of stouter fibre than Jess Smith; in

Attorney-General Harry M. Daugherty (right) and Jess Smith.

Daugherty frazzled nerves took the form of irritability. His wife was sick for months in Johns Hopkins hospital at Baltimore; Daugherty used to go to see her week-ends; he was often ill himself. His work as Attorney-General was strange to him; he knew there was mistrust of him because of the newspaper criticisms of his earlier career. Always he was under fire, from newspapers,

from individuals and committees in Congress. Aside
from these harassments of his own, he was troubled
about some ominous developments he knew were arising
within the Harding Administration, and some close to
himself. The feeling of strain grew upon him:

During the illness of Mr. Daugherty's wife he had become
cross and irritable, which Jess said was quite foreign to him.
Jess said he was always very courteous and polite to him. One
thing which impressed Jess so much, and why Jess was so willing to serve him and do anything for him, was his courteousness
to him always. For instance, if Mr. Daugherty wanted Jess
to do anything he wouldn't say, "Do that," he would say,
"Would you like to do this for me?" or "Would you mind doing that?" or he would wire Jess at home, "I am awfully
lonesome without you; will be so glad when you come back;
will you be back Monday?" He wouldn't say "Come back."
Jess wouldn't have gone then. Jess adored Harry Daugherty,
he wanted to shield him in every possible way, he lived for him,
he loved him. On Friday, the last Friday Jess was alive, Mr.
Daugherty and Jess went out to the shack.

The shack on a farm near Washington Court House,
to which Daugherty and Smith had long been in the
habit of going for rest after their forays in politics; the
shack at which, years before, Daugherty used to say to
Smith, "He'd make a great President — some day we'll
put it over, Jess."[4]

They were out there since Friday, or Thursday, I believe.
Friday or Thursday, I am not quite sure. That afternoon —
Mr. Daugherty always had the habit of taking a nap after
lunch and this was about 1 or 1.30 — he was taking a nap, and
there was a gentleman came down from Columbus and wanted
to see Mr. Daugherty; and Jess as I have said before, he was
Mr. Daugherty's bumper and he would arrange this or that
for him and he said, "He is asleep and he can't be disturbed."
And the gentleman was so persistent, and he was an old friend
of Jess's too, and Mr. Daugherty's, and so he insisted, and so
Jess finally went upstairs to Harry's room and aroused him
and told him this man wanted to see him. And Harry im-

[4] See Chapter 2.

mediately flew off and abused Jess unmercifully for arousing him from his sleep; and he swore at him and talked to him disgracefully; and he got up and he put his clothes on and started to leave, got his driver and his car, and Jess didn't have a car there, and he was going to leave Jess there at the shack by himself. He was mad and was going to leave Jess there by himself. And so Jess called up several people to come and bring him from the shack. But finally Mr. Daugherty waited and took Jess, and took him to Washington Court House. And Jess got out of Mr. Daugherty's car and walked right to the hardware store and got a gun. He had made his decision. Harry had been so unkind to him that he had made his decision what he was going to do.

That evening Jess went to see Roxy:

This time he came down the street his old self, his head up, and just like as if he were happy and everything, and I saw such a change in him, and I said, "Are things all right now, Jess?" And he said, "Yes, they are all right now." And that is the first time in months he would walk straight and carry his head up. Yet he was making all this preparation.[5]

The following night, Jess took the train to Washington. At the apartment he and Daugherty shared he was alone — Daugherty had gone to the White House to stay. The following night Daugherty asked his secretary, Warren F. Martin, to stay in the apartment with Smith — Daugherty was worried about him. The next morning Martin heard a crash, he thought it was a door slamming or that a waiter had dropped a tray; but he could not get to sleep again and he went into the sitting-room. Looking into the other bedroom, he saw Jess Smith slumped on the floor his head in an iron waste-basket and a revolver in his right hand.

That night, as usual, Daugherty — still a guest of the White House — dined with the Hardings. Mrs. Harding, as if she sensed the gloom that must be upon

[5] Quoted from the testimony of Roxy Stimson, U. S. Senate Hearings, Investigation of the Attorney-General, 1924.

the two men, with their intimate memories of Smith and
happy times, invited two guests from outside, a couple
who were close friends of the Hardings. The device did
not help much. The guests, far from being able to bring
cheerfulness to the table, were suffused with the numb
despair of the hosts; for the rest of their lives the two
guests — they happened to be a sensitive couple — remembered that night. At the dinner table, only fragmentary sentences were spoken. Afterward, a private
showing of a motion-picture in the upstairs hall furnished no real diversion — but did happily provide a
darkness to five harassed souls, a darkness that saved each
countenance from sight of the others. No one spoke.
Only from one person came any sound; from time to
time Daugherty uttered a long-drawn-out "O-o-o-o-
o-o-o." For the ordinary blows of fate, Daugherty had
stoicism unlimited; but this wound to his affections
broke his defences. At the end of the motion-picture,
the guests shook limp hands with white-faced hosts.

VII

For Harding's distress at Jess Smith's suicide, there
was enough reason in the personal affection he had had
for him, the old associations, and the very great affection
which Harding knew Daugherty had felt for him.

There was justification for another reason: Harding
had heard that Smith had been keeping company that a
man in his position ought not to keep, that he was much
with lobbyists and fixers, that there was ominous talk
about it; Harding had told Daugherty that he must send
Jess away from Washington, and Daugherty had told
Jess he must go back to Washington Court House. Now
Harding could not know how much Smith's suicide
might be due to humiliation over Harding's saying he

must leave Washington — Harding, more than almost
any other man would have hated to think that. Harding
could not know how much Smith's suicide might be due
to that, how much to ill-health, and how much might
perhaps be due to guilty conscience in Smith — to what
degree Smith might have become seriously involved
with the lobbyists and fixers and might have been in
fear of exposure.

But Smith's had been the second suicide in the Harding circle within three months; and in connection with
the other one, Harding had convincing evidence that
there were dubious conditions in an important department of his Administration.

VIII

Of all the appointments Harding had made on a personal basis, from among his own circle of friends and
acquaintances, he had taken almost the greatest pleasure
in giving the office of head of the Veterans' Bureau to
an acquaintance he had made on a trip to Honolulu,
Colonel Charles R. Forbes.[6] Harding had taken pleasure
in making the appointment and later took pride in
Forbes's work. Forbes was a bustling energetic person,
with a glib and convincing tongue; he kept telling
Harding how fast he was getting hospitals built — Congress had appropriated $36,000,000 for the purpose and
Forbes was making the money fly; these reports Harding used to take pleasure in repeating to newspapermen
at his press conferences. One observed during the early
months of Harding's Administration that whenever he
mentioned Forbes's work he looked pleased; here was one

[6] See Chapter 8.

part of his Administration, Harding felt, that was clearly making good.

One day, Harding's personal physician, Doctor Charles E. Sawyer, whom Harding had brought from

From a photograph by Keystone.

Charles R. Forbes.

Marion and who was alert for Harding's interest, heard information that made him suspicious about Forbes. Sawyer looked into it enough to become more suspicious, and then went to the other old friend who was watchful for Harding, Attorney-General Daugherty. Sawyer told Daugherty facts which suggested strongly that Forbes had corrupt relations with the contractors to whom he let out the building of hospitals, and with others, to whom he was selling excess supplies left over from the war.

Daugherty decided to tell Harding. He hated to, he knew it would hurt Harding. But he went to the White House.

He found Harding having his portrait painted; it was by Howard Chandler Christy, and Mrs. Christy was there. Daugherty killed time with the group and then got Harding alone. "Mr. President," Daugherty said — at all times there was, between the two, a formality of address and manner, odd considering their intimacy; always Harding was "Mr. President," always Daugherty was "General," abbreviation for Attorney-General. "Mr. President," Daugherty said, "I have a very unpleasant duty to perform." Harding said, "Shoot" — that was his habitual word to any one seeking to talk with him. Daugherty told Harding what he had heard about Forbes. Harding grew red; it was the first time he had heard any intimation of anything wrong in his Administration, and to blush, or flush, was usual with him when he was embarrassed or disturbed. He said, "That can't be." Daugherty assured him he had looked into it enough to be convinced; and suggested that Harding should have an investigation of his own made. Harding was partly depressed; partly irritated. He let Daugherty go home without inviting him to remain at the White House for dinner; the omission was significant — it was the first time Daugherty had been at the White House at that time of day and not been asked to stay to dinner. The next day occurred another omission, even more pointed. There was, between Harding's office in the White House and Daugherty's office in the Department of Justice a special private telephone; it was the only phone going out of the White House that could be operated direct, without going through any switchboard or being touched by any employee. Ordinarily, Harding called Daugherty from five to twenty times a day. This day, no call came to Daugherty. The second day, Harding sent for Daugherty. When Daugherty arrived, Harding put his arm around Daugherty's shoulders and said, "Old man, did I hurt your feelings the last time you were here?" It was the first time, in all their years of association, that Harding had addressed him so intimately. Daugherty, concealing embarrassment by friendly brusqueness, said, "Oh, you couldn't hurt my feelings." Harding told Daugherty he had had an investigation, as Daugherty had told him to do, and had found that what Daugherty had said about Forbes was true. "I am heartsick about it," Harding told Daugherty.

Harding sent for Forbes and had an interview with him (from which Harding returned to sit through a dinner with friends in the White House without saying a word); he arranged with Forbes that the latter should go abroad, and while abroad should resign; this Forbes did.[7] Within a short time, the gossip about Forbes reached a point at which a Senate investigation of the Veterans' Bureau was inaugurated.[8] Twelve days after the investigation was authorized, Forbes' closest assistant, legal adviser to the Veterans' Bureau, Charles F. Cramer, asked his wife one night to take the midnight train to New York with a message Cramer said was important. The next morning, Cramer's cook, surprised by his not coming down to breakfast, found him on the bathroom floor, shot, a suicide. To Harding, suicide of one high in the Veterans' Bureau, and close to Forbes, at the time investigation of the Bureau and Forbes was beginning, could not help but be ominous.

[7] February 15, 1923.   [8] March 2, 1923.

The incidents had not, as yet, made much impression on the public; they were chiefly subjects of gossip in small circles. But Harding had begun to learn something of the conditions they implied.

IX

To only a slight degree was Harding temperamental; life did not translate itself to him in terms of being happy or unhappy. But the Presidency weighed on him. The work of it was more arduous and continuous than he had been accustomed to. The hard work, the limitations on his ease and freedom, wore him down. As he worked harder, he pursued his diversions harder, golf two or three times a week, poker and whist at night. The speed, the tempo, was so contrary to Harding's nature that it alone was enough to weaken him physically, distress him spiritually.

During his 27 months in office, frustration and disillusion beset him. He had generous impulses, he had supposed the White House would be a place where he could exercise them more than ever before, but he found that in fact he could not. In some instances in which he had been generous, he now knew, his generosity had done harm to his beneficiaries, to himself, and to the country. He learned that what his friends had always told him was his weakness actually *was* a weakness; somberly he realized that some of his loyalty to friends, some of his trust in human nature, was going to turn out tragedy to himself and to the country. It was not in his nature to try to put upon others the blame for acts of his own which turned out badly. At a Press Club dinner in Washington a year after he became President, he said, "If there is anything wrong with the White House job, it is the inability to be a human being." He was learning the truth expressed in the concluding line of a novel that Samuel Hopkins Adams was later to write about his administration, "Friendship in

Photograph © by Edmonston.

One of the few photographs of Harding and Coolidge together. As the photograph suggests, Harding, but for a fatal streak of softness, was the bigger man, the larger personality. As between the two, it was Harding who looked the President. The qualities that enabled Coolidge to make the better record were caution, coldness, a canny shrewdness. This photograph was taken shortly before Harding started on his ill-fated trip to Alaska in June, 1923. At this time, as the expression of strain on his face indicates, he was well on in his *via crucis.*

politics undermines more principles than fraud, and gratitude is a worse poison than graft."

He was conscientious, according to his own standards — which is the only way anybody can be conscientious; and he was irked, a little shamed, by the compromises he had frequently to make between what he liked to do and what his office obliged him to do, or what he felt was due to his office. Once, after he had sent for me and we had sat on the South portico of the White House, talking about a serious railroad strike, he wished to offer me a drink. He, with Mrs. Harding, took me into their bedroom, saying they felt that since national prohibition was in effect, they ought not to drink in the ordinary rooms of the White House, nor offer drinks to their friends, but that in their bedroom they might properly follow their personal standards.

Of all Harding's escapes from weariness, the one he liked best was to go out into the country and make speeches. He felt he spoke well, it was the sole thing he was vain about. Modest to the degree that he blushed when other accomplishments were attributed to him, he would say, to friends sufficiently intimate, "I really think I know how to deliver a good speech." The ability to please his audience and the response, the sympathy he got from the crowd, stimulated him. So he liked to do it, he had a word for it; his expression was, "I like to go out into the country and 'bloviate.'"

Some of this feeling moved him, in the spring of 1923, to plan a trip to Alaska. As the time approached, it happened that he completed negotiations begun by two men who had wished to buy the Marion *Star;* the price was large, for the *Star* was a fine property, the contract included an arrangement by which Harding, when he should complete his Presidency, would write for it. To close up the negotiations and write the contract, he had Daugherty in the White House for a day, it was the day before he was to start for Alaska. He took advantage of Daugherty's presence to have him write his will.

12

LAST DAYS

Harding, Depressed and Very Tired, Seeks Stimulation by Contact with the People. He Travels Across the Continent, Making Many Speeches; He Goes to Alaska for Recreation, but on His Return Falls Ill. His Private Car, Named the *Superb*, Becomes a Funeral Car. The Return Across the Continent; Scenes at the Capital, and Finally at Marion

THE trip to Alaska began on June 20, in the car "Superb" — ornately named — attached to a special train. In the party were Doctor Hubert Work, Secretary of the Interior, Doctor Sawyer, the President's physician, George Christian, Secretary to the President, and their wives; Doctor Joel T. Boone, and a few personal friends; and in addition secretaries, stenographers, newspapermen, Secret Service men, a Navy band, and a trained nurse for Mrs. Harding. Mrs. Harding had just recovered from a serious illness and had insisted on accompanying her husband despite the fears of the latter that the strain of the long journey would be too much for her.

At the start, the crowds meeting the train in cities and towns were small and apathetic, but as Washington was left farther behind they grew in size and enthusiasm. Had the circumstances of the trip been different, Harding would have got enjoyment from it. As it was, he was miserable. Physically he was tired out, tired beyond the point where recuperation would be possible short of a long period of absolute quiet and rest. And matching his physical discomfort was mental un-ease. The President was distraught, restless. He disliked being alone, and when alone brooded. He wanted to be playing bridge all the time; to the others it became a chore. Except when at the bridge table he wanted to talk, and that was most unlike him; he never remained long in his seat, but moved about, peering through the windows, changing from one side of the car to the other. The train, after reaching the Middle West, struck a heat wave which lasted all the way to Denver. Doctor Sawyer, concerned, urged Harding to relax, take things easy, but at every town and village where the train stopped, Harding appeared on the rear platform, made a speech, shook as many hands as he could reach, posed for photographers, stood bare-headed in the sun's glare. On a day of killing heat, at Hutchinson, Kan., after making a long address to a gathering of farmers, Harding went to a wheat field and drove a binder.

Before leaving Washington, Harding had written a number of speeches for delivery along the way. By 1923, the radio had developed to the stage where it was an adjunct to oratory; in some of the places where Harding talked microphones and amplifiers were installed. These were new to Harding and it was noticed that using them cost him a double expenditure of effort. He was irritated, felt that his delivery was made ineffective. That distressed him. His delivery was the one thing he was proud of.

In set speeches, at St. Louis, he dealt with the World Court; at Kansas City, with railroad consolidation; at Hutchinson, Kan., farm problems; at Denver, Prohibition[1]; at Salt Lake City, taxation.

From Salt Lake City, the party made a side trip to Zion National Park; and from Helena, Mont., another side trip, to the mines at Butte. Both excursions were

---

[1] He was enthusiastically applauded when he said that no one alive would ever see any political party declare for repeal.

strenuous and it was noticed that neither the President nor Mrs. Harding bore up well.

At Meacham, Ore., one of the last stops before taking ship for Alaska, a pageant of the Old West was staged. Harding chuckled when told of a difficulty the managers of the pageant had had. One of the scenes was to be a hold-up of a stage coach by Indians. When Indians were sought for to play the rôle of savage Redskins, it was found that the only ones in the neighborhood were a few old fellows who were in jail for bootlegging. Amiably the authorities granted temporary paroles in the interest of fidelity to historical atmosphere.

By the time the train reached Tacoma (where the party was joined by Secretary of Commerce Herbert Hoover and Mrs. Hoover) everybody was fagged out; all looked forward to the prospect of rest and cool weather during the four days they would have at sea going to Alaska.

In Alaska travel proved to be more of a strain than had been anticipated. The President grew more and more tired. A plan to return by way of the "Richardson Trail" was given up in favor of the route by rail, which was more direct and would more quickly get Harding to the quiet and rest of the sea trip aboard the Transport *Henderson*. But the few days at sea on the *Henderson* were too short. At Vancouver, where the party landed on July 26, tremendous crowds welcomed them; but Harding's effort to respond to their enthusiasm was pitiful. Next day at Seattle, he spoke in the Stadium, bareheaded, under a burning sun. Members of the party observed that several times he faltered, as if about to collapse. By now everybody on the Presidential train felt acute concern; everybody except Harding thought that the trip should now be given up.

That night from the President's room a hurry call was

sent out for Doctor Sawyer. Doctor Sawyer found Harding in great pain. He thought it due to ptomaine poisoning caused by eating tainted crabs. Others had eaten the crabs but had not been made ill.

From a photograph by Brown Brothers.

Harding in Alaska.

Harding insisted that the journey be resumed. On the way to San Francisco, he remained in bed in his stateroom. Repeatedly he expressed distress because of the disappointment he was causing the crowds by not being able to show himself.

San Francisco was reached on Sunday morning, July 29. Harding dressed himself and walked unaided through the station to the street. Reporters said in their stories that he looked "gray and worn."

At the Palace Hotel, Harding went at once to bed, but sent out word that after resting he would be all right and that he would surely deliver an address he had scheduled for the following Tuesday. Over the week end he

From a photograph by Underwood & Underwood.

The last photograph of Harding, taken at the end of the Alaskan trip as he was entering the Palace Hotel in San Francisco, from which he was to be borne out on a bier. There is a melancholy interest in comparing this with earlier photographs of Harding on preceding pages.

failed to improve. "His acute illness came to a peak on Monday night with the rapid development of a bronchial pneumonia. The quick, irregular, and labored breathing distressed him and when, by stimulation, he had been relieved after a sharp attack of breathlessness, he said, 'I feel much relieved, but, oh, so very tired.' "[2] On

[2] Doctor Ray Lyman Wilbur, a California physician called into consultation by Doctor Sawyer, in an article "The Last Illness of a Calm Man," in *The Sat-*

Tuesday he was seriously ill. The doctors said his heart
was weak. Wednesday he showed "remarkable improvement," was able to sit up in bed, read the papers,
take solid food. Wednesday afternoon Doctor Sawyer
announced that the crisis had passed and that the President was on the road to recovery. Thursday the bulletins
announced continued, though slow, improvement. Thursday evening at about half past seven, Mrs. Harding was
reading aloud to him an article about himself by Samuel
G. Blythe in *The Saturday Evening Post* — the editors
had captioned it "A Calm View of a Calm Man."
When Mrs. Harding paused a moment, Harding said,
"That's good! Go on, read some more." As he uttered
the words, a shudder passed through his body. Then he
relaxed.[3] Mrs. Harding ran out into the corridor crying,
"Call Doctor Boone; call Doctor Boone."

I have said that Harding's last words were a request to
his wife to continue reading to him. Those were the last
words from his lips. But at the very moment when he
died, Harding's secretary, George Christian, taking his
sick chief's place, was reading an address written by
Harding to a gathering of Knights Templar at Hollywood. One passage read — in a public sense these were
Harding's last words:

I am a confirmed optimist as to the growth of the spirit of
brotherhood. Science and genius are lending their aid to the
removal of the obstacles to intercourse and mutual understanding among the peoples of the world. We do rise to heights, at
times, when we look for the good rather than the evil in others.

---

urday Evening Post, October 13, 1923. Doctor Wilbur was a former president
of the American Medical Association, president of Leland Stanford University,
and later Secretary of the Interior under President Hoover.

[3] Harding was "struck down by apoplexy and lost his gallant battle against
death from pneumonia just when victory seemed to be his." — Doctor Wilbur.

II

August 3, early in the morning, the body of the President was delivered into the hands of the embalmers. Afterward, clothed in a cutaway morning coat and black trousers, it was placed in a casket in the big drawing-room of the Presidential suite in the Palace Hotel. There was little funereal about the scene; had it not been for the subdued demeanor of the people coming to pay their respects, the occasion might have been a quiet commemoration of some not unhappy event. This effect was increased by the many wreaths of flowers heaped about the casket and overflowing into the other quarters of the suite. The room itself was a cheerful place, large, high-ceilinged, spacious, with many tall windows through which the golden California sunshine beamed. The casket was situated not in the centre but close to a wall, in a place where the sunlight pouring in through the open windows radiated an effulgent brightness. Callers, passing by the casket, could see the President's features clearly, and noticed that his face had a placid and un-worried look.

Mrs. Harding, under orders from her physician, remained in bed all morning. To such friends as were permitted to see her she talked unceasingly of "Warren." Her lips trembled constantly, and there was fear she might collapse before the long journey back to Washington could be made.

In San Francisco, stores, banks, and schools were closed — the only activity visible were squads of workmen tearing down the gay bunting that had been put up in honor of the President's coming. Over the doorway of the Palace Hotel crêpe was hung. The President's flag had been hauled down and an American flag hung at half mast.

At five in the afternoon, with only members of the Presidential party and a few others present, the Reverend James S. West spoke a simple prayer:

The great and beloved Chief Magistrate of our nation has suddenly fallen. . . . Our hearts are broken; we are sore stricken with the sense of loss. . . .

Among the small number present, the most intimate, aside from Mrs. Harding, was Harry Daugherty. When Harding was leaving Washington for Alaska he had asked Daugherty to meet him on his return to San Francisco. It was twenty-three years since the two had come together in a little hotel at Richwood, Ohio.

III

The Funeral Train

Harding was the first President who had died in office in twenty years, since McKinley, and the fifth in the history of the country. The event provided one of the rare occasions America has for national emotion. The circumstances — the death in San Francisco, the long journey of the funeral train across the continent, the ceremonies at Washington, the journey from the Capital back to Ohio, the burial at Marion — prolonged the emotion as few emotions are, enabled scores of separate communities to have a direct part in it, and made of the whole an event not before duplicated and not in the future likely to be.

At seven P.M. the cavalcade, with a hearse bearing the President's body at its head, started on the half-mile journey from the Palace Hotel to the station of the Southern Pacific Railway, where the special train was waiting. A pall of quiet hung over the city. As the procession, escorted by a Marine Corps detachment, moved through streets solidly banked with people, the only sounds were Chopin's "Funeral March" and "Lead. Kindly Light," played by a Navy band which had been with the Presidential party from the start at Washington. (This band had been a special favorite of Mrs. Harding, playing for her frequently the two songs she liked best, "The End of a Perfect Day" and "La Paloma.")

At the station the casket was carried into the car "Superb" — the name had a melancholy significance now — and mounted just above the level of the windows where it could be seen from outside.

To avoid the ferry crossing of San Francisco Bay, a detour was made down the peninsula and around east and north to the Overland Limited line.

The itinerary of the cross-continental run had been arranged in advance on a fixed schedule, and newspapers had given wide publicity to it. Thus it was possible for people living long distances from the route to be on hand to see the train as it passed by. Multitudes came — estimates put the numbers as high as 3,000,000. The spectacle was a unique one. Newspaper men aboard the train, some of them veterans who had witnessed most of the important happenings in America during twenty years past, said they had never seen anything to compare with it.

In towns, as the train passed through, practically the whole population assembled at the stations. In cities, so vast were the crowds at the stations and along the tracks that the train could only creep along. Even in the open country there was hardly a mile of the continent-wide journey without its fringe of on-lookers.

"The silent reverence of the crowds, the men with their hats off and the women frequently with tears on their cheeks, was tremendously impressive. . . . By the thousands they stood, in the hot sun, their heads uncovered. At every town were groups of war veterans and boy scouts who dipped their flags. Soldiers from occasional posts stood at attention."[4]

Despatches sent out to the press associations by local reporters described scenes in their communities:[5]

Stockton, Calif. — Fifteen thousand persons were at the station. . . . Bells in the city tolled. Theatres, restaurants, and all-night stores were closed.

Auburn, Calif. — Although it was nearly 1 A.M. when the Harding funeral train passed through here this morning, 300 persons, or one-fourth of the adult population, were at the depot. The crowd bowed in silence as the train passed.

Reno, Nev. (5:50 A.M.) — As the train approached the city limits the bells of the churches began to toll and every head among more than 2000 who had gathered at the depot was bared.

Sparks, Nev. — The sun was just breaking over the horizon as the long funeral train drew out of the hills and came to a stop. Flowers in abundance were put aboard. Hundreds gathered with uncovered heads.

Omaha, Neb. — Forty thousand persons, including almost as many women as men and thousands of children, kept a vigil until 3 o'clock this morning to watch the funeral train pass. Silent, respectful, the mere bulk of them gradually pushed the lines of soldiers back, not from elbowing or crowding by those in front, but from the irresistible pressure of those behind stretching back beyond the limits of view.

[4] Carter Field, correspondent of the New York *Tribune,* who was aboard the train.

[5] The descriptions here given, of scenes along the route of the funeral train, at Washington, and at Marion, are from newspaper accounts, most of them by correspondents who accompanied the train, some by local correspondents who sent out despatches from their towns and villages as the funeral train passed through. The web of them, here woven, composes, in a way, an orderly narrative of the nine days during which the funeral was the focus of national interest. Many of the quoted accounts, as printed here, are paraphrased slightly.

The interest of these extracts lies mainly of course in the scenes they picture; but they have also an interest as illustrations of newspaper work, of how the details of an important and engrossing spectacle were put before the public through the press, at the time when the press did not share its function with the radio.

From Nebraska eastward, as the train entered the more thickly populated Middle West, the crowds increased in size.

Chicago, August 6. — The Harding funeral train arrived in the Western part of the city at 5:50 P.M., 2 hours and 20 minutes behind time. One of the largest throngs that has gathered in Chicago in many years was massed about the station and along the tracks. Other thousands assembled at other vantage points. The funeral party was met by a special aldermanic committee bearing a great white wreath of roses and lilies. A dirge of tolling bells and sounding of steamboat sirens were heard as the train moved slowly along. Salutes of 21 guns were fired by the 122d and 124th Field Artillery, Illinois National Guard. The same silent, reverent attitude was observable here as elsewhere. Within the crush along the tracks were people from more than a score of races and nationalities — Poles, Bohemians, Jews, Italians, Turks, Armenians, Dutch.

Entering Ohio, the President's native State, Mrs. Harding asked that the train travel slowly, with frequent stops.

Newton Falls, Ohio, Aug. 7. — The funeral train passed here at 8:42 o'clock this morning, hours behind schedule. All night long thousands slept or rested at the station on railway trucks, in autos, and on lawns. Hundreds of persons placed coins on the tracks and scrambled for them as mementos after the cars had flattened them.

IV

At the Capital

Washington was reached at 10:22 P.M. August 7. For hours thousands had been jammed in the station concourse, packed against the iron fence shutting off the train platform. The train entered rear-end first so that the funeral car with its flag-draped casket would be near the exit. Mrs. Harding was the first to descend, leaning on the arm of George Christian, Doctor Sawyer at her other side. President Coolidge and a small group of high officials were waiting. There was no sound but the throbbing of an air pump on an engine. The band in the concourse began "Nearer, My God, to Thee." As the solemn strains of the comforting old hymn filled the station the casket was gently lifted down from the special door cut in the side of the "Superb." On the great flag spread over it a single wreath was laid.

The military guard assumed position. The uniformed men raised their burden and began walking slowly through the station. Outside a squadron of cavalry and a battery of field artillery stood at attention. The casket was placed on a caisson. A low-voiced command brought sabres flashing to salute. The cavalcade swung into column formation and the slow march to the White House was begun.

The following day a clock in a tower near the White House was striking ten when the great doors of the main entrance were thrown open and a detachment of soldiers, sailors, and Marines appeared with the casket. Piled high upon it were gladioli — they were from Mrs. Harding.

A mounted artillery officer gave a low-voiced command. Riders of six sleek brown horses pressed their knees to their horses' sides and the black-draped caisson rolled into position. The casket was lifted to its place, a tall bluejacket watching to see that the colors were not disarranged. Black straps were adjusted, a bugle quavered a single note. As the vehicle cleared the tall columns of the White House portico, there appeared a group of men in morning coats and with silk hats held against their breasts. These were the honorary pallbearers: Senators Lodge, of Massachusetts, Curtis, of Kansas, Watson, of Indiana, Overman, of North Carolina, Fletcher, of Florida, and Kendrick, of Wyoming; Speaker Gillett of the House, and Representatives Burton of Ohio, Butler of Pennsylvania, Cooper of Wisconsin, Garrett of Tennessee, Garner of Texas, and Haugen of Iowa. Mrs. Harding, clinging to the arm of Secretary Christian, appeared in the doorway, and

stepped forward into an automobile with drawn blinds. After
her came other members of the dead President's family. Then
came the new President, Coolidge, and after him Chief Justice Taft of the Supreme Court, who had been President a
dozen years before, and after him, Woodrow Wilson, war-
time President; it was the first and only time in American
history when four men who had been honored with the nation's

From a photograph by International News Photos, Inc.

The return to the White House.

highest political office had come together. The Members of the
Cabinet took their places, Secretary of State Hughes well forward, and behind him Attorney-General Daugherty and Postmaster-General New.

Out in Pennsylvania Avenue bayonets were sweeping by,
slanting with an odd appearance of rain in a summer shower.
Far ahead an army band was playing a dirge. The 2d squadron
of the 3d Cavalry was moving at a walk; a battalion of the
13th Engineers just behind them.

Then came the Marine band playing "Onward, Christian
Soldiers," with a swing that is not heard in churches. Marines
and bluejackets stepped forward, the caisson moved out of the

White House grounds into the procession. As it rumbled through the gate, where Harding had passed nodding and smiling and waving happily so many times, the crowd massed there behind steel cables was as silent as mortals can be. . . .

Half way down Pennsylvania Avenue the artillery horses were halted. A host of children were singing "Nearer, My God, to Thee." As they sang, those nearest the street tossed flowers beneath the wheels of the caisson. Again the horses moved on. Ahead the troops were moving up the hill to the Capitol. . . .

At the Capitol the casket was placed in the center of the domed rotunda. Around the walls had been distributed ten truckloads of flowers from the White House. . . . President Coolidge appeared, the gathering rose to its feet. He laid a wreath on the bier. A clergyman prayed. Then, abruptly, the dimly shadowed rotunda was filled with music. Voices were singing "Lead, Kindly Light." Ears alone could not have located the source of the music, but roving eyes could see four male singers standing against the wall close by a great sculptured head of Lincoln, whose body, not so long ago in the life of the nation, had lain on the same catafalque in the same spot where now reposed the form of Warren Gamaliel Harding.

When the short service had come to an end the chairs were folded up and cleared away and then at a signal an almost endless column of people, four abreast, swept into the building, and filed by the casket which now was opened.

At about 4:45 P.M. the military escort which had accompanied the caisson to the Capitol in the morning drew up into formation in the plaza facing the steps to the rotunda.

Fifteen minutes later President Coolidge, the Cabinet, honorary pallbearers, and the guard of honor of general officers of the Army and admirals of the Navy entered to bid official farewell to their dead chief. Attorney-General Daugherty, bent with grief, was a pathetic figure.[6]

V

The Return to Marion

The journey of the funeral train from Washington to Marion was like the trip from San Francisco east. At Baltimore, York, Pa., Harrisburg — everywhere the

[6] Boyden Sparkes, in the New York *Tribune*, August 9, 1923.

tracks were lined with people. Frequently the train stopped and did not arrive at Marion until noon, August 9, hours behind schedule.

Marion's reception to her dead was severely dignified. The

From a photograph by International News Photos, Inc.

The casket being carried into the home of President Harding's father at Marion, after the journey from Washington.

cortège, hearse, and motor cars bearing the family and official party moved slowly through a city of whispers nearly a mile to the home of the late President's father, Dr. George T. Harding, on Center Street.

The crowd gathered early. At 4 A.M., when Ohio National Guardsmen went to the Station to clear its precincts they were forced to evict a score of persons who had remained up all night to hold points of vantage.

Through the morning the roads leading to Marion were

choked with automobiles. Many persons brought lunch bas-
kets. Whole families with small children early took up places
in store entrances and on the lawns of residences along the
route. . . .

Inside the plain home of his father, where Warren Harding
lived as a young man, in the sitting-room, the President's body
lay in its great bronze casket. At the head and foot of the bier
stood soldiers and sailors at attention, the only sign that the
occupant of that little sitting-room had been President of the
United States. Looking down from the walls, unnoticed in the
removal of the furnishings, was a crayon portrait of Dr. Harding and a print of the familiar painting, Watts' "Hope." As
the steady line of mourners moved through the room, light from
two tall electric candelabra shed a dim glow over the settled
features, softened by the heavy glass separating them from
those who gazed. . . .

Outside, under the low boughs of a maple in the front yard,
scores of floral pieces were densely heaped.

Warren Harding had been a front-porch man, the sort who
sits and rocks after supper and goes across lawns at dusk to
chat with the next-door neighbor. It was front-porch folk
who made up the wet-eyed procession that passed through the
little house today, plain people, of the same simple stock as the
late President. There were men from the fields with the deep
tan of outdoor work under the blazing sun; young women bearing infants; shy, elderly women; gray, gaunt men supporting
their feebleness with canes; boys and girls unwontedly subdued.[7]

Next day was the burial —

In front of Dr. Harding's house, from the curbing to the steps
of his porch, a carpet of green matting had been laid. Inside
the house were the close relatives of the dead President and
every high officer of the government. A gun boomed, the flag-
covered coffin appeared in the doorway. In the yard a few
women sobbed.

Ohio Guardsmen in wrinkled, slept-in uniforms stood guard
in lines stretching along both curbs as far as the eye could
reach. Behind them, on the lawns of houses on both sides of
the wide, brick-paved street, were massed uncounted thousands of people.

A sailor, a chief petty officer in white duck bearing a great
blue banner, the eagle-crested flag of the President of the United
States, appeared in the street. He was marching slowly ahead

[7] Forrest Davis, New York *Tribune,* August 10, 1923.

of a gray automobile hearse. It stopped with its rear doors abreast of the spot where Dr. Harding usually leaves his mare and phaeton. The casket was borne down the three or four steps from the porch. Ahead walked Major Ora Baldinger, his hair as red as when as a newsboy he delivered damp copies of *The Star*. Beside him, also in white duck, was Captain Adolphus Andrews, commander of the Presidential yacht *Mayflower*. Over their shoulders one could see four streaks of steel, the bayonets of the men who were keeping the last vigil by the body of their late commander-in-chief.

Other enlisted men, whose uniforms fairly sagged with medals, stepped unevenly beneath the weight of the coffin.

Just behind the casket walked the President of the United States and the Chief Justice of the Supreme Court. Both Mr. Coolidge and Mr. Taft held their silk hats close to their breasts, their eyes on the starred field of the flag on the coffin. Behind them came Secretary of War Weeks and Attorney-General Daugherty. Four other members of the Cabinet were there, and Albert Cumming, president pro-tem of the Senate, and Speaker Gillett of the House of Representatives.

A bluejacket placed his shoulders against the coffin and pressed it into the hearse.

Men in silk hats were still coming from the house, two by two. There was the tall figure of Governor Pinchot of Pennsylvania; Governor Donahey of Ohio, and George Harvey and Will Hays. Standing at one side was a group of men who had no place in this line dictated by years of precedent, but who, in the heart of the Hardings, stood well at the top of the list. There was "Jim" Prendergast, who believed Mr. Harding was going to be President back in the days when Ohio failed to elect him to the governorship. Orley Rapp was there and "Dick" Crissinger, now governor of the Federal Reserve Board. Their eyes were swollen.

Now another white uniformed military aid pressed forward, escorting a slender black-clad woman who took her place beside the President of the United States. It was Mrs. Coolidge and she was assisted into the first automobile that drew up beside the curb. President Coolidge and the aide followed her and the automobile moved slowly on.

Secretary Hughes and Chief Justice Taft entered the next car, and in succession the other dignitaries.

Slowly the procession formed, and then, when the men of the government were all in line, the widow emerged walking beside George Christian. With them, too, was Brigadier General Sawyer, but wearing black clothes as though he no longer cared for the military trappings that had become his through the power of his late friend.

The automobiles were moving slowly enough for the sentries to keep their places at each corner of the hearse. Just at the rear of the hearse walked Ferguson and Daly of the Secret Service, keeping their places beside their late chief as though he still required their presence to protect him.

The crowds on the sidewalks were silent when the big gray car passed, but buzzed into comment as they caught sight of and identified some of the personages following the casket. Now the procession was passing a weather-worn brick building, a rectangular structure that was the foundation of Warren Harding's career. It was the plant of the Marion *Star*, hung with mourning drapes of black and white. Its presses were silent, its door closed.

The sailor holding high the flag of the President turned the corner into South State Street, passing the Marion Hotel, the shabby old building that the citizens have been promising to renew during all the months since their fellow townsman was nominated at Chicago. Today, its windows were filled with visitors. Just beyond was the barber shop that is always pointed out to visitors because it was there that the editor of *The Star* always went for a shave.

Across the street, on the second floor, were windows draped with purple and black, the local lodge of Elks. Not just an ordinary Elks Lodge, but the one to which Brother Harding belonged.

The hearse crossed Church Street, out of which so many delegations of pilgrims had marched to 380 Mt. Vernon Avenue in the days of the front-porch campaign. Throughout the journey of nearly a mile and a half the way was lined by massed thousands who stood silent, while the cortège passed.

Now it came to the gates of the cemetery. Here the foot soldiers were augmented by troopers mounted on black horses. Cannon boomed at regular intervals. Great trees arched overhead; to the branches clung a host of boys.

The hearse had halted. The car containing the President and Mrs. Coolidge stopped just behind it. Again the President and the Chief Justice stood together while the others of the Cabinet stepped up behind them. Mrs. Harding, escorted by Mr. Christian and Dr. Sawyer, arrived. The coffin bearers drew their burden from the hearse. Three clergymen began to walk slowly down an avenue bordered by graves to a graystone, peak-roofed mausoleum, its entrance an ivy-covered portico.

The sailor with the President's flag stepped after them. Then came the coffin supported by soldiers, sailors, and marines, guarded on one side by six major generals, on the other by five admirals and the commandant of the Marine Corps. The President and the Chief Justice walked just behind. Next were the Cabinet, and then Mrs. Harding and the family.

From a photograph by International News Photos, Inc.

Thousands of people from Marion and the surrounding country visited the home of Doctor Harding, where the late President's body lay in state for a day.

The iron gates of the tomb had been opened inward. The bleak interior was softened now by flowers piled almost to the roof.

The bearers placed the coffin on a brown velvet catafalque just in front of the tomb. The President, the Chief Justice, and the members of the Cabinet lined up in two rows facing the grim structure.

On a hillside just beside the tomb a group of young men and women in white, the Trinity Baptist Choir, began "Lead, Kindly Light."

The Reverend Dr. George Landis, pastor of Trinity, stepped into the space between the coffin and the entrance to the mausoleum. He began to pray.

Mrs. Harding had turned and was facing the minister. Her eyes did not waver. Just at her shoulder Mrs. Coolidge watched her sympathetically.

Some one was sobbing. It was Dr. Harding. Now, it seemed, he was thinking not of the President of the United States, but of a little fellow not four years old who came calling him out of the long ago, shouting: "Pappy, I kin read!"

"Yes, sir," the old doctor had loved to relate, "that little tyke had learned to read. His mother taught him his letters from the copy of the Marow County *Sentinel* that was pasted on the woodbox beside the kitchen stove."

There was an interval of silence. The bearers shuffled into place trying to walk noiselessly. They lifted the coffin and then two by two mounted the single step into the tomb. They were concealed from view for almost a minute. Only the brown catafalque remained. Then they reappeared. A soldier stepped to the doorway and faced the President of the United States. He lifted a silver cornet to his lips. At times the notes quavered so that it seemed the music would break. He was playing "Taps."

Mrs. Harding's handkerchief was pressed to her lips. The musician finished and stepped from view. Major Baldinger, who had gone into the tomb, emerged and approaching Mrs. Harding whispered to her. She stepped into the thick odor of flowers within the small stone building. She remained there several minutes.

The President of the United States, the Chief Justice, and all the others waited patiently. Then she reappeared. She walked firmly, her chin lifted, her eyes shining.[8]

[8] Boyden Sparkes, New York *Tribune,* August 11, 1923.

13

COOLIDGE BECOMES PRESIDENT

In a Ceremony so Simple that Its very Simplicity was
Striking, Coolidge Is Sworn in as President by His Father.
He Issues a Statement Which Quiets Public Nervousness
and by His Comportment Wins the Confidence of the People.

On the night of August 2, 1923, Calvin Coolidge, Vice-
President of the United States, went to bed at nine
o'clock. That was his customary bed-time when on
summer visits to his father's house at Plymouth in the
Vermont mountains. During the evening, at about half
past seven, he had received a report, telephoned from
the near-by general store, about President Harding's condition. He had been told that the physicians attending
the President at San Francisco had issued a bulletin stating that the President was on the road to recovery.

Then, at half past two in the morning ———

I was awakened by my father coming up the stairs calling
my name.[1] I noticed that his voice trembled. As the only
times I had ever observed that before were when death had
visited our family, I knew that something of the gravest nature had occurred. . . . He must have been moved by the
thought of the many sacrifices he had made to place me where
I was, the twenty-five-mile drives in storms and in zero weather
over our mountain roads to carry me to the academy, and all
the tenderness and care he had lavished upon me in the thirty-
eight years since the death of my mother, in the hope that I
might some time rise to a position of importance.
He told me that President Harding had just passed away.
My wife and I at once dressed. Before leaving the room I
knelt down and, with the same prayer with which I have since
approached the altar of the church, asked God to bless the
American people and give me power to serve them.

[1] The Autobiography of Calvin Coolidge.

Accommodations for visitors at Plymouth were limited, and the Vice-President's assistant secretary and his chauffeur were lodged at a hotel in Bridgewater, eleven

From a photograph by Brown Brothers.

Coolidge while Governor of Massachusetts spent vacations on his father's farm at Plymouth, Vermont. In this photograph he is wearing his grandfather's boots and smock.

miles away. Also at this hotel was William H. Crawford, a journalist. Mr. Crawford wrote:[2]

E. C. Geisser, assistant secretary to the Vice-President, and Joseph N. McInerney, his chauffeur, rushed into my room at the hotel, saying: "Wake up! Did you know President Harding has died?"

"How do you know?"

"We have just received a telegram from George Christian saying that the President died at 7.30 o'clock."

[2] *Collier's Weekly,* May 25, 1923.

Hurriedly dressing, we covered the eleven miles to the Coolidge home in less than that many minutes. The telephone operator at Bridgewater also sent a messenger to advise Mr. Coolidge of the President's death. The elder Coolidge was the first one awakened.

The Vice-President and his wife came down the rickety stairs. Mr. Coolidge was one step in advance. The stairway is too narrow for two abreast.

I greeted him with: "Good morning, Mr. President," the first time he had ever been so addressed. His face was a character study. He mechanically shook hands with me, and there was a slight lowering of his voice as he said: "Is this information authentic?"

The telegram was handed to him by Mr. Geisser. He took it, walked over to the small center table on which a kerosene lamp was burning, having just been lighted by his father. Its wick had not been properly trimmed and the light was poor. Mrs. Coolidge said: "I'll get the lamp from our room, Calvin." Returning in a moment, she placed it also on the table.

During the interval the President had not said a word. Then he read the message over carefully and passed it to me. There was an awed silence. The reporters who had by this time come from Ludlow at breakneck speed gathered near the door. Mrs. Coolidge seated herself on the arm of a chair and rested her clasped hands on her knees, while the elder Coolidge tiptoed nervously around the room.

Suddenly the President said: "I will dictate a statement." And then he retired with his secretary. We could hear the typewriter clicking away on the first message ever given out by President Calvin Coolidge.

Mrs. Coolidge, in order to break the nervous strain, began a conversation with the newspaper men. She spoke of her sympathy for Mrs. Harding and expressed her belief that so brave a woman would resolutely bear up under her burden.

Presently the President came out and handed us his first message, which was entirely characteristic:

"Reports have reached me, which I fear are correct, that President Harding is gone. The world has lost a great and good man. I mourn his loss. He was my Chief and my friend.

"It will be my purpose to carry out the policies which he has begun for the service of the American people and for meeting their responsibilities wherever they may arise.

"For this purpose I shall seek the co-operation of all those who have been associated with the President during his term of office. Those who have given their efforts to assist him I wish to remain in office that they may assist me. I have faith that God will direct the destinies of our nation. . . ."

Coolidge, at the moment he issued this statement, was not President. He was still Vice-President and he would not be President until he took the oath of office. During

From a photograph by Brown Brothers.

Coolidge and Mrs. Coolidge with their sons Calvin Jr. and John. Calvin Jr. died while the Coolidges were in the White House.

the interval of several hours between Harding's death and Coolidge's taking of the oath, the Government of the United States was without a head.

A consultation, including Coolidge, his father, and his wife, took place over what the necessities of the situation required. When an elected President takes office, the oath is administered to him by the Chief Justice of the United States Supreme Court. Should Coolidge wait then until he reached Washington and take the oath there? Would it be legal if his father, a notary public, should administer the oath? What was the wording of the oath? What did the Constitution say on the point? A copy of the Constitution was found, and Coolidge read:

Article II, Section 1, paragraph 8. Before he [the President] enter on the execution of his office he shall take the following oath or affirmation:

"I do solemnly swear (or affirm) that I will faithfully execute the office of President of the United States and will, to the best of my ability, preserve, protect, and defend the Constitution of the United States."

That language did not clarify the confusion in Coolidge's mind. He decided, however, with some misgivings, to have his father administer the oath. Later, at Washington, the ceremony could be repeated, if that should be called for.[2a]

The scene now enacted in the little sitting-room of the old farmhouse was impressive for its simplicity. Coolidge and his father, their faces reflecting the sobering thoughts passing through their minds, stood beside a small table on which rested the two kerosene lamps and a Bible which had belonged to Coolidge's mother. About the walls of the old-fashioned room were hung a few pictures of the sort which might be found in any farmhouse, among them several charcoal portraits of Coolidge's farmer ancestors. Behind the stairway leading to the second floor was an alcove fitted with bookshelves on which rested the family's photograph albums. The elder Coolidge stood squarely erect facing his son. Adjusting his spectacles, he read the words of the oath, his son repeating them after him: "I do solemnly swear that I will faithfully execute the office of President of

[2a] The ceremony was repeated, without publicity, after Coolidge reached Washington. The oath was administered by A. A. Hoehling, Justice of the Supreme Court of the District of Columbia.

the United States. . . ." At the conclusion there was a moment of silence. Then came the clatter of running feet as newspaper men rushed across the porch to their cars for the race to Bridgewater to get their stories

From a photograph by Underwood & Underwood.

Painting by Guido Boer of the swearing in of Coolidge as President by his father, some time after midnight on the morning of August 3, 1923. The painting was made, of course, after the event. Coolidge, in his autobiography said charitably that while the likenesses of the figures were poor, the details of the scene were accurate.

started to their papers. Only the family and the Secret Service men remained, the latter to continue at Coolidge's side as long as he should be President. Silence settled again on the old farmhouse.

The time of the taking of the oath which made Coolidge President was 2:30 o'clock on the morning of August 3, 1923. A few hours later he left Plymouth to begin his duties as the nation's head. On the way he made one stop —

> I turned[3] aside from the main road to make a short devotional visit to the grave of my mother. It had been a comfort to me during my boyhood when I was troubled to be near her last resting place, even in the dead of night. Some way, that morning, she seemed very near to me.

[3] Autobiography of Calvin Coolidge.

From a photograph by International News Photos, Inc.

Coolidge after he had been President about a year.

14

THE OIL SCANDALS

An Obscure Citizen of Wyoming Writes a Complaining Let-
ter to His Senator, and Thereby Sets in Motion a Chain of
Events Which Has Somewhat the Nature of a Powder Train,
Beginning in Tiny Sputterings and Ending in a Vast Ex-
plosion. The Lease, by Secretary of the Interior Fall, of Two
Oddly Named Tracts of Land, Teapot Dome and Elk Hills.
Opportunity Knocks at the Door of Senator Thomas F.
Walsh, a Frontier-Trained Lawyer. A Drama Involving in
Its Cast of Characters a Wide Variety of Personalities, from
Walsh, the Austere Inquisitor, to Fall, Who Goes to Jail for
Fraud, and Sinclair, Who Goes to Jail for Contempt of the
Senate; and Doheny, Who Seeks Great Advantage but Is
Balked and in the End Receives Only Grief and Contumely.

HARDING was in his grave. Dying, he had known
that some of his friends and appointees, some that were
closest to him personally, had betrayed him, that scandal
was brewing and must in time explode. But of that the
country knew nothing; its emotion about Harding's
death was unqualified, a fine outpouring of the nation's
pride and simple faith; the country thought of Harding
as a capable and deserving President who had died mid-
term of a worthy administration.

Hardly had grass taken root above him when, through
a long series of Congressional investigations and criminal trials — installments of them continued as late as
the 1930's — the country saw one after another of Harding's appointees, some his close friends, brought under
accusation of crime, three convicted of crime.

II

A Citizen of Wyoming Writes a Letter

In a chain of events, after it has stretched out over a
period of years, and turned back on itself, and wound

over and under itself, and become twisted into knots, with some links not only joined to those before and after but also welded by time and rust to many others, until the whole is an intricate tangle — in such a chain, it is not easy to identify the first link (if, indeed, it is ever possible to say there was a "first link" in any chain of events or circumstances).

In telling the tale that came to be known for an American decade as the "oil scandals," we may begin with an obscure citizen of Wyoming, his name buried somewhere in dusty files, whose part consisted merely in writing a letter to his Senator. His motive was self-interest. Self-interest, indeed, in varying degrees of praiseworthiness — or the opposite of praiseworthiness — is, in this narrative, the practically uninterrupted *motif*. It would be difficult to find another drama in which any kind of disinterestedness is so rare.

The Wyoming citizen was in the oil business. In the circles where his calling took him he heard early in April, 1922, gossip that certain oil land belonging to the government and known as "Teapot Dome" — that odd and vivid name of a queer-shaped Wyoming hill was destined to ease the daily stint of many a cartoonist and newspaper paragrapher — was being leased by the Secretary of the Interior to a private corporation, that the leasing was being done secretly, and that the private beneficiary of the lease was a corporation called the Mammoth Oil Company, which was, in effect, a corporate alias for a bold and successful oil producer and promoter named Harry F. Sinclair.[1]

That the story should provoke curiosity was natural. The government had held the oil lands for many years — why should it now part with them? And why should

[1] Throughout this chapter, for brevity and to achieve clearness, the name "Sinclair" or "the Sinclair Company" is used as the equivalent of "the Mammoth" and the other companies that composed Sinclair's interests.

the negotiations be secret — the usual way of the government, imposed by law as a rule, is to conduct such transactions by public bidding? The negotiations on the

Page in the Louisville "Courier Journal."

The shape of a butte on the oil reserve leased by Fall to Sinclair provided the name for the reserve and provided opportunity for cartoonists.

side of the government were being carried on, so the story said, by the Secretary of the Interior, Albert B. Fall — why should that be? It was for the Navy that the oil lands had been set aside; if they were to be leased at all, why should not the Secretary of the Navy[2] do the leasing?

These questions, the suspicions that accompanied them, the surmises they gave rise to, and miscellaneous fragments of sinister rumor, were written by the Wyo-

[2] Edwin N. Denby.

ming citizen to one of the State's Senators at Washington, John B. Kendrick. From other Wyoming citizens came similar intimations, the whole suggesting a condition of the sort that slang of the day described as "dirty work at the cross-roads."

Senator Kendrick, being a Democrat, felt under no obligation to pigeon-hole a matter that threatened embarrassment to the incumbent Republican administration. Yet it was largely in the spirit of a perfunctory gesture, as a guerilla shot, that he wrote to Secretary Fall. Would Fall, Kendrick asked, explain these stories; would Fall give him a detailed and complete statement of the facts and of Fall's intentions?

Fall did not reply. Thereupon, Kendrick introduced[3] in the Senate a formal resolution calling upon Fall as Secretary of the Interior (and also upon the Secretary of the Navy, Edwin N. Denby) to advise the Senate whether the government oil lands were being leased to a private corporation. The resolution was adopted, perfunctorily, in the spirit in which the Senate amiably accommodates a desire of one of its members in a matter affecting his own State.

Still Fall remained silent. But in about a week his Department, the Interior, issued[4] a public statement over the signature of an under official.[5] This announced not only that Teapot Dome had already been leased to the Sinclair Company but added that a second lease was in preparation, of the Elk Hills reserve in California, to the Pan-American Petroleum and Transportation Company,[6] of which Edward L. Doheny was head. For

[3] April 15, 1922.   [4] April 19, 1922.   [5] Judge Finney.
[6] Throughout this chapter, for brevity and to achieve clearness, the name "Doheny" or "the Doheny Company," is used as the equivalent of "Pan-American Petroleum and Transportation Company" and the Doheny oil interests generally.

justification, the statement alleged "that oil was being drained from these reserves in very large quantities, amounting to millions of dollars of loss up to the present time, by wells on adjoining lands, and that within a few years the government reserves would be depleted."

The explanation was plausible. Everybody was familiar with similar situations, in which the owner of one plot of oil land was obliged to develop it as a defense against neighboring owners who set up rows of wells along the boundary line.

Two days later,[7] Fall made a belated reply to Kendrick. He confirmed the statement that Teapot Dome had been leased to Sinclair. The leasing was — so Fall's attitude implied — an act of executive discretion, which the Senate must not question. He admitted it had been done secretly, without bidding. In justification, he intimated that matters of great moment were involved, the naval preparedness of the country, the safety of the nation.

That explanation seemed plausible too. At all times there was intermittent apprehension about war with Japan, in which, conceivably, Fall's leasing of the reserves might better equip America for naval operations in the Pacific. At this particular time, early 1922,[8] the apprehension was acute — Japan was expanding her navy and expanding her ambitions in various parts of the Pacific. If Fall's leasing of the oil reserves to private interests would facilitate our preparedness, the leasing had not only a plausible justification but a meritorious one.

To one man in the Senate, however, the plausibility

[7] April 21, 1922.

[8] For an account of the delicate relations between the United States and Japan in 1921–1922, see Chapter 9.

was not sufficient. To Robert M. LaFollette[9] plausibility
was never sufficient. LaFollette had spent much of his
career lifting the cloak of speciousness from innocent-
seeming transactions to seek for sinister reality beneath,
and had been made sardonic by so often finding the hand
of Esau associated with the voice of Jacob. To LaFollette, any transaction in which government makes a grant
to a corporation was prima facie suspicious. He now set
in motion one of the most potent known mechanisms for
extracting information from unwilling possessors of it
— he introduced and successfully piloted through the
Senate a resolution ordering the Committee on Public
Lands[10] to investigate, and calling upon the Secretary of
the Interior to send to the Senate all documents and other
official data connected with "this entire subject of leases
upon naval oil reserves."

Chairmanship of the investigating committee would
ordinarily have devolved upon LaFollette himself; but
he, busy with his miscellaneous crusadings, had not
enough time to pursue this trail. He was content to let
the headship pass to one in whom he had confidence,
Senator Thomas J. Walsh, Democrat, from Montana.

III

*Divagation, Which While Essential to This Narrative,
Goes Somewhat Afield, as Far as to Frontier Days in
Montana, in Order to Explain an American Who, Already a Useful Public Servant, Becomes, by Conducting the Oil Investigation, an Eminent One. The Character, Training and Intellect of Thomas J. Walsh*

Thomas James Walsh, by his inherent quality, ready
now to be evoked by high events, was worthy of the

[9] The senior LaFollette, who served in the Senate from 1905 to 1925.
[10] A Republican, Reed Smoot of Utah, was chairman.

Senate at its best at any time. For his ability, the sort of training he had had was largely responsible. Not his academic training — many a Senator and many a lawyer had had schooling as good in quality and greater in quantity. What gave Walsh much of his precision of mind and clarity of expression — and particularly gave him his extraordinary grip on basic principles — was the experience he had had in his young manhood, an experience that could only have occurred in the America of an older day, an experience at all times unusual, and by the year this history was written, not to be had.

Walsh was born, a year before the Civil War began, in a tiny, cold Wisconsin hamlet — Two Rivers. He got such education as the local schools afforded; in his teens he became himself a teacher and saved enough money to go for a year to the University of Wisconsin. Upon graduating in law at the age of 25 he looked, as was common with young men in that day, toward the new lands, farther west. He began practice in a small community called Redfield in what was then Dakota territory, at a time when Indian warfare, of the degree of Custer's massacre, was only seven years past. At Redfield, Walsh, for a few years of his young manhood, participated in the organization of community life, during a period when the territory was developing to that degree of self-government at which statehood would be attained. By this experience, Walsh saw, and participated in, and was a leader in, the evolution of a microcosm of frontier society.

In 1891, Walsh moved still farther westward, to Helena in Montana, which had just achieved statehood. There he became the State's ablest lawyer, got together a modest competence, and began to take part in politics as a Democrat. In 1913, he was sent to the United States Senate, for a period which his loyal fel-

low-Montanans, by three re-elections, made a life tenure — a contribution to the nation, by a small, sparsely-
populated State, of a public man of the very highest
rank.[11]

In those pioneer communities where Walsh spent his

From a photograph by Brown Brothers.

Thomas J. Walsh at the time he came from Montana to the Senate.

early professional years, law, as law, had little standing
— and lawyers, as lawyers, rather less. It was not
enough for a lawyer to emit a Latin legal maxim, and
expect a jury to be impressed; nor for a political speaker
oratorically to belch the word "constitution" and expect
his audience to genuflect. Not even was it enough to

[11] A contribution duplicated in many circumstances by Idaho with Senator
William E. Borah.

recite the statute. The fact that a law had been enacted by a legislature at the State capital, or, during territorial days, by the Congress at Washington, did not carry undisputed authority, unless the statute conformed to local common sense. Those frontier settlements had rigid notions of right and wrong and about the protection of property; and in dealing with infractions of their simple code they were more severe, and more prompt, than older communities. Swiftness and certainty in the meting out of justice were often assured, indeed, by a spontaneous informality which the law might later sanctify as a "posse comitatus," but which the communities described as a "vigilance committee," or, more colloquially, as a "lynching bee"; these, in many places, regarded death by hanging as the appropriate punishment for horse-stealing.

Had those little pioneer communities been isolated, had they composed new and independent units of government, they would have evolved gradually their own laws and institutions, and these would have become much the same as those that England had evolved and America inherited. But when the inherited laws and institutions were brought in to these frontier communities as finished things, the communities would accept them only so far as they saw that the laws were merely their own common sense crystallized, and that they composed a reasonable and satisfactory body of rules for conducting community affairs. To make the frontiersmen see that the common law was merely common sense codified, became the necessity of the local lawyer. Unless he could do that, he lost his cases.

Those little pockets of new American life in the Rocky Mountains went through in one generation the experience that in England had consumed centuries, the experience of crystallizing common sense into law, and the average man's sense of justice into judicial institutions. In the process, the lawyers of the frontier communities had to be teachers. To one beginning practice in one of those territorial villages, it was not enough that he had learned the law well in school. He had to know what the law ought to be, and had to explain to the jury why it ought to be. By that, the young practitioner was obliged to pass the law through the prism of his own mind, and thereby to learn it for himself, as not all lawyers in older communities do. Granted a good mind to start with, the frontier training was one to produce a great mind.

Walsh was called austere; discussions about him that were wholly friendly held it strange that this man of pure Irish extraction seemed to resemble that figure in history whom the Irish most detest — Cromwell. During his conduct of the oil investigation especially, newspapers, in the newspaper way which sometimes sacrifices exactness to spectacular phrase, conferred on Walsh dramatic adjectives — "cold-steel mind," "relentless prosecutor," "stern inquisitor." Only to the extent that he had extraordinary clarity of mind, extreme precision of language, native restraint of manner, did Walsh deserve these adjectives. What seemed austerity was in large part, and curiously, a consequence of affection, sentiment. In Walsh, affection went out, in part, to principles, to abstractions, to institutions. His attitude toward justice and law was sentimental; he had an emotion of affection for integrity.

For America and its institutions Walsh had a love that second-generation Irish-Americans often have; he had seen his father come to America an immigrant workingman — and his father's son free to climb as high as ambition and ability could carry him. America was a good country; to regard it with affection and pride was a satisfying pleasure; to honor it, and especially to safeguard its institutions, was a sacred duty; to keep its public life pure, its paths of justice clear, was a personal responsibility.

Walsh was austere, in the sense that his mind was exact. His intellectual austerity gave him the reputation of being temperamentally cold but that he was not. He was an earnest adherent of his church, the Catholic, got spiritual uplift from regular attendance upon its rituals. Evenings he liked to invite friends to dinners of two at his apartment. Afterward, swaying gently in his rocking-chair, he would talk of the day's news, and of old times, of "singing geography" in the country schools of the 1880's, and "recitation day" on Friday afternoons; of neighborhood "spelling bees" on winter nights; skating in winter on the solidly frozen streams near his birthplace; his eager interest in the first street-car he saw; court-room scenes in early Montana; his youthful adventures in the law.

One story Walsh used to tell was about himself and his brother searching among the new prairie towns of Dakota territory for a place to locate. Prospecting thus, they inquired about opportunities not only in the law, but in politics, particularly Democratic politics. Once, having spent a forenoon making inquiries in Fargo, they walked out of the town to the bridge over the Red River. Sitting on the edge of the bridge, eating lunch from a paper bag, they discussed Fargo as a place for two young Democratic lawyers to settle. Unable to come to a decision, their eyes looked outward to the scene before them. Walsh noticed his brother gaze intently at the river below, then look at the sun, then look again at the river and again at the sun. "Tom," said the brother, "isn't that river flowing North?" Walsh, after similarly surprised observation, said it was. There was a moment of ruminating silence. "Tom," said the brother, "let's go on; I don't feel right about a place where rivers run North and Irishmen vote the Republican ticket."

To Walsh, always the path of duty was perfectly

From a photograph by Wide World Photos.
Thomas J. Walsh while conducting the oil investigation.

clear, always he followed it without consciousness that any other path existed. Once, in 1924, he was for nearly three weeks presiding officer over a Democratic national convention, famous for its prolonged tension, in which one of the largest elements of strife was between two groups, of which one wished to vote condemnation by name of the Ku Klux Klan, and the other wished not to mention it, the one group largely Catholics,[12] the other prevailingly non-Catholics. So evenly balanced were the two groups that in the deciding ballot only one vote separated them in a total of 1088 — 544½ to 543½. Over that angry controversy, tense with emotion, the convention a turbulent uproar, the presiding officer was Thomas J. Walsh, chosen for the post by reason of his knowledge of parliamentary law and his clear-minded administration of it. From minute to minute Walsh had to pass on motions, rule on points of order, impose parliamentary discipline. Never did accusation enter any mind, at a time when those inflamed minds were abnormally receptive to suspicion, that there was anything but cool and even-handed fairness in Walsh's choice of whom to recognize among the many that clamored simultaneously for the right of the floor. Never did any delegate protest against his level-voiced "The gentleman is out of order." That Walsh was a Catholic, and an earnest one, every one knew; but every one knew also that Walsh would not remember the fact.

IV

Such was the man who was made head of the Senate sub-committee to investigate the oil leases. With quiet deliberateness, Walsh went about the work. To examine the evidence, to familiarize himself with so technical a subject, and otherwise prepare for public hearings, would take time — it turned out to be a year and a half.

He was left to do the work in quiet. Newspapers and public forgot the early flare-up.

So far as the Administration was concerned, President

[12] It is desirable not to over-state the religious element in the controversy over the Ku Klux Klan resolution in the Democratic National Convention of 1924. Some of those most determined to censure the Klan were non-Catholics, and many Catholics were in the group that voted against mentioning the Klan.

Harding ended the matter with a brief assertion of rectitude: "The acts," he declared,[13] "have at all times had my entire approval." That, at a time when the Administration was still comparatively new, and high in favor and respect, was sufficient.

Newspapers printed, without unusual conspicuousness, such items of news as bore on the leases. Fall completed the Elk Hills lease to Doheny.[14] When outsiders embarrassed Sinclair's occupancy of Teapot Dome, the Navy Department, through Assistant Secretary Theodore Roosevelt, Jr., sent[15] a detachment of Marines to eject trespassers and protect the Sinclair Company in developing the field.

The oil leases were taken for granted, as an accepted thing, presumably a worthy and useful thing.

v

The slow deliberateness that caused Walsh to consume some eighteen months in preparation was in part his mental habit; in part, perhaps, it reflected, at the beginning, lack of strong conviction that corruption could be shown. With characteristic thoroughness, he began by re-familiarizing himself with the laws affecting public lands — he had known them fairly well in his private practice — and with the history of them. The background went as far into the past as the beginnings of the country.

The Subject-Matter, the So-to-Speak Bone of Contention, of the Oil Investigation

The nation had acquired great tracts of land by purchase, or by driving the Indians off, or by a combination

[13] June 7, 1922.   [14] April 25, 1922.   [15] July 28, 1922.

of both methods. Most of the lands west of the Mississippi had been acquired by purchase from France; thereafter, from time to time, the Indians were driven off or herded into reservations. The land thus cleared was thrown open to settlement and private ownership. Lands capable of cultivation could be acquired by one method, timber land by another, grazing land by another; land believed to contain minerals by yet another. All the ways were easy — the universal purpose, for a century, was to get the public domain developed. Yet by 1900 there still remained great areas for which no one cared enough to take the small trouble necessary to acquire ownership.

About that time rose a consciousness that the public domain was a diminishing heritage; the feeling expressed itself in a policy called conservation.[16] In pursuit of that policy President Roosevelt withdrew much of the remaining public land from settlement, and President Taft some more.

About the same time, oil began to be adopted as fuel for ships, instead of coal. About 1909, some 12 years before Harding took office, it was suggested that some of the withdrawn lands, believed to contain oil, should be specifically dedicated to the use of the Navy, to provide an adequate supply for its future needs. The intended method was to keep the oil in its natural deposit until such time as the Navy should need it. The Elk Hills field in California was set aside in 1912 (together with another California field which does not figure in this narrative). The Teapot Dome field was set aside in 1915 under the Presidency of Wilson. Control over the reserves was vested by Congress in the Secretary of the Navy.

The policy adopted was to keep the reserves as nearly

[16] For an account of the conservation policy, see "Our Times," Vol. III.

intact as was practicable. During the World War the Navy obtained all the oil it needed from the more than abundant commercial sources, and there had been no need to tap the reserves; the policy of conservation, of holding the reserves for some further emergency, was adhered to.[17] The policy was followed strictly by Wilson's Secretary of the Navy, Josephus Daniels, who took scrupulous care to keep the reserves as what they were intended to be, storehouses for future use.

This was not, however, completely possible; oil was not like a solid substance, oil would run. At spots along the edges of the reserves were wells in private ownership, which drained from within the reserves; at isolated locations inside the reserves were flowing wells operated by private individuals who asserted title to them, and some long-standing claims to drilling rights, about the validity of which there was dispute. These were an embarrassment to the integrity of the reserves. To deal with them and to achieve flexibility and efficiency in the management of the reserves, Congress in February 1920 passed a "General Leasing Act" (supplemented later in the same year by another act) giving to the Secretary of the Navy the authority to make leases on the reserves if and when in his judgment the best interests of the nation required such action. The powers given the Secretary of the Navy, in order to be flexible, had to be broad. Under them, Secretary Daniels in the Wilson Administration made some isolated leases on some of the reserves. It was never contemplated, however, that any of the reserves should be leased as a whole.[18]

17 There was one exception which does not figure in this narrative. It had proved impossible to save Reserve No. 2, in the Buena Vista Hills section in California. These Buena Vista lands, at the time of their withdrawal from public entry, had been literally honeycombed with privately held patents and claims and wells that were actually running oil.

18 The intent of Congress in enacting this legislation was later an important factor in the suits at law growing out of the oil scandals, for which reason it

This was the status when, a year later, the Harding Administration took office. The reserves were an empire. A sense of the sacredness of a trust for the future attached to them. It is little wonder that any suspicion of improper disposition of them should give rise to concern.

VI

Fall

Walsh, after his 18 months of quiet preparation, called the first public hearing.[19] As the first witness he called Fall.

Among Senators and others in the committe room who were on the inside of the Washington scene, there was some partisanship for Fall. Here was a Senator, Walsh, summoning one who very recently had been a fellow-Senator, to testify upon what amounted to an accusation.

Fall bore himself with somewhat more than his usual touch of quiet arrogance. At all times, Fall's bearing attracted attention rather favorable. The feature of him most arresting to a stranger was his eyes, which were bright blue, and the direct gaze of them, a gaze that comes to many persons who have spent much of their lives in the out-of-doors and in a country where the horizons are distant. Persons not familiar with the reason for that habitual look in Fall's case assumed it to be an expression of special candor, simplicity, forthrightness, courage. For this reason, and whatever others, courage was a quality commonly attributed to Fall; legend, possibly having no more authentic basis than his Ken-

will be well here to cite the exact language of the act. It authorized and directed the Secretary of the Navy "to conserve, develop, use and operate" the Naval Reserves "in his discretion, directly, or by contract, lease or otherwise, and to use, store, exchange or sell the oil and gas products thereof, and those from all royalty oils from lands in the Naval Reserves, for the benefit of the United States."

19 October 25, 1923.

tucky birth and his upbringing in the Southwest, said Fall was a man who would shoot in defense of his honor.

Marks of the Southwest were upon him, and caused him to stand out from the crowd, the wide-brimmed

Photograph from Acme Newspictures.

Secretary of the Interior Fall leaving White House after cabinet meeting
January 2, 1923.

felt hat, the bronzed skin, the agreeable drawl, the erect body and head, as of a man who had spent much time in the saddle. Legend said he had been a prospector in his youth, and people associated him now with mining, ranching, stock-raising. He let it be understood these were his occupations, though much of his life he had spent in office-holding; before coming to the Senate he had been a member of the New Mexico Legislature, twice attorney-general of the State, a justice of the State supreme court.

Many in Washington who knew him well liked him. He had a gift for being a crony; was a quietly agreeable companion for hours of recreation; in the Senate he had been one of the group that included Harding. He was loyal to those who herded with him; whoever is that is certain to be liked by his own crowd.

If anybody had doubt about Fall, it was about his political ethics; and if this was under any suspicion, that again was explained by his life in New Mexico. If Fall had a special code of politics — and no one in Washington knew if he had — it was assumed to be a natural fruit of the political soil from which he had come. In New Mexico large numbers of the voters were aliens, natives of Mexico, unable to read or write English, or even to speak it. If, to get the votes of that kind of electorate, a man ambitious for high office found it necessary to use methods which some other communities would consider unconventional, no one in Washington thought the less of him. As between Fall, and Senators who got their majorities from the big cities in the East and North, Fall was not likely to have been the greater sinner against meticulous standards.

In short, Fall did not stand badly. So far as the flare-up about his leasing the oil reserves had caused any to give a thought to his integrity, there was a possible explanation, an innocent one. One felt that Fall, coming from the West, might share a common view of that section about public lands; that he might, by reason of his associations and background, be unsympathetic to the policy of conservation; that he might hold the view that the public domain was meant to be opened up to private development. Indeed Fall, being rather truculent about his views, might conceivably have leased the oil fields partly as a flaunting gesture of defiance to the conservationists, as a sign that the policy was to be modified. That, many assumed, might be the explanation of Fall's leasing the oil reserves, if explanation were needed.

VII

Fall Denies

Fall, facing Walsh, accepted full responsibility — not only accepted it, seemed to court it; he had an air of pride in having done something fine and farseeing for the United States, and almost of pity for any one so lacking in vision as to question either the usefulness of what he had done, or its propriety. Fall defended not only his action but his way of doing it:

Senator Walsh — Your reason for not calling for bids was what?

Mr. Fall — Business, purely. I knew I could get a better price without calling for bids.

Senator Walsh — Do you think if you had advertised, designating whatever terms and conditions you saw fit, and invited bids, that you would not have gotten any?

Mr. Fall — Oh, I might have gotten bids. There was only one bid I could have gotten that I could have considered, however, in my judgment, and that is the bid that was finally accepted.

Senator Walsh — Who was the authorized legal adviser of the Interior Department?

Fall, with almost the manner of Louis XVI declaring "*L'état, c'est moi*," replied: "The Secretary of the Interior, largely himself."

Walsh asked:

In this matter what other oil companies did you consult?

But Fall would be no tattler of official secrets:

Unless this is considered absolutely necessary for the purposes of the hearing, I prefer not to name the oil companies.

Walsh turned to the secrecy of the transaction —

Walsh — What objection was there . . . to giving to the public immediately upon the execution of this contract information that the contract was, in fact, executed, inasmuch as the public would necessarily know as soon as Mr. Sinclair began work?

Fall — Certainly no sinister purpose could have been served by it.

Walsh — Was there any purpose not sinister?

Fall, with a manner of being very patient, re-cited the reason he had cited before, the reason of state, the reason that had to do with foreign relations and possible war:

Fall — Now, you are going into the policy which I had in mind with reference to this thing. I have undertaken to explain that I regarded myself as a business agent of the Secretary of the Navy, acting in what I regarded as a military matter under the President of the United States. I did not propose, so far as I am concerned, to call attention to the fact that contracts providing for enormous storages of oil for future use in a crisis were being made off the coast or in certain parts of this country. That was what I had in the back of my head.

It would not be Fall who would needlessly make known a naval policy which a foreign nation might interpret as a threat. If others revealed it, let that be on their consciences. Fall could only be responsible for himself; he would follow the path of personal propriety; and self-approval, conformity to his personal code, would be his only reward. He said:

If that information should be given out . . . it must be by the parties who were interested in it more than I was. I did not suggest it to them. It was up to them. I had my own ideas.

That was that.

Walsh turned to the fact that Fall after resigning

from office had made a trip to Europe on business for the man, Sinclair, to whom a year before he had leased Teapot Dome.

Fall — Yes. I did not go under any terms of employment at all. . . . My expenses were paid by the [Sinclair] syndicate — $10,000. I have never even suggested any compensation and have received none.

Walsh queried him about his relations with the beneficiary of the other oil lease, Doheny.

Walsh — It has been stated that you are under some employment, or have been, from the Doheny interests?
Fall — That is incorrect. I have been advising Mr. Doheny with reference to some other important matters, of which I think our government is informed, but without any compensation at all.

Fall's denial was complete, absolute. He had received no compensation of any sort, for any service, from either Doheny or Sinclair. He had received no money from Doheny at any time. From Sinclair he had received nothing until after resigning from the Cabinet and then only expense money covering a business trip to Russia in Sinclair's interest.

On the whole, the impression Fall made on his hearers was distinctly favorable. There was nothing in what he said, or in his manner, to excite suspicion. His gaze was direct; his replies came easily. To observers, even cynical ones, including shrewd and hard-boiled newspaper men, the occasional hint of sharpness in Fall's voice seemed merely honest indignation which any faithful public servant might feel at having his motive questioned. The despatches that went out to the country intimated that Walsh was on a preposterously false trail.

VIII

Denby

Walsh called the Secretary of the Navy, Edwin N. Denby.[20] Walsh asked Denby why it was that oil reserves committed to the care of the Navy had been transferred to the Interior Department; why the leasing of them, which ought to have been done by Denby if by anybody, had actually been done by Fall.

Denby didn't exactly know. He truly did not know. He had assented to what Fall had suggested without understanding much about it; he had signed important papers as if they were routine memoranda. Did he ever submit the matter to the General Board of the Navy? — "Not to my recollection." Did he ever submit it to the council of bureau chiefs? — "Not that I recall." Had he ever examined the act of Congress that made him custodian of the oil reserve (Denby ought to have been as familiar with that as with his official commission)? — "I do not recall." Did he know anything about the policy of the Navy with respect to the oil reserves? — he did not. Did he remember when he signed the leases? — he did not.

Denby was not "stalling." He literally did not know. He was perfectly honest — and perfectly inept. His "I don't know's" and "I don't remember's" were not the evasion of the guilty; they were the simple directness of the dumb.[21] Quickly Walsh realized what sort of

[20] October 25, 1923.

[21] "Stupidity is the high crime and misdemeanor of which the Senate accuses Mr. Denby, and the only one." — New York *Tribune,* February 12, 1924.

"He was pitifully credulous." — United States Senator George Wharton Pepper of Pennsylvania.

"Of all the motley army of witnesses assembled by the Senate Committee, none presented such a pitiable spectacle. He seemed a butterfly on the wheel. He was bewildered, helpless, pathetic, dumb. His ignorance, his weak memory, his irresponsibility, his feeble grasp of facts and their significance, his gullibility, and withal his cocky self-assurance would have discredited a junior clerk. —"The Story of Teapot Dome," Marcus Eli Ravage, 1924.

man he had on the stand, abruptly thanked him and let
him go.

We, too, can let him go, as respects the oil leases,

From a photograph by Brown Brothers.

Edwin Denby, Secretary of the Navy in Harding's Cabinet. He looked the part
more fully than he was able to live up to it.

though as one who held high office he calls for explanation.

In looks, Denby was the most adequate Secretary the
navy ever had; his countenance expressed power, poise,
dominance. But looks were about all he had. His tragedy was that nature, after giving him features that
would have fitted a Bismarck, had neglected to fill the
space behind his features with Bismarck material.[22] He
took the most impressive photograph of any man in

---

[22] There was a parallel in recent American history, accompanied by similar
tragedy, in the case of William Sulzer. Nature had given Sulzer the features
and forelock of Henry Clay. That, capitalized by Sulzer, pieced out by an
oratory and a frock coat of the Clay model, carried Sulzer through four terms
of Congress, and into the office of governor of New York. There, lack of Henry
Clay brains led to his impeachment.

public life (and how he liked to!). Somehow the camera lens and the silver screen can frequently transmute weakness into ruggedness, vacuity into substance. Motion picture actors need only to look their parts, not be them. But the public expected Denby to be what the camera said he was — and he could not. He did not have the stuff.

Denby had been appointed Secretary partly because of an incident which reflected the best that was in him — and there was much good, though not the kind of good that makes an adequate tenant of high public office. At the time the Great War broke out, Denby had been in Congress six years, was 47 years old, and was overweight. Nevertheless, as a genuine expression of patriotism he enlisted in the Marine Corps as a private and rose through the non-commissioned grades to be major. He had won affection and respect, and had been strikingly useful in building up the morale of the Corps.

When Harding was making up his Cabinet, he came to within a few days of inauguration before filling the final post, Secretary of the Navy. In his hurry, he consulted John W. Weeks, whom Harding had already chosen as Secretary of War. Weeks, mentally running over possible material, remembered Denby for his unique contribution in the war, and also as a member of Congress. Further reflection recalled that Denby had done something of the same kind in the Spanish War, had volunteered as a common seaman and ended as a gunner's mate. He was now practicing law in Detroit. He was a graduate of the University of Michigan where he had played football — he would! His father had been United States Minister to China. Because of Denby's record, Weeks recommended him, and Harding, being in a hurry, appointed him. He made a great cheer leader at the navy's football game with West Point.

IX

The Worthies — of Varying Worthiness

The men involved in the oil scandal, those who began it and those drawn into it; those who caused it, like
Fall, as well as those who exposed it, like Walsh; those
who were tempted and fell, and those who were tempted
but were too virtuous — or too worldly-wise — to fall;
those at the bottom of it, like Sinclair and Doheny, and
those blamelessly touched by the flying spray of it, like
McAdoo and George Creel; those whose rôle was sinister, and those whose rôle was innocent — all had one
quality in common, an indigenous trait of outstanding-
ness. As each stepped on to the witness stand, all who
watched recognized that here was an exceptional personality — the quality of the personality might be one
thing or the other, but the quantity of it was undeniable.

In the fauna of American society, they belonged
among the genera of the grizzlies and the bison, the
Hereford bulls and the timber-wolves — including that
species which American slang calls the bear-cat. No
three-hour drama on the stage could have accommo-
dated such a parade of characters. From the aggregate
of them one could select, from here a trait and there
a trait, the materials to assemble a gallery that would
include much of Napoleon and St. George, Cromwell
and Clive, Machiavelli and de Medici. Sinclair in a
different era and place might have been a Cecil Rhodes,
Walsh a St. Ignatius Loyola. Those who were weak
were spectacularly weak, those who were strong a little
too strong for an age that has left the Napoleons behind it. The liars were magnificent liars; the truth-
seekers were similarly eminent on the side of virtue.
(Though the truth-seekers, as we shall see, were not

quite a match for the liars.) Even the one who provided a nation-wide laugh, Ned McLean the playboy-
lout who almost became a principal in the drama but
scurried back to safety — even he was facile princeps
among his kind. And the one who played nit-wit, poor
Denby, was after all a rugged nit-wit.

x

Walsh Calls Experts

Walsh called technical witnesses, from the Navy and
from scientific branches of the government, to find out
whether the leasing of the reserves was wise and in the
best interest of the navy; whether leasing was necessary to present depletion of the reserves by drainage
from outside wells; whether, in short, there had been
any sound reason of public interest for the leasing.

Walsh called an admiral, R. S. Griffin, who had had
charge of the naval reserves for some ten years until
he was removed a few months after the Harding Administration went into office. Admiral Griffin stated
and stated strongly that he regarded the leasing as a
mistake; that he had opposed and opposed strongly the
transfer of the reserves to the Interior Department
which had made the leasing possible; that he had repeatedly warned Secretary of the Navy Denby that if
the reserves should be taken out of the navy's control
"we might just as well say goodby to our oil"; that he
had said to Denby "I did not agree that these were
public lands, that I thought that after they had been
withdrawn from entry and set aside for the exclusive
use of the Navy they were as much naval property as
were the navy yards."

Walsh called Commander H. A. Stuart of the bureau

in the navy which had had control over the reserves. Commander Stuart stated that he had "been very much opposed to the transfer of the naval reserves to the Interior Department"; that because of this Secretary Fall had urged Secretary Denby to have him "detached and sent out of Washington." He added that on account of Secretary of the Interior Fall's "antipathy" to him he had been given orders "not to have any communication with the Interior Department or to go into the building."

Walsh called K. C. Heald, chief of the Oil and Gas Section of the United States Geological Survey:

Senator Walsh — What occasion did you see, if any, for the leasing of the entire reserve [Teapot Dome]?

Mr. Heald — I could see no reason for leasing the entire reserve . . . I am positive about it. I can see no reason whatever for leasing. I think that other geologists will concede that.

Senator Walsh — What have you to say as to the extent of the drainage occasioned by the wells in the Salt Creek field outside the Teapot Dome?

Mr. Heald — The drainage would not be serious.

Walsh called Admiral Robison who had had charge of the oil reserves for a few months before they were transferred to the Interior Department. Admiral Robison said he had favored the leasing of the reserves because he believed they were being drained by outside wells. Walsh asked him on what he based his belief. He replied that Edward L. Doheny had told him so in a casual conversation six years before.

Walsh called the chief geologist of the United States Geological Survey, Doctor W. C. Mendenhall. Doctor Mendenhall stated that in his "opinion fear [of drainage] was unjustified and that any leasing in consequence was unjustified."

XI

Doheny Denies; Sinclair Denies

Walsh called one of the two beneficiaries of the two leases, Doheny.[24] Doheny told little more, that bore importantly on the point, than that the leases had been made and that he regarded them as wise on the part of the government.

I claim my lease was made in the interest of the United States Government. . . . You cannot get me to admit that it is a bad lease, because I certainly do not think it is.

In reply to questioning, Doheny stated that he expected the reserve leased by him would yield the staggering quantity of 250,000,000 barrels of oil, and, even more amazing:

I would say that we will be in bad luck if we do not get $100,000,000 profit. . . .

Walsh called the other beneficiary, of the other lease, Sinclair. Walsh questioned Sinclair about a visit he had made to Fall's ranch some time before the lease to him was made. Sinclair's answer was direct:

I went to Three Rivers to discuss with Senator Fall the leasing of Teapot Dome.

Sinclair was then asked specifically, directly, comprehensively, the question that covered everything:

Senator Lenroot — Mr. Sinclair . . . is there any profit to be received in this transaction, that Mr. Fall received, any benefits or profits, directly or indirectly, in any manner whatsoever in connection with you?

Sinclair's reply was as direct as the question; and

[24] December 3, 1923.

question and answer were all-embracing, composed a complete denial:

Sinclair — No, sir, none, unless he had received some benefit from the cattle.[25]

Walsh read into the record a statement made by Sinclair before another Senate committee, telling of the profits he expected to make from the Teapot Dome lease.

Mr. Sinclair — Well, I did not say positively . . . that there was $100,000,000 of value in the Teapot Dome. I told you it was a guess, but it was my opinion that the Teapot Dome properties would be worth more than $100,000,000. . . .

Walsh had called the government official who made the leases, Fall, and had uncovered nothing. He had called the two beneficiaries and uncovered nothing from either.

XII

But Walsh, in prosecuting the investigation, was favored by one condition, a condition that never fails to emerge in similar circumstances, a condition familiar to every committee chairman who ever conducted an investigation, to every lawyer who ever prosecuted a sensational case, to every editor who ever conducted a newspaper crusade.

Whichever way we look at it, whether the righteous see it as a beneficence aiding the operation of punitive justice, or the cynical see it as a manifestation of a less lovely part of human nature — in either case, it is the experience of all who ever conducted a *cause celebre* that once the victim is on the rack, once the mills of ex-

---

[25] The reference was to a shipment of blooded stock from Sinclair's farm in New Jersey to Fall's ranch early in 1922, which witnesses had dealt with earlier.

posure are set in motion, the materials to keep them going come in from every quarter. So surely does this occur that a prosecutor with experience will sometimes begin an inquisition without having the key evidence in hand, trusting to chance that the needed stone for his arch of proof will come to him some day in a telephone call from a stranger, or a letter, or a whisper from a caller. Once the newspaper headlines begin to send accusation out upon the winds, volunteer offerings of evidence blow in from every point of the compass. From a wide variety of persons it comes, and through many kinds of motive, from furtive busybodies writing anony. mous letters, to vain exhibitionists eager to get in the limelight that shines upon a witness stand. Those who had business relations with the victim years before, and remember the outcome as unsatisfactory, now see a chance to even the account; those who have had neighborhood feuds with him, or acquaintanceship that terminated in ill-feeling, now see opportunity for spite; those who have had contacts with his uncles or his cousins or his aunts recite allusions to the victim that they had heard which throw suspicion on him; old acquaintances of the victim who "knew him when" recall incidents of his boyhood which foretold an evil end; every one who happened to see a letter, or overhear a telephone conversation, comes forward with testimony. Much of it, of course, is chaff; yet in some such way, in many a famous case, has come the particular bit of evidence that made the difference between conviction and acquittal.

From such volunteers there came to Walsh's office evidence that Fall had lately experienced an access of affluence not explainable by any apparent source of legitimate income. Two years before, an editor[26] in New

26 Carl Magee.

Mexico stated of his personal knowledge, Fall had been "broke."

Some of the signs of Fall's new affluence were comparatively trivial; they turned out to be material for a smile, or at the most, unconvincing evidence of corruption. Some blooded stock had appeared among the flocks and herds on Fall's New Mexico ranch, stock of a lineage more high-bred than Fall had hitherto owned. The number was small, only — as it turned out when their association with crime subjected them to precise enumeration — only 14 heads extraordinarily assorted; six hogs, a stallion, six heifers, and a bull. And the total value was only some fourteen hundred dollars. But there was information that the freight car which had brought the animals across the continent had begun its journey at Ramapo Hills, New Jersey, where there was a stock farm owned by Harry F. Sinclair. And there was information that Sinclair and his wife had been visiting at Fall's ranch not long before the blooded stock arrived.

Sometime after that evidence came out, a rather distinguished volunteer witness appeared. Archibald B. Roosevelt was a son of the late Theodore Roosevelt; it was immaterial to the case, but provocative of added interest, that young Roosevelt's brother, Theodore Roosevelt, Jr., was Assistant Secretary of the Navy. Young Roosevelt, pale and nervous, asked to be allowed to take the stand and make a statement. He was, he said — or had been until the day before — an employee of Sinclair, vice-president of a subsidiary of Sinclair's oil company. His sudden termination of the connection had been, he said, of his own accord; he had resigned because of a remark that had been made to him by another Sinclair employee. Sinclair's confidential secretary, G. D. Wahlberg — so young Roosevelt stated — had hinted to him that "somebody might have lent Mr. Fall money," and had mentioned a payment of $68,000 to the foreman of Fall's ranch.

Next day Wahlberg appeared on the stand. It was true, he said, he had talked with young Roosevelt about Fall and Sinclair. But he denied ever having mentioned $68,000. Roosevelt had misunderstood him. He had spoken about "six to eight cows" — not "sixty-eight thous'."

The incident, at the time, led to not much more than expressions of cynicism about the accuracy of Mr. Wahlberg's enunciation, coupled with smiles at young Mr. Roosevelt's panic over an innocent association with sin.

But some of the statements about Fall's new affluence were more convincing. From the treasurer of Fall's county in New Mexico came information, later put in affidavit form, that in 1922 Fall had paid the back taxes on his ranch, some of them in arrears for ten years. From neighbors of Fall in New Mexico came information that he had bought a ranch adjoining his own for $91,500, and other land costing $33,000, and had installed a $40,000 electric light and power plant on his ranch, and made other expenditures, for repairs to buildings, new construction, fencing, and the like, the whole approximating an outlay of $175,000.

XIII

Fall Explains

To Walsh and his committee, $175,000 seemed a good deal of money; under the circumstances, they judged, the source of it should be cleared up. They wrote to Fall, who was then at his ranch in New Mexico.

Fall made no immediate reply. Friends told him he must reply, for the sake of his own reputation, and that

of the administration of which he had been a part. Fall
wired from New Mexico that his son-in-law would go
to Washington. The son-in-law did not appear. Presently Fall began a lagging and reluctant journey in the
direction of Washington. Newspapers reported him in
Chicago, in New York, at Atlantic City. Finally he
reached Washington, went to the Wardman Park Hotel
and stayed there.

His health, he said in reply to the committee's request for his appearance, was such that he must remain
quietly in bed. He did, however, prepare and send[26a] to
the committee a long letter.

"It is difficult," Fall began, "for me to understand
the theory upon which this evidence [concerning his
private finances] has been adduced."

But . . . the gentleman from whom I obtained it [$100,000]
and who furnished me the cash was the Hon. Edward B.
McLean of Washington, D. C. . . . It should be needless for
me to say that in the purchase of the Harris ranch or in any
other purchase or expenditure I have never approached E. L.
Doheny or any one connected with him or any of his corporations, or Mr. H. F. Sinclair or any one connected with him or
any of his corporations; nor have I ever received from either
of said parties one cent on account of any oil lease or upon
any other account whatsoever. . . .
I shall go into no further details in discussing this matter.
The entire subject, of course, is more or less humiliating even
to refer to.

XIV

The Scion of a Brief American Dynasty

To Washington, Fall's statement about the source of
his funds seemed completely convincing. It was the sort
of explanation that might have occurred to any one, but
which, once mentioned, carried the conviction of complete naturalness.

[26a] December 26, 1923.

McLean was a well-known Washington figure, somewhat better known to that portion of the city that went to the race-track than to the Y. M. C. A. He and Fall, in spite of a great difference in age, were friends, cronies, and often seen together. Their intimacy was re-enforced by the intimacy both had had with Harding — both were among the most frequent participants in the White House bridge and poker parties that were Harding's principal evening diversion. If Fall was in difficulties, McLean would be likely to help him, not only because he was McLean's friend but also because he was Harding's. If Fall needed money, it would be natural for him to ask it of McLean; and it would have been natural for McLean to lend it. Both natural and possible. McLean was very rich, and, by streaks, open-handed. His wealth he had inherited — much of Washington thought that if he had not inherited it he probably would not have it.

Edward Beale McLean was the second generation of one of those brief American dynasties that arose between the Civil War and the end of the century. His father, John R. McLean, was the familiar type, a strong man, with ability and character of the sort that forceful men and rough men understand. He had started in Cincinnati, had owned the *Enquirer* there and had made it extremely profitable. He had become powerful in Ohio and national Democratic politics; during the 1880's and 1890's he was occasionally mentioned as a possibility for the Vice-Presidential nomination on the Democratic ticket. He had marched on Washington, bought the Washington *Post*, and projected himself into forms of money-making which at that time went with power in politics and ownership of a leading newspaper. He had become a principal owner in the gas company, the street railway company, the leading bank and the leading trust company. He built a house covering half a city block. A horse-and-carriage journey outside the city he built a great country palace, called "Friendship,"

From a photograph by Underwood & Underwood.

The wife of Edward B. McLean, Mrs. Evelyn Walsh McLean, wearing the "Hope" diamond.

where, about the turn of the century, he entertained the great in politics and finance. All this, when he came to die, he left to his only child, not directly, but in the custody of a trust company, and carefully surrounded with conditions which suggested he may have apprehended that his son might turn out to be less competent in guarding against the dissipation of the fortune than the father had been in acquiring it.

Young McLean had acquired much of his knowledge

of life in quarters less sheltered than schools; he had never gone to college and in Washington, as a young man, had acquired a reputation more extensive than conventional. He seemed to have suffered more than usually from the handicaps that sometimes attend a rich man's only child. After his father's death, he tried to get control of his inheritance, and his effort had ended in a compromise by which he was permitted to be a co-trustee, and to have charge of the two newspapers, and of the rest of his fortune, under the scrutinizing eyes of a considerable retinue of lawyers, bankers, business managers, confidential personal employees and other mentors. Upon his marriage to the heiress of a fortune as great as his own, and as new, his wedding present to his bride was the "Hope Diamond," a gem with a history bizarre in proportion to its size and cost; the legends associated with it made it a standard topic for page-stories in Sunday newspapers; one of the legends said that ownership of it was accompanied by bad luck. (In later years McLean had occasion to remember that legend.) With marriage, young McLean became less unconventional, gave more work to his newspaper properties and took pride in them. Washington thought of him as trying earnestly, according to his lights, to live up to the responsibilities attending ownership of great newspapers. His ownership of the Cincinnati *Enquirer* brought him into association with Warren Harding as a Senator; McLean became one of the most intimate of the coterie that included the Ohioan. Since Harding's elevation to the Presidency, McLean was higher in prestige and in the esteem of the community than he had ever been.

In short, Washington felt young McLean was just the kind of person who would be likely to lend Fall $100,-000. Every one, when he heard Fall's explanation, said, "Ah, of course," and thought the mystery of Fall's funds completely ended.

When Walsh seemed disposed to pursue it further, much of Washington thought him obsessed, a reformer become fanatic. Throughout the country the oil investigation as a spectacle teetered toward the status of comedy; in the newspapers there was a trace of jeering.

Walsh, however, went quietly on. Having lived with the oil scandals a year and eight months, he knew or could infer more than he was able, as yet, to get into the record; he could, moreover, sense things from the attitude and manner of men whose tongues were evasive, or silent.

XV

A Young Man with the Jitters

McLean, when he was named by Fall as the source of Fall's funds, was at Palm Beach, Florida. It was obvious he might be summoned before the committee to confirm Fall's statement. McLean did not wait for a subpoena. But neither did he come forward to testify. On the contrary he became instantly and extremely active in forestalling a subpoena. Before Walsh could issue a formal summons, McLean began bombarding the committee with requests that he be excused from appearing. He sent the committee a statement saying "I loaned Fall $100,000 on his personal note in 1921. . . ." This statement he repeated in many communications. But he begged that he be excused from appearing personally before the committee, as "it would be very difficult for him to come to Washington." He said his health was not good. He sent a lawyer to the committee, a Democratic lawyer,[27] presumed to be agreeable

27 A. Mitchell Palmer.

to Walsh, to ask that the committee accept a statement from him, a disposition if necessary — anything to relieve him from appearing in person. He sent a second lawyer,[28] one of his regular staff. He sent a statement from his physician. In message after message he stated formally that "I loaned Fall $100,000 . . ." but asked that the committee excuse him from appearing before it because of his health. He was very sick, he was extremely sick, he had "severe sinus trouble." Besides, his wife was sick, too. He was willing to state, and repeat, and to promise to amplify in an affidavit, that "I loaned Fall $100,000." But he did not wish to appear personally before the committee. McLean's messages to the committee, and the formal appearances of his lawyers, were public and were entered on the committee's proceedings.

To Washington, all this was not necessarily suspicious. McLean was a strange person with many queer traits; Washington could well understand that he might be thrown into a panic by the mere prospect of having to appear before any kind of committee in any circumstances.

Walsh knew, however, as the public did not, that McLean, in addition to his open and formal efforts to avoid cross-examination, was in secret feverishly pulling wires. Walsh instinctively felt that some of the Senators who approached him in the interest of "Poor Ned's Health" had been inspired to it by McLean. Furtively as well as openly, McLean was as energetic as only a badly scared man can be. He kept the telegraph wires to Washington busy with appeals to his friends. He got in touch with prominent Democrats he knew, and asked them to help him get immunity, told them that "my doctor here informs me on account of my health it will be impossible

[28] Wilton J. Lambert.

for me to go to a Northern climate until spring." [29] He asked the editor of his Washington newspaper to see Senators who might influence the committee to grant him immunity. He kept several secretaries and members of his newspaper staff busy informing him about the progress of the case and the probability of his being called, and the actions and plans of Walsh. He had them send him scores of telegrams every night. Most of the telegrams were in code.

XVI

To Walsh it was quite apparent that McLean, whether sick or not, was extremely scared, was extremely loath to endure cross-examination. He decided that if McLean could not come to Washington, he, Walsh would go to Florida. He had himself appointed a one-man sub-committee, packed his modest grip, and took the train to Palm Beach.

As Walsh lay in his berth in the train rolling Southward, there passed along the wires overhead a telegram to McLean, sent by one of his secretaries at Washington. It was in code; it read:

WASHINGTON, D. C., JANUARY 9, 1924
EDWARD B. McLEAN, PALM BEACH, FLORIDA:
JAGUAR BAPTISTICAL STOWAGE BEADLE 1235 HUFF
COMMENSAL FITFUL LAMBERT CONATION FE-
CUND HYBRIDIZE.[30] W. O. D.

Walsh, arriving at Palm Beach, went to McLean's house. There—

Senator Walsh — Mr. McLean, did you loan $100,000 to Mr. Fall?
Mr. McLean — I did, yes, sir, in checks.
Senator Walsh — Whose checks?
Mr. McLean — My own checks.

29 Telegram to Francis McAdoo.
30 The translation of this telegram will be found on page 314.

Senator Walsh — Drawn on what bank?

Mr. McLean — Drawn, to the best of my recollection, on the Federal, the Commercial — and there might have been a smaller one drawn on one other third bank which was a very small amount.

Senator Walsh — Have you got the checks?

Mr. McLean — I do not think so — I am not positive.

Senator Walsh — Were they returned? What became of them?

Mr. McLean — Senator Fall returned them to me.

The next question Walsh asked is proof that he knew[31] what he was going to find. McLean's answer, that "Fall returned them to me" had been extraordinary — when one man gives checks to another, they do not come back from the beneficiary; they go through the bank and it is the bank that returns them to the maker. McLean's answer was astonishing, but had Walsh been astonished by it his next question would have expressed surprise and mystification. But what Walsh asked, calmly, was:

Senator Walsh — When?

Mr. McLean — In the last part of December, 1921, sir — the last week — I am not positive as to date.

Seantor Walsh — They never did go through the bank?

Mr. McLean — No, sir.

Senator Walsh — So that so far as you are concerned you did not give him any cash?

Mr. McLean — Cash? No, sir.

That answer was the first climactic sensation of the oil scandal. McLean had given no money to Fall. So far as anything about money had occurred between Fall and McLean, McLean had given checks to Fall and

---

[31] Ex-Senator Irvine L. Lenroot, who was Chairman of the Committee that investigated the oil scandals, having read the proof of this chapter, wrote me: "When Walsh went to Palm Beach to take McLean's deposition, it was not a blind guess. Walsh had received what he thought was fairly accurate information that at the time McLean said he gave Fall the hundred thousand dollars he, McLean, did not have anything like that amount on deposit in the banks in Washington."

Fall had returned them without using them. Many wondered if, indeed, even that much had occurred. Washington and the country buzzed with surmise.[32] Had

*From a photograph
by Underwood & Underwood.*

*From a photograph
by Underwood & Underwood.*

Senator Walsh on his trip to Palm Beach, Florida, to extract unwilling testimony from an oil scandal witness.

Edward B. McLean, an oil scandal witness who contributed involuntary comedy.

Fall made his statement about McLean without consulting the latter? Had McLean generously undertaken to "go down the line" for Fall — and then got cold feet

[32] Subsequent testimony showed that McLean's story was quite true, that Fall had asked him for the money, that McLean had given Fall the checks, and that Fall, a few days afterward had returned them, telling McLean he was getting the money from another source.

when he faced the pitilessly cold eyes and pitilessly cold
mind of Thomas J. Walsh? The sophisticated reflected
that to lie for a friend might have been within Mc-
Lean's code — but to commit perjury and obstruct justice might send a man to jail.

In any or all events, it was certain Fall had lied. He
had not received $100,000 from Edward B. McLean.
He must have received it from some one else. And the
some one else must be one whose name Fall dared not
reveal. Fall had lied in order to conceal the real source
of his affluence.

XVII

After Walsh returned to Washington, and after Mc-
Lean's health improved — he now had no reason to continue to be sick — Walsh brought him to Washington
and put him on the stand. But first Walsh read into the
record the code telegram that had been sent to McLean
in Florida by one of his secretaries in Washington on
the night Walsh was on his way to examine McLean:

WASHINGTON, D. C., JANUARY 9, 1924
EDWARD B. McLEAN, PALM BEACH, FLORIDA:
JAGUAR BAPTISTICAL STOWAGE BEADLE 1235
HUFF COMMENSAL FITFUL LAMBERT CONATION
FECUND HYBRIDIZE.
                                         W. O. D.

Decoded, that message revealed the minuteness, even
if it did not conceal the ineptness of McLean's amateur
secret service:

WALSH LEAVES COASTLINE TONIGHT 12:35 IN-
STEAD OF SEABOARD. LAMBERT ON SAME TRAIN.
                                         W. O. D.

One wonders by what aptness of accident Walsh became, in the code, "Jaguar." It was a fit word for the
beginning of such a message. For to the miserable Mc-

Lean the message, understood in the light of the circumstances, as McLean understood it only too well,
meant that: Thomas J. Walsh, head of the investigating
committee, leaves tonight 12:35 by the Atlantic Coast
Line to put you under oath and interrogate you on Fall's
statement that you loaned him $100,000; but be of
good cheer, Lambert [one of McLean's many lawyers]
is on the same train.

Walsh then read into the record all the other telegrams
that had passed to and from McLean in Florida when
the latter had been trying frantically to avoid testifying.
There were hundreds of them.

McLean was a lavish user of the telegraph at all
times, and when jittery about being called before the
committee he kept the wires hot. There were scores of
messages to and from his secretaries, his employees on
The Post, his lawyers, friends who might help.

Most of the messages were in code, indeed, in three
different codes. Walsh subpoenaed the chief of the code
section of the Chief Signal Officer of the War Department and set him to work. Thereby was the public given
an extraordinary peep into the intimacies of a rich play-
boy with the jitters; and of his employees eager to calm
him, to please and flatter him, to commend themselves
to him by sending assurances of his safety, and of their
diligence in lobbying to save him from going on the
stand, together with cheering messages from friends in
public life and miscellaneous gossip, the whole assuringly
interspersed with expressions of their admiration, loyalty
and encouragement, which were not the less warming
when clothed in such uncouthnesses as "opague," "bolog"
and "bial."

As the coded messages and the translations of them
emerged serially in the newspapers a national smile

spread from Passamaquoddy Bay to the Gulf of California. At first millions of brows furrowed, then millions of faces grinned, at such cryptic confidences as:

HAXPW SENT OVER BY BONKA AND HOUSEHOLDER BONKA SULTRY TKVOUEP PROZOICS SEPIC BEPELT GOAL HOCUSING THIS POUTED PROPONENT.

The names which the codes gave to prominent men had the humor of grotesqueness. McLean himself was TKVOUEP, which would seem sufficiently to conceal any one. Walsh, after being a ferocious "Jaguar" in the menagerie code, was in another WYCGO. Lawyer Lambert was WFGE. Attorney General Daugherty was SONATONE; one of his messages sent to McLean through his secretary said, "Tell Ned not to worry." In one code, Fall was "Officialize," in another, the horticultural code, he was "Apples." Other public men were "Peaches," "Prunes," "Cherries," and "Apricots." But no power of Walsh's probing, and no diligence of his decoders, was able to discover to whom those charming designations referred.

The editor of The Washington *Post* was "the Count," McLean's secretary was "the duck." McLean himself was "the chieftain" — described in one passionate tribute from an emotional employee as the "beleaguered chieftain."

XVIII

McLean Testifies as Much as He Can

To explain the whole thing, or as much of it as he could grasp or remember after such tenseness of trouble as he had been through, McLean himself was put on the stand. He repeated what he had said from the beginning, that he had given Fall checks for $100,000 and that Fall had returned them unused. His repetition was convincing; even Walsh was convinced, though at the beginning he had been skeptical. Aside from that, the sum of McLean's contribution of enlightenment was that "I don't know what on earth the whole thing is about."

And the truth is, he didn't. His ignorance, and his candor, saved him, caused the committee and the country to warm toward him. He told Walsh yes that Fall had asked him to deceive the committee, but that he had said to Fall, when the situation became tense, "Albert, this thing has gone as far as it can go; I have gone down the line for you; I have done everything, but it has come to the point where I have got to tell the truth."

Walsh asked him a few questions, but—

I'll be goldarned if I know, Senator, but I am telling you the absolute truth . . . Senator, so help me God, I don't know . . . I have read so many of these telegrams my head is dizzy, Senator, trying to figure them out . . . Senator, I'll be doggoned if I know what the trouble was . . .

Senator, I was trying to go down the line as far as I could for a friend. I have never done a dishonest thing in my life, financially. I have never had anything to do with this darned Teapot Dome thing. That is really the truth, Senator. You can decode telegrams, you can look through them for the next year, and you can never find anything dishonest I have done.

Walsh believed him fully, and smiled; the committee smiled, Washington smiled, the country smiled — all with friendliness. They recognized that McLean was a "boob," a "dub," [33] but that he had had no sinister part in the oil scandal. In his simplicity he was rather en-

[33] "It may seem extraordinary to describe the owner of the Washington *Post* and the Cincinnati *Enquirer* as a 'dub' of such degree of 'dubship' as his present predicament implies, but it must be remembered that Mr. McLean acquired these two newspapers as an inheritance from his father. Most persons in the newspaper business are of the opinion that if young Mr. McLean hadn't inherited them he wouldn't have them." — Mark Sullivan, New York *Tribune,* March, 1924.

gaging; the country regarded him as a generous contributor of comic relief to a drama otherwise, so far, almost too tense for the national nerves. In the parade of extraordinary characters that the oil scandal threw on the national screen, McLean was the unintending and unwilling antic.

XIX

On the night of the day McLean admitted he was not the source of Fall's $100,000, humming telegraph wires carried the latest development to every city and town; newspaper headlines blared it. Many read it with fascinated interest; of them all, few with as much interest as an inconspicuous little old man with mild blue eyes and a drooping white moustache who lived in Los Angeles.

Edward L. Doheny, after brooding for some two weeks, went to see his lawyer. He went for the purpose with which many men seek lawyers, for peace of mind — lawyers are consulted for sleeplessness as often as doctors. Doheny's lawyer was a big-framed, burry-voiced, very able Scotchman named Gavin McNab; his pronunciation of his name, "Gahvin Mucknob" carried a suggestion of the combination of force and charm that made him one of the great lawyers of his generation.

McNab told Doheny he must go to Washington, at once, by the quickest possible route. Doheny said he would not go without first telling Fall what he was going to do. Long distance telephones buzzed with inquiries for Fall's whereabouts, inquiries discreetly phrased to say no more than merely that Doheny wanted to see him — the grim matter now afoot was not for the ears of telephone operators. Fall was located in New Orleans — he had reached the point of spiritual disintegration where he seemed to be aimlessly wandering about the country.

Doheny, accompanied by McNab, left for Washington, by way of New Orleans. At New Orleans they went to see Fall. They told Fall — MacNab did most of the telling, Doheny really liked Fall and could not be harsh with him — that he, Fall, must go before the Senate committee and tell the true source of the money. Fall said he would think about it. Doheny and McNab waited a day. They could get no answer from Fall; first he would and then he wouldn't; what with despair and desperation Fall was incapable of acting rationally.

XX

Doheny

Doheny and McNab went on to Washington. McNab, going before the Committee, asked for his client the privilege of appearing as a voluntary witness. That was the most dramatic event, so far, in the oil investigation.[34]

As the news flew out that Doheny had asked the committee for permission to make a voluntary statement, Washington speculated eagerly about what would develop and reviewed what it knew of Doheny. Doheny had been in Washington during the War and after, and all that Washington knew of him was creditable. He was a millionaire many times over and he had come up from a very lean youth, but he was no "coal-oil Johnny." [35] As between Doheny and Sinclair — there was no connection between them and the association of both with Fall and the oil scandal was mere accident — as

[34] January 24, 1924.
[35] "Coal-oil Johnny" was the name given in the 1860's and 70's to rough men who struck oil, or on whose farms oil was found, in the early days in Pennsylvania when oil was called "coal oil," and who became extravagant spenders.

between the two, it was Sinclair who lived up to the picture of the new rich. But Doheny — "If you should meet Doheny and talk with him and did not know his background," wrote a journalist[36] of that day, "you might think he was a professor of philosophy at some small backwater college." He was distinctly a man of thought, with enthusiasm for ideas. Though he had had little formal education, he liked to talk with scholars, with men of talent. "What he had to say about his own experiences was interesting and colorful; what he had to say about the abstractions of human life was stimulating. . . . Russia about that time, and its adventure in a new form of society was much in the public mind, and Doheny, in his dinner-table conversations with friends, would set out with clarity and force the various theories of society. He spoke of the democratic form as being like a tight-rope, with Socialism on one side and the extreme individualism of anarchy on the other; he used to talk of the difficulty of maintaining a balance between them, and of the duty of thoughtful men not to fall on one side or the other.

"Doheny had spent most of his formative years, not in schools, but as a lonely, grub-staked, poverty-stricken wanderer on the desert. Doubtless it was in the quiet of those lonely days and nights that he became a man of reflection. For twenty years he prospected for gold and silver. Then he turned to oil, and found it in several places in our own Southwest and Mexico. He found one spot where a well poured forth upward of two thousand barrels of oil every hour for months and years. After he found his oil he organized his companies with business skill. All his energies were in those companies. He cast away none of his vitality in dissipation; hardly did he give any time to recreation. At no time was he a new-

[36] Mark Sullivan.

rich splurger. He built a fine home in California, but aside from that he lived simply. He was utterly unostentatious. He seemed neither to care for money for the sake of keeping it, nor for the sake of ostentatious display. He made some gifts to technological schools. He seemed a kindly, simple, modest man of intellectual tastes."

XXI

Doheny Admits

That was the picture of Doheny that Washington had, and the country also, so far as the country knew much about him. Now he was asking to be heard as a voluntary witness in what everybody felt by this time must be a colossal scandal:

Walsh — I asked the Committee to meet this afternoon because I was informed that Mr. Doheny desired to come before the committee to make a statement. If he is present we would like to have him now.

Mr. Doheny (who stands up in the crowded room)—All right.

Doheny had a prepared statement which he asked the Committee's permission to read:

I wish to state to the Committee and to the public the full facts. . . . [37]

I regret that when I was before your Committee I did not tell you what I am now telling you. When asked by your chairman whether Mr. Fall had profited by the contract, directly or indirectly, I answered in the negative. That answer I now reiterate.

I wish first to inform the committee that on the 30th of November, 1921, I loaned to Albert B. Fall $100,000 upon his promissory note to enable him to purchase a ranch in New Mexico. This sum was loaned to Mr. Fall by me personally. It was my own money and did not belong in whole or in part

[37] Throughout this history, the appearance of three periods thus: . . . in a quotation means that part or parts of the quotation has been omitted.

to any oil company with which I am connected. In connection with this loan there was no discussion between Mr. Fall and myself as to any [oil] contract whatever. It was a personal loan to a lifelong friend. We had been friends for more than thirty years. Mr. Fall had invested his savings for those years in his home ranch in New Mexico, which I understand was all that remained to him after the failure of mining investments in Mexico and nine years of public service in Washington, during which he could not properly attend to the management of his ranch. His troubles had been increased in 1918 by the death of his daughter and his son, who up to then had taken his place in the management of his ranch. In our frequent talks it was clear that the acquisition of a neighborhood property controlling the water that flows through his home ranch was a hope of his amounting to an obsession. His failure to raise the necessary funds by realizing on his extensive and once valuable Mexican mine holdings had made him feel that he was a victim of an untoward fate. In one of these talks I indicated to him that I would be willing to make him the loan, and this seemed to relieve his mind greatly. In the autumn of 1921 he told me that the purchase had become possible, that the time had arrived when he was ready to take advantage of my offer to make the loan. . . .

Following the reading of his statement, Doheny was questioned:

Walsh — How were the negotiations carried on?

Doheny — By telephone. He [Fall] telephoned me he was ready to receive that loan if I was still prepared to make it, as I had proposed to do some time earlier than that. If you will bear with me I will tell you something about the conditions that led up to the making of the proposal. I had known Senator Fall for about thirty years or more. We had been old-time friends. We both worked in the same mining district in New Mexico in 1885. In those days the Indian troubles were still on the country, and we were bound together by the same ties that men usually are, especially after they leave camp where they have lived under trying circumstances and conditions. Sometimes when men are in camp where their conditions are hard, and where the struggle for a living is precarious and the danger from Indians is bad, they do not have such a very great feeling for each other; but after they leave there they become warmer friends by reason of having associated under the same conditions.

Furthermore, I studied law at the same time that Senator Fall did. I practiced for a short time in the same district that he did. I watched his career all through the development of it, as district attorney, judge, and United States Senator. I was very much interested in him on account of our old associations. I, myself, followed prospecting. I was fortunate, and when he was telling me about his misfortunes, and at a time when it was coupled with his misfortune of having to bear the loss of his two children — two grown children — I felt greatly in sympathy with him. He was telling me about his hope of acquiring this ranch, and being of an impulsive nature I said to him, "Whenever you need some money to pay for the ranch I will lend it to you."

He said something about giving the ranch as security. I said, "I will lend it to you on your note. You do not need to give the ranch as security."

That relieved Senator Fall greatly. Later on he telephoned to me that the time had come when the ranch could be purchased. When he telephoned to me about it I sent him the money. I sent it to him right away, I think the next day, or within a couple of days.

Walsh — How did you transmit the money to him?

Doheny — In cash.

Walsh — How did you transport the cash?

Doheny — In a satchel. The cash was put up in a regular bank bundle, and taken over and delivered to him.

Walsh — Who acted as your messenger in that matter?

Doheny — My son. . . .

Walsh — You are a man of large affairs, and of great business transactions, so that it was not unusual for you to have large money transactions, perhaps, but it was, was it not, an extraordinary way of remitting money?

Doheny — I do not know about that. I will say that I think I have remitted more than a million dollars in that way in the last five years. . . . In making the decision to lend this money to Mr. Fall, I was greatly affected by his extreme pecuniary circumstances, which resulted, of course, from a long period, a lifetime of futile efforts. I realized that the amount of money I was loaning him was a bagatelle to me; that it was no more than $25 or $50 perhaps to the ordinary individual. Certainly a loan of $25 or $50 from one individual to another would not be considered at all extraordinary, and a loan of $100,000 from me to Mr. Fall is no more extraordinary.

Walsh — I can appreciate that on your side, but looking at it from Senator Fall's side it was quite a loan.

Later in his testimony Doheny remarked: "There is nothing extraordinary about me; I am just an ordinary, old-time, impulsive, irresponsible, improvident sort of a prospector."

Doheny was asked whether he considered there was any impropriety in loaning "money to an officer of the Government with whom you had very large business transactions."

Doheny — No, sir, it did not. And it does not now, Senator, with all due respect to your question. If I were limited in my lendings of money to people with whom I had no connection I would have to hunt up some agent to find objects of charity to give it to. I do not lend any money to anybody except those I am associated with and that I know through old friend-ship. I have an army of old prospectors, nearly every name on the calendar that are hunting around in my place to get money from me. They do not get it because they are entitled to it, because they have anything I am after; they get it be-cause of old friendship. And I lend money in quantities that would surprise some of you gentlemen here if you knew it and that $100,000 I loaned to Mr. Fall at that time was not an extraordinary thing at all to me.

Walsh asked Doheny about the note Fall had given him in exchange for the loan of $100,000:

Walsh — Where is the note now?
Doheny — It is at home. I looked for it the day I started over here, but it was impossible to locate it, and there was a question between my wife and myself whether it was in New York, in my private box, or in Los Angeles. We came to the conclusion that it was in New York, so we gave up looking for it at home, and I decided to look for it in New York, when I get there tomorrow or next day. . . .

Some of the investigating committee asked questions which implied skepticism on their part about Doheny's having any note from Fall. Doheny said he believed the note was in his New York office, said he would search for it on going to New York the next day, and that if

he could find it he would produce it at a subsequent
meeting of the committee.

Six days later[38] Doheny returned with the note. He
had only part of it — Fall's signature had been torn off.
Doheny explained:

I came today prepared to make a statement with regard to
the note which I got from Mr. Fall when I loaned him the

Photograph by United.

A $100,000 Scrap of Paper.

Albert B. Fall's note to Edward Doheny. The signature was torn off according
to Doheny so that in case of his death his executors could not press Mr. Fall
for payment. Doheny later produced the signature.

$100,000. I brought with me all of that note that is in my pos-
session at the present time. I had the entire note in my possession in December, 1921, and my wife and I on the eve of our
departure for California were going through some papers and
I found this note in my pocketbook. I remarked to her that
inasmuch as I had made this loan to Mr. Fall to help him out
of a difficulty, it would not much help him out of a difficulty if
anything happened to us and the note became the property of
executors; it would mean that he would be pressed upon for the
payment of it, and that the note instead of being a service to
him would be an injury. So I divided the note into two parts.
I gave her one part to keep, and I have the other part here to
present to the committee. . . . The remainder of the note, I
believe, is in California, in Los Angeles. I searched for it in
New York, but I failed to find it there. I went to the private
box that Mrs. Doheny and I have access to, and in which we

[38] February 1, 1924.

keep such papers as that, and the fragment was not there. . . . With the entire note in the possession of my family, whenever we wanted to collect the note we had the note to show that the money was due on the note, but if it should happen to go into the hands of our executors, in case something happened to us, they would not be able to press Mr. Fall and make the loan an injury instead of a help to him. . . . If anything happened to us the two fragments of the note would still remain in our possession, wherever we were with our bodies, if we were in a railroad wreck, and our heirs, my son, would have gotten hold of the pieces and he would have known what they meant, but executors wouldn't; they would force payment of the note upon Mr. Fall. My son knew that the note was given for the money, and he knew it was Mr. Fall's intention to pay the note, and we believed that he could get a new note from Mr. Fall by asking for it. That is what is in my mind.

Senator Pittman of the committee became harsh with Doheny, accused him of not having been frank on his previous appearance before the committee.

Senator Pittman — You did not tell the whole truth, did you?

Doheny — Are you trying to get me to admit that I lied about it? Because there is no use; if I lied about it, I lied about it. I don't need to admit it to you. It is in the evidence, whatever I said, and my admitting it doesn't make any difference.

Pittman — I was trying to see if you are as innocent as you are pretending to be.

Doheny — Well, I am quite sure that when I was here before, Mr. Pittman, that you were going to be disappointed when I produced the note.

Pittman — I have no doubt about it. I want to read a little of that examination to show how disappointed I am.

Doheny — Yes, sir.

Pittman — I tried to make it very plain to you, Mr. Doheny ——

(Doheny (interposing) — That you didn't believe me.

Pittman — Yes.

Doheny — And you did make it very plain to me that you didn't believe me.

Pittman — Yes, I did. . . . It was known that this committee was suspicious about the very existence of a note. . . .

Doheny — My dear sir, I am not here attempting to answer

questions as to whether I told the truth or not. I am here to answer questions as to the note I received from this loan, and that is no evidence before this committee as to whether I told the truth or not. I told the truth then as I saw it, and I tell the truth now as I see it. I have got the note Fall gave for that loan, if it is in fact a note without the signature. I had that with me when I was before the committee before. I didn't produce it at that time because I thought I could produce a note in the form that would allay suspicion. I could not produce the whole note until I got back to California, if I can at all, so I produced what I have got for what good it will do. . . . It is the note for what I loaned him; that is all there is to it. All your questions cannot make me admit that I perjured myself.

(Subsequently, in one of the lawsuits that arose out of the oil investigation, Doheny produced the missing signature of Fall that made the note whole.)

XXII

On the night of the day this testimony was made public Fall arrived in Washington. To reporters he said only: "I am a very sick man." The next day a subpoena was served on him. February 2, Fall faced the committee. That was one of the most tragic spectacles Washington ever saw, a former Senator appearing before his former associates under what amounted to a charge of crime; a former Cabinet-officer already plainly guilty of a lie and by all appearances guilty of having accepted a bribe.

Fall entered the committee room piloted by Senate attendants who elbowed a path through the dense mass of avid spectators that overflowed the room, crowded the doorway, and milled in the corridor. He leaned on a cane — in his best days he had carried one, but then jauntily, as an ornament for virility; now it was a support for feebleness. His blue serge suit was creased and baggy, the outer surface of inner demoralization. As he approached the witness-chair, he almost tottered; all the lines of his features and figure bent downward, the bars of his gold-framed spectacles made a downward

From a photograph by Underwood & Underwood.

Former Secretary of the Interior Albert B. Fall and his wife at the opening of his trial.

line from his ears to his eyes; the ends of his mouth drooped, his cheeks hung limp, everything about him sagged. Around him his lawyer bustled, almost as much nurse as lawyer. Pulling himself together for a moment Fall read, in a voice that was clear enough but totally

without resonance, a statement that his lawyer had prepared. With the opening words every Senator and lawyer recognized the words of the traditional legal form
and knew what it signified:

I decline . . . to answer any questions, on the ground that
it may tend to incriminate me, and on the further ground . . .

Concluding, he did not look at his fellow Senators or
at any one else. Eyes looking downward, he turned,
took the arm of his lawyer and moved slowly toward
the door. The crowd, turning to watch him, was so
silent that the tapping of his cane could be heard as,
with shuffling feet, he moved slowly down the corridor.

XXIII

Walsh said — and who could know better — that
"it was Fall's parading of his new-found wealth among
his neighbors in New Mexico that led to the exposure." [39]
That was not only the immediate cause of his exposure, it was a clue to the remoter and fundamental
cause of his tragedy. Not that Fall was specially ostentatious. But his whole personality was a curious combination of façade that seemed one thing and reality
that was another. He was a synthesis of integrated os-
tensibles. He was ostensibly a rich man, but actually
not; he was ostensibly courageous but actually a coward;
ostensibly he seemed a man with an exceptional code of
pride, including what is commonly called honor, but
actually he was a liar.
The ostensible part of him, the façade, was convincing. Men who for six years sat beside him in the Senate,
and lounged beside him in the cloak-room, exceptionally
shrewd and worldly men whose careers in politics had de-

39 Thomas J. Walsh, New York *Times*, February 10, 1924.

pended in large part on their insight into other men, had
taken Fall as what he appeared to be. Some of the ablest
men in America, who for two years had sat 'round the
table with him twice a week at Harding's Cabinet meet-

From a photograph © by Underwood & Underwood.

Two "old prospectors," Albert B. Fall on the reader's left and Edward L. Doheny
on the right, with their lawyer, Frank J. Hogan, taken at the time of
the trial of Fall and Doheny.

ings, accepted him at the valuation that seemed to go
with his exterior. Perhaps the reason they were misled
was that by reason of his background, the Southwest and
the desert, he was an unfamiliar type. Coming from
New Mexico, wearing the soft felt hat of an older West,
having the mannerisms and locutions of the vanished
frontier, telling stories of early prospecting days, describing[40] himself as "engaged in farming, stock raising
and mining," men thought of him as a survival from the

[40] "Who's Who in America," 1920–1921 and later.

West of the past, and credited him with the glamour and the ruggedness and the code of the pioneer. Perhaps Fall romantically thought of himself as what he was not, and thus became more convincing to others.

His façade had made him; it was his reality that destroyed him. Had he had true pride, he would not have sought or accepted money from Doheny to parade in false pride as a lord of lands and herds. Had he had courage he would not, when exposure threatened, have told the lie about getting it from McLean, but would have told the truth. And had he told the truth at that time he might have saved himself. Had Fall told the very version that Doheny told later, the picture of two old friends and fellow prospectors, desert bedfellows under blankets spread beneath the stars, of whom one became rich and the other remained poor; and of the Mæcenas wishing to make it easy for his former companion to live in ease and dignity — had Fall told that story, the country might have accepted it, might even have felt sentimental.

XXIV

Partial Picture of a Midas

Up to this point, and indeed through to the end of the long and sorry chapter, it was possible to make a distinction between Fall and Doheny.[41]

As to Fall the condemnation was severe. For him

41 The author of this history, who knew Doheny and liked him, wrote in the New York *Tribune,* February 2, 1924:

"I asked Doheny once, when he was telling his difficulties with the then government of Mexico, why he kept it up — why should he, then sixty-five years of age, stick to the harassments of hustling back and forth from Mexico to Washington, to Los Angeles, to New York, fretting his spirit and wearing himself out to safeguard his corporations? Why should he not "cash in" — for five millions, for ten millions, for twenty millions, for whatever it might be, and enjoy the ease and reflection for which apparently his temperament and his habit of thought fitted him? He merely smiled and said something about obligations of loyalty to associates whose prosperity was bound up with his.

"One wonders if he wishes now that he had retired. There is something almost

Washington had no excuse or condonation. He was an experienced public man who knew the law and the proprieties. He had been holding public office at a time when he asked and received $100,000 from a man to whom, in his official capacity, he was about to grant a valuable lease. Also, Fall had lied about the money, had said he got it from one man and later admitted he did not get it from that man. Fall had initiated the transaction, had asked for the loan.

As to Doheny, one could see how he might have made the loan on the basis he put it on, namely, that this old friend and companion of his desert prospecting days had said he needed the money and Doheny wanted to let him have it for old times' sake. One could even construct a case for Doheny to the effect that he might have realized the impropriety of what he was doing but might have been too generous, in a sense too manly, to plead impropriety or danger as an excuse for declining to loan the money to an old friend in hard luck who said he needed it.

Some days later when Doheny was on the stand again,

---

pitiful about this old man of sixty-eight rushing up and down the country. One thinks of him not as owning his possessions, but as being owned by them, driven and harassed by them.

"Doheny thought passionately that he had a correct philosophy for the world, but one wonders if he really had a correct one for himself. When you saw him going in and out of the committee room you wondered if he was really as happy as one of the elderly watchmen who read the newspaper at their ease and doze the afternoon away in freedom from care.

"A good deal of Doheny's thought ran in the direction of maintaining democracy and the whole present system of organized society. He dreaded the thing that was being attempted in Russia — dreaded it not so much for the sake of his own possessions, but dreaded it rather as fatal to all that he regarded as being of human good. When Mexico tried an experiment looking in the direction of Communism, Doheny felt it was another menace to civilization.

"And now the ironic fact is that this unostentatious man, who seemed less concerned about money for his personal sake than about individual ownership as a theory of organized society — this man is one of the central figures in a scandal about which it has been said that no propaganda coming out of Russia has done as much to undermine public confidence in government and big business as has the oil scandal."

he forfeited much of the good impression that in the beginning he had made — forfeited it not by any change
in the substance of his story of the relation between himself and Fall, but by a change in his manner — and especially by his woefully unnecessary expansion of his testimony in other fields having no relation to the oil
scandals. Departing from his relation to Fall, which was
the subject of the investigation, he volunteered testimony
about matters quite different.

He was a hot-tempered old gentleman and he had
been made extremely angry by the questions asked him
by Democratic Senators, and by speeches made by Democrats in the Senate, by doubts they raised about his ve-
racity, slurs they put upon him. In his anger he was
willing to hurt himself for the sake of "getting back"
at his Democratic critics. His revenge consisted of testifying that at various times he had prominent Democrats, former members of Wilson's cabinet, on his
pay-roll. He put his employment of them on the worst
possible basis for himself — he seemed to take a per-
verse pleasure in making it look as bad as he could. In
describing the nature of his employment of the Democratic ex-office-holders, the kind of services he expected
from them, he used over and over such bald phrases as
"I paid them for their influence." If some hostile lawyer of great subtley had set out to put the most damaging
possible words into Doheny's mouth, he could not have
done more harm than that. After those later hearings,
Doheny went almost as low in the estimation of Washington as Fall. It was patent that if he wanted to defend
himself, to make out a better case for himself, he could
have described his transactions with the Democratic ex-
Cabinet members and others in such a way as to suggest
no odium either on himself or on the men he employed.
Or he need not have mentioned his employment of

Democrats at all. But he did not take that line. He seemed to exult in making the case seem as bad as possible for the Democrats — and therefore for himself.

Now Doheny's money went through a reverse alchemic transmutation. Having been oil turned into gold, it now became gold turned into oil. Every one touched by it was tarred. It was as if Doheny's gold, transmuted back into oil, was a gusher, drenching all who came near. The investigation became like an immense Dutch windmill; the great fan-blades as they went through their downward arc, dipped into tanks of greasy oil; as they arose they flung the oil in every direction that the wind would take it. Some fell on innocent bystanders. Any one who had ever received a dollar from Doheny felt under the necessity of explanation. Doheny named quite a few, partly in angry resentment at the attacks that Democratic Senators and others had made on him; partly in naïve eagerness to show that big men were associated with him, many of them under obligation to him, employed by him. Doheny, it was apparent, modest in most matters, almost shy, had one marked trait of egotism; he liked to be able to show that he, as a great money-maker, could hire and have around him as subordinates men who had come to distinction in fields where Doheny could not function. He called the roll of them like an ostentatious king giving an inventory of his possessions, like a parvenu art collector calling the roll of his Rembrandts and Van Dyck's.

He got pleasure out of having such men on his payroll, regardless of any exceptional service they could render him, or that Doheny expected. Many of these were Democrats — Doheny had culled the cabinet of Democratic former President Woodrow Wilson when that Administration went out of office; four former

Cabinet members had been retained by him as lawyers,[42] and one other close associate of Wilson, George Creel, in some kind of literary capacity.

XXV

Oil Spatters Everywhere

As the whirling wings of the investigation spattered oil on Democrats, the public and the newspapers, like a crowd at a Roman holiday, shrilled at this unexpected and dramatic addition to the entertainment. The association of the prominent Democrats with Doheny was entirely innocent and regular, had no faintest touch of what was the distinguishing and damning feature in Fall's case, the essential taint, the fact that Fall had been in office when he took money from Doheny, and that Fall could give no service in return except a corrupt one. The Democrats had been employed by Doheny only after they retired from office and upon a basis that no one could impugn. Yet impugnment was feared by them.

To one of them, William G. McAdoo, son-in-law of Wilson and Secretary of the Treasury in Wilson's Cabinet, Doheny's mention of his name was acutely embarrassing, for McAdoo was now a candidate for higher office, was an active and quite promising aspirant for the Democratic Presidential nomination. McAdoo's name, mentioned by Doheny as retained by him for legal services at $25,000 a year, led to newspaper headlines in which "McAdoo" was coupled with the deadly combination "oil" and "money" in a proximity dictated more

---

[42] They were William G. McAdoo, former Secretary of the Treasury; Franklin K. Lane, former Secretary of the Interior; Thomas W. Gregory, former Attorney General; and Lindley M. Garrison, former Secretary of War. Ex-Secretary Garrison denied the allegation and it was later proved that his employment by Doheny had not been direct.

by the enforced brevity of headlines[43] than by meticulous regard for fine shadings of exactness. For twenty-four hours, the most thoughtful politicians and ob-

© *N. Y. "Tribune."*

The First Good Laugh They've Had in Years.

Cartoonist "Ding" satirizes the exhilaration of the Democrats over the oil scandal in the Harding administration.

servers of politics, familiar with the truth, but familiar also with the public atmosphere, thought McAdoo was doomed. Some of his closest friends, and some of the most important figures in the Democratic party, advised him to give up the race. McAdoo, however, tenacious

[43] The headline in The Cincinnati *Times-Star* read, with gross, even if unintended, injustice: "McAdoo received $250,000 from the Doheny interests; was paid $50,000 a year 'on outside' while he was Secretary of the Treasury."

and daring, demanded a hearing before the Committee. He was successful, and retrieved much for himself when he showed that his retainer from Doheny had had nothing to do with the leasing of Naval Oil Reserves. But he lost something when he added that promptly on reading Doheny's story of his loan to Fall he had severed all connections with the man who for years had been paying him a handsome retainer. Persons who looked at the matter from the standpoint of human relations felt that right now, when Doheny was in a desperate situation, was no time for one of his lawyers to quit him.

McAdoo's testimony cleared him utterly of taint;[44] but it is not certain the explanation headlines ever caught up with the accusatory ones; the incident may have accounted for the comparatively small margin of which McAdoo missed the Democratic Presidential nomination of 1924.

Sheer mirth attended the case of another of Doheny's employees, the emotional and spectacular former Chairman of Wilson's wartime committee on Public Information, George Creel. Creel, demanding to be heard, testified that he had been in Doheny's employ three months and had then resigned. Doheny, he said, "had the clearest blue eyes I ever saw, the most childlike

---

[44] A contemporary despatch, written by the author of this history and published in the New York *Tribune,* February 11, 1924, states:

"William Gibbs McAdoo did very well for himself at his appearance today before the Senate Committee. . . . As his tall form entered the door, his face turned as if instinctively not toward the committee but toward the crowd. In response to Mr. McAdoo's friendly glances toward the audience, it applauded. It had been completely realized that however inexpedient McAdoo's relationship to Doheny was in a political sense, and however it affected his political availability for the Democratic nomination, it was entirely blameless in his rôle of man and lawyer. Senator Lenroot had the air of almost apologizing on behalf of the committee for having drawn Mr. McAdoo into the matter. Lenroot asked McAdoo if the latter did not think the committee was obliged to do what it did. McAdoo replied courteously that of course the committee could not have done otherwise. McAdoo as a man and as a lawyer cleared himself beyond any doubt."

candor, and he fascinated me to a point where I really wanted to write his life as a textbook." However, this good opinion of his patron did not endure. "He was a man," he explained, "who seemed utterly unable to view anything except in the light of his own desires. Whatever he wanted was right; whatever was opposed to him was the work of enemies and devils." That characterization of Doheny was not accurate; it was rather the improvisation of Creel at a time when he was ready to hit Doheny with the first verbal brick that came to his mind.

XXVI

A Senate investigation that had gone so far afield as to call on the completely innocent to swear to their innocence, was now, of course, almost in the area of hysteria. Even Walsh, clear-minded and self-disciplined though he was, caught the crowd-psychology; he passed the point at which men's minds, under the influence of excitement around them, break loose from the restraints of fact and expand into a state in which they treat almost anything as credible. Walsh was excusable. Where so much that was incredible had proved to be true, who could doubt anything? The lines of the scandal had spread out in so many directions, it had turned out to be so enormous — could it be possible, where so much was infected, that anything was not?

Moreover, events were now hurrying at a pace far beyond that when Walsh had been able to give a year and a half to preliminary exploration before calling his first witness. No longer, in the flow of rumor that flooded his office, did he carefully sift innuendo from fact, and the absurd from the probable. Without adequate preliminary examination he sent subpoenas for all against whom the most irresponsible fingers pointed and permitted almost any exhibitionist volunteer to go on the stand.

An ex-train robber turned reformer, Al Jennings of Oklahoma, took the stand to assert that a rich and vulgar Oklahoma oil promoter, Jake Hamon, now dead,

From a photograph by International News Photos, Inc.

"Jake" Hamon, a newly-rich oil operator in Oklahoma, whose alleged actions and utterances figured in the oil investigation. Hamon was murdered under sensational circumstances by a woman.

had told him that he, Hamon, had spent a million dollars to nominate Harding for President. Once that was in the record, a considerable portion of the male population of Oklahoma had to be called, some to support the tale, others to denounce it as a fantastic yarn. The residuum of truth seemed to be adequately described by one witness who said that "when Jake had a few drinks of scotch he talked pretty big."

Walsh came to the point where he really thought Harding personally might be involved, and even Harding's successor, now in office, Coolidge. Coolidge's secretary, Bascom Slemp, was called on to explain that a Christmas trip he had taken to Florida had been for recreation only and had not had any connection with the Fall case; the committee had to satisfy itself that the trip had not been to see Edward McLean and stiffen his backbone to stick to his story about having loaned $100,000 to Fall. Walsh summoned the White House secret service man, Col. Starling, to explain a telegram he had sent to McLean — it was about a private employee of McLean whom Starling had recommended. Walsh summoned the head telegrapher at the White House, E. W. Smithers, to explain his employment during evenings as a telegrapher for McLean's newspaper — it was to eke out his salary of $2,500, he needed the money. Walsh summoned the White House doorkeeper, "Pat" McKenna, to explain a telegram he had sent to McLean — it was an innocent message of routine sort informing McLean that Bascom Slemp was leaving Washington and would arrive at Palm Beach at a certain hour.

XXVII

Poor Denby, in the excitement that was flaring, was hounded. The House of Representatives threatened to impeach him. The Senate passed a resolution calling on President Coolidge to dismiss him. Coolidge felt that Denby was innocent, and felt that the Senate had no right to tell him to dismiss a Cabinet member. But calm as Coolidge ordinarily was, he had been made jittery about the scandals involving high Republican office-holders and party officials. While Coolidge was hesitating, Senator Borah happened to call at the White House. Coolidge told Borah his troubles. Borah had no high opinion of Denby, and Borah was loyal to the prerogatives of the Senate when the Senate was in the right. But Borah was equally scrupulous about the prerogatives

"Whiter Than Snow" — Cassel the cartoonist here satirizes the outcome of one of the oil scandal cases which favored the defendant.

of the Presidency, and he knew the Constitution and knew where the dividing line was. Borah told Coolidge he ought by no means to obey such a resolution from the Senate, but on the contrary ought vigorously to defend the rights of his office. Coolidge, relieved, his mind made up for him, asked Borah to draft a letter for him to send to the Senate. Borah did so. It was a strong letter, and the Senate backed down.

But Denby knew the fire was too hot. He resigned, telling Coolidge that his continuance in office "would increase your embarrassment." In one of the many court procedures that later arose out of the oil scandals, the Supreme Court, almost with a manner of going out of its way to exonerate the innocent, said that Denby "took no active part in the negotiations."[45] The rest of his life he passed rather obscurely, in Detroit.

XXVIII

By now, public emotion was beginning to be sated a little with the sight of victims on the rack, bored a little with a bizarre that could not become more bizarre. Part of public opinion turned to distaste for the extravagances of some of the Senate committee's divagations. There was, in some quarters, something like approval for Sinclair when, called[46] again before the committee, he refused to answer questions. Sinclair did not give the rea-

[45] "Mr. Denby is neither a martyr nor a scoundrel. He was dismissed, not because he corruptly betrayed his trust, not because an aroused people demanded a scapegoat, but purely and simply on his record. His record demonstrated him to be ludicrously unfit for his post. The man merited neither tears nor prosecution. He deserved to be laughed out of the Cabinet." — Marcus Eli Ravage, "The Story of Teapot Dome."

"No man could have had a truer and higher conception of duty and integrity. I would as soon have held Denby guilty of complicity of a fraud against the country he had shown he loved so well as St. Peter in cahoots with Judas Iscariot." — J. Mayhew Wainwright, Assistant Secretary of War in the Harding Administration, and long a member of the House of Representatives, in a letter to the author.

"Poor Denby! There was never a more honest man. I have known two men in my life who suddenly and unexpectedly found themselves under attack, neither of whom had committed any wrong, but who, under the circumstances, seemed to go completely 'blah'; whose mental processes appeared to cease to function. That was the case with Denby. He just did not seem to know what it was all about, but no man can ever make me believe Ned Denby knowingly ever did anything contrary to the best interests of his country. None who knew the man will ever think otherwise." — Harry S. New, Postmaster-General in Harding's Administration, in a letter to the author.

[46] March 21, 1924.

son that Fall had given. Fall had put his reason in a familiar formula of law, "on the ground that it might tend to incriminate me." That reason amounted almost to confession of crime and made it practically certain that Fall would later be in the criminal courts; but it was a complete excuse for Fall as respects the Senate proceedings — the committee could only let him go.

But Sinclair did not say that. Sinclair specifically refrained from saying that. Sinclair said: "I do not decline to answer any questions on the ground that my answers may tend to incriminate me, because there is nothing in any of the facts or circumstances of the lease of Teapot Dome which does or can incriminate me."

Having made that clear, Sinclair stated just why he declined to answer the Senate committee's questions. He said that he would "reserve any evidence I may be able to give for those courts to which you and your colleagues have deliberately referred all questions of which you had any jurisdiction and shall respectfully decline to answer any questions propounded by your committee."

Ten times, Walsh asked Sinclair a question. Ten times Sinclair replied, "I decline to answer on advice of counsel."

For that Sinclair was subject to contempt. The committee itself could not punish him. It could only report Sinclair's recalcitrant taciturnity to the Senate. This the committee did. The Senate, by a vote of 72 to 1, cited him for contempt. "Citing" meant that Sinclair was turned over to the criminal courts, charged with refusal to answer questions asked by a duly authorized committee of the United States Senate. In the criminal courts, Sinclair was indicted for contempt of the Senate and released on $1,000 bail.

There followed much argument in the courts, and appeals from court to higher court, on the right of the

Senate to ask the particular questions they had asked Sinclair, on whether Sinclair's refusal was contempt of the Senate, and on whether contempt of the Senate under these circumstances constituted a crime. In the end, Sinclair was tried on the contempt charge, convicted, and

From a photograph by Brown Brothers.

Harry F. Sinclair.

sentenced to pay a fine of $1,000 and spend three months in jail. He was confined in the District of Columbia jail, where he reverted to the occupation of his youth, making up pharmacal prescriptions for prisoners, who came to like him.

In the wise-cracking of the time, Sinclair was given a curiously inverted eminence and credit. He had proved the negative, so the epigram said, of an aphorism that had long been serviceable to cynics and radicals, the assertion that "you can't put a million dollars in jail."

Sinclair had another minor distinction. He served his

sentence for contempt of the Senate. Then, later, he was put on trial for the real criminal charge involved in the oil scandal, the charge that he and Fall had conspired to defraud the government. In the course of that trial, Sinclair employed detectives to shadow the jury. This was discovered and reported to the court, which regarded Sinclair's action as contempt of court, and sentenced him to six months in jail. By that, Sinclair achieved a unique eminence; he was the only man who ever succeeded in getting himself in jail twice for contempt of two separate bodies, the United States Senate and the courts of justice. (Fall, later, achieved a zenith of ignobility. He became, in the whole history of the United States, the first cabinet officer to go to jail.)

XXIX

The trial and conviction of Sinclair for contempt of the Senate was, of course, not much more than an incident of procedure. The trial of him for the substantial crime involved, and the trials of Fall and Doheny, and the civil suits to recover the oil lands for the government, must come later.

Normally, with the conclusion of the Senate investigation, the cases would have gone to the Department of Justice. But the Senate lacked confidence in the Department of Justice, because its head, the Attorney-General, was Harry Daugherty, and Daugherty had himself gone through the wringer of a Senatorial investigation — he and his Department had been under almost continuous attack and criticism. Even Senators belonging to Daugherty's own political party were disinclined to leave the prosecution of the oil scandals to him. Accordingly, the Senate on February 2, 1924 (and the House one day later), passed a joint resolution calling on the President, Coolidge, to appoint special counsel independent of the Department of Justice. Coolidge first named former Democratic Attorney-General Thomas W. Gregory, but it turned out he was lawyer for an oil company in Texas. Coolidge named Republican Silas H. Strawn of Chicago, but it turned out he was counsel for a trust company which was trustee for a bond issue put out by an oil company. The objection was fantastic, the relations of both Strawn and Gregory to oil were remote — but by this time, so much did oil smell, so agitated was public opinion, that it was almost an impediment ever to have bought ten gallons of gas at a filling station. Finally, Coolidge named a Republican lawyer from Philadelphia, not then nationally known,[47] Owen J. Roberts, and a Democratic ex-Senator, Atlee W. Pomerene of Ohio. Even with these, Walsh was not satisfied, in the Senate he voted against confirmation of both; he, and everybody knew the defendants would have the best legal talent[48] money could hire. Walsh's long concentration upon the oil scandals had almost taken him, for the time, out of the field of calm judgment; he thought Pomerene, on account of his service in the Senate, had been too long out of practice of the law, and he thought Roberts ought to be familiar with the western land and mining law, which of course he was not. Walsh forgot that Roberts's work in the oil cases would be ordinary criminal and civil law.

To Roberts and Pomerene, President Coolidge gave strong, continuous and vigilant support. Coolidge made just one public statement about the oil scandals; the guilty would be brought to justice and the government's

[47] But destined to be. After his work in the oil cases made him nationally known, he was appointed, by President Hoover, a Justice of the Supreme Court.

[48] One of them, Frank Hogan, was said to have received a fee of $1,000,000 from Doheny. "Frank Hogan's million dollar fee" was for years a subject of Washington quips.

interests would be protected; thereafter, Coolidge's record was one of inaction. His quietly firm support of the prosecution, and his attitude about the government's business altogether, brought to the public an assurance

From a photograph by Underwood & Underwood.

Counsel for the government in the civil suits to recover the oil reserves in the criminal prosecutions of Fall, Doheny, and Sinclair. On the left, Owen J. Roberts, later Justice of the Supreme Court, on the right, Atlee W. Pomerene, former Democratic United States Senator from Ohio.

which, after the now revealed record of the Harding Administration, the public greatly needed.

Roberts and Pomerene settled down to long and arduous work. The two proved to be a good combination. They had their desks side by side in the same office, plans and policies were formed jointly in conference between the two and between the men whom each had brought to assist in the work. With much patience and resourcefulness they dug up evidence which showed that Doheny's loan of $100,000 to Fall was almost simultaneous with Fall's first gestures toward leasing Elk Hills to Doheny, a bit of evidence which went far toward taking the $100,000 transaction out of the category of "loan" and into a category more sinister. With much ingenuity and persistence, Roberts and Pomerene discovered evidence that was new and vital, deposits of some $200,000 in Liberty bonds that had been made to Fall's credit, or to the credit of his son-in-law, in various western and southwestern banks. Through work that took months they traced the bonds back to Sinclair, whereupon explanation was set up that Sinclair had intended to make Fall's New Mexico ranch into a pleasure resort, and that his payments to Fall had been on account of that enterprise.

Suit to annul the lease of Teapot Dome to Sinclair was entered in the United States District Court at Cheyenne, Wyoming, March 13, 1924. June 12, 1925, Judge T. Blake Kennedy upheld the legality of the lease. On appeal, the United States Circuit Court of Appeals cancelled the lease of Teapot Dome on the ground that it had been obtained as the result of "collusion and conspiracy" between Fall and Sinclair.

Suit to annul the lease of Elk Hills to Doheny was entered in the United States District Court at Los Angeles, California, March 17, 1924. June 19, 1925, Judge McCormick found that the payment of $100,000 by Doheny to Fall was against good morals and public policy; that the payment constituted a fraud on the United States Government, rendering voidable all contracts. On appeal to the United States Circuit Court of Appeals in California, Judge McCormick was upheld (January 5, 1926), and the findings of both courts were upheld by the United States Supreme Court, December 28, 1927. The Supreme Court held that the lease to Elk Hills had been secured through "fraud and corruption" and ordered the property returned to the United States Government.

Fall, Sinclair, Edward L. Doheny, Sr., and Edward L. Doheny, Jr., were indicted June 5, 1924, in the District of Columbia Supreme Court, Fall and the elder Doheny charged with conspiracy, Fall and Sinclair charged with conspiracy, and Fall and the two Dohenys charged with bribery. April 3, 1925, Chief Justice McCoy dismissed the indictments on a technicality. May 27, 1925, new indictments were returned. Doheny and Fall, tried on the charge of conspiracy to defraud the Government, were acquitted December 16, 1926. On November 1, 1927, during a trial of Sinclair and Fall before the District of Columbia Supreme Court on the charge of conspiracy to defraud the United States Government, Prosecutor Roberts presented affidavits showing that the jury was being shadowed by detectives employed by Sinclair. A mistrial was declared. A retrial of the case resulted, April 21, 1928, in the acquittal of Fall and Sinclair. In October, 1929, Fall after long delay was put on trial for having accepted a bribe. On October 25, the jury after deliberating a day and a night brought in a verdict of guilty but with a recommendation of mercy. Fall was sentenced to a year in jail and fined $100,000. After many delays Fall went to jail in July, 1931, serving until May, 1932, when he was released, his sentence shortened by his record of good behavior while a prisoner. March, 1930, Doheny was acquitted, following a trial by jury before the District of Columbia Supreme Court, on the charge of bribing Fall.

15

TRAGEDY COMPLETED

Other Scandals Emerging after Harding's Death Which Involved Persons High in His Administration and Close to
Him Personally. For a Time, Some of the Scandals Seem,
to an Appalled Nation, to Involve Harding Himself. Including a "Woman Scandal" which Actually Did Touch
Harding. An Incident in a Senate Investigation, Which
Drew the Searchlights of the World upon Harding's Reputation and Revealed Nothing to His Financial Discredit.

ONE scandal, because it accused Daugherty, and because
of a remarkable reason Daugherty gave for not going
on the witness stand, seemed to come close to Harding
personally.

When America entered the war, the government took
over all property of Germans in the United States. One
piece was the American Metal Company, said to be
owned by the Metallgesellschaft and Metall Bank, of
Frankfort-on-Main, Germany. This the government
seized and sold, investing the proceeds in Liberty bonds
which were sequestered in the Treasury. The price received, $6,000,000, amounted, through accretions of
interest, to $6,500,000 in 1921. This the owners wished
to get back. They claimed the American Metal Company had not really been owned by the German Metallgesellschaft, nor by any other Germans, it had been
owned by Swiss, with a French name, the Société Suisse
pour Valeurs de Métaux. The facts and the law are not
material to the present narrative.

Representing the owners, Richard Merton (born
Moses) came from Frankfort-on-Main to New York.
There he inquired among acquaintances in the financial

district for — so he put it in his testimony later —
"some one who could pave the way," some one who
could get "speed" in the Alien Property Custodian office at Washington.

Merton's financial friends sent him to John T. King.
King was a figure who kept one hand in high finance,

From a photograph © Underwood & Underwood.
John T. King.

the other in Republican politics, making each serve the
other and both serve himself. In the financial district,
his contacts included large-scale speculators and others
identified with the less conservative side of finance. In
Republican politics, King's associations were with the
highest. He had been close to Theodore Roosevelt and
if Theodore Roosevelt had lived King would probably
have managed a campaign on his behalf for the Republican Presidential nomination in 1920. After Theodore
Roosevelt died, King managed the campaign of General

Leonard Wood, until Wood discovered that King had been making promises which would embarrass Wood if the latter should become President. King later associated himself with Harding, he was on occasion a dinner guest of Harding at the White House. King, in the line he followed, was able, a "big shot." He was what slang of the day called a "smoothie," suave, soft-spoken, well-dressed, well-educated. He was unobtrusive in manner but energetic in action, slow in speech but quick in mind, always a formidable combination.

King and Merton arranged that King would undertake to get the American Metal Company out of the Alien Property Custodian's office. The employment was proper enough, or could be if carried out through regular and legal channels.

The process consisted of first getting the consent of the Alien Property Custodian's office to release the property, and then getting approval by the Attorney-General's office. Presently this was done. Merton paid King $441,000, said "auf wiedersehen," and departed for Europe.

Of the $441,000 which King received, $391,000 was in Liberty bonds. After a time, $50,000 of these bonds was found to have reached the hands of the Alien Property Custodian, Thomas W. Miller. Miller was indicted, convicted and sent to jail. Fifty thousand dollars more (at least) was found to have reached the hands of Jess Smith. Because Smith was close to Daugherty, suspicion was directed at the latter. The suspicion was increased by the disposition Smith had made of the bonds, he had deposited them in a bank at Washington Court House, Ohio, of which the head was Daugherty's brother, "Mal" Daugherty. He had deposited them to the credit of an account labelled "Jess Smith Extra No. 3." (Smith had two other accounts in the bank, a personal one and one for the department store he had until recently owned.) The account "Jess Smith Extra No. 3" was a "political account." It was managed by Jess Smith — he collected contributions for it, made deposits in it, and drew checks on it. But above Smith, the account was directed by Harry Daugherty. Daugherty had opened it when he started to make Harding the Republican Presidential nominee. Contributions Daugherty received for that purpose were deposited in the account, disbursements paid out of it.

These conditions, the circumstantial evidence, pointed toward indictment of Daugherty and this a New York grand jury did, the charge being that in his action in the American Metal case, Daugherty had conspired to "defraud the United States of its governmental functions and rights and of the honest, impartial and unprejudiced services and 'judgment" of Daugherty as Attorney-General.

At the trial, Daugherty produced strong testimony to show that he personally had had nothing to do with releasing the American Metal Company except the perfunctory signing of his name to decisions made by other government officials. The managing director of the Alien Property Custodian's office took the stand and assumed full responsibility for the original decision that the American Metal Company be released. The assistant to the Attorney-General, Guy D. Goff, a man of high standing, took the stand and accepted full responsibility for the approval given by the Attorney-General's office.

This testimony seemed to cover the matter of the decision. As respects the disposition of the $50,000 given Smith,[1] Daugherty produced testimony from his brother showing that Smith had been personally in de-

[1] Smith had committed suicide long before the trial took place. Another whose testimony might have clarified the case, John T. King, had also died.

fault to the account "Jess Smith Extra No. 3," that Harry Daugherty and "Mal" Daugherty had both pressed him to make an accounting, and that Smith had deposited the $50,000 to make good his default to the account.

But the circumstantial evidence against Daugherty was so strong that everybody considered he was called upon to take the stand and submit to examination. This he did not do. When the time came when he should do so, he picked up a pencil and wrote:

Having been personal attorney for Warren G. Harding before he was Senator from Ohio and while he was Senator, and thereafter until his death,
And for Mrs. Harding for a period of several years, and before her husand was elected President and after his death, . . .
And having been attorney for the Midland National Bank of Washington Court House, Ohio, and for my brother, M. S. Daugherty,
And having been Attorney General of the United States during the time that President Harding served as President,
And also for a time after President Harding's death under President Coolidge,
And with all of those named as attorney, personal friend and Attorney General, my relations were of the most confidential character as well as professional,
I refuse to testify and answer questions put to me, because: The answer I might give or make and the testimony I might give might tend to incriminate me.

To the public Daugherty's reason for not taking the stand was appalling — it seemed clearly to imply scandal involving Harding personally. The shock was increased by the fact that Daugherty had destroyed the records of "Jess Smith Account No. 3" — that, again, seemed to imply that this "political account" must contain something which, if revealed, would reflect on Harding. The shock was intensified when Daugherty's lawyer,[2]

[2] Max D. Steuer.

explaining his client's failure to take the stand, said after the case was ended:

It was not anything connected with this case that impelled him to refrain from so doing. He would have been glad to have Mr. Buckner ask him anything that had a bearing upon the case. He feared, however, . . . that Mr. Buckner would cross-examine about matters political that would not involve Mr. Daugherty concerning which he knew and as to which he would never make disclosure. . . . The destruction of the ledger sheets did not conceal anything that had the slightest bearing on this case. . . .

If the jury knew the real reason for destroying the ledger sheets they would commend rather than condemn Mr. Daugherty, but he insisted on silence.

And the shock was rather increased when the jury did not convict Daugherty — after deliberating 66 hours they disagreed. The public felt, as it was put by a writer in the *Nation:* "The jury decided that a President's good name was at stake." And the public felt, about Daugherty's remarkable statement and that of his counsel, that "what Mr. Steuer was trying to say politely was that the bank records contained material reflecting on Daugherty's great friend . . . Warren G. Harding." [3]

The implication was plain that Daugherty was either (a) safeguarding guilt of his own by hiding behind the dead Harding (and the dead Mrs. Harding) or (b) that there were matters in the bank accounts, and in his testimony if he had submitted himself to examination, which actually would have involved Harding. Politicians who knew Daugherty well, knew his daring and knew his code, which included utter loyalty to friends and especially to Harding, felt the second surmise must be the true one, that there were matters which would have reflected on Harding. But the politicians also knew

[3] Bruce Bliven in *The New Republic,* October 27, 1926.

Harding, and felt he was incapable of any breach of financial integrity. In this situation, many politicians who had been close to the inside of things surmised another reason for Daugherty's destroying his political bank account and declining to take the stand.[4] They concluded that the political bank account, and Daugherty's testimony, if he had given it, might have brought up, not anything to the dead President's discredit, but certain "woman stories" about Harding; perhaps some of the payments out of the political account had had some connection, without Harding's knowledge, with a "woman story." Stories of this kind were in quiet circulation among persons close to the Harding régime.

This surmise was increased by the appearance, a little

[4] What was Daugherty's motive in not taking the stand, when his refraining presumably increased his risk of being found guilty, remains, as respects the author of this history, as inexplicable as it was at the time. I have read most of the testimony in the trial of him, and all the hearings in the Senate investigation of him and the House attempt to impeach him. In addition, in the year in which this history is written, I asked him many questions by letter and had long replies from him, and I spent two days with him at his home in Columbus. He was then 75 years old, but still salient, self-reliant, defiant of any standards except his own. I felt that he lived by a code of his own; if his code did not happen to be identical with the world's conventions, so much the worse for the conventions. When I asked him straight whether he had stayed off the witness stand and destroyed bank records because he feared cross-examination of him might reveal some "woman story" about Harding, he looked me straight in the eye and said: "If there was any 'woman scrape' in Harding's life I never knew it, and if there had been one Harding would have told me." Letting his cold eye become humorous for a moment he added, "I know there was never any woman scrape in my life." When I tried to press the matter, he quoted an aphorism from his code, "I never talk about dead men or living women."

Just what was Daugherty's motive, what might have been revealed by court examination of him and the records of the political account he kept in his brother's bank, I do not know. Conceivably it may have been nothing very portentous. Daugherty was capable of going to fantastic lengths to keep a secret, even though the secret were unimportant, just because he had promised some one he would never tell it.

Of one thing I am sure, none of the money Jess Smith got to facilitate the American Metal case went into Daugherty's pocket. Daugherty, when in Harding's cabinet, and at all times with respect to Harding, prized Harding more than he prized anything else. To suppose that, in this respect or as respects any action of his, he would have consciously done for his personal benefit a thing that would bring discredit on Harding would be to indict not only his morals but his loyalty and his intelligence.

later, of one of the most sensational books ever circulated in America.

II

During 1927 there appeared in the advertising offices of New York newspapers copy submitted as advertisements for a book called "The President's Daughter," written by Nan Britton, and published by the "Elizabeth Ann Guild, Inc." In one case the advertisement, going through routine channels under the eyes of clerks too busy to more than glance at it, appeared in print.

Inquiry led to hurried consultations by editors and business managers. Where the advertisement had not been originally refused it was dropped after one or two publications. Editors of book review departments debated whether to review the book; whether they were excused from that function by the fact that the organization putting it out was not a standard publishing firm, whether it belonged in the category of books in the conventional sense. In the channels where books are sold there was similar perturbation; many booksellers, horrified, refused to handle it; such as did hid it on lower shelves beneath the counter, like contraband.

Readers to whom the book came spoke of it in horrified whispers — whispers penetrating enough, however, to give the book ultimately a circulation of some 90,000 — and probably never did a book have so large a number of readers in proportion to the number sold, for the volume was passed from hand to hand, was abstracted from a drawer of the desk in the sitting room to be read by adolescents away from the parental eye; or was devoured by eager-eyed servants in the absence of the family. At such libraries as acknowledged they had it, or were willing to handle it as they did ordinary books, there were waiting lists. One way or another "The President's Daughter," by the time it had been out for about a year, had probably been read by more persons than commonly read the most widely and openly circulated best-sellers.

The book had as its frontispiece a photograph of a little girl some six years old, upon which readers, after they had absorbed the book, looked intently to see if they could find likeness to Warren Gamaliel Harding. There was a

DEDICATION

THIS BOOK IS DEDICATED
WITH UNDERSTANDING AND
LOVE TO ALL UNWEDDED
MOTHERS, AND TO THEIR
INNOCENT CHILDREN WHOSE
FATHERS ARE USUALLY NOT
KNOWN TO THE WORLD. . . .

NAN BRITTON

and a prefatory declaration of "the author's motive" which, according to the author, was, of course, completely high-minded. She had written the book, she said, for the Cause (capital "C"), the Cause of illegitimate children everywhere, that of all such "the name of the father be correctly registered in the public records," that every child born in the United States of America be recorded as legitimate, whether born within or without wedlock.

In the book Miss Britton recited:

That she had been brought up in Marion, Ohio, the daughter of a physician; that when she was fourteen — and Harding a more than middle-aged man, nearly fifty, running for Governor of Ohio — she had conceived an infatuation for him; that she used to phone his house frequently hoping he might answer the phone;

that she decorated her bedroom with photographs of him cut from campaign posters bound in frames the child bought at 5 and 10-cent stores; that she used to stand in a doorway across the street from the office of the Marion *Star*, watching Harding in his office on the second floor — Harding's habitual pose, she wrote, was with his feet on his desk; when she saw his feet leave the desk she knew he was about to walk home, and she would follow him at a distance; that Harding at this time was completely unaware of the child's long-distance adoration of him and never spoke to her except as he might casually greet the not very distinctly recognized child of a neighbor.

She recited that after the death of her father she went to work in New York in 1916; that she wrote a letter to Harding, then in the Senate, asking him to find her a position; that Harding replied that he would do so and, on a trip to New York, told her to come and see him at his hotel; that at once the relation was put upon a sentimental basis; that Harding decided he should get her a position in New York rather than in Washington, as in New York he would be under less observation; that Harding got her a position with the United States Steel Corporation at $16 a week; that once when Harding was making campaign speeches at Indianapolis and Rushville, Indiana, Miss Britton accompanied him, being registered at the hotel and introduced by Harding to his friends as his niece; that Harding visited her many times in New York, the two stopping at various hotels; that she used to receive letters from him as much as sixty pages in length (though no love letter, nor any part of one appeared in the book); that she made frequent visits to Washington to see Harding, and that the two met at the Ebbitt House or in apartments that Harding borrowed for the day from various friends; that once she visited him in his Senate office.

On October 22, 1919, Miss Britton declared in her book, when she was 23 and Harding 54, she had a baby, born at Asbury Park, New Jersey; that Harding treated her generously, sending her $100 to $150 every week or so; that in June, 1920, when Harding was in Chicago at the convention at which he was nominated for the Presidency, he visited her several times at her sister's apartment; that after Harding was nominated she went to the Adirondacks for a rest, leaving her child in Chicago; that while she was in the Adirondacks and Harding campaigning for the Presidency, Harding sent her money, the money being brought by a secret service man[5] to whom Miss Britton gave the name Tim Slade (a pseudonym easily decoded by any one familiar with the secret-service staff at the White House). After Harding was elected, Miss Britton said, she visited him secretly at Marion, where Harding gave her three $500 bills; she said that after Harding was in the White House, she, in June, 1921, made a trip to Washington and met Harding at a tryst in the White House; that she corresponded with Harding constantly, the letters being sent in care of the secret-service man whom she called Tim Slade; that in January, 1922, Miss Britton's child was formally adopted by her sister, Mrs. Willits, and her husband; that Harding had never seen the child; that Miss Britton continued to pay occasional visits to the White House; that in 1923 she took a trip to Europe, Harding bearing the expense, and was in France when Harding died.

Soon after Harding's death, Miss Britton said in her book, she married a Swedish ship captain. Soon the two

[5] The rule of the secret service is that from the hour a candidate is nominated for the Presidency by either party, he comes under the protection of the secret service and is attended by regular relays of them.

separated. Miss Britton said she began to make inquiry
whether Harding had made any financial provision for
her and her child. "Tim Slade" was unable to discover
any one to whom Harding had entrusted any such fund.
Thereupon, Miss Britton said, she decided she should
approach Harding's family; she said that she wrote
many letters to Harding's sisters, Miss Daisy Harding
and Mrs. Heber Votaw. At first, she said, Miss Daisy
Harding was sympathetic, gave her, on different occasions, sums amounting to a few hundred dollars, but
rather abruptly ended the gifts when Harding's brother,
Doctor George Harding, took hold of the situation. Doctor Harding met Miss Britton, so she complained in her
book, with a cold eye, a notebook on his knee. He asked
her for letters — she had none; Harding, she said, had
asked her to destroy them, and she could produce only
a few impersonal notes. Doctor Harding remained
"stonily impassive." He asked her for dates, places.
"When was that?" "Where did that meeting take
place?" Miss Britton "wondered vaguely at his wanting
these so definitely." At the end Miss Britton thanked
him for the interview. Doctor Harding showed impatience. She did not see him again. The Harding family
did not give her the $50,000 she asked.

III

Upon Harding's reputation, upon the memory of him
— he was three years in his grave — the effect was terrible. The Nan Britton book, coming after exposures
of financial corruption on the part of members of his
Administration, made Harding's memory almost a rag
in the gutter. Omitting the Nan Britton book, listing
only the proved crimes or undisputed facts, the country
saw:

Harding's friend and appointee as Secretary of the

Interior, Albert B. Fall, convicted of accepting a bribe[6] and sentenced to jail.

Harding's friend whom he had appointed[7] to be head

A cartoon famous during the Presidential campaign of 1924. The oil scandal had been exposed and the Republicans were necessarily in the position of promising future honesty. The theme was taken from a song widely known at the time "It Ain't Goin' to Rain No Mo'."

of the Veterans' Bureau, Charles R. Forbes, convicted of defrauding the government and sentenced to jail.

Harding's appointee as Alien Property Custodian, Thomas W. Miller, convicted of accepting money to influence an official action, and sent to jail.

Harding's intimate associate, the promoter of his Presidential nomination, his appointee as Attorney-General,

[6] For an account of Fall and the oil scandals, see Chapter 14.
[7] See Chapter 11.

highest law officer of the government, Harry M. Daugherty, accused, indicted and put on trial for faithlessness
to duty. Even though Daugherty had not been convicted,
the incident was sufficiently sordid.

An intimate of the Harding entourage, Jess Smith,
revealed as having accepted more than fifty thousand
dollars to facilitate a case before the Alien Property Custodian; Smith had committed suicide, and everybody
felt the self-destruction had been in anticipation of exposure.

The bald, proved facts were awful enough. Because
of circumstances associated with some of the cases, rumor
expanded even beyond the facts. The suicide of Jess
Smith, intimate of Attorney-General Daugherty, the
suicide taking place in Daugherty's apartment, led to
stories that he had been murdered[8] to still his tongue
about tales he might tell, and that Daugherty had been
party to the murder — the innuendo was plainly made
on the Senate floor by Heflin of Alabama and others; by
word of mouth it was broadcast. The fact that another
suicide, Charles F. Cramer,[9] assistant and counsel to
Forbes in the Veterans' Bureau, had had a financial
transaction with Harding — he had bought from Harding the Washington house Harding had occupied when
a Senator and his suicide took place in this house — gave
rise to suggestions that Harding himself had been involved. In the inflamed state of the public mind, sufficiently shocked by the facts and even more appalled by
the rumors, the story that Harding had been involved

---

[8] The freedom with which newspapers and persons expressed belief that Jess
Smith had been the victim not of suicide but of murder, is illustrated by an article
in *The New Republic,* October 27, 1926, in which Bruce Bliven said: "Jesse
Smith, who committed suicide — or was murdered — when the operations of the
Ohio gang grew to such huge dimensions that exposure seemed inevitable."

[9] For more about Cramer's suicide, see Chapter 11. So far as my researches
have gone, I found no concrete charge against Cramer.

personally was given momentum by publication of a statement that Mrs. Harding, before she died in 1924, had destroyed his private papers.

Presently, many of the rumors began to centre round Harding, especially after they began to include "woman stories" about him. Word-of-mouth whisper said the President had killed himself, other whispers said he had been murdered.[10] A book, "The Strange Death of President Harding," plainly implied that Mrs. Harding had poisoned him — not all who read the book,[11] or heard similar stories, knew that the writer, Gaston B. Means, was the most monumental liar and facile criminal of his time. Another book, "Revelry," [12] by a reputable author, Samuel Hopkins Adams — who did not purport to write more than fiction based on the facts and rumors of the Harding Administration — added momentum to

[10] A recollection of my own that remains vivid is about a colored bootblack at the old Shoreham Hotel, the compromise he made between his native delicacy and his curiosity. He knew me well, we talked familiarly, but he felt embarrassment in asking me about a thing which in all circles was restrained to hushed whispers. Drawing his bootblack's cloth back and forth across the instep of my shoe, and refraining from looking up, he said: "You know, Mr. Sullivan, some folks — just common, rough people, of course — are saying Mr. Harding was 'bumped off.'"

[11] The intimation that Harding had killed himself, or been murdered, has been given credence by even authentic histories, and by other books taken seriously:

"Without accepting the most sensational of the stories of his death, it must be admitted that the mystery of it has never been cleared up. . . ." — "The March of Democracy," James Truslow Adams.

"Before these scandals came to light, Harding died, with suspicious suddenness." — "The Post War World," by J. Hampden Jackson, History Master at Haileybury College, England.

"A rumor that the President committed suicide by taking poison later gained wide currency. . . . Gaston B. Means, a Department of Justice detective . . . implied only too clearly in 'The Strange Death of President Harding' that the President was poisoned by his wife. . . . Both the suicide theory and the Means story are very plausible. . . ." — "Only Yesterday," Frederick Lewis Allen.

For these assertions and intimations about Harding's death, there is no faintest justification. When James Truslow Adams said 'the mystery of it has never been cleared up," was he aware of the clear, detailed and explicit account by one of the attending physicians, Doctor Ray Lyman Wilbur, who was at the time President of Stanford University, and had been President of the American Academy of Medicine, and of the council on medical education of the American Medical Association?

[12] Published 1926.

the story that Harding's death had been suicide. "Revelry" was made into a play and a motion-picture.

By this time, the Harding scandals were a conspicuous feature of the time. Everybody heard them. Some cynically believed all. Others, their finest sensibilities wounded, hating to believe but unable to deny, refused to talk about them or listen to them. The effect on the country's morale was definite, visible, and most damaging. Some of Harding's friends had undertaken to erect a great memorial at his grave in Marion; confident in their faith in his public integrity, they loyally went through with it, but much of the public smiled wanly and some newspapers felt they were discreet in not giving much space to accounts of the project.

IV

The Exoneration of Harding

The charge, rather the intimation, that Harding personally had been involved in corruption, emerged in print in February, 1924. A retired New York banker, Frank A. Vanderlip, was invited to make a Lincoln Day address at Briarcliff, N. Y., before a Rotary Club. His subject was "Courage and Leadership."

Lincoln Day morning Vanderlip telephoned a friend of his, an editor on the New York *Tribune*, telling him of his engagement and suggesting that "it would be an interesting speech . . . to report." The editor, not expecting anything very exciting from a speech about "courage and leadership," but on the theory that Vanderlip was an important man whose utterances had news value, sent a reporter to Briarcliff. *The Tribune* man, picking out the parts of Vanderlip's address having most public interest, wrote his story and sent it in to the office

— it arrived there about 2 A.M., too late to make any but the fourth and final edition of the paper. Through processes familiar to the craft, other New York newspapers learned about the story but prudently decided it was too dangerous to print without verification by Vanderlip; and Vanderlip had gone to bed and could not be reached. The Associated Press put the story on its wires but had a cautious second thought and before it could be printed sent out a flash to "kill."

Vanderlip, arriving at his office the following morning, found it crowded with reporters and press association men who clamored at him to make a statement. Confused by the uproar the reporters were making, not prepared for the whirlwind of excitement into which he had stepped, not certain himself what *The Tribune* story contained, for he had not had an opportunity to give it careful reading — Vanderlip incautiously permitted the reporters to infer that he stood squarely behind the speech as *The Tribune* had printed it. That was enough, and all that the reporters wanted. They rushed out to telephone their managing editors.

The lid was off. Noon and afternoon editions of newspapers in every large town and city in the country printed conspicuously on their first pages a New York despatch to the effect that Frank A. Vanderlip, distinguished New York banker, had said in a public speech, among many other sensational things, that:

A certain Marion newspaper sold for $550,000, when it was known to every one that it was not worth half that sum.

Two young men of no financial standing purchased it. Everybody in Washington, including the newspaper correspondents, knows this, but no one wants to look under the edge of a shroud.

Where did the money come from? Where did it go? These are matters of public interest. The last administration stands challenged. We cannot wait for Congress or the courts, especially when we remember that Mr. Daugherty is Attorney-General. . . .

The Senate did not go further in investigating Secretary Fall, because Fall was ready to peach, and what he would have said would have gone into high places. They didn't dare.

The despatch nowhere mentioned the name of Harding, but practically everybody knew at whom the

Cartoon by Orr in the Chicago *Tribune* when the oil scandal had reached the stage in which some innocent victims were tarred.

phrase, "no one wants to look under the edge of a shroud," pointed. Everybody knew and understood that a "certain Marion newspaper" meant the Marion *Star*, which the late President had sold a few days before leaving on his trip to Alaska to two young newspaper men, Louis H. Brush and Roy D. Moore. The plain implication was that the price paid for the *Star*, alleged to have been excessive, was a "cover," a means by which Harding had been given money for a corrupt reason.

In the telegraph room of *The Star* at Marion a man "taking" news on the Associated Press wire suddenly grasped the sheets of a despatch he had just typed and dashed to the office of the paper's new owners. There Brush and Moore, their faces registering dismay and indignation, read the statements about their purchase of *The Star* made the night before by Vanderlip. They had cause for indignation. Their acquiring *The Star*, a very sound and prosperous newspaper property, had been absolutely bona fide. They themselves were men of substance, owners of a chain of small-town papers in Ohio and upper New York State. They had financed *The Star's* purchase not with money from some mysterious source, as the Vanderlip speech hinted, but with their own funds. As a condition of the sale they had arranged with Harding to conduct an editorial column in the paper, which they believed would give *The Star* a unique status as a sort of national newspaper with a nation-wide circulation, which they hoped would make their investment an exceedingly profitable one.

Quickly Brush and Moore prepared and gave to the Associated Press a statement denying the allegations of mystery in their purchase of *The Star*. At the time, the Walsh Committee investigating the oil scandals was in session at Washington. To the committee Moore and Brush sent a telegram demanding that the committee call Vanderlip before it and question him. To this demand the committee agreed and a subpoena was telegraphed Vanderlip.

Vanderlip, anxious and disturbed, almost sick, took the witness chair at 10 A.M., February 15. He did not have a thing to support his reported assertions and did not pretend to have anything. Frankly he said so. He said his purpose had been to lift the story out of the area of whispered rumor into print and cause investigation of it:[45]

What I said was that there are rumors emanating from Washington, becoming current throughout the United States, deeply affecting the public mind. . . . I said most emphatically that I knew nothing whatever about the facts. I believed that out of respect to Harding's memory that thing should be brought up to close scrutiny, and the scandal should be downed. No one knew the truth; every one seemed to have heard it. I have no legal information of any kind. I have no information at all as to the value of the paper. The statement I made was that this is current rumor. . . . I thought that by bringing it out in this public manner you gentlemen will bring out the truth, and the truth ought to clear the slander.

The two hours Vanderlip spent before the committee were probably the most uncomfortable of his life. He was given an unmerciful grilling, rather worse than the treatment any of the principals in the oil scandals had received. One after another members of the committee forthrightly said they did not believe his story

[45] A despatch written for the New York *Tribune* by the author of this history on the evening of the day Vanderlip's speech was published in the newspapers pictures the sense of relief which official Washington felt over the publicity given this one of the many rumors then having wide circulation about financial corruption associated with the name of Harding.

"Expressions of indignation over Frank A. Vanderlip's dragging the Harding rumors into the light were quite natural. The writer is free to say that when he read the despatch his feeling was one of definite relief. These rumors have been current in Washington for weeks. Many thought they ought to be ignored. . . . Some persons thought their very gravity was such that they ought to be suppressed for the benefit of society.

"The writer has felt sure that as a matter of fact, suppression was impossible and that as a matter of good policy suppression was undesirable. The rumors had been brought to the attention of the investigating committee. Some of the committee shared the feeling that the stories were really too terrible to be given further momentum. The committee gave earnest thought about their duty. To whatever extent they may criticize Mr. Vanderlip for the precise words and manner in which he dragged the rumors into the light, probably the real truth is that the committee in their hearts felt the same sense of relief that some of the rest of us did. It was utterly impossible to suppress these rumors or ignore them permanently. Their circulation had been too wide-spread. For weeks the writer has found them in Washington, in Philadelphia, in New York and elsewhere. The only possible cure for the situation was to let in the light. That was the only true disinfectant."

that he had been misquoted, and each and all of them read him a lecture on ethics and conduct and the obligations attaching to a man of his prominence in business and public life:

Would it not have been a more friendly act if, after making an investigation — and if you were a friend of Mr. Harding, you would certainly be anxious to ascertain the truth — after ascertaining whether or not there were any proofs or evidence or anything tangible that would support a slander, and if the absence of the possibility of obtaining any such facts, would it not have been a more friendly act to have denounced the slander?

Harsh as the committee's treatment of Vanderlip was, there was worse yet to come. When the Senators had exhausted their wrath, a lawyer representing the owners of the Marion *Star* was allowed to interrogate him, and the grilling was gone through once more.

Vanderlip's failure even to attempt to prove the truth of the rumor which his speech had broadcast, together with the later appearance of Brush and Moore before the committee with adequate and convincing proof that their acquisition of the Marion *Star* had been entirely above-board and legitimate, completely disposed of this one among the many ugly rumors now current about the dead President and his Administration. But for Vanderlip, the episode did not end so happily. For him the ordeal before the committee had been merely the prelude to worse trouble — it had been, figuratively and almost literally, the frying pan; now he was in the fire. Suit for $600,000 damages was brought against him by Brush and Moore, which friends acting for him eventually settled out of court.

Vanderlip's innuendo against Harding, the printing of it, the instant examination into it, the complete refutation of it, had a wholesome result. It ended forever all whispers of financial scandal in connection with Harding. If Harding had not been an impeccably honest man, if any faintest financial corruption had ever touched him, the glare of searchlights which the oil investigation was would have brought it out.

On June 16, 1931, nearly eight years after Harding's death, after the memorial to him at Marion, Ohio, had been long completed but had for several years stood undedicated, President Hoover, with former President Coolidge also present, performed the duty of a living President to the memory of a dead one; he paid just tribute to the fine qualities in Harding, and said:

> We came to know that there was a man whose soul was being seared by a great disillusionment. We saw him gradually weaken not only from physical exhaustion but from mental anxiety. Warren Harding had a dim realization that he had been betrayed by a few of the men he had trusted, by men he had believed were his devoted friends. It was later proved in the courts of the land that these men had betrayed not alone the friendship and trust of their stanch and loyal friend but they had betrayed their country. That was the tragedy of the life of Warren Harding.

It was Harding's tragedy, but the country's also. Harding's ended with his death; a nation is a constantly developing organism, wounds to a national spirit may modify its ethos for a long time. The injury to the national morale by such conditions as arose in Harding's Administration could not be wholly cured by the austere disinfectant that the Administration of Coolidge was. When, in the early 1930's, depression came; when depression caused discontent, and discontent expressed itself in the discrediting of government by plays, books, and the intellectuals — in that condition the willingness of the public to tolerate the demeaning might have been less, but for the recollection of the Harding scandals, which seemed to justify it.

16

SOME NEW THINGS IN BOOKS DURING THE TWENTIES

The "War Books." Novels, and also Plays, Which Dealt
with the War, or Had the War as Their Background. The
Effect Made upon National Thought by the Fact that
the War Books Were Unanimously Grim and Realistic in
Their Descriptions of the War, Uncompromisingly Stern.
The "Lost Generation." And the "Younger Generation,"
Together with the Novels about Them — and by Them.
"Sex Stuff," Which Was Written by Exploiters; and also
the Treatment of Sex by Sincere Writers. The Credo of
the Young Intellectuals. A Trend in Literature Which Displaced the Legendary "Old South." Some Important Novels
of the Period. The Diffusion of Culture, of Varying Kinds.
The Processes Through Which the Average Man Is Influ-
enced by Books He Never Read, Authors of Whom He
Never Heard. The Prolongation of Youth. Autobiographies without "I." And the Poetry — Including the
"Light Verse."

THAT the War should give rise to books and plays was
natural. That the output would be large was to be expected — the age was vocal. What constituted a phenomenon was that the "war books" unanimously took
one view of the war, the bitter view. All pictured war
grimly — a horrible, destructive experience for those
who lived through it; a loathsome, useless death for
those who died. The figures whom literature about
former wars had made to seem romantic, glamorous —
Kipling's dashing young subalterns, Richard Harding
Davis's gallant captains, even Rupert Brooke's eager
young patriots — all these seemed a thousand years away
from the stony disillusionment expressed in the novels
and plays about the Great War.

When the war books turned out to be very grim, and

yet best sellers, there was argument about what inference should be made, what the phenomenon might portend. Some, pacifists especially, believing that the wide reading of works picturing war in its most horrible aspects might mean popular hatred of war, thought, perhaps too sanguinely, that the revulsion would bring permanent world peace. Others, perhaps too gloomily, inferred that, since authors wrote war books because the public liked to read them, it must be that the public liked war. "People," said one critic,[1] do "not read what they do not enjoy reading; the success of war books is due to the fact that people like them; this truism reveals an appalling truth — war books are a success because people like war."

Somewhere between those two extremes lay the correct interpretation. It was nearer to the former. True, the average person enjoyed war books avidly — the sales proved that; books treating war with unrelieved realism were immensely popular. But it is possible to enjoy art without necessarily wishing to experience what the art portrays. Many a reader of war books reflected, "So that is war! Thank God I wasn't there!" And the average reader said further — this was one contribution of the war books to national policy — "We must see to it that America gets into no more wars."

This disillusionment, the unanimity of it, and the force with which it was expressed, gave to the war books as a group an importance unique in the literature of the time. The importance had no relation to the literary value of the books. The importance was not in the field of literature; it was in the world of national point-of-view. The war books at once expressed and helped to create the national thought about a national question; they had weight in determining the country's attitude about

[1] Salvador Madariaga in the *Saturday Review of Literature*. Here condensed.

its relations with the world, and about some phases of domestic policy.

II

The War Books

Apart from their importance in expressing and determining national thought, it happened that many of the war books[2] were good as literature. "All Quiet" — so the title was abbreviated[3] — by a German, Erich Remarque (read in America more than any war book by an American), managed to convey the most revoltingly loathsome details of life in the trenches with a philosophical, an almost tranced detachment, infinitely more moving than indignation. The spirit of the book, comparable to the calm centre of a cyclone, was conveyed in the solemn rhythm, the sardonic irony of its title "All Quiet on the Western Front," a title most fortunately retained when the book was made into a very successful film,[4] where its influence on national thought was expanded.

There were very few novels in the early twenties which had not some war episodes or background, but

[2] The novels of the war here mentioned are but a few of the many. When Willa Cather described the experiences of a Nebraska boy, in "One of Ours," the Pulitzer committee in 1923 awarded her the prize for the best fiction of the year. Actually, Miss Cather's war novel was inferior to every one of her other, and earlier, novels in which she stayed with the background she knew best, the prairie life of Western Nebraska.

An attempt to rate Miss Cather's novels in the order of their value would probably place first "Oh Pioneers," with "My Antonia," "The Song of the Lark," and "A Lost Lady," close behind, and all four much better than "One of Ours."

[3] The original title, in German, was "Im Westen Nichts Neues" — "Nothing New in the West."

[4] Transition from print to celluloid was very frequently accompanied by an alarming change in the title of the work. One of the most startling metamorphoses was accomplished when Cecil B. de Mille, presumably after prayer and anguished thought, transformed Sir James Barrie's "The Admirable Crichton" into "Male and Female." The same type of "movie-mind" was epitomized in the *New Yorker* cartoon which showed one little lady explaining to another, "In the book it's a gun-boat, in the movie it's a woman."

"Three Soldiers," by John Dos Passos, was probably the first outstanding American novel written entirely about the Great War and life in the army. This record of what one reviewer called "the seamy side of experiences with the A.E.F." was obviously autobiographical

John Dos Passos.

in part — Dos Passos, as an ambulance driver, had seen the worst of war. The three soldiers he selected for artistic presentation of war's horrors were types of the A.E.F. — a city boy, a country lad, and a musician. They had gone into the war gaily, in the spirit of another Dos Passos character who wanted to get in quickly "before the whole thing goes belly up." But soon: " 'Fellers,' Fred Summers was saying, 'this ain't a war, it's a goddam madhouse.' "[5] Still later: "I can't explain it but I'll never put a uniform on again." Their final desperation, the strain that passed the stage where war's

[5] Quoted from Dos Passos, "1919."

horrors were intolerable and reached a point where even the routine of army life was unendurable, was expressed, with appealing poignance, in, "I've got to a point where I don't give a damn what happens to me; I don't care if I am shot or if I live to be 80; I'm sick of being

"War—sure—is—hell."

One of Captain John W. Thomason, Jr's. drawings for his book of the war "Fix Bayonets."

ordered around; one more order shouted at my head is not worth living to be 80."

A play about the War, "Journey's End" by R. C. Sheriff, achieved its sombre spirit without stressing war's physical horrors; there were no sordid details to be, so to speak, risen above; Sheriff's art, suggesting the Greek classics, made the very fact of war seem more tragic and terrible than any mere wounds to the physical body or any sights of carnage. The struggle between man and the terrific forces that were utterly beyond his control, and between man and the varying facets of his own nature when under the strain of war — all that Sheriff portrayed with a verity, and a beauty of writing and characterization, which achieved something close to greatness.[6]

Another play dealing entirely with the War, "What

A scene from the motion picture made from "What Price Glory."

Price Glory," by Maxwell Anderson and Lawrence Stallings, achieved prominence by genuine gusto and merit — and also achieved notoriety by the profusion and pungency of the soldier profanity pressed into service by the authors. A joke current during the vogue of "What Price Glory" was about two old ladies who, when they went to see the production, were as lady-like as old ladies should be, but who entered into the spirit of the

[6] Sheriff's art was able to make the drama completely adequate and compelling although there were only male characters in it.

play so thoroughly that, at the end, one said to the other, "Shall we get the hell out of here?" "Not," replied her elderly companion, "till I find my goddam glasses."

Of all the American writers influenced by the war and articulate in varying degrees, the one who was most acclaimed as the historian of the generation that reached maturity during the war, the one who summed up with final authority and greatest effectiveness the judgment of the most sensitive of that generation, was Ernest Hemingway. His early stories, beginning about 1925, although obviously a result of post-war disillusionment and of a passion for naturalism fed by the war, did not deal explicitly with war experiences. His later pronouncement about the war itself, coming ten years after it had ended, in 1929, was "A Farewell to Arms." The story begins in the Italian army where the hero, an American, is an officer in an ambulance unit. He is wounded and falls in love with a nurse. He deserts and they go to Switzerland where they pretend to be married and where the nurse dies in childbirth.

As to the war:

You did not know what it was about. You never had time to learn. They threw you in and told you the rules, and the first time they caught you off base they killed you. . . . I was always embarrassed by the words "sacred," "glorious," and "sacrifice," and the expression "in vain." We had heard them sometimes standing in the rain almost out of earshot, so that only the shouted words came through, and read them, on proclamations that were slapped up by billposters over other proclamations now for a long time, and I had seen nothing sacred, and the things that were glorious had no glory and the sacrifices were like the stockyards at Chicago if nothing was done with the meat except to bury it. There were many words that you could not stand to hear, and finally only the names of places had dignity. Certain numbers were the same way and certain dates, and these with the names of the places were all you could say and have them mean anything. Abstract words

such as glory, honor, courage or hallow were obscene beside
the concrete names of villages, the numbers of roads, the names
of rivers, the numbers of regiments and the dates.

When Hemingway spoke thus of the war he spoke
not only for himself and for other writers whose temperament led them to express themselves differently,
perhaps less poignantly. He spoke also for hundreds of
thousands of men, white and black, who shared to the
full his emotion. Some were unable to read or write,
most of them would have found that passage completely
unintelligible, but translated into their terms they would
have agreed. Hemingway spoke for an era.

III

The "Lost Generation"

The direct effect of the war on the generation that
lived through it was not the whole consequence. The
war affected every aspect of their lives, it would continue to affect them until they died; it affected and
would continue to affect the whole national spirit.

The war, carried on by draft on the whole country,
took in a representative cross-section of every class,
every type, every temperament. Some were exceptionally sensitive; among these would be the generation's
writers, artists and playwrights. As such they would
— and during the Twenties did — at once reflect the
mood of the generation and in part create it. Into the
books they wrote they put the effects of the war on
their own acute sensitiveness, and also the point-of-view
about the world and society which their revulsion to
war had caused in them; the books, being read, stimulated the same point-of-view in others. The writers and
artists were not the whole of the generation; many, differing in temperament, did not share their emotions
during the war, nor after the war share their disillusion-

ment, sense of frustration, and cynicism. Great numbers, an overwhelming majority, indeed practically all of the generation, lived lives normally contented.

But the writers and artists, though numerically only a tiny fraction of the generation, had an influence greater than their numbers. With perhaps too much con-

Ernest Hemingway.
From a photograph by Helen Breaker taken in Paris during the late Twenties.

fidence in their franchise to speak for all, and with some Byronic self-consciousness and romantic self-pity, they called themselves "the lost generation." That phrase was invented and applied to them, so gossip among writers said, by one of their idols, Gertrude Stein, in a conversation with Ernest Hemingway. And Hemingway it was who, in "The Sun Also Rises," wrote the most complete expression and description of the "lost generation." For the function, Hemingway was especially equipped, by temperament, by the reaction of his temperament to his own experiences in the war, and by his style (a greatly simplified and articulated derivation from Gertrude Stein's early principles) which, though it becomes occasionally monotonous, has an individual rhythm and power. Like a mental surgeon in a sardonic mood, Hemingway cut away ideals, introspection, analysis, subtlety, national or class roots, and left his characters reduced to the simplest terms. He believed in a world in which the only conceivable good is an intensification of stoicism, courage to endure rather than courage to do. Of this rather primitive attitude "The Sun Also Rises" is the outstanding expression. It deals with a group of expatriates in Paris — Jake, Bill, Brett Ashley, Robert Cohn and their friends — artists and writers who feel that life is too complicated to think about and who endlessly pursue some unobtainable anodyne for their bored and rootless spirits. Terse and quick-witted, they drink incessantly, sobering up occasionally only to get drunk again as soon as they realize that the world about them is still too much with them — and for them. Any diversion which will prevent thought is desirable. Introspection is absolutely useless, to be avoided at any cost.[7]

Those who, like the characters in "The Sun Also Rises," were made by the war into neurotics, were a small number. The writers who wrote about them were an even smaller number. But the historian must always consider the right of the current books of any period to be accepted as the reflectors and records of the period, as well as its guides and teachers. Rather more in the 1920's than in other periods did books clearly establish the inevitability of their inclusion in an adequate his-

[7] Other books by Hemingway were "Men Without Women" (1927) and "Death in the Afternoon" (1932).

tory of the times. An author might take refuge in an ivory tower to avoid the rub of the world, yet he could not help reflecting the world. Even less could he avoid influencing it. Permeation of his ideas was facilitated by new mechanisms for the spread of the written word. A book was written; by highly organized business methods it was spread and sold; accompanying distribution as a book, it was disseminated far and wide by serial publication in newspapers and periodicals; if successful it was imitated; the imitations were put through the same processes; both original and imitations were made into motion pictures. By the sum of these processes, ideas in books spread out, during the 1920's, to a larger proportion of the population[7a] than in any other country or time. Indeed, dissemination of the ideas in any really popular book was close to universal. Many a father had to tolerate a conversation overheard in the sitting room between eighteen-year-old Nelly and her beau, a conversation which shocked the old gentleman — because a man he never heard of named Hemingway wrote a book he never heard of called "The Sun Also Rises."

[7a] The interest in books during the decade can be judged, not only by the opinions of historians of literature or social life, but by figures. In 1919 American publishers put out 5,741 new titles; in 1929 the number had almost doubled, increasing to 10,187. In 1919 E. Haldeman-Julius founded, in the little town of Gerard, Kansas, what was to become almost an American institution, the library of Little Blue Books, paper-bound volumes which sold first at ten cents the copy and later at five. Between 1919 and 1929, one hundred millions of these were sold. In 1926 was founded the Literary Guild, an association sponsored by Carl Van Doren, Joseph Wood Krutch, Elinor Wylie, Zona Gale, Hendrik van Loon, and Glenn Frank, who considered each month the newly published books and sent one which they selected as the best to their subscribers. A year later the Book of the Month Club was sponsored by Henry Seidel Canby, Christopher Morley, Heywood Broun, Dorothy Canfield Fisher, and William Allen White. This association had the same purpose as the Literary Guild and a more appealing title. The name, in fact, had the happy fortune to become a vogue — dresses were advertised as "The Dress of the Month." The First Edition Club and the Limited Editions Club were designed for the book collector rather than the reader. The Modern Library, a collection of reprints of distinguished books begun in 1918, was still tremendously popular seventeen years later.

IV

The "Younger Generation"

The average thoughtful American had, when the World War broke out, reached a place where he had attained enough material prosperity to enable him to have the leisure to reflect on the world about him. This release from the stress of making a living and gaining security for himself and his children was interrupted by the war. Not only was his leisure taken from him by the stress of world problems but his inclination to think of himself was taken from him by the daily reading matter of tragedy, by the vitalness and the starkness of the life that the daily press placed in front of him for four years or more.

When the war and its problems seemed to have been temporarily shelved, he found that he had more leisure than he had had before, and that he could give his children the opportunity for education and development that he himself had been deprived of by the exigency of making a living. He could give his children some protection from the necessity of making a living until they had obtained a college education, in some cases until they had attempted to find their place in the world through extra post-graduation years at universities; in remarkably many cases he could keep them from the necessity of facing the workaday world until they had had a chance to travel extensively through the civilized world. Of course, this was not true of a majority of the fathers of families in the United States, but it was true to some degree for a large part of the young generation maturing between 1919 and 1929.

Youths who, if born a generation before, would have been behind the plow at fifteen, remained in high school until seventeen, or in some cases went to college until twenty-three, or even to post-graduate school until close to thirty. The prosperous condition of the entire American business world made it possible for many young men and women, whose families formerly could not have supported them after they were through high school, now either to earn their way through college, or borrow the money, or acquire scholarships. Many could earn their way to Europe, either as stewards on transatlantic liners, or by playing musical instruments for the entertainment of other young people travelling "Students Third," or by conducting the children of wealthier parents to Europe, or by working for the numerous American business concerns that needed young people to handle the affairs of fellow Americans travelling on the Continent.

Also after the war an emphasis was placed on the young, simply because they were young, that has probably never been equalled in the history of the world. Anthropologists say that the more highly developed forms of animal life can be distinguished, among other marks, by the length of the period in which they protect their young. If this analogy can be carried over to a race that prolongs the care of its young, then the 1920's was a period of an exceptionally high civilization. Partly because of the number of youths lost through the war; partly because of the emphasis that psychology and psychoanalysis placed on training the individual when he is young, before his habits are set; partly because of the premium that the inventions of the machine age placed on the younger person — it was difficult for an older man to adjust himself to the dexterity demanded in handling new machinery — partly for these reasons, but mainly because of the wish and the means to gratify it, this generation gave its youth unheard of opportunities for education and advancement. The decade was the decade of the young. It was natural that the literature of the period would be occupied, more than is generally the case, with the contrast between an older and a younger generation.

It was natural that youth, having the advantages that

"It's broccoli, dear."
"I say it's spinach, and I say the hell with it."

This illustration, printed in the *New Yorker,* became famous. The firmness and definiteness of the child's expression of opinion, together with the forcefulness of language, was accepted as the complete picture of the mental attitude of the "younger generation."

the parents had not, would measure the parents by a new standard and find them lacking. Youth felt superior. Always youth is a little defiant, always it has an adolescent conviction of its own importance; and the American youth of the Twenties found in the world about him many circumstances that tended to confirm this conviction. Pathetically, in many cases, the parent fed the natural arrogance of the youth, subscribed to the superiority which youth claimed for itself. The Twenties, reversing age-old custom, Biblical precept and familiar adage, was a period in which, in many respects, youth was the model, age the imitator. On the dance-floor, in the beauty parlor, on the golf course; in clothes, manners, and many points of view, elders strove earnestly to look and act like their children, in many cases their grand-children. The egotism thus stimulated was increased by the ease with which young folks could achieve economic, and therefore to a large extent, moral and intellectual independence. Everywhere, youth was flattered. In Italy, Mussolini, with Latin extravagance, adopted as his national anthem a song beginning, "Youth, youth, springtime of beauty." And there was one supreme cause for the ascendancy of youth: youth had fought the war; no matter what his years, any male who had gone through the war was a man, chartered to talk, think, and write like a man.

An opening gun in the pro-youth, pro-freedom, and anti-Puritanism campaign was fired in 1920, with the publication of "This Side of Paradise," a book which had the distinction, if not of creating a generation, certainly of calling the world's attention to a generation. The author was F. Scott Fitzgerald, aged 24.[8] While it was felt that the book was not literally autobiographical, still, alarmed elders felt that Fitzgerald knew of what he wrote. It was a curiously chaotic and formless novel, with almost every fault except lifelessness. The central character, Amory Blaine, a young man of great beauty and sensitiveness, finds himself facing a world in which all gods are dead, all wars fought and all faiths in man shaken. World-weary as he considers himself to be, he manages to enjoy several love affairs of extraordinary

[8] Youth is a relative term for every age. Elizabethan young men were commonly through their education and launched on the world at seventeen.

subtlety and sophistication. The theme gave Fitzgerald an opportunity to record college life in the jazz age without falling into either of the two great errors, belligerent hedonism or comstockery. But Fitzgerald's readers were unable to preserve so detached a point of view. Young people found in Amory's behavior a model for

F. Scott Fitzgerald, author of "This Side of Paradise."

their conduct — and alarmed parents found their worst apprehensions realized.

The interest created by "This Side of Paradise" stimulated imitation.[9] Lynn and Lois Montross wrote lightly mocking stories of life in a small coeducational college in the West, where their protagonists had formed themselves on Fitzgerald's model; the principal character was Andy Protheroe, a perpetual senior. Charles Wertenbacker with a novel called "Boojum" caused a sensa-

[9] The novels about youth and college, here mentioned as successors to "This Side of Paradise," give a straight account, according to the authors' ability, of life as the younger generation lived it. As such, this group of novels is to be clearly distinguished from the pornographic, or pathological, or excessively realistic sex novels mentioned elsewhere in this chapter.

tion, as limited geographically as it was intense emotionally, by his description of life and liquor at the University of Virginia, where, according to this author, alcohol for the time had taken the place of the ideals of Thomas Jefferson and snobbishness had replaced chivalry.[10]

An English equivalent of "This Side of Paradise" was "Dusty Answer," by Rosamond Lehmann, which became a best seller in America. Either because of the passage of time — "Dusty Answer" was published in 1928 — or because of the difference between the American and British temperaments, there was at Oxford, according to Miss Lehmann, little or no jazz or drinking or petting parties or use of a "line."[11] The leading trait of the British young, Miss Lehmann's book implied, was a peculiar and involved — the unsympathetic might say neurotic — sensibility and subtlety; they "suffered."

v

The Younger Generation in Black and White

Supremely, the artist of youth in the jazz age, in words as well as drawings, was John Held, Jr., whose sardonic sketches of "flappers," "jelly beans" and "drug store cowboys" were a caricature gallery of the youth of the period. Held's drawings became a proof of Oscar Wilde's contention that nature imitates art far more than art imitates nature. As the Gibson girl and the Gibson man had been the ideal for the youths and maids of the 1890's, so Held's drawings were the archetype of the

---

[10] Other novels of the same general type as "This Side of Paradise" included "The Wife of the Centaur" by Cyril Hume, "What Happens" by John Herman, "Spirals" by Aaron Marc Stein, "The Plastic Age" by Percy Marks, "Glitter" by Katherine Brush, "The Barb" by William McNally.

[11] "Line" was collegiate for a stereotyped conversational pose; each youth aspired to have an individual one.

late Twenties. On every street corner was the Held male, buried in a raccoon coat, with patent leather hair, wrinkled socks and bell-bottomed trousers. Frantically bidding for the superior creature's attention was the Held flapper — stubby feet, incredibly long and brittle

John Held, Jr.'s drawings of the younger generation for Scott Fitzgerald's "Tales of the Jazz Age."

legs, brief and scanty skirt, two accurate circles of rouge just below the cheek bones, and a tight little felt hat like an inverted tumbler. The apotheosis of an attitude heralded its passing.

VI

The Intelligentsia

The attitude of the Twenties' younger generation was not caused wholly by the war, nor was it as new with them as they thought. The causes went as far back as

Darwin in the 1860's, and included the doctrines of Freud about sex which came to America in 1910, the reading of the hedonistic quatrains of Omar Khayyam about the same time, the jeering at conventionality that Bernard Shaw had kept up for more than a generation, the novels of H. G. Wells. All these influences and many others, growing cumulatively, came to a climax in the Twenties. To these were added the effect on young American minds of seeing what was happening in Russia. Here was being put in practice a new conception of society and government, a conception which not only ran counter to, but denied, opposed, and regarded as its enemies, nearly everything that, in other forms of society and government, were regarded as fundamental. The new Russian conception fought religion, called it the "opium of the masses," exterminated private property, introduced new and startling practices about marriage and family life.

The ferment of all these influences in the world could not help but affect young Americans greatly. The "younger generation" in combination with the "lost generation" took the new ideas, and themselves, most seriously. A group of them — authors, poets, playwrights and artists — inhabited a purlieu of New York, a modern American version of Bohemia, called Greenwich Village. Some so-to-speak cousins of them lived in the Latin Quarter in Paris. The ideas they advanced, the convictions they held, amounted about 1920 to a doctrine, a system, which, one[12] of them said years later, "could roughly be summarized as follows":

1. *The idea of salvation by the child.* — Each of us at birth has special potentialities which are slowly crushed and destroyed by a standardized society and mechanical methods of teaching. If a new educational system can be introduced, one

[12] Malcolm Cowley. The statement, here condensed, is taken from Cowley's "Exile's Return."

by which children are encouraged to develop their own personalities, to blossom freely like flowers, then the world will be
saved by this new, free generation.

2. *The idea of self-expression.* — Each man's, each woman's,
purpose in life is to express himself, to realize his full individu-

"*But Mater, this is life in the raw.*"

A drawing by Van Buren in the "New Yorker."

This cartoon "But Mater, this is life in the raw" pictured another form of self-
expression on the part of the youngish generation.

ality through creative work and beautiful living in beautiful
surroundings.

3. *The idea of paganism.* — The body is a temple in which
there is nothing unclean, a shrine to be adorned for the ritual
of love.

4. *The idea of living for the moment.* — It is stupid to pile up
treasures that we can enjoy only in old age, when we have
lost the capacity for enjoyment. Better to seize the moment
as it comes, to dwell in it intensely, even at the cost of future
suffering. Better to live extravagantly, gather June rose-buds,
"burn our candle at both ends."

5. *The idea of liberty.* — Every law, convention or rule of
art that prevents self-expression or the full enjoyment of the

moment should be shattered and abolished. Puritanism is the great enemy. The crusade against Puritanism is the only crusade with which free individuals are justified in allying themselves.

6. *The idea of female equality.* — Women should be the economic and moral equals of men. They should have the same pay, the same working conditions, the same opportunity for drinking, smoking, taking or dismissing lovers.

From a drawing by Alice Harvey in the "New Yorker."

The child's request, "Mother, when you're dummy, will you hear my prayers?"
was a biting satire on the vogue of bridge and the devotion
of parents to pleasure.

7. *The idea of psychological adjustment.* — We are unhappy because we are maladjusted, and maladjusted because we are repressed. If our individual repressions can be removed — by confessing them to a Freudian psychologist — then we can adjust ourselves to any situation, and be happy in it. . . .

8. *The idea of changing place.* — "They do things better in Europe." England and Germany have the wisdom of old cultures; the Latin peoples have admirably preserved their pagan heritage. By expatriating himself, by living in Paris, Capri or the South of France, the artist can break the Puritan shackles, drink, live freely and be wholly creative.

The influence of the intelligentsia went far. One of the Greenwich Villagers, Edna St. Vincent Millay, a distinguished poet, wrote a stanza which became a battle cry of freedom for young people from the Atlantic to the Pacific:

> My candle burns at both ends;
> It will not last the night;
> But ah, my foes, and oh, my friends,
> It gives a lovely light.

That, during the early 1920's, could be recited by more young persons than could repeat the formalized codes of more orthodox authorities.

To put forth codes and *credos*, to give their ideas the form of pronunciamentos, proclamations of revolt, *defis* to the elders was one of the traits of the young moderns. Their opinions were collected into a "credo of the intellectuals" by an author of the period, Frederic Lewis Allen,[13] who said that "not many of them accepted all the propositions in the following rough summary, yet it suggests, perhaps, the general drift of their collective opinion":

1. They believed in a greater degree of sex freedom than had been permitted by the strict American code; and as for discussion of sex, not only did they believe it should be free, but some of them appeared to believe it should be continuous. . . . From the early days of the decade, when they thrilled at the lackadaisical petting of F. Scott Fitzgerald's young thinkers and at the boldness of Edna St. Vincent Millay's announcement that her candle burned at both ends and could not last the night, to the latter days when they were all agog over the literature of homosexuality and went by the thousand to take Eugene O'Neill's five-hour lesson in psychopathology, *Strange Interlude*, they read about sex, talked about sex, thought about sex, and defied anybody to say No.

2. In particular, they defied the enforcement of propriety by legislation and detested all the influences to which they attributed it. . . . They pictured the Puritan, even of Colonial days, as a blue-nosed, cracked-voiced hypocrite; and

---

13 In "Only Yesterday." Here condensed.

they looked at Victorianism as half indecent and half funny.
. . . Some of them, in fact, seemed to be persuaded that all
periods prior to the coming of modernity had been ridiculous
— with the exception of Greek civilization, Italy at the time
of Casanova, France at the time of the great courtesans, and
eighteenth-century England.

3. Most of them were passionate anti-prohibitionists, and

From "Judge."

"Mother, you've been gypped! This is the expurgated edition."

A pungent satire, from *Judge,* of the period of "sex novels" and the "younger
generation."

this fact, together with their dislike of censorship and their
skepticism about political and social regeneration, made them
dubious about all reform movements and distrustful of all reformers. They emphatically did not believe that they were
their brothers' keepers; anybody who did not regard tolerance
as one of the supreme virtues was to them intolerable. . . .

4. They were mostly, though not all, religious skeptics. If
there was less shouting agnosticism and atheism in the nine-
teen-twenties than in the eighteen-nineties it was chiefly because disbelief was no longer considered sensational and because the irreligious intellectuals, feeling no evangelical urge

to make over others in their own image, were content quietly to stay away from church. It is doubtful if any college undergraduate of the nineties or of any other previous period in the United States could have said "No intelligent person believes in God any more" as blandly as undergraduates said it during the discussions of compulsory college chapel which raged during the 'twenties. Never before had so many books addressed to the thinking public assumed at the outset that their readers had rejected the old theology.

5. They were united in a scorn of the great bourgeois majority which they held responsible for prohibition, censorship, Fundamentalism, and other repressions. . . . Those of them who lived in the urban centers prided themselves on their superiority to the denizens of the benighted outlying cities and towns where Babbittry flourished; witness, for example, the motto of *The New Yorker* when it was first established in the middle of the decade: "Not for the old lady from Dubuque."

6. They took a particular pleasure in overturning the idols of the majority; hence the vogue among them of the practice for which W. E. Woodward, in a novel published in 1923, invented the word "debunking." Lytton Strachey's "Queen Victoria," which had been a best seller in the United States in 1922, was followed by a deluge of debunking biographies . . . for a time it was almost taken for granted that the biographer, if he were to be successful, must turn conventional white into black and vice versa.

7. They feared the effect upon themselves and upon American culture of mass production and the machine, and saw themselves as fighting at the last ditch for the right to be themselves in a civilization which was being levelled into monotony by Fordismus and the chain-store mind. . . . The intellectuals lapped up the criticisms of American culture offered them by foreign lecturers imported in record-breaking numbers. . . .[13a]

If all this seems pretty jejune, a justified answer on behalf of the young American intellectuals might say they had a right to be surprised at their moderation. Their sincerity, their effort to pass the new ideas through the prisms of their own minds, to reflect upon them and reduce them to *credo* was a credit to them. They had

[13a] And bought, in great numbers, books about America by visiting foreign authors, such as "America Comes of Age," by André Siegfried.

recovered from the immediate war mood of Dos Passos'
soldier, "I don't give a damn what happens to me." They
cared very much what happened to them; they cared
very much what happened to the world, and with complete sincerity wished to make the world over according to what they conceived to be a better pattern. But
this charitable and consoling reflection did not occur to
many parents, who merely knew that, as it was often put,
the Twenties were a hard time for raising children.
Young persons in school and college, too immature to
understand the new ideas fully or reflect on them or
examine them as a code, merely said, with a kind of
diffident defiance, "I have a right to do anything that
doesn't harm any one else" — that was heard often by
parents in the Twenties, it was a kind of slogan of the
adolescent. With maturity, the young folks learned it is
not easy to live by so simple a formula, not easy for an
individual to be sure what acts of his will or will
not harm others, not easy indeed to be sure what acts will
or will not harm himself. Both to individuals and to
the "younger generation" as a group, passage of a little
time brought clear thinking, sobriety, and a sense of responsibility. The casualties attending the impact of new
ideas about morals were not more numerous than under
the old code. Indeed, I think that at any time during
the Twenties the essential standards, and the practices
under them, were on the whole rather more wholesome
than in the past.

VII

Sex as Best Seller

The practice of writing is in actuality a profession
like any other, in spite of the efforts of some practitioners to make it seem special or even supernatural. As
among lawyers there are shyster lawyers, as among phy-

sicians quack physicians, so there are literary quacks, men who, having some slight or even marked talent for writing, seize on literary trends and fads, and capitalize them. To such facile artisans, the Twenties were a period peculiarly favorable. A great demand for books of all degrees of merit, and many new and strongly

"May I assist you, madam?"
"N-no—I'm just on my way to the religious books."
A drawing by Helen Hokinson for the *New Yorker,* showing that the older generation was not unsusceptible to the vogue of sex novels but felt it proper to practise a little Victorian hypocrisy.

marked developments in the field of literature, gave them an unparalleled opportunity, and they took it.

In 1919, an honest artist, Sherwood Anderson, wrote "Winesburg, Ohio," and in all earnestness and sincerity recorded the life of an American middle western village as he believed it to be, its inhabitants preoccupied either consciously or unconsciously with sex. Contemporary with Anderson, and sharing his sincerity, several others — notably Theodore Dreiser and John Dos Passos in America, and Somerset Maugham and D. H.

Lawrence in England — wrote about sex with fidelity
to artistic integrity and to the validity of factual and
emotional realism.

Taking advantage of the honest pioneering done by
these valid artists, came the quacks. Warner Fabian, in
"Flaming Youth," made three motherless sisters the
puppets about which he wove an improbable tale almost
exclusively concerned with sex and alcohol, its high spot
a moonlight bathing scene. It is most unlikely that Mr.
Fabian believed that such characters existed anywhere
in the length and breadth of the United States, but he
knew the bans had been raised and that all through the
country men and women, who would not read Anderson's sober and troubling book, would devour with las-
civious excitement Fabian's glib and highly spiced account of the improbable and erotic adventures of
incredible people. In a second novel, "Unforbidden
Fruit," Fabian, using college life as a background,
achieved an even greater apotheosis of pruriency, and a
second time made the best-seller list.[14]

Of all the sex books, the one that attracted the most
attention, one that for a time had the ecstatic adulation
of much of the intelligentsia, was "Jurgen," by James
Branch Cabell. Upon its publication in 1920, it was
suppressed. Moved perhaps by anger towards the
authorities, or possibly by regard for the painful efforts
at a style which the book showed, the literati of the
United States hailed a masterpiece. Not without dissension even within the ranks of the elect, however. While
one critic praised it as written "with phallic candour"
another felt that it had been written "with a smirk" —
precisely between those two characterizations lies the

14 From the deluge of novels emphasizing sex, I confine my allusions here to
those which at one time or another figured in best-seller lists. And of these I
have not mentioned all.

line that separates honest realism from deliberate lasciv-
iousness. On the whole, the group who insisted that
"Jurgen" was honest "phallic candour" won the day,

Drawing by Helen Hokinson in the "New Yorker."

"Avez-vous 'Ulysses'?"

When James Joyce's "Ulysses" was barred by the censors from sale in America,
Americans hunted for it in Paris book stores.

until they rather lost interest when the book was released for free circulation in 1923. The book is the
story of the adventures of a young man named Jurgen
in "the heaven of his grandmother and the hell of his
fathers" and a great many other strange and exotic
regions as well. Examined with more detachment twelve
years later, there seems little unique about it save a

curious use of rather strained erudition; "Jurgen" is an elaborately veiled and long-drawn-out smoking-room story which proves practically nothing save that Cabell had some acquaintance with the works of Anatole France. The book could, for the purpose of any examination of the literary trends of the era, be entirely disregarded save for two facts. The first is that it proves the self-consciousness of the breakdown of former reticences, and the second is that "Jurgen" was to some extent the forerunner of a curious little group of novels characterized by an immense and blasé cynicism and a fevered preoccupation with sex for sex's sake.

Sex, the subject of universal interest since time and man began, had an additional fascination for a generation recently and abruptly released from the prohibitions of Victorianism.[15] Eagerly certain types of writers catered to the demand. To satisfy it came sex in Paris as portrayed in Victor Marguerite's "The Bachelor Girl," with its extremely liberal heroine and the apartment in which she played hostess in extraordinary episodes; sex in college as portrayed in the career of Hugh Carver in "The Plastic Age"; sex on the desert as portrayed in "The Sheik," with its scenes of passion between a young English woman of title and an amorous Arab; sex in high-life London as portrayed in the luxurious milieu and sophisticatedly casual affairs of Iris March in Michael Arlen's "The Green Hat" — the vulgarity was increased by the Armenian author's awed admiration for the titled and the wealthy.

"Eric Dorn," by Ben Hecht was a story of neurotic people written in a choppy exotic style; when the same

[15] The release was not yet complete; such books as "The Sheik" and "Simon Called Peter" had to be smuggled into many a conservative house — the young people steering a course between the standards of their "set" and the standards of their parents.

author the following year published "Gargoyles," even the advanced minority group of the intelligentsia could find little to praise and contented themselves by mentioning that the characters were obsessed with sex. "Peter Whiffle," by Carl Van Vechten was a tenuous story of an idler among the sophisticated, a story so very attenuated and removed from ordinary life that it scarcely existed at all. "The Tattooed Countess" by the same author described the extremely dull seduction of a young boy in a midwest town by a countess with the appropriately gaudy name of Ella Nattatorini. "Blackguard," by Maxwell Bodenheim, a poet of some ability, and the same author's "Georgie May," the story of a prostitute in a Southern city, showed marked peculiarities of style and subject matter, subject matter which if treated differently would have been as permissible as any other, but which, as treated by Bodenheim, indicated a neurotic tension.

One novelist who dealt almost exclusively with manifestations of the sexual impulse, but who, due possibly to a less "high-brow" attitude, found a far wider audience than the others, was Elinor Glyn. All her books were utterly worthless, and all were tremendously popular. A perfectly fair sample of the Glyn dialogue is taken from "Man and Maid" in which the hero murmurs thoughtfully to the heroine, "You have had immense experience of love, Coralie, haven't you?" Mrs. Glyn's most lasting achievement was in a field not necessarily literary; like the man who had "quiz" written on all the walls of Dublin, like the unfortunate Captain Boycott, like the estimable Mrs. Bloomer and the industrious Macadam, Mrs. Glyn added a word to the English language. Rather, she added a meaning to the simple pronoun "it," transmuting that neutral little

word into a noun and making it, for the younger generation at least, a symbol for the most desirable thing the
gods could give. Mrs. Glyn used the word — with these

From a photograph by Underwood and Underwood.

Elinor Glyn, author, who introduced a new meaning for the pronoun "It"; and
Clara Bow, who became known as the "it girl in motion pictures.

especial connotations — for the first time in a short story
called "The 'It' Girl" to indicate a tremendous attraction for the opposite sex. In schools and colleges, classes
voting upon which of their members was most likely to
succeed, gravely included in their tests of distinction the
choice of the fellow-student fortunate enough to pos-
sess the most "It," sometimes translated as "sex appeal"

and abbreviated as "S.A." The sex books finally inspired
Samuel Hoffenstein to a couplet:

> "Breathes there a man with hide so tough,
> Who says two sexes aren't enough?"

VIII

A Minor Literary Iconoclasm of the Twenties

All "lost causes," if they are lost definitely enough,
whether by clearcut decision or by the passage of time,
become objects of romance and glamour. Bonnie Prince
Charlie is a story-book hero, William of Orange a
dull figure in history; Napoleon is a superman, Wellington just another general; Lee a legendary knight,
Grant a drab President. Inaccurate as these estimates
are, they are the snap judgments of the average man, or
his spontaneous feelings, and they would have to be
greatly changed before the love letters of the victorious
Duke of Wellington would be published serially in the
newspapers — as the defeated Napoleon's were in 1935.

Of this tendency to exalt the vanquished, the South,
after the Civil War, was one beneficiary. In imagination and in literature, the great houses became greater,
the lovely women lovelier, the chivalrous men more
chivalrous, the happy darkies happier.

This legend was accepted not only in the South but
perhaps even more wholeheartedly in the North. O.
Henry observed that when the band played "Dixie" in a
New York café about the turn of the century, the man
who leaped into the air with a wild yell, waved his hat
and then buried his face in his hands and burst into tears
— such a man said O. Henry cynically, is usually an
inhabitant of Keokuk, Iowa. Dixie was not alone the
song of the South, it was a symbol of romance for the
whole country.

This disposition of the whole nation to cherish the Southern legend was natural. We were a new country, our heritage of tradition was relatively scant, we lacked romantic associations, we had no sagas. We hungered for glamorous tradition, for legends of "home scenes and places and familiar names." To feed our hunger we accepted the tradition about the South and magnified it.

As for the South its circumstances drove it in the same direction. Prevented by superior force from actual secession, it sought solace in spiritual secession. Completely impoverished, the best of its manhood gone, the one way of life it knew destroyed, the South turned its face backward and created a legend of the past. For half a century, Southern authors — Thomas Nelson Page, F. Hopkinson Smith, George W. Cable, Mary Johnson, Joel Chandler Harris, even the "Little Colonel" books and the "Elsie Dinsmore" series — created, added to, and intensified a vision of life in which crino-lined maidens, hanging on the arms of gallant soldiers, walked forever beneath magnolia trees; where white-mustached and always courtly colonels drank an eternal julep brought to them by their devoted body-servants, where the laughter and the singing of the darkies was only interrupted to listen to the softer singing of birds.

To this picture, the first modification was brought by Ellen Glasgow. Born in Richmond, Va., self-educated there and remaining there, she became, in literature, a bridge between the old South and the new, the novelist of transition. Knowing the old South and loving it, yet seeing it clearly, she looked with equal clearness upon the coming of the new. Her "Deliverance" was the story of the passing of a plantation from one of the old families, the Blakes, incompetent to adjust themselves, to one of the new, wealthy families, the Fletchers. Miss

A scene from the stage presentation of Erskine Caldwell's "Tobacco Road," dealing with "poor whites" in the new South in literature.

An illustration by C. K. Linson for "In Ole Virginia," by Thomas Nelson Page, depicting life in the older, romantic South.

Glasgow treated both with objective fairness: "If a Fletcher can come by property honestly, all right; but if he is a vulgarian he will not sit at Miss Glasgow's dinner table. A Blake may sit at her table, rich or poor; but if he has lost his estate through his defects as a man, Miss Glasgow will tell him, somewhere between soup and nuts, that he deserved to lose it." [16]

It was Miss Glasgow who, precisely through her artistic objectiveness, did most to shatter the sentimental tradition of the South; certainly she was the first to crack it. Then in 1915, a younger author — he happened to be a relative of Miss Glasgow — James Branch Cabell, wrote a novel whimsically entitled "The Rivet in Grandfather's Neck," in which he told Richmond some quite unpleasant home truths. This was the beginning of the almost complete breakdown, so far as contemporary literature was concerned, of the legendary South. [17]

Presently, a critic, Henry L. Mencken, was hurling bricks, almost literally, at the Virginia legend: "not a single contribution to human knowledge has come out of her colleges in twenty-five years; she spends less than half upon her common schools, per capita, than any Northern state spends. In brief, an intellectual Gobi or Lapland."

It was in this spirit that the new South, in the person of its own writers, began to deal with the homeland. While the better ones preserved much of what was fine and true in the old picture, the South as a whole had the feeling of being subjected in literature, to what in politics and economics, in the North of twenty years be-

[16] Quoted from Grant Overton, here slightly paraphrased.

[17] A story told to express the former view of the old South was of the southern mammy who, instructing her white charge, said to the child "Never ask any one where they were born, honey; if they were born in Virginia they'll tell you, and if they weren't they don't want to talk about it."

fore, had been called "muckraking." Some of the new Southern writers seemed to take a sadistic, perverted pleasure in what an old phrase described as "fouling his own nest."

Taking the deep South as background, William Faulkner wrote, in "The Sound and the Fury," of a family in which one member was an idiot, one a prostitute, and one committed suicide; in "Sartoris," of a returned soldier who after several unsuccessful attempts, manages to accomplish, by his own suicide, the wiping out of a worthless and degenerate Southern family; and in "As I Lay Dying," the journey of an insane and revolting family of degenerates as they cart a putrefying corpse half across the state to bury it. As Granville Hicks said, "The world of William Faulkner echoes with the hideous trampling march of lust and disease, brutality and death." A less authentic artist, Erskine Caldwell, again with the deep South as background, achieved what would seem to be the ultimate in horror writing. In fact the horrors described by Caldwell were so extreme as to border on the grotesque. After reading one of his stories the exclamation of the average reader, uninfluenced by the idea that any pronouncement on art was necessary, would probably be, "Oh, now, honestly!" uttered in a tone of indifferent incredulity. In an effort, presumably to give some order to the chaotic and obviously overdrawn world that he created, Mr. Caldwell injected a little of the fashionable "class-consciousness" of the early depression years into his work — without, however, bringing his efforts any closer to literature.

Not all the realistic writing about the new South was sordid. Much of it merely applied correction to the earlier picture. DuBose Heyward in "Porgy" and "Mamba's Daughters," wrote of negroes as complicated characters, rather than colored puppets; and Julia Peterkin in "Green Thursday," "Black April"[18] and "Scarlet Sister Mary," which won the Pulitzer prize for 1929, did the same with greater realism. In 1929 Thomas Wolfe published a book having its background in North Carolina, which should rank as a great American novel,

Thomas Wolfe.

"Look Homeward, Angel." The sense of time and the universe, the beauty of writing and the deeply-rooted Americanism made the book great, at once a best seller and a favorite with the critics. No reader of the book could forget the vitality of the Pentland clan, the howling imprecations of W. O. Gant, the laconic and hidden love of Ben for his young brother Eugene, and the pathos of the little school that Eugene attended. So faithful was the book to the city of Asheville that it

[18] Of this book, with its story of the life of a South Carolina lowland plantation, one reviewer said this is "African life in what may be roughly called the first stage up from the jungle."

was said that touring busses conducted "Look Homeward, Angel" tours about the city, pointing out the scenes described in the book.

The novels of exceptionally high quality, having the South as their background, published during the 1920's,

Richard B. Harrison as "de Lawd" in Marc Connelly's Pulitzer prize play, "Green Pastures," based on "Ol' Man Adam an' His Chillun."

were many. Among the best were: "Avarice House," by Julian Green, "The Time of Man," by Elizabeth Madox Roberts; "The Romantic Comedians," and "They Stooped to Folly," by Ellen Glasgow; "Drums" and "Marching On," by James Boyd; "In Abraham's Bosom," by Paul Green, and "Teeftallow," by Thomas Stribling. "Ol' Man Adam an' His Chillun," by Roark Bradford, was adapted into the exceptionally popular and moving play, "Green Pastures," which had one of the longest runs in American dramatic history.

IX

Sinclair Lewis was a tall, lean, freckle-faced, red-haired young man with a temperament kin to the color of his hair. He had been born in a characteristic American small town, Sauk Centre, Minnesota; had gone through the local high school and through the other boyhood experiences of the community, with a nervous, restless, rebellious mind. He went to Yale University, learned much there, but was in constant irritation against many of the student-body's conventionalities; went to a Socialist and Utopian colony in New Jersey, where he stoked the furnace and ran the patent washing machine; passed some ten years, in different cities, in newspaper reporting and editorial work to which he was unsympathetic and at which he was neither very good nor very successful. Having by nature a mind that saw things in lights and colors different from those in which the average and complacent youth sees them, and having an innate distaste for the usual, the accepted, in way of life or point-of-view, Lewis, by the time he was thirty, had acquired a considerable number of rasping experiences, and a quite fat mental portfolio of keenly observed American types, many of them, to him, irritating. These he put into a number of novels. Since Lewis had an extraordinary gift for mimicry, the characteristic types in his novels were universally recognized, by themselves with resentment, with hilarity by those who disliked them. Lewis's novels became the most discussed fiction of the Twenties.

In "Main Street," Lewis introduced a gallery of typical characters of a small American town — the doctor, the undertaker, the storekeeper, a score of others — all painted unsympathetically except one, the doctor's wife, Carol Kennecott, a misfit dreamer, whose sensitiveness brought out the contrast with the self-satisfied provincialism of the others.

In "Babbitt" (George Follansbee Babbitt, leading realtor of Zenith), Lewis caricatured the small-city business man; he ridiculed Babbitt's pride in his city, his pride in his association with prominent persons of his small world, his pride in his up-to-date-ness, his pride in his automobile, his pride in his white-tiled bathroom —and, as a symbol of all that Babbitt represented, ridiculed his pride in his membership in Rotary. In "Elmer Gantry," Lewis lashed out at the clergy; inventing one whose major interest in his profession was material, and sensual; whose eye constantly moved from the sermon on his lectern to the figure of the most susceptible choir-girl; whose religion consisted of the art of showmanship; whose career was a constant juggling between his undisciplined desires and the necessity for deceiving his parishioners. In "The Man Who Knew Coolidge," Lewis achieved a composite of many types; Lowell Schmalz, oracularly pontificating to a group of fellow-Americans in a Pullman car, "does not stop talking after describing his intimate relations with Mr. Coolidge; he tells what he considers a funny story; he holds forth on women, California, relatives, touring, birth control, psycho-analysis, undertaking parlors and cafeterias."

Lewis's novels were prodigiously talked about; many who never read the books came to know the characters. "Babbitt" passed into the common tongue, like Hamlet, Don Quixote, and Sherlock Holmes; in American print and talk of the Twenties, "Babbitt" became almost a common noun, almost it could be spelled with a small "b"; the derivation "babbittry" was frequent. The term "Main Street" was recognized and used, by persons who never heard of the book, as a generic term for small-town ways, institutions, and personalities.

Of the types that Lewis satirized most fiercely, many were mainly in the world of business, the "go-getter," the smug success, the "human dynamo," the "mixer," the man who could "sell himself," the one who could "put his message across." As a consequence of the satires

Sinclair Lewis (left) and James Branch Cabell.

by Lewis and others — combined with several contemporary actualities, over-emphasis on salesmanship, over-respect for business success — and also some contemporary scandals in business and politics — it resulted that some American types formerly treated with deference, even in some cases awe, found themselves, by the end of the 1920's, occupying pedestals lower than those to which they had been accustomed. The process went hand in hand with the debunking of history which was also a characteristic of the period.

X

Mencken of Baltimore

To write of Henry L. Mencken as a literary figure is completely appropriate and accurate — yet inadequate. He was a national character, and the magazine he edited, the *American Mercury*, a national institution, one with an influence projecting into the future, for, said a teacher at the University of Chicago, an elderly conservative alarmed for youth, "the one thing that makes me fear for the future is the number of our students who read the *American Mercury*; on the campus you see it under every arm; they absorb everything in it." And a clergyman, the Reverend S. Parkes Cadman of Brooklyn, appealed to "pastors and orators" to talk at colleges, that students "be saved from the beliefs preached by H. L. Mencken." Another clergyman, the Reverend Louis L. Neuman of San Francisco, partly in satire, partly in unwilling concession, gave to Mencken and his magazine the rank of a cult: "Mercurianity is the name of a new religion, the Bible of which is a green-covered monthly magazine."

Mencken was a Baltimorean by birth, and, as he reiterated in his diatribes against New York, by preference. Even during the some fifteen years he edited magazines published in New York, he commuted twice a week or so from Baltimore, retaining, by his residence in the latter city, a contact with a more average American background, an immunity from infection by the metropolis, a detachment from the influence of New York's literary cults and fads — which fortunate dissociation was part of his uniqueness and his strength. His innate ruggedness hated the esthetic pose; while he knew intimately the most elevated stratum of professional writers, and held their exceptional confidence in his taste and judgment, yet by instinct he spent many of his hours of diversion, much of that part of his time not devoted to writing and editing, in the company of persons remote from the esoteric.[19] He maintained his connection with workaday newspaper circles, kept his hand in by regular contributions to the Baltimore *Sun*; at political conventions he was present as a working reporter. By instinct he stood apart from the rather effete or neurotic self-styled "intelligentsia" of the period; when they were writing about sex and shrieking against Puritanism, and clamoring for more freedom, Mencken thought they "have just about as much freedom as is good for them,"[20] as much as their literary horse-power could make good use of. Mencken was too vital to have any kinship with the defeatists who wrote much of the fiction of the "lost generation," too normal and wholesome to have much communion with the neurotics who wrote many of the novels of the "younger generation."

One other immunity Mencken had; he had never gone to college, and thus he became an outstanding one among those occasional personalities that are the better for not having been subjected to formal academic training, "a good brain not spoiled by education." As a youth and as a young man working on the Baltimore *Sun*, his native instinct for excellence led him to find standards of his own; his mind, curious, acquisitive for knowledge, and virile and conscientious, grew sturdily, with a confidence, and ultimately a sure-footed facility, that might not have come to him had his information and standards, and his art, been handed down to him. With Mencken, information, knowledge, standards of taste, judgment

[19] Once he told me he had never attended a "literary tea" (Prohibition era euphemism, partly sarcastic, for a literary cocktail party).

[20] Though he once challenged arrest in the interest of resistance to censorship.

about books and about men — these grew, with Mencken, as with a coral, through slow acquisition accompanied by sure digestion into an integral possession of his own. The understanding of words, prosody, style, which many college students fail to acquire from a score of

H. L. Mencken.

teachers and text-books, Mencken distilled for himself from one self-found book, Sidney Lanier's "Science of English Verse." He became one of the most skilled craftsmen of his time. As a stylist, his every sentence was firm and intelligible; he had a genius for the striking word and the effective phrase, an instinct for musical sentences; he knew how to make punctuation an effective accessory to his art, he used it perhaps more meticulously than other writers of the Twenties; he achieved the most forthright, clear and provocative writing done in America during his time. His style was a complete expression of his personality, and was therefore brilliantly effective for what he had to say.

Meeting Mencken, sitting down opposite to him at table (usually there would be a stein of beer or a bottle of wine between) one would, if given twenty guesses about his occupation, have said business man, or lawyer, or doctor, or any other of seventeen. In appearance he was stocky, almost chunky, his head round, his eyes blue-gray and direct, his mouth humorous. Once, practising the humorous candor and engaging intimacy that was an alluring part of his art, he described[21] himself:

> ... Five feet eight and half inches in height and weighs about 185 pounds. In 1915 he bulged up to 197 pounds, then he took the Vance Thompson cure and reduced to 175, rebounding later. He has good eyes and a gentle mouth, but his nose is upset, his ears stick out too much, and he is shapeless and stoop-shouldered. One could not imagine him in the movies. He wears a No. 7½ hat. He is bowlegged. He is a fast walker. He used to snore when asleep but had his nasal septum straightened by surgery, and does so no longer. He wears BVD's all the year round, and actually takes a cold bath every day. He never has his nails manicured, but trims them with a jackknife. He works in his shirt-sleeves and sleeps in striped pajamas.

That physical averageness was accompanied by intellectual normalcy; Mencken was the normal American, essentially an American archetype — energetic, logical, entirely practical, curious, unbiased, loving liberty and scorning sentimentality and hypocrisy. In short, he applied to literature those habits of mind usually employed by Americans in the pursuit of business. A steel manufacturer would weigh no more impartially a proposition for doubling production than Mencken weighed the ideas current in his time. He loathed nothing more than "an endless series of false assumptions and nonsequiturs

21 In "Pistols for Two."

— bad logic piled recklessly upon unsound facts." He
was in incessant warfare upon "hampering traditions of
any sort." He was a firm believer in self-help and self-
reliance as the only necessities for personal advancement,
as firm a believer in them as were any of the Rotarians
whom he zestfully jibed at. He stood for progress, de-
ploring the tendency of the mob to cling to its delusions;
he was an individualist, believing that the rewards for
extraordinary efficiency should be without limit; he was
an admirer of the early heroes of America, because,
among other reasons, "The Fathers of the Republic
. . . not only sought to create a governmental machine
that would be safe from attack without; they also sought
to create one that would be safe from attack within;
they invented very ingenious devices for holding the
mob in check, for protecting the national policy against
its transient and illogical rages. . . . Nothing could
have been further from the intent of Washington, Hamilton and even Jefferson than that the official doctrines
of the nation, in the year 1922, should be identical with
the nonsense heard in the Chautauqua, from the evangelical pulpit and on the stump."

He distrusted Idealism — that is, self-conscious Idealism, Idealism with a capital I — that, Mencken called
"bilge." He hated prudery, and the censorship with
which prudery seeks to protect itself; the contemporary
symbol of prudery and guardian of it, Anthony Com-
stock, Mencken called a "damn fool," an "imbecile."
He hated slipshoddiness, in work, in morals, in thinking,
in style; the speeches of President Harding drove him to
fury: "Harding writes the worst English I have ever
encountered; it reminds me of a string of wet sponges;
it is so bad that a sort of grandeur creeps into it." But
equally Mencken hated meaningless mellifluousness;
turning from Harding to his predecessor in the White

House, Mencken wrote: "Almost I long for the sweeter song, the rubber stamp of more familiar design, the gentler and more seemly bosh of the late Woodrow." Even more did Mencken dislike Bryan: "Bryan was the most sedulous fly-catcher in American history and in many ways the most successful; his quarry, of course, was not *musca domestica* but *homo neandertalensis*; for 40 years he tracked it with coo and bellow up and down the rustic back-waters of the Republic."

Mencken attacked moralists, progressives, reformers, patriots, boomers; from the beginning of his career, he said, his general aim had been "to combat, chiefly by ridicule, American piety, stupidity, tinpot morality, cheap chauvinism in all their forms."

All these, and sundry miscellaneous disapprobations, Mencken set down in a series of books which, with a candor at once engaging and provoking, he labelled "Prejudices" — *Prejudices: First Series; Prejudices: Second Series; Prejudices: Third Series*, and so on to sixth, with, as a kind of compendium, a seventh volume called *Selected Prejudices*.

The particular disapprobation that brought Mencken most attention was that which became familiar through his newspaper reports of the Scopes trial. Mencken thought of Fundamentalism as largely one with Prohibition and the Ku Klux Klan, and at these he fired his biggest guns. Mencken's was not a fight against religion so much as one in behalf of tolerance; it was a fight largely in behalf of religious minorities — including that minority which believes in no religion:

After all, no human being really *knows* anything about the exalted matters with which all religions deal. The most he can do is to match his private guess against the guesses of his fellowmen. For any man to say absolutely, in such a field, that this or that is wholly or positively true and this or that is utterly false is simply to talk nonsense. Personally, I have never en-

countered a religious idea—and I do not except the idea of the
existence of God—that was instantly and unchallengeably
convincing, as, say, the Copernican astronomy is instantly
and unchallengeably convincing.   But neither have I ever encountered a religious idea that could be dismissed offhand as
palpably and indubitably false.   In even the worst nonsense
of such theological mountebanks as the Rev. Dr. Billy Sunday,
Brigham Young and Mrs. Eddy, there is always enough lin-
gering plausibility, or, at all events, possibility, to give the
judicious pause.   Whatever the weight of the probabilities
against it, it nevertheless *may* be true.

Mencken's reports from the Scopes trial, his attacks
upon Fundamentalism, Prohibition, and the Ku Klux
Klan, his thrusts at the rural sections, especially the
Southern sections — he called the South "the Bible-
belt" and its people "the boobery"; as individuals,
"boobus Americanus" — caused him to be noticed by a
wider audience than would have observed his more
purely literary productions. His victims fought back,
with blistering ferocity.

In the combat, necessarily the weapons had to be
words; and, compared to Mencken's arsenal, his adversaries were poor in vocabulary. They managed, however, to find a considerable number of simple, primitive
epithets, which they used with a force that, they hoped,
would offset Mencken's superiority in artistic deftness.
Many of the epithets were taken from the terminology
of the less esteemed species of the animal kingdom. The
aggregate of these zoological appellations — had Menck-
en been at one and the same time all the animals his adversaries called him — would have composed a truly
terrifying miscegenation. To the Tampa *Times*, Menck-
en was, by a curious mesalliance of disparate parentages,
at once "this maggot, this buzzard." To the Jackson,
Mississippi, *News*, he was "a howling hyena." To the
San Francisco *Chronicle* he was, simply, "a pole-cat."
Charitably the Philadelphia *Inquirer* said that "perhaps

society needs Mencken as nature needs mosquitoes." To the Minneapolis *Journal* he was — strange achievement in mongrelism — "wasp and pole-cat purely." To the Norfolk *Virginian Pilot* he was, with some aptness, "the literary man-eating tiger." The *Diapason* (Chicago) compared him to "flies that gather about the garbage in summer, and delight in what they can discover." To the Nashville *Tennessean* he was a "mangy ape"; to the Iowa *Legionaire*, "a mangy mongrel." A clergyman, the Reverend Charles E. Jones, D.D., writing in the *Gospel Call*, chose the buzzard metaphor, but carried it to artistic completeness: "If a buzzard laid an egg in a dung-hill and the sun hatched a thing like Mencken, the buzzard would be justly ashamed of its offspring." Other clergymen, seeking arts of repartee, found happy significance in the fact that the initials of Mencken's name, printed with a dash between "H—L," composed the accepted euphemism of print for an undesirable region. The Knights of the Ku Klux Klan of Arkansas formally "Resolved: that we condemn in the strongest possible language the vile mouthings of this writer, to whom virtue, patriotism and decency are only a subject upon which to expend the venom of a poisonous pen, and that we protest against the calumny as too degrading and false to come from the heart of one who is not himself a moral pervert."

Some of the retorts to Mencken came from discriminating sources: British author Arnold Bennett said that Mencken was "violent, farcical, grotesque and intellectually unscrupulous." British author J. B. Priestley called him "a roaring and bellowing democrat; the clown of an intellectual pantomime, who, while he merely touches up the policeman with a red-hot poker, sees himself as Lucifer dismantling Heaven." William Allen White, while using one of the zoölogical metaphors,

gave Mencken credit for much justification and usefulness: "With a pig's eyes that never look up, with a pig's
snout that loves muck, with a pig's brain that knows only
the sty, and a pig's squeal that cries only when he is
hurt, he sometimes opens his pig's mouth, tusked and
ugly, and lets out the voice of God, railing at the white-
wash that covers the manure about his habitat."

All of which, and some 130 printed pages of similar
epithets and miscellaneous objurgations, Mencken, with
the humorous gravity that was one of his charms, collected and published in a volume which he called
"Menckeniana, A Schimpflexicon," saying suavely, in
a prefatory note, that "this collection is not exhaustive,
but an effort has been made to keep it representative."

But one observed that Mencken's hospitality to his
enemies was not broad enough to include in his Schimpflexicon what many thought the sharpest arrow ever
aimed at him. When he, and a literary partner he had
for a time, were at the height of their vogue; and when
they seemed, to fellow-craftsmen, in some danger of
accepting too seriously the rôle of omniscience that current valuation set on them, a young woman[22] deft with
words, intent upon saving Mencken and his partner
from self-overestimation, wrote a biting couplet:

> Mencken and Nathan and God;
> Yes, probably, possibly, God.

XI

New Points of View in History and Science

What mainly characterized the books of the Twenties
was new point of view. New point of view is much the
same as obsolescence of old point of view; or worse than
obsolescence, disappearance; or, worse than death and

[22] Elisabeth Cobb, daughter of Irvin S. Cobb.

decent burial, jeering at the old. And one kind of passing or another was the fate, during the 1920's, of many old points of view — they went to the intellectual scrap-heap as rapidly as old designs of machinery, old conceptions of physics in the material world.

I have mentioned, in Chapter I, some changes that had taken place in the material world, many accompanying the war, some the result of influences going farther back — changes in the boundaries of nations, their forms of government, their relations to each other; changes in the map of commerce, changes in the values of currencies; advances in science, new inventions. Changes equally striking had taken place in the world of ideas, the patterns and channels and beaten ruts of man's thought. The two groups of changes are in this history, for convenience sake, categorized separately. But the separateness in nature is not so distinct. Change in the material world works change in men's minds, change in men's minds results in change in the world about them. The invention of the airplane became as much a modification in man's way of thinking as it was a change in time and distance. Since the childhood of the race, man had been told he could not fly; it was a fixed immutability, as certain as death. Now, man did fly. If that immutability was mutable, how about other negations and affirmations hitherto accepted as infallible, laws of science, dogma of theology, familiar axioms?

The emergence of new points of view was expressed in the writing of the Twenties. So great was the accumulation of them, so widely did they depart from the old, that much of the history of the race was re-written; partly, of course, in the light of new information, for some new had been discovered by the researches of archæologists and other scholars, but more in the light of new points of view, new theories about the forces that make history,[23] new hypotheses in science, new theories about men's motives and about human conduct.

The extent and rapidity of the writing from the new standpoints were matched by the avidity with which the public consumed it. Man was as eager to learn about his relation to cosmos as writers were industrious in providing him with the information. Subjects which in previous generations would have got into print only in the form of treatises that would have reposed on the shelves under such titles as "paleontology" or other words ending in "ology," were now among the books most in demand at public libraries. The average American, having achieved through his own efforts safety and prosperity, having created his own cosmos, was anxious for drapings to cover the bare flesh of his mind. Too busy in most cases to have attended college himself, he packed his sons and daughters off to have an education pumped into them, and settled down by his own fireside to repair his cultural deficiencies. There was a certain pathos about these efforts; too often they represented the tragedy of the tired business man who recognized his inability to amuse himself after office hours; too often they were founded in a pathetic but fundamentally weak fear that he would be unable to keep up not with the mythical Jones but with his own sophisticated children.

[23] Several histories written in America during the period had high quality. "The hunt for a civilization in the United States," said Carl Van Doren in 1927, "began with fresh energy about half a dozen years ago." Among important histories written during the Twenties were:

"The Frontier in American History,"	Frederick Jackson Turner
"The Founding of New England,"	James Truslow Adams
"New Viewpoints in American History,"	Arthur M. Schlesinger
"Main Currents in American Thought,"	Louis Vernon Parrington
"Our Times,"	Mark Sullivan
"The Golden Day,"	**Lewis Mumford**
"Rise of American Civilization,"	Charles and Mary Beard
"The Party Battles of the Jackson Period,"	Claude Bowers
"The New History and the Social Studies,"	Harry Elmer Barnes
"Domestic Architecture of the American Colonies and the Early Republic,"	Fiske Kimball

The first effort systematically to round up knowledge, throw it and hog-tie it, was made by H. G. Wells when he published the "Outline of History," two stout red volumes that covered quite adequately a big field. The "Outline of History" probably set a record for popularity, remaining on best-seller lists from 1920 to 1924. Following came "The Outline of Science" by J. Arthur Thomson. "Outlines" bceame a literary vogue; there was an "Outline of Literature" by John Drinkwater, and an ambitious, indeed over-ambitious, "Outline of Man's Knowledge" by Clement Wood. Accompanying the "Outlines" and similar to them were the "Stories": "The Story of Mankind" by Hendrik Willem Van Loon; the "Story of Philosophy" by Will Durant; "The Story of the World's Literature" by John Macy.

In 1923 appeared "The Humanizing of Knowledge" by James Harvey Robinson, a plea for the popularizing of science and learning, an eminently readable and authoritative justification for the outline system. In science, there was "The New Decalogue of Science" by Albert Edward Wiggam, "The Universe Around Us" by Sir James Jeans; "Our World Today and Yesterday" by James Harvey Robinson; "This Believing World" by Lewis Browne, an account of the great religions man has subscribed to; "The ABC of Atoms" by Bertrand Russell, a summary of recent knowledge about the constitution of matter; "Microbe Hunters" by Paul Henry De Kruif, stories of the pioneer bacteriologists who, during a brief new segment of history, had enlarged and greatly changed man's understanding of disease. All these were, in a way, brief notes from a ruler to the people, some explanations of the working of science to an age more influenced by science than by any other single force.

Psychology, in the Twenties, suffered a sea change,

a change for the better. Instead of preoccupation with
the pathological, psychology began to take an interest in
the average man, to explain to him what he was, to show
him profitable ways of thinking and conducting himself,
to act as a guide to every-day behavior. There was "The
Mind in the Making" by James Harvey Robinson, a
serious and worthy examination into man's failure to
solve his problems; "Why We Behave Like Human Be-
ings" by G. A. Dorsey, a study of the endocrine glands
and the mechanism of adjustment, and "The Hows and
Whys of Human Behavior" by the same author; "The
Art of Thinking" by Abbé Ernest Dimnet, an effort to
teach the unteachable; "The Fruit of the Family Tree"
by Albert Edward Wiggam, a study in heredity; "The
Doctor Looks at Love and Life" by Doctor Joseph Collins; "The Conquest of Fear" by Basil King; "Outwit-
ting Our Nerves" by Jackson and Salisbury; "The
Dance of Life" by Havelock Ellis. Psychology invaded
the field of biography; Gamaliel Bradford wrote
"American Portraits," which he described as psycho-
graphs or psychological portraits.

XII

New Viewpoints in Biography

Biography, also, was rewritten — in some cases in a
strongly critical, even sardonic spirit. In most cases not
much new information was sought, what was new was
the interpretation of old information. The actions and
motives of old heroes were subjected to new critical
standpoints, were interpreted in the light of new
theories, particularly new theories of psychology, including theories about human behavior which had been
put forth by Freud about 1910, and by others later. In
the process the old worthies suffered, for some of the

new biographers did not stop with mere application of
new understanding to old facts; some of them seemed to
take a pleasure in demeaning old heroes. This school of
biography reversed that dictum of St. Paul, which had
said "Whatsoever things are true, whatsoever modest,
whatsoever just, whatsoever holy, whatsoever lovely,
whatsoever of good fame, think on these things." The
up-to-date biographer, said the Dublin *Standard* (condemning, unfairly, Francis Hackett's "Henry the
Eighth") goes by the contrary rule, "Whatsoever things
are false, or immodest, or unholy and unlovely, whatsoever may be unjust to the fame of men and women long
since dead — above all, if there be any vice — on these
things he dwells." For the new way of writing biography a word was coined, "debunking," a 1920's equivalent for the "muckraking" of the early 1900's. The
biography that gave rise to the word was W. E. Woodward's "George Washington." A biography to which
the term was applied, not with complete justice, was
Rupert Hughes's "George Washington." Edgar Lee
Masters wrote "Lincoln the Man" in a manner which
caused a shocked reviewer to describe it as a "thorough-
going indictment of the man who is generally regarded
as one of our greatest statesmen."

A more gentle and delicate dissection was Lytton
Strachey's "Queen Victoria"; Strachey, said a reviewer,
taught that "something besides good might easily and
properly be said of the dead." By no means could the
term "debunker," in its popular connotation, be applied
to Strachey; he was an austere scholar with a fine and
accurate mind, quite lacking in prejudice or sensation-
seeking traits.

There were during the Twenties an exceptional number of excellent biographies: Amy Lowell's magnificent

"John Keats"; Albert Beveridge's "John Marshall"; Carl Sandburg's "Abraham Lincoln"; Burton Hendrick's "The Life and Letters of Walter H. Page"; Harvey Cushing's "The Life of Osler"; Hervey Allen's "Israfel The Life and Times of Edgar Allan Poe"; Henry James's "Charles W. Eliot." These were written with fidelity to the classic manner, using the mental habits of the era, rather than being used by them.

XIII

Fictionized Biography

Among literary experiments made during the decade was a curious hybrid, the novelized biography; as novel, diluted; as biography without pretense to scholarship and inaccurate by the nature of the case; as a whole worthless. In essence the author blandly invented conversations which might have taken place, scenes which would have been vastly effective, and even incidents which would have been extremely interesting. Pioneer among artisans of it was E. Barrington (a pseudonym). Most familiar of her half dozen books were "The Glorious Apollo," the life of Byron; "The Divine Lady," the romance of Nelson and his Lady Hamilton; and "The Exquisite Perdita," story of the love affair between George IV and the actress, Mrs. Robinson. The romantic and adoring titles are clues to the nature of the books; E. Barrington's geese were not only swans but magically beautiful and heroic swans. In 1925 André Maurois joined the field of sentimental biographers with "Ariel," a highly colored and rather inaccurate life of Shelley.

It is difficult to recapture at this later date the reason for the popularity of these works. They gave no particularly clear picture of the times which they set out to portray, nor did the principal characters seem startlingly alive. Perhaps their wide popularity was due to the fact that, as easy to read as any light novel, still they dealt more or less with facts and gave some information, and so fitted in with the desire for information which was a characteristic of the decade.

Remotely related to these "novelized biographies," but much better, were the novels of John Erskine. The difference was that Erskine, instead of romanticizing facts, merely — but ably and successfully — put legends through a process of pert modernization. In a spirit of sophistication, precisely and cleverly attuned to the times, he wrote "The Private Life of Helen of Troy"; its prompt emergence on best-seller lists was deserved by its excellence, but without doubt many bought the book expecting to get a choice example of the sex literature that was then flamboyantly current. Erskine's second book, "Galahad, Enough of His Life to Explain His Reputation," won its best-selling position presumably without adventitious aid from purchasers seeking the pornographic.

XIV

Autobiographies Without "I"

In the judgment of many persons of reflective temperament, the best autobiography ever written by an American (some thought it the best ever written by any one) appeared in 1919. (There had been a private publication some years before.) That it remained on best-selling lists for 18 months is a tribute at once to the quality of the book and to the taste of a large segment of American readers — compensation for the popularity conferred upon many trivial or foolish volumes, even undesirable ones. It remained in 1935 among the few books of the 1920's that seemed most likely to endure, or the best deserving to endure. One might use, as a test of the cultural standard of Americans having some eleva-

The Memorial to Mrs. Henry Adams, in Rock Creek Park, Washington, D. C.
By Augustus Saint-Gaudens.

tion of taste, two questions: did they read and appreciate "The Education of Henry Adams?" And did they know, actually or in pictorial reproduction, and were they moved by, the bronze statue of "Grief" [24] in Rock Creek Park, Washington, D. C., which Henry Adams had the

[24] Adams preferred to call it "The Peace of God."

sculptor Saint-Gaudens make as the tombstone for his wife?

Henry Adams came of the best stock America possessed, received the best education America afforded, experienced the most cultivated associations and followed one of the most elevated careers. Grandson of one President of the United States, great-grandson of another, member of the American family that has had the most sustained vitality and has contributed the largest number of members to the public service, he was born under the shadow of the State House in Boston; spent much of his youth with his grandfather, the sixth President, in retirement at Quincy; listened as a child to the table-talk of the statesman, Charles Sumner, the historian John G. Palfrey, and the writer, Richard Henry Dana;[25] was educated at Harvard, where his teachers included the scientist, Louis Agassiz, and the poet James Russell Lowell; was further educated in Germany; served as secretary to his father, Charles Francis Adams, when the latter was American Minister to Great Britain during the stirring period of our Civil War; taught history at Harvard; edited the *North American Review* when it was the most distinguished literary periodical in America; wrote authoritative books in a wide variety of fields — "Essays on Anglo-Saxon Law," "Life of Albert Gallatin," "Life of John Randolph," a nine-volume "History of the United States," a study of mediæval life and philosophy called "Mont-Saint-Michel and Chartres"; wrote two novels under a pseudonym; travelled — often, extensively and thoughtfully — throughout Europe, in the Caribbean, in the South Seas; and spent his later years in Washington as the closest friend of John Hay and a familiar in a group of similar spirits. More than any other man of his generation,

[25] Author of an American classic, "Two Years Before the Mast."

Henry Adams had known the finest and most thoughtful minds in America and Europe, had known them intimately; more than any other man, he had participated in the most elevated intellectual and artistic life of his day; more than any other, he had had variety and depth of intellectual experience.

Out of that experience, in a spirit of seeking to distill what he had seen and felt and participated in, trying to find some lesson in it, seeking to extract from it some design for living — or the reason for lack of a design, Adams wrote his autobiography. What grandiose self-complacency a man of ordinary clay would have made of it, one can surmise. The mood in which Adams went about it is suggested by his eliminating the pronoun "I," writing it in the third person, and calling it "The Education of Henry Adams." In the book, the events and conditions he saw and shared, the exalted experiences he had, are used by him as merely the framework upon which he builds the record of his intellectual development. In a man of Adams' type it could not be otherwise. More truthfully than any man of his generation, he could have said — though his diffidence would have prevented him from saying: "cogito, ergo sum." His life was a life of the mind. All his years he had searched, and now in his confession he recorded his search, for the laws of life, to discover them and apply them.

The autobiography resolved itself, in large part, into an account of the difference between him and his environment, between his mind and the time he lived in, between his spirit and the spirit of the age. His mind had been determined by his education, the education he had received through contact with the elders of his family, and the formal education he received in the schools that were dominated by the same Puritan spirit. His

ancestors had, almost literally, worshipped duty as the
"Stern Daughter of the Voice of God." His father had
once written in his diary, after a day's fishing " . . . but
why not take some of life for simple enjoyments, provided they interfere with no known duty?" This austere
conception of life and duty was transmitted almost un-
changed to the sensitive son who was torn by doubts
unknown to them. The very landscape and familiar
scenes of Henry Adams' childhood, the granite hills and
stone-walled fields of New England, imposed austerity,
assumed a word in which right and wrong were always
and clearly distinguishable. The sobriety of the New
England scene, the temperament of the Puritans, the
severity of a classical education, the consciousness of
duty to himself and to his family, all these had led
Adams throughout his life, in spite of Hamlet-like
doubts and questionings, toward one pattern of life. The
education he had received through heredity, from the
conscious intent of his parents, and from his early environment, was to fit him to live in a world in which the
right course of action for a responsible man was ascer-
tainable, and the only problem was to follow this right
course through the vicissitudes and temptations of cir-
cumstance. But Henry Adams felt and saw clearly that
the world in which he spent his life was one in which
values and criteria were in such flux as to make the education he had received obsolete. Not only had the standards changed, they constantly continued to change; almost each day he awoke in an altered world. The
horizons of man's knowledge had been extended more
rapidly than man's ethics could keep pace with. The
change from the world in which his grandfather, the
President John Quincy Adams, consumed six weeks in
travelling from Boston to Washington, to the world in
which Henry Adams made the same journey in one day,

had brought corresponding disruption in the intellectual and spiritual pattern of life.

So, at the end, Adams felt that he had failed, that he

A photograph of Henry Adams taken by himself in his study in Washington about 1903. In the possession of Mrs. Ward Thoron.

had been obliged to fail. His conclusion, possibly too broad, possibly too large a generalization from one individual's experience, was that, "In plain words, chaos was the law of nature, order was the dream of man." Probably it is best to regard Adams' "Education" as one man's confession of futility, rather than accept it, in the way some have, as an affirmation of defeatism in the sense of a universal philosophy.

xv

"The Americanization of Edward Bok"

The readers who made "The Education of Henry Adams" a best-seller for eighteen months were a special stratum in American culture. Not only were those who read it a definite cultural group; those who liked it were mainly persons of a special temperament, kin to Adams' own. They were — in the throbbing, material, worldly American Twenties — a group apart, almost, in the American scene of that day, exotic.

Much more diverse, and more characteristic of the whole of America, were the different group — one is quite sure they were a different group — who kept another autobiography, "The Americanization of Edward Bok," a best-seller for the longer period of thirty months. That the Pulitzer committee awarded the prize for the best autobiography to the Adams book in 1920, and the following year to the Bok one, is a comforting testimonial to the catholicity of the judges, if not to their enduring critical discernment. About all the two books had intrinsically in common was the device of the author referring to himself as "he," a device intended to create deprecation, the deprecation being in Adams' case an actuality, in Bok's a simulation. It would take far more than substitution of "he" for "I," far more than any literary gadget could accomplish, to confer any aura of modesty on Bok's naïve view of his achievements. One felt Bok used the "he" to enable him to speak with more freedom concerning the hero about whom he wrote. Bok's achievements were great, he knew it and he exulted in it. In him was no sense of futility, no troubling doubts about whether life had been worth while. To Bok, life had been a grand good thing, and he said so, said it with childlike, undisguised admiration — admiration for his career and of the conditions that had made it possible, the America that was the golden land of opportunity.

Born in Holland, coming to America at the age of six, a literally penniless immigrant, Bok had as a boy striven desperately under the goad of poverty and the lure of ambition; at school he strove prodigiously for education and in spare time did odd jobs that yielded him 50 cents or a dollar a week; he collected autographs of celebrities and devised ingenious ways to make a special impression on each of them; became a stenographer, worked in publishing houses; became, at the age of 25, editor of *The Ladies Home Journal*; made it the leading periodical for women and one of the half-dozen most popular and successful of any class; raised the standard of living — and also the standard of taste — in American homes; exercised a deep and useful influence in America for more than a third of a century; conducted a crusade against patent medicines and in favor of the pure food law; promoted movements for social betterment and civic beautification — once he set out to persuade all the railroads to plant their bare, ugly embankments with wild roses; was at once public spirited and self-centered; Bok would make the world a better place — but the world must understand that Bok knew what was best for it. As an editor, he sought contributions from the most eminent authors and paid the highest prices for them, did the same with Presidents and ex-Presidents and other public characters, took pride in association with the great of his time. He was an editor who looked like a corporation president, he was very successful, he became wealthy, he gave generously to good causes. At the age of 60 he retired, looked backward upon his career, and wrote "The Americanization of Edward Bok."

It was Americanization not merely in the ordinary sense of an immigrant boy becoming an American; it was Americanization in the sense of taking on supremely the most prevailing ideal of the America of the period. Bok represented the most prized virtue of the American system — he was in the fullest sense of the word a self-made man, one who had risen from obscurity to fame, from weakness to power, from poverty to great wealth. It was possibly with the idea of discovering Mr. Bok's secret that American readers kept his book on the best-seller lists for two and a half years. Reflecting on the book fifteen years later, one realizes that Bok embodied American ideals and traditions of his time; an America that believed in strenuous striving, approved of competition, practiced it, enjoyed it; did not welch or repine when the other fellow won, rather on the contrary took pleasure in seeing the prize go to the hardest striver. But one realizes also that Bok as a man was tactless, "bumptious." The young Americans who read his book to find a recipe for success, and the young French boys and the Italians and the Argentinians and the Portuguese and the Greeks — the book was translated into I do not know how many tongues — may have incorrectly assumed that all of Bok's qualities were essential in the formula.

XVI

Some Other Autobiographies

Another autobiography of an immigrant, "From Immigrant to Inventor," winner of the Pulitzer prize in 1924, told the story of Michael Pupin, who as a lad in Serbia had been told, and believed, that thunder is the noise made by Jehovah's chariot as it dashes about the heavens, and who, in America, became one of the world's leading authorities on the science of sound; a contributor of many inventions to the telephone and radio. Pupin was a wholesome, fine-spirited, generous, tolerant man, fully entitled to be called great. . . . "The Autobiography of Margot Asquith," a best-seller in 1921, was a record of the contacts of an English woman, later Lady Oxford and Asquith, with English political and literary celebrities; an American reviewer of the book, Dorothy Parker, said that "the love affair of Margot Asquith with Margot Asquith will go ringing down the ages." . . . "We" by Colonel Charles Lindbergh appeared in 1927; every one understood the implication of the title — one of "We" was the youth who had made the first flight from America to Europe, the partner to whom he gave an equal share of fame was his plane, known as "The Spirit of St. Louis."

XVII

Poetry

They said the Twenties was a material age, that it was dominated by business, that much of the imaginative in man and the spiritual had been diverted into making business "go-getters"; that what the Twenties meant by "a man with a mission" was a man with a mission to sell more automobiles, more chewing gum, more shaving soap.

They said these things, and these things were true. They said also — foreigners said it and Americans[26] said it — that the triumph of industrialism in America had been at the expense of art; that life in America was so

---

[26] Even so loyal a partisan of America as Stuart Sherman, as late as 1922, thought: "It has never been hard for the native-born American to hold America 'first' in political affairs; but . . . men of letters, as such, cannot, without straining the meaning of the word, hold her first till her national genius expresses itself as adequately, as nobly, in literature, as it has, on the whole, in the great political crises."

bleak, so lacking in intellectual depth, so lacking in encouragement for the artistic life, that the few sensitive, refined minds America produced were forced to flee to Europe to escape spiritual starvation. They had been saying this for a long time. A distinguished author of American birth had said it; one of the highly developed intellects that had escaped the American wilderness to the security of England, Henry James, had written: "One might enumerate the items of high civilization, as it exists in other countries, which are absent from the texture of American life, until it should become a wonder to know what was left: No sovereign, no court, no personal loyalty, no aristocracy, no church, no clergy, no army, no diplomatic service, no country gentlemen, no palaces, no castles, no manors, nor old country-houses, nor parsonages, nor thatched cottages, nor ivied ruins; no cathedrals, nor abbeys, nor little Norman churches; no great universities nor public schools — no Oxford, nor Eton, nor Harrow; no literature, no novels, no museums, no pictures, no political society, no sporting class." Henry James had said that during the early 1900's, and it continued a high-brow thing to say until the 1920's. What they implied was that without the accessories Henry James catalogued, art could not thrive.

Yet the fact is that during the period following the war, the poetry written by Americans was more important than that written by the poets of any other country. And the renascence of poetical writing was accompanied by spread of popular acquaintance with it. "Suddenly after 1912 poetry began to pour out a flood of volumes and to compete even with the novel as a marketable commodity. For the first time since 'Hiawatha' a book of poems entered the list of the best sellers. Seemingly a poetic renaissance had opened, and everywhere it was hailed with enthusiasm. Poetry during the five years after 1912 came surging out from the vacant niches where so long it had furtively lurked, into an unheard-of prominence. It was a subject now for newspaper front pages even, and popular weeklies. Everybody[27] was reading it or professing to read it. It burst even into the Sunday "funnies" and the comic journals:[28]

> There's a grand poetical "boom," they say,
>   (Climb on it, chime on it, brothers of mine!)
> 'Twixt the dawn and the dusk of each lyrical day
> There's another school started, and all of 'em pay.
>   (A dollar a line!
> Think of it, Ferdy, a dollar a line!)[29]

For the emergence of an unusual number of exceptionally talented poets, one would hesitate to venture a reason. It is not the sort of phenomenon that can be explained. Historically we can say there had been a prolonged period of sterility, and that abundance followed. The burgeoning began about 1912. It came after almost half a century of sterility. The New England poets who had created the nineteenth century's golden age of verse had ceased to be productive about

[27] Not quite everybody. Once, soon after Coolidge became President, he sent for the author of the present volume and, after some talk, asked: "Have you any ideas about this job of mine?" There followed some discussion of policies. As I was about to leave, I made a suggestion for another field. "I have always thought," I said, "that a President ought to use his office to confer distinction on men eminent in their lines; Theodore Roosevelt used to do it, he was always having authors and artists and scientists, all sorts of persons like that, to stay at the White House. If I were President, especially if I were a President from New England as you are, there is one thing I'd do, I'd have some of those New England poets come and visit the White House." Coolidge, with laconic directness, asked, "Just what poets do you have in mind?" "Oh," I said, "any of the New England ones—Robert Frost, Edwin Arlington Robinson, Edna St. Vincent Millay—she was born in Maine." "Frost? Robinson?" asked Coolidge meditatively, searching his memory—"I never heard of them. There was a fellow in Boston when I was in the legislature that used to write poems—he was a newspaper man—his name was McCarthy." (Dennis A. McCarthy was a minor poet of parts, but Coolidge's acquaintance with him hardly made up for his lack of having heard of Robert Frost and Edwin Arlington Robinson.)

[28] Quoted from Fred Lewis Pattee.

[29] The verses are quoted from Don Marquis.

the time of the Civil War. There followed a quarter century during which the only American poets of any consequence were Walt Whitman and Emily Dickinson. From 1890 for a score of years there was only Edwin Arlington Robinson in his early phase. Then, during about five years, from 1912 to 1917 came spate: In 1914, Vachel Lindsay's "General William Booth Enters Into Heaven" and "The Congo and Other Poems"; in the same year, Amy Lowell's "Sword Blades and Poppy Seed"; in the same year, Robert Frost's "North of Boston." In 1915, Edgar Lee Masters' "Spoon River Anthology." In 1916, Carl Sandburg's "Chicago Poems." In 1917, Ezra Pound's "Lustra"; in the same year Edna St. Vincent Millay's "Renascence." These all continued to produce into the 1920's; so did also Edwin Arlington Robinson, improving always.[30] They were joined, during the 1920's, by Elinor Wylie, E. E. Cummings, T. S. Eliot, Conrad Aiken, Archibald MacLeish, Stephen Vincent Benét, William Rose Benét, and the young negro poet, Countee Cullen.

These, not recognizing fatal handicap in the lack of Henry James's "no palaces, no manors, nor thatched cottages nor ivied ruins" — these American poets found adequate inspiration in familiar American scenes:

Robert Frost in the New England countryside:

> The woods are lovely, dark and deep,
> But I have promises to keep,
> And miles to go before I sleep,
> And miles to go before I sleep.

Edwin Arlington Robinson in the ruin of a farm-house on a New England hill:

> They are all gone away;
> The House is shut and still.
> There is nothing more to say.

[30] So much so that he took the Pulitzer poetry prize three times during the 1920's.

Why is it then we stray
  Around that sunken sill?
They are all gone away.

There is ruin and decay
  In the House on the Hill.
They are all gone away —
There is nothing more to say.

Carl Sandburg in the life and language of the Middle West:

A code arrives; language, lingo; slang;
behold the proverbs of a people, a nation:
Give 'em the works. Fix it, there's always
a way. Be hard boiled. The good die young. . . .

Good morning, America!
Morning goes as morning-glories go!
High noon goes, afternoon goes!
Twilight, sundown, gloaming —
The hour of writing: Good night, America!
Good night, sleep, peace, and sweet dreams!

T. S. Eliot in a skeptical interpretation of a certain New England culture:

When evening quickens faintly in the street,
Wakening the appetites of life in some
And to others bringing the *Boston Evening Transcript*,
I mount the steps and ring the bell, turning
Wearily, as one would turn to nod good-bye to Rochefoucauld,
If the street were time and he at the end of the street,
And I say, "Cousin Harriet, here is the *Boston Evening Transcript*."

Vachel Lindsay in scenes in the Mississippi valley:

Booth led boldly with his big bass drum —
  (Are you washed in the blood of the Lamb?)
The Saints smiled gravely and they said:
  "He's come."
  (Are you washed in the blood of the Lamb?)

XVIII
Light Verse

Among writers of light verse there was one who achieved supremely what light verse (of the ironic kind) is supposed to do. Here was an age intent upon striving, regarding diligence as the most worthy of virtues, giving to optimism almost the standing of religion, making a god of success. About all that, Mrs. Dorothy Parker wrote verses which began with apparent sharing of the universal reverence:

> If I should labor through daylight and dark,
> Consecrate, valorous, serious, true,
> Then on the world I may blazon my mark —
> And what if I don't and what if I do ?[31]

More direct was the thrust — the Twenties would have called it a "swift punch" — that Mrs. Parker delivered upon her own and related professions, in which, during the period, many of the practitioners tended to be more self-conscious than talented:

> Authors and actors and artists and such
> Never know nothing, and never know much
> Sculptors and singers and those of their kidney
> Tell their affairs from Seattle to Sydney.
> Playwrights and poets and such horses' necks
> Start off from anywhere, end up at sex.
> Diarists, critics and similar roe
> Never say nothing, and never say no.
> People Who Do Things exceed my endurance;
> God, for a man that solicits insurance!

One of Mrs. Parker's distinguishing traits was an application to the art of verse of the O. Henry trick-ending technique, long familiar in short stories. She gave delight to college students with a rondelle in which she dwelled sentimentally and demurely on the theme "She's passing fair," and then ended,

> But if the passing mark be minus D,
> She's passing fair.

She wrote a conventional, fairly charming lullaby, ad-

[31] "Enough Rope." 1926.

dressed to a lovely young lady — but in the last two lines reveals the reasons for her tender solicitude:

> When you're awake, all the men go and fall for you,
> Sleep, pretty lady, and give me a chance.

She wrote a poem which the reader might suppose to be a charming love lyric, but which in the last line hit him in the eye with:

> She will always wait,
> By the same old gate —
> The gate[32] her lover gave her.

Integral in Mrs. Parker's art was a talent for titles. Under the caption "Two Volume Novel," she wrote merely:

> The sun's gone dim, and
>   The moon's turned black;
> For I loved him, and
>   He didn't love back.[33]

More commonplace in style were the epigrammatic poems of Samuel Hoffenstein which appeared in 1928, in a volume grumpily entitled "Poems In Praise of Practically Nothing." Hoffenstein's terse verses were widely read and quoted by the generation just too young to consider Edna St. Vincent Millay as a beacon light. His poems had a quotability and a cold-blooded cynicism about sex that appealed to a rather callow generation. College men, as they styled themselves, loved to assure each other in Hoffenstein's words that

> Nothing from a straight line swerves
> So sharply as a woman's curves.
> And having swerved no might or main
> Can ever put them straight again.

---

[32] In slang of the Twenties, to be given the gate was to be dismissed, from a relation of love, or from a business position, or from any other relation more desired by one party than the other. Equivalents were "given the air," or "given the bum's rush." Slang for voluntary retirement was to "walk out on him" or to "leave him flat."

[33] "Sunset Gun." 1925.

17

TUNES OF THE TWENTIES

"The history of a country is written in its popular songs;
from time immemorial current events have found lyric expression through the people's self-appointed troubadours,
and such vocal outbursts have often had a real significance
in reflecting the spirit, the atmosphere, the customs,
the manners, and morals of the day."—SIGMUND SPAETH.

SERIOUS acceptance of the theory that "the history of a
country is written in its popular songs" would lead to
distortion of a sort not uncommon when history is made
to conform to a formula, and facts ingeniously mobilized
to support a theory. But, accepting popular songs as a
facet of the times, we might say, without too much
straining, that the decade of the 1920's had as its overture
the serene and confident *Smiles*,[1] that it rose to a for-
tissimo which might be expressed in a pæan of exuberant
affluence, *My God, How the Money Rolls In*,[2] and that it
ended, after the panic of 1929, with a crashing finale —
"crashing" is in this connection an especially apt adjective — the universally familiar and uniquely appropriate
song of indigence, *Brother, Can You Spare a Dime?*[3]

[1] There are smiles that make us happy,
There are smiles that make us blue,
There are smiles that steal away the teardrops
As the sunbeams steal away the dew,
There are smiles that have a tender meaning,
That the eye of love alone may see,
But the smiles that fill my life with sunshine
Are the smiles that you give to me.
1917. Reproduced by permission of the copyright owner, Remick Music Corp.
[2] An old American ditty revived during the 1920's.
[3] 1932.
Throughout this chapter, the year named in connection with the title of a
song is the year of copyright.
Writers of plays and novels sometimes use the volumes of OUR TIMES as a

Brother, Can You Spare a Dime? was a true "topical"
song, had a direct and intended relation to the time. It
was composed during the depression, was inspired by the
depression, and reflected the depression mood. The song
was an essential part of the depression years, as characteristic, and as familiar, as bank-closings, money-hoard-
ing, and seedy-genteel men selling apples on street-
corners. As music, or as verse, the song was not much.
What mainly gave it the vogue it had was the unique
appropriateness of its title.

After a while the title cut itself loose from the song

Broth-er, can you spare a   dime?____

and acquired a standing of its own. The words "Brother,
can you spare a dime?" became a saying, a comment, the equivalent of a shrug of the shoulders, serving
for the depression years the same function that "c'est la
guerre" had filled during the Great War. The words
"Brother, can you spare a dime?" with the tone in
which they were said, the union of appeal for help with
resignation to adversity, made it the complete and adequate summary of the spirit of the day. Occasionally it
was said with bitterness; but it conformed more closely
to the American spirit on the more frequent occasions

---

source for material with which to create the atmosphere of a year or a period,
the songs that were sung, the books and plays that were popular, and the like.
To these, and to others using Our Times as books of reference, it is desirable
to give a guide: While as a rule the year of a song's popularity was the year
of its copyright, or the year following, there are occasional exceptions, in
which the apex of popularity did not come for two or more years after publication. There are exceptions still more extreme. For example, any novelist
seeking to create the atmosphere of 1922 would be likely to mention a revue
produced by Russians, Chauve Souris, and a musical number which was one
of its most agreeable features, *The Parade of the Wooden Soldiers*. This piece
had been composed and published, however, eleven years before, in 1911.

when it was spoken with humor, humor sustained under hard conditions.

For a song to express the boom-peak of the decade, we should be obliged to go back to an old ditty which during the Twenties experienced a revival and an adaptation. *My God, How the Money Rolls In*, sung with exuberant gusto, was an accurate expression of the late 1920's, but the original words had been written many years[4] before:

> My sister she works in the laundry,
> My father he fiddles for gin,
> My mother she takes in washing,
> My God! how the money rolls in!

By changing the second line to

> My father sells bootlegger gin

or

> My father makes synthetic gin,

the Twenties gave to the song a timeliness which related it to the "easy money" phase of the decade, and also made it appropriate to another aspect of the period. The allusions to specifically described sources of easy money provided humor to a generation just becoming familiar with outlawed — but not successfully exiled — substitutes for liquor. A good many Americans of 1920 and subsequent years never heard the word "synthetic" except as an adjective describing gin.

Change of yet another line of *My God, How the Money Rolls In* introduced an additional modern allu-

---

[4] Carl Sandburg, in his American Song Bag, says that *My God, How the Money Rolls In* is very old. He classifies it among "railroad and work-gang songs" and believes, accurately I think, that it was originally written in a spirit of mordant satire, a "bitter ditty of low life," an analogue to Hood's "Song of the Shirt."

sion, and gave to the adaptation that attraction which the younger generation during the Twenties seemed to find in songs (and novels) about an area which their parents described as "low-life" [5] — partiality of "high life" for "low life," a wish of the former to seem the latter, was one expression of the pose of daring which was a vogue of young folks during the Twenties.

My sis-ter, she works in a laun-dry; ____ My fa-ther, he fid-dles for gin. ____ My moth-er, she's tak-ing in

For the full understanding of the 1920's version of *My God, How the Money Rolls In*, it may be desirable to explain that "snow" was argot for cocaine, and "snow-birds" for its addicts. Since sale of the former to the latter was illegal, the traffic was remunerative; it became one of the ways in which "easy money" was achieved. The enumerated sources of revenue in the Twenties' version ran:

> My sister sells snow to the snow-birds,
> My father makes bootlegger gin, . . .
> My mother she takes in washing,
> My God! how the money rolls in!

[5] The outstanding expression of this taste of young folks during the Twenties was the revival of "Frankie and Johnny," a bawdy ballad of many generations before, in which the heroine lived, and had her career, in a brothel, and the hero — if he could be called that — was her faithless lover.

II

A period which made its money in the spirit of *My God, How the Money Rolls In,* spent it, naturally, in the spirit of *Makin' Whoopee.* As the former reflected economic exuberance, so did the latter express spiritual recklessness. The words of *Makin' Whoopee* were merely some cynical, gay verses about marriage, divorce, and alimony; it was the music that expressed the whole spirit of noise, abandon, recklessness, and excitement which were implied by the song and were characteristic of large segments of life. The phrase "makin' whoopee" became a part of the common tongue; any person or group who dismissed restraint and threw themselves with loud and feverish gusto into any area of activity — a visitor spending freely in a night club, a farmer "on a tear" in the city, a husband on the loose, a politician starting an insurgent movement, a banker banking recklessly, a business man imprudently expanding — all were "makin' whoopee." Nearly everybody did it; few, during those flush years, escaped the infection that made men act with an impulsiveness which did not sufficiently calculate the consequences:

> Weddings make a lot of people sad,
> But if you're not the groom, they're not so bad . . .
>
> Picture a little love-nest
> Down where the roses cling.
> Picture the same sweet love-nest —
> Think what a year can bring:
> He's washing dishes and baby clothes,
> He's so ambitious he really sews.
> But don't forget folks,
> That's what you get folks,
> For makin' whoopee.
>
> Another year, or maybe less,
> What's this I hear? Well, can't you guess? . . .[6]

[6] 1928. Sung by Eddie Cantor. Reprinted with permission of copyright owner, Donaldson, Douglas and Gumble.

"Making whoopee" was associated with night clubs, features of city life, especially New York City life, which sprang up as incidents of national prohibition —

Underwood & Underwood photo.

Texas Guinan — night club hostess — as she sailed with her entertainers for London.

De Mirjian photo.

Helen Morgan — a torch singer well known on the stage and in the night clubs of the period.

institutions designed to provide illicit and therefore alluring access to stimulation by alcoholic beverages, accompanied by associated forms of gaiety. The most lavish patron of night clubs in New York, the one who provided most conspicuously the wherewithal upon which and for which whoopee was made, was the rich visitor from out of town; his rôle was recognized with disarming audacity by a famous night club hostess, Texas Guinan, whose technique was to address loudly the prospective spender as "Hello, Sucker!" So strange was the spirit of the time that the customer was pleased by the conspicuousness, and proceeded to act the part which the hostess had conferred on him. Generically, the free spender, especially if elderly and a little obese, became known as a "big butter and egg man"; geographically he was usually described vaguely as "from the West." About him a song was written:

CHORUS

1. The big but-ter and egg man from Crack-er-town P   A

> The big butter and egg man from the West,
> He carries his produce on his vest . . .
> He turns the city upside down
> And drinks up all the wine in town.
> He just throws his dough away . . .
> He bought a chorus girl a pup,
> Next day the price of cheese went up.[7]

III

On the theory that popular songs reflect the spirit of the day, there should have been many about liquor, drinking; for national prohibition — and the violation of it — composed a large part of the atmosphere of the twenties. But neither did the legal absence of liquor give rise to madrigals about sobriety, nor did the illegal presence of it inspire songs about inebriation. Wine there was, in large quantities, and woman had not diminished from her usual proportion to the population, but the

[7] *The Big Butter and Egg Man.* 1924. The version printed here varies slightly from the published version. Reproduced by permission of the copyright owner, Jerome H. Remick & Co.

song that is supposed to complete the delectable trinity was not present. At least it was not present in the sense of new drinking[7a] songs emerging. The old ones may have been sung with as great frequency and as much gusto as ever; indeed the revival of an old University of

From a photograph by Globe Photos.

Rudy Vallée with copies of his famous "Stein Song" as it was published in five different countries.

Maine "Stein Song," and the frequent singing[8] of it by Rudy Vallee, was almost as conspicuous an incident of the musical history of the Twenties as the appearance of any new song.

> Drink to all the happy hours,
> Drink to the careless days . . .
> To the trees, to the sky!
> To the Spring in its glorious happiness,
> To the youth, to the fire,
> To the life that is moving and calling us!
> To the Gods, to the Fates,
> To the rulers of men and their destinies;

[7a] Two songs celebrating illegal access to liquor were "The Bootlegger's Daughter" and "Good-bye, Broadway; hello, Montreal."

[8] Singing in this case — not crooning.

To the lips, to the eyes,
To the girls who will love us some day!
Oh fill the steins to college days,
Shout till the rafters ring![8a]

A college periodical portrays an example of identity between art and nature in
these drawings of college students. On the left as they were depicted
and on the right as they actually were.

From "College Humor."

A pictorial joke of the twenties based on the vogue of college students of
"decorating" their raincoats.

[8a] This University of Maine *Stein Song* had distinguished authorship, in
Lincoln Colcord. Written originally in 1909 it had only local popularity until
revived and sung by Rudy Vallée in 1927. Reproduced by permission of the copyright owner, Carl Fischer, Inc.

Another song about drinking frequently sung during the Twenties was:

> Show me the way to go home,
> I'm tired and I want to go to bed;
> I had a little drink about an hour ago,
> And it went right to my head.[9]

One song of the Twenties may serve posterity as a partial record of the manners of college students, their

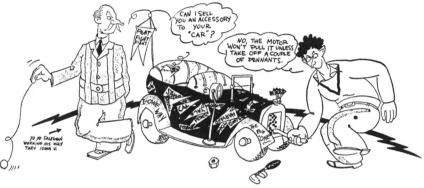

From "College Humor."

College youths prized their automobiles as much for their decorations and the legends the students painted on them, as for their ability to run.

attitude toward life, and their clothes, especially their clothes. In many a previous period, of course, it has been the desire of college youths to attain one kind or another of outre-ness. In the twenties, the ambition took a direction and went to a length which caused visitors to a college campus to wonder sometimes whether they had by mistake stumbled upon the poorhouse, or perhaps the insane asylum. The age, unkemptness and scantiness of college students' attire — it was the pose in all colleges, men's, women's, and co-ed — did not reflect poverty or parsimony upon the part of their parents. On the con-

[9] *Show Me the Way to Go Home* (1925).

trary, the Twenties was a time when lavishness toward children at college was part of the universal disposition toward liberal spending. No, the students chose that sort of clothes because they liked them; it was the vogue, there was a kind of competition in uncouthness. It was described in *Collegiate*[10] — in which the spelling was as eccentric as the collegians' clothes:

C'lle-giate, c'lle-giate. Yes! we are collegiate!
Nothing in-ter-med-jate, No ma'am.
Trousers baggy and our clothes look raggy,
But we're rough and ready, Yea!
   (spoken) Hot Dog!
Garters are the things we never wear . . .
We're col-le-giate! Rah! Rah! Rah! Rah!

Slickers, knickers, we can't do without;
And we wouldn't care if there were
   No suspenders!

IV

Songs sometimes reflect the emergence of inventions that impress the age. In the early 1890's, a song called *Daisy Bell* alluded to the tandem bicycle, then novel and striking; in the chorus, the youth told the maid that "it won't be a stylish marriage, we can't afford a carriage, but you'll look sweet, upon the seat of a bicycle built for two." The automobile brought a ditty describing a frequent experience the drivers of early automobiles were obliged to have, *You've Got to Get Out and Get Under*. With the flying machine came two love songs, *Come Josephine In My Flying Machine*, and *Come*

[10] 1925. Reprinted by permission of the copyright owner, Shapiro, Bernstein and Co., Inc.

Take a Trip in My Airship. The 1920s' equivalent of those songs associated with new inventions was *If I Had a Talking Picture of You.*[11]

> If I had a talking picture of you,
> I'd play it every time that I felt blue.
> I'd sit there in the gloom of my lonely little room;
> I would have three shows a day,
> And a midnight matinee.

V

A visitor from Mars — that often conscripted but, I hope, not overworked servitor of historians — the visitor from Mars who should have surveyed America in the year 1923 might have concluded that the place of exalted and mystic significance which in Greece was occupied by the lotus, in France by the lily, and in Japan by the chrysanthemum, must be in America occupied by the banana. From almost every lip he would have heard song about that humble fruit, song expressed in a locution so contorted that hardly any amount of grammatical diligence on the part of the Martian visitor would have enabled him to understand just what this ditty meant, or why it was sung.

About the origin of the phrase "Yes, we have no bananas today," there is dispute, the final arbitration of which would consume time which in this book it seems best to reserve for issues more simple to solve. Some said the phrase came into existence as the response of a Grecian vendor of fruit, or perhaps an Italian one, whose regretted inability to supply the particular fruit requested by a customer was expressed in a phraseology designed to soften disappointment with Levantine graciousness. After the phrase became familiar, it served

11 1929. Reproduced by permission of the copyright owner, DeSylva, Brown & Henderson, Inc.

as the point of many quips that amused the early Twenties. One of these purported to repeat a laconic conversation, alleged to have taken place in that fecund source of much American folklore and slang, the messkitchen of an army post, a conversation in which the captain undertook to impress on the private that punctilio of army life which requires that the reply of a subordinate to a superior must end with "sir":

Captain (sternly): "Do I understand there is no dessert today?"
Private: "Yes."
Captain: "Yes, what?"
Private: "Yes, we have no bananas."

Whether the phrase preceded the song and inspired it, or whether the song came first and the widespread currency of the phrase was an outgrowth — about that there is uncertainty as insoluble as that about the relative priority of egg and hen. About how the song arose, what queerly impish inspiration dragged the strangely assorted words of it into their extraordinary conjunction, I pretend no austere historical authority. As to the music, divers analysts of tune, expert in the genealogy of melody, have asserted that *Yes, We Have No Bananas* was sired — or should we say dammed? — by the *Hallelujah Chorus*. Others have assigned the banana song's paternity to *I Dreamt I Dwelt in Marble Halls*. This attribution of noble ancestry to a humble tune involves no shame to the descendant; it is familiar that nearly all new music, even the proudest, bears some degree of family resemblance to earlier classics. In music, adaptation may be as much a work of talent as invention. By so capable an authority as Irving Berlin it has been said that "there is no such thing as a new melody." [12]

[12] "We depend largely on tricks, we writers of songs. There is no such thing as a new melody." — Irving Berlin in *The Greenbook Magazine*.

Yes, We Have No Bananas,[13] during 1923 and soon after, was sung infinitely more often than *The Star-Spangled Banner*, and more often than all the hymns in all the hymnals of all the churches combined. If European visitors assumed it to be the national anthem, maybe

they were not wholly wrong; perhaps the song which during any period is the most generally sung deserves to be regarded, for the time, as the musical expression of some temporarily forward phase of the national spirit. What queer momentary aberration of the American national ethos the banana song may have reflected is beyond the ability of this historian to say. Indeed, to say anything about *Yes, We Have No Bananas* is futile surplusage. It so fully speaks for itself. To paint the lily, to add gilt to gold, would be justifiable adornment, compared to adding yellow to the banana song. I reproduce it, with its strange and inexplicable bizarreries of spelling and lettering, just as it was printed on the millions of

13 Copyright 1923. Reproduced by permission of the copyright owner, Skidmore Music Co.

sheets of it that were sold during 1923 and for a short
time after:

YES! we have no bananas, we have no bananas to-day.
We've string beans and HONions, cabBAHges, and scallions,
And all kinds of fruit they say.
We have an old-fashioned toMAH-to—
Long Island poTAHto; but YES! we have no bananas —
We have no bananas to-day.

That was the chorus. So widely appreciated was it
that many other stanzas were devised. It was clear that
a wide area of American taste found humor and entertainment in the names of familiar articles of food —
when mispronounced, and sung to music that was a
variation of the *Hallelujah Chorus:*

YES! we have no bananas; we have no bananas to-day.
We'll sell you some Swiss cheese — when you open up this
   cheese
It gets up and walks away.
We got those IM-ported STRUM-berries,
COO-cum-bers and cherries,
But, YES! we have no bananas; we have no bananas to-day.

Eight such stanzas were included in the song as formally published. When appreciative audiences indicated
that eight were less than an adequate musical meal, generous and ingenious caterers of song improvised yet more.
Always the concluding stanza extended an invitation to
the audience; always the invitation was enthusiastically
accepted:

YES! we have no bananas; we have no bananas to-day.
This song isn't pretty, but still it's a ditty
That grows on you day by day.
And you can all do something for us,
Just join in the chorus.
       (Spoken) *All together!*
YES! we have no bananas; we have no bananas to-day.

What the banana song signified as a phenomenon; whether Sigmund Spaeth could in this case prove his generalization that popular songs "often reflect the spirit, the atmosphere, the customs, the manners and morals of the day" — about all that I am unequipped to be authoritative. Possibly America sang *Yes, We Have No Bananas* to disprove any suspicion of cultural effeteness — that instinct for a kind of flaunting earthiness was widely current during the Twenties, especially among young folks.

If that was the motive, many other songs of the dec-

CHORUS

Hors-es, Hors-es, Hors-es, Nut-ty o-ver Hors-es, Hors-es, Hors-es, Goof-y o-ver

ade served the same purpose. No nation could be charged with having "gone high-brow" that sang, as much as America did sing, *Horses*.[14]

Horses, Horses, Horses! Nutty over Horses, Horses, Horses!
    Goofy over Horses, Horses, Horses!
She's a little wild over Horses, Horses, Horses, Horses; daffy
    over Horses, Horses, Horses,
Silly over Horses, Horses, Horses . . .
At the altar, altar, altar, maybe she will falter, falter, falter,
Then I'll get the halter, halter, halter, just to make her mind.

Horses was sheer nonsense; the verses made no sense and did not pretend to. The song was intended as silliness, and, as such feats can be when well done, was amusing. There were many nonsense ditties in the Twenties — it was a high-spirited age and could enjoy fun made for fun's sake. Young persons liked to sing a couplet[15]

14 1926. Reproduced by permission of the copyright owner, Leo Feist, Inc.

Though the words of *Horses* would seem to acquit it of any charge of classic taint, the music is said by the erudite to have its inspiration in Tschaikowsky's *Troika*.

15 From *Who Takes Care of the Caretaker's Daughter*, 1925. Reproduced with permission of the copyright owner, Shapiro, Bernstein & Co.

whose attractiveness lay mainly in its verbal rattle of sound:

> Who takes care of the caretaker's daughter
> While the caretaker's busy taking care?

Sometimes modified to:

> Who oversees the overseer's daughter
> While the overseer's busy overseeing?

As at all times, one of the convenient vehicles for nonsense was parody. The elevated *Volga Boat Song*[16] —

1925. Copyright, Robbins-Engel, Inc.

much emphasized during the Twenties by the Russian singer, Chaliapin, and appreciated by discriminating musical taste — was caricatured for the common in *Oh, How I Love My Boatman*:

> Oh how I love my boatman, my great big vulgar boatman,
> He's a rushin', crushin', mushin', Russian from the sea.

VI

Next to *Yes, We Have No Bananas,* or possibly exceeding it in far-flung familiarity during the early 1920's, was *Mister Gallagher and Mister Shean.*[17] In the cases of both men, it was "Mister," as spelled here, not "Mr." That fulness of title was appropriate to the

[16] Reproduced by permission of copyright owner, Robbins Music Corporation.
[17] These gentlemen were not mere inventions of song; Ed Gallagher and Al Shean were flesh and blood; they were vaudeville actors, a team, and the song was by them and about them.

wisdom, philosophy, and humor of the two characters, whose allusions to events of the day were widely quoted, as humorous epitomes of the popular judgment. Always their song began with a stanza which, so to speak, set the stage:

There are two funny men, the best I've ever seen;
One is Mis-ter Gal-la-gher, the other Mis-ter Shean.
When these two cronies meet, it surely is a treat —
The things they say, and the things they do, and the funny
    way they greet:
"Oh! Mis-ter Gal-la-gher! Oh! Mis-ter Gal-la-gher!"
"Hel-lo what's on your mind this morning, Mis-ter Shean?"

Then ensued the dialogue, which versatile singers varied to cover whatever was the question of the day. National prohibition, comparatively new in 1922, and the ensuing expensiveness of alcoholic exhilaration, was deemed to be a misfortune:

Everybody's making fun
Of the way the country's run . . .
Why Mister Shean, why Mister Shean,
The day they took away our old canteen,
Cost of living went so high
That it's cheaper now to die.

Always these confident affirmations of judgment ended with a formula of mutual and emphatic agreement:

Positively! Mister Gallagher!
Absolutely! Mister Shean![18]

Only once was this completeness of agreement interrupted. It was when Mr. Shean addressed Mr. Gallagher on a personal matter.

If you're a friend of mine
You'll lend me a couple of bucks.
I'm so broke and badly bent,
And I haven't got a cent.

[18] 1922. Reproduced by permission of the copyright owner, Jack Mills, Inc.

To which the reply was

> Oh! Mister Shean, Oh! Mister Shean,
> Do you mean to say you haven't got a bean?
> On my word as I'm alive,
> I intended touching you for five.
> Positively, Mr. Shean! Absolutely, Mr. Gallagher.

The simplicity of the music and the formula of the words — mutual greeting, dialogue, and mutual agreement — lent itself to amateur adaptation; *Mister Gallagher and Mr. Shean*, parodied with local variations

By permission of King Features Syndicate, Inc., drawings by Billy DeBeck.

An example of the newspaper "comic strip" in which the characters were Barney Google and his horse "Spark Plug."

and personal allusions, served as a vehicle for much of the wit and entertainment at "smokers," dinners, club-meetings, and other forms of gregarious conviviality.

Similar in eminence to Messrs. Gallagher and Shean was a fictitious character known as "Barney Google." Barney, with a racehorse he had, called "Spark Plug," had become familiar to the public as the hero of a "funny," a "comic strip" in the daily newspapers. The hold on popular affection that Barney and Spark Plug won by their pictorial adventures and misadventures — led to transcription of their experiences into song:

> Barney Google bet his horse would win the prize;
> When the horses ran that day,
> Spark Plug ran the other way . . .
>
> He got odds of five to eight —
> Spark Plug came in three days late.

On another day potential victory for Spark Plug was balked by a malevolent spectator, with a rudely shouted reminder of an earlier career in which Spark Plug had been engaged before he went on the racetrack, a career in which excellence lies not in speed, but in steadiness, and a stop at every kitchen door:

> Spark Plug ran as fine as silk,
> Until somebody hollered "Milk."[19]

Zest about Barney's experiences on the racetrack led to stanzas which carried him into other fields and elevated him to the status of a national character:

```
CHORUS
Bar    ney   Goo - gle   with his   Goo  Goo  Goo  gly
Bar    ney   Goo - gle   with his   Goo  Goo  Goo - gly
```

Who's the most important man this country ever knew?
Who's the man our Presidents tell all their troubles to? . . .
I am mighty proud
That I am allowed
A chance to introduce
Barney Google with his goo-goo-googly eyes.

In his ampler rôle, the hero had many up and downs, through all of which Barney won as much affection for his triumphs as for his disasters:

> Barney Google is the luckiest of guys;
> If he fell into the mud,
> He'd come up with a diamond stud.

VII

Search among the tunes of the Twenties for ones having a union of popularity with superior quality would

[19] *Barney Google,* 1923. Reproduced by permission of the copyright owner. Jerome H. Remick & Co.

give consideration to *The Japanese Sandman*,[20] of which some three and a half million copies were sold:

Here's the Japanese Sandman
Sneaking on with the dew,
Just an old second-hand man
He'll buy your old day from you.

And a *Russian Lullaby*[21] that Irving Berlin wrote:

Where the dreamy Volga flows, there's a lonely Russian Rose,
Gazing tenderly down upon her knee,
Where a baby's brown eyes glisten, listen —

Ev'ry night you'll hear her croon a Russian lullaby.
Just a little plaintive tune when baby starts to cry,
Rock-a-bye, my baby, somewhere there may be a land
That's free for you and me and a Russian lullaby.

Quality of a different kind, indeed, a really elevated kind, was in *That's Why Darkies Are Born*,[22] a song sufficiently faithful to reality to deserve almost the status of poetry; its superiority was recognized by Lawrence Tibbett, who sang it often:

Someone had to pick the cotton, someone had to plant the
　　corn,
Someone had to slave and be able to sing, that's why darkies
　　were born.

[20] 1920. Reproduced by permission of the copyright owner, Jerome H. Remick & Co.

[21] 1927. Reproduced by permission of the copyright owner, Standard Music Publications, Inc.

[22] 1926. It was sung in the "George White's Scandals" of that year. Reproduced by permission of the copyright owner.

Someone had to laugh at trouble though he was tired and worn,
Had to be contented with any old thing; that's why darkies
    were born.
Sing, sing, sing when you're weary, and sing when you're blue.
Sing, sing, that's what we taught all the white folks to do.
Someone had to fight the devil, shout about Gabriel's horn. . . .
That's why darkies were born.

VIII

Ol' Man River

In accepting, so far as we dare accept, the theory that
popular songs reflect the spirit of the age, we must always bear in mind that in any age there may be a surface
spirit, and also an inner one. If during the 1920's, any
ordinary artisan of tune had set out merely to imitate the
music of the day and push the current vogue to a greater
height, he would have been likely to give his creation a
rapid tempo, and fill it with noise — he would have
tried to out-whoopee whoopee. Many did that, and
wrote ordinary songs, destined to ephemeralness followed by desuetude. One person, however, seeing more
of the age than its surface, wrote a song which, eight
years after it was composed, had a degree, and kind, of
appreciation which seemed to forecast for it an enduring
position in the classics.

To compose a song that adequately reflects the spirit
of an age is rare and distinguished. But to compose one
which probes through the surface spirit down to a mood
that the age itself has not yet recognized — to accomplish that calls for such prophetic insight, such instinctive understanding, such kinship with the inner soul of
a generation as is indisputably genius.

The late 1920's was the peak of the boom, a time
when, any ordinary observer would have said, the spirit

of America was supremely one of concern with things, possessions, buildings and bonds and barter; with size and speed, a time when the ambition of every American was to acquire, by processes faster and faster, more and more of whatever material accumulation was his private zest, and a time when the more and more seemed so easy of attainment that all were, or thought they were, happy in the achievement.

Into the very vortex of that whirling-dervish time

came, in 1927, a song of longing for repose and peace, a song which exalted detachment from the hurly-burly, contentment with little:

Ol' man river, dat ol' man river, he must know sumpin', but
    don't say nuthin',
He just keeps rollin', he keeps on rollin' along.
He don't plant 'taters, he don't plant cotton, an' dem dat
    plants 'em is soon forgotten
But ol' man river he jes keeps rollin' along.
You and me, we sweat and strain, body all achin', an' racked
    wid pain.
"Tote dat barge! Lift dat bale!"
Git a little drunk an' you'll land in jail.
Ah gits weary an' sick ob tryin', ahm tired of livin' an' feared
    of dyin',
But ol' man river he jes keeps rollin' along.[23]

Doubtless *Ol' Man River* is timeless; no doubt it would have taken high place had it emerged in the time

[23] 1927. Reproduced by permission of the copyright owner, T. B. Harms.

of Thomas Moore or Christopher Marlowe or Horace; and no doubt fifty years hence or a hundred it will have its place among that very small number of permanent classics of popular song, in which high musical merit goes hand in hand with the tunefulness that appeals to the mass. But can any one doubt that the instantaneous and universal appreciation which *Ol' Man River* received in 1927 was due to a special condition, a reason deep in the spirit of the times? Perhaps a beginning disillusionment with the material abundance that was supposed to be the pride of the age, a disrelish for the hurry and fret with which that material abundance was achieved, a questioning of the complexity and the feverish tempo that the Twenties imposed, a longing for the serenity and imperturbability, the self-sufficient philosophy of

Ol' man river, he jest keeps rollin' along.

Almost with the dignity of an Old Testament prophet, *Ol' Man River* stood up before an America frantic with hurry, and told it what was its true heart's desire.

To *Ol' Man River* several of the best talents of the time contributed: One of the great story-tellers of the generation, Edna Ferber, wrote a novel of life on the Mississippi, "Show Boat"; the most expert showman of the time, Florenz Ziegfeld, adapted the novel into a musical play; the words of the lyrics were written by Oscar Hammerstein, 2d, the music by Jerome Kern. One other contributor there was, one who, curiously, did not see the song nor hear it sung until it was completed, but whose personality had been in the mind of the composer from his first inspiration, a great negro singer, Paul Robeson, who, Kern had hoped, would have a rôle in the play, but was unable to.

IX

Ol' Man River was a great song, and the musical play from which it came, "Show Boat," was the parent of four other genuinely good songs. Always musical plays — musical comedies, light operas and operettas as well

Paul Robeson as he sang *Ol' Man River.*

as operas — have been fruitful sources of popular songs. It was so as long ago as when *Then You'll Remember Me* and *I Dreamt I Dwelt in Marble Halls* had been sung in "The Bohemian Girl." In American light opera, Robin Hood produced two of the best-liked and most enduring songs of the 1890's, *Brown October Ale* and *Oh, Promise Me.* "Erminie," "Florodora," "The Merry Widow," and many other light operas had made contributions to the best and most long-lasting American popular songs. As it happened, the musical plays of the 1920's included several of high quality, and those gave rise to some of the best songs of the period.[24]

In the late Twenties, a new source of popular songs arose. When motion pictures became talking pictures,

[24] *Musical Play*   *Songs*

As You Were (1920–1921)   *If You Would Care for Me*
Mary (1920–1921)   *Love Nest*
Sally (1920–1921)   *Look for the Silver Lining*
                                 Sally
Blossom Time (1921–1922)   *Song of Love*
Bombo (1921–1922)   *April Showers*
Follies (1921–1922)   *My Man*
Music Box Review (1921–1922)   *Say It With Music*
Lady in Ermine (1922–1923)   *When Hearts Were Young*
Music Box Review (1922–1923)   *What'll I Do?*
Orange Blossoms (1922–1923)   *Kiss in the Dark*
Kid Boots (1923–1924)   *Some One Loves You After All*
No, No, Nanette (1923–1924)   *Tea for Two*
                                 I Want To Be Happy
Student Prince (1923–1924)   *Deep in My Heart*
                                 Serenade
Lady Be Good (1923–1924)   *Lady Be Good*
Rose Marie (1923–1924)   *Indian Love Call*
                                 Rose Marie
Countess Maritza (1926–1927)   *Play Gypsy*
Desert Song (1926–1927)   *One Alone*
                                 Desert Song
The Girl Friend (1926–1927)   *Blue Room*
Peggy Ann (1926–1927)   *Tree in the Park*
Connecticut Yankee (1927–1928)   *My Heart Stood Still*
Hit the Deck (1927–1928)   *Hallelujah*
                                 Sometimes I'm Happy
My Maryland (1927–1928)   *Mother*
                                 Silver Moon
Rio Rita (1927–1928)   *Rio Rita*
                                 Rangers' Song
Show Boat (1927–1928)   *Ol' Man River*
                                 Bill
                                 Can't Help Lovin' That Man
                                 Why Do I Love You
                                 Make Believe
Good News (1929–1930)   *Varsity Drag*
                                 Good News
                                 Best Things in Life Are Free
Sweet Adeline (1929–1930)   *Why Was I Born?*
                                 Here Am I
New Moon (1929–1930)   *One Kiss*
                                 Lover Come Back to Me
Nina Rosa (1929–1930)   *Nina Rosa*

theme songs were written for them. By this, the talking picture stepped alongside the musical show of the regular stage as a source of popular songs. From talking pictures came several of the songs that became familiar after 1928. (In some cases, talking pictures were made from stage productions that had preceded, and the songs had been popular before they were heard from the screen):

Talking Picture	Song
Street Angel (1928)	Angela Mia
On with the Show (1928)	Am I Blue?
Singing Fool (1928)	Sonny Boy
Shopworn Angel (1928–1929)	Precious Little Thing Called Love
Sweetie (1928–1929)	My Sweeter Than Sweet
Love Parade (1928–1929)	My Love Parade
Sunny Side Up (1929)	Sunnyside Up
	Picking Petals Off o' Daisies
	If I Had a Talking Picture of You
The Pagan (1929)	Pagan Love Song
Broadway Melody (1929)	Broadway Melody
	You Were Meant for Me
Hollywood Revue (1929)	Singin' in the Rain
Syncopation (1929)	Jericho

X

Analysis of the popular songs[25] songs of any period, if any one should attempt so grisly a ghoulishness, would reveal that an immense majority of them deal with love, and that the purpose these mainly serve in cosmos is that

[25] A test of relative popularity, not necessarily associated with merit, was sales of phonograph records. During the 1920's, the ten best selling Victor Records were:

	Approximate Sales
The Prisoner's Song	1,519,000
My Blue Heaven	1,446,000
Three O'Clock in the Morning	1,427,000
Valencia	1,381,000
Whispering	1,327,000
In a Little Spanish Town	760,000
Sleepy Time Gal	627,000
Blue Skies	454,000
The Doll Dance	318,000
Hi-Diddle-Diddle	269,000

of aid to lovers and sweethearts. (Those old English words were, during the Twenties in America, translated into "boy-friend" and "girl-friend.") Swains moved by sentiments which, they feel, are beyond any inventiveness of expression in their poor possessions are happily enabled, by one song or another, to achieve a sublimity of utterance adequately proportioned to the immensity of their emotions.

Many popular songs are, in short, for humans, the equivalents of the love-calls of birds and animals; equivalents more elevated to be sure — or can we be sure about that? Is *Gimme a Little Kiss, Will Ya, Huh* really any more elevated than the cry of a whip-poor-will to his mate? When, in the trees of the front yard, a biped with feathers expressed himself in the soft "coo" of the dove, while on the porch a biped without feathers poured out his cosmic urge in *I Gotta Have You,*[26] who can say which came out best in the musical comparison? At least the feathered one performed on his own steam; he patronized no Tin Pan Alley to tell him how to tell his love. The words and musical notation of *Love, Your Spell Is Everywhere,* may be more intricate than the spring call of the bull moose, but it means much the same — the function of the two is identical.

For this happy service the love songs of the 1920's provided a felicitous abundance: *The Love Nest* (1921). . . . *Hot Lips* (1922). . . . *Burning Kisses* (1924). . . . *Kiss Before Dawn* (1927). . . . *Sweet Man* (1925). . . . *Crying for You* (1923). . . . *Two Sweet Lips* (1921). . . . *Let Me Linger Longer in Your Arms* (1924). . . . *Baby Face, I Need Lovin'* (1926). . . . *Last Night I Dreamed You Kissed Me* (1928). . . . *Tonight You Belong to Me* (1926). And so on and so on — the number of them was legion.

[26] 1929.

Some love-songs of the Twenties were dainty, and would not have shocked a Victorian lady. But some went far in approximation to the equivalent vocalizations of cosmic urge in the animal species below the primates. The Twenties were a decade of frankness, daring, realism, earthiness. The younger generation, taught by Freud and other influences, went far toward assuming there was little distinction, if any, between sentimental love and physical. Elders, brought up in an age more delicate — the younger generation said, more hypocritical — were shocked. Complaint arose from churchmen, and from others having a sense of responsibility about standards of public manners. A Catholic periodical [27] uttered a protest against the double sin, carnality and banality:

Popular songs never did pretend to be much, either from the poetical or the grammatical standpoint. But in the days when pupils learned something of grammar, rhyme, rhythm, reason, and ordinary decency in the public schools, there would have been a riot over the perpetration of an atrocity like:

> "He's my boy friend, I'm his sweetie.
> When we dance my heart gets leapy.
> He's so amorous
> He gets me glamorous!
> Oh, my!
> I
> Wanta die
> With my boy friend
> Right then!"

XI

A venture into discrimination between good songs and not good, or less good, was made by a periodical for women, [28] which in 1933 assembled the judgments of

[27] *The Fortnightly Review,* September 15, 1928.
[28] *The Woman's Home Companion.*

three hundred and seventy musicians and orchestra leaders to make up a list of the ten greatest songs of the
preceding decade. The élite thus selected were:

> *Tea for Two* (1924)
> *I'll See You in My Dreams* (1924)
> *The Man I Love* (1924)
> *When Day Is Done* (1926)
> *Ol' Man River* (1927)
> *Russian Lullaby* (1927)
> *My Blue Heaven* (1927)
> *Lover Come Back to Me* (1928)
> *Star Dust* (1929)
> *Good Night, Sweetheart* (1931)

Not all would agree with that selection. "Greatest,"
or "best" in connection with popular songs, is an elastic
word. Some like their songs for humor, or gaiety; others, especially the young, for sentiment. The judgment of musicians does not always coincide with that of
hearers, or amateur performers. Only the coldly un-
sentimental can base their judgments wholly on austere
standards of harmony in music and prosody in words.
To most of those who lived through the 1920's, especially those who were young and knew love, the "best"
popular song of the time is the one they heard under
the most sentimental circumstances, on the occasion —
or occasions — when they were in love.

XII

To say which was the best love-song of the Twenties
would be an exercise of judgment which should not be
entrusted to either a historian or a musician. To every
youth and lass who lived through the period, the best
love-song was the one which to them had the particular
associations that compose "love and youth and that sweet

time." Possibly as often as any, the song that acted as precipitant of young love was *Who?*[29]

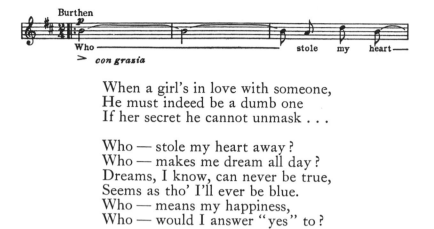

When a girl's in love with someone,
He must indeed be a dumb one
If her secret he cannot unmask . . .

Who — stole my heart away?
Who — makes me dream all day?
Dreams, I know, can never be true,
Seems as tho' I'll ever be blue.
Who — means my happiness,
Who — would I answer "yes" to?

Almost equally serviceable as a way of telling love was *Valencia:*[30]

In my dreams, it always seems,
I hear you softly call to me,
Valencia!

In *Valencia* the youth was singing to the maid. Among songs with which the maid could hint an unmistakable "come hither" to the man, perhaps *The Man I Love*[31]

[29] 1925. Sung by Marilyn Miller in "Sunny." Music by Jerome Kern. Words by Oscar Hammerstein, II. Reproduced by permission of the copyright owner, T. B. Harms.

[30] 1926. Reproduced by permission of copyright owner, Harms, Inc.

[31] 1924. The words were by Ira Gershwin; the music by his brother, George. The song was distinguished and had a high degee of originality. Reproduced by permission of copyright owner, Harms, Inc,

served that purpose of coy beguilement as often as any other:

Some day he'll come along, the man I love;
And he'll be big and strong, the man I love.
And when he comes my way, I'll do my best to make him
    stay . . .

In *Ramona*[32] love was the theme, but it conscripted as accessory lures the glamor of Spanish romance, the peal of mission bells, the aroma of flowers, and a suggestion of the climate of California:

Ramona, I hear the mission bells above;
Ramona, they're ringing out our song of love.
I press you, caress you and bless the day you taught me to
    care;
To always remember the rambling rose you wear in your
    hair . . .
Ramona, I need you, my own.

Love in a lighter mood was in *Tea for Two:*[33]

Picture you upon my knee,
Just tea for two and two for tea,
Just me for you and you for me, a-lone.
Nobody near us to see us or hear us,
No friends or relations on week-end vacations,
We won't have it known, dear, that we own a telephone,
    dear . . .

In a yet lighter mood was *You're the Cream in My Coffee*[34] — indeed it was well over the borderland of

---

[32] 1928. Reproduced by permission of copyright owner, Leo Feist, Inc.

[33] 1924. From the musical comedy "No, No, Nanette." Reproduced by permission of copyright owner, Harms, Inc.

[34] 1928. Reproduced by permission of the copyright owner, DeSylva, Brown & Henderson, Inc.

nonsense. But it was also love, love expressed in metaphors which could be either the sincerity of simplicity, or agreeably ridiculous — it was love with a laugh. As such, *You're the Cream in My Coffee* must have served a good many lovers well; with it, a suitor could achieve a titillating tentativeness and the lady could take it as either serious declaration or whimsical humor, each able either to make the occasion serious, or laugh it off:

You're the cream in my coffee, you're the salt in my stew,
You will always be my necessity, I'd be lost without you.
You're the starch in my collar, you're the lace in my shoe . . .

Many of the songs of sentiment took a familiar form, nostalgic longing for love remembered:

Though the days are long, twilight sings a song,
Of all the happiness that used to be.
I'll see you in my dreams . . .
Lips that once were mine, tender eyes that shine;
They will light the way tonight; I'll see you in my dreams.[35]

My Blue Heaven[36] was about love that succeeded and became permanent, married love:

Just Mollie and me
And baby makes three
We're happy in my blue heaven.

Jilting of the swain by the sweetheart — "running out on him" the Twenties called it — was recited, with gusto and good humor, in:

My sweetie went away,
But she didn't say where,
She didn't say when,
She didn't say why.[37]

[35] *I'll See You in My Dreams,* Isham Jones, 1924. Reproduced by permission of copyright owner, Leo Feist, Inc.

[36] 1927. Reproduced by permission of copyright owner, Leo Feist, Inc.

[37] *My Sweetie Went Away,* 1923. Reproduced by permission of copyright owner, Mills Co.

And the more slangy

> Somebody stole my gal, . . .
> Somebody came and took her away.
> She didn't even say she was leavin' . . . [38]

In one song the jilted suitor soothed his pride with sarcasm:

> I offer you Con-grat-u-la-tions . . .
> You found somebody new,
> What else is there to do,
> But offer you con-grat-u-la-tions ?[39]

XIII

What the fraternity of professional song writers know as "kid songs" was represented by *I Faw Down an' Go Boom:*

> I played horsie down the street
> With my broom,
> Down the street;
> When somebody moved the street,
> I faw down an' go boom

Other verses described disasters accruing to children of greater years, one of them the misadventure of an impecunious swain:

> I took sweetie out to dine,
> Out to dine,
> She said "Fine."
> When she ordered up some wine,
> I faw down an' go boom.

Another adult tragedy was described in:

> I played the market down the street,
> That's a game I thought I'd beat,
> I bought Amalgamated Heat —
> I faw down an' go boom.[40]

[38] *Somebody Stole My Gal,* 1923. Reproduced by permission of copyright owner, Denton & Haskins Co.

[39] *Congratulations,* 1929. Reproduced by permission of the copyright owner.

[40] 1928. Reproduced by permission of the copyright owner, Donaldson, Douglas and Gumble.

A truer type of song about children expressed the love of parents for them. Commonly, in popular songs, parental love is a monopoly of the mother; but during the 1920's Al Jolson made song of father-love very popular, *Sonny Boy:*[41]

When there are gray skies, I don't mind the gray skies

When there are gray skies . . .
You make them blue, Sonny Boy.
My friends may forsake me . . .
You'll pull me through, Sonny Boy.

XIV

The type of music that was supposed to be essentially characteristic of the Twenties was jazz. And in truth, one of the definitions of jazz, "brazen defiance of accepted rules," would have served equally well to describe the spirit of much of the generation. The eccentricity of syncopation which jazz achieved is suggested by the happily apt title of a piece written in 1921 to adapt jazz to the piano, *Kitten on the Keys* — in which the startling effect was achieved by triple rhythm with the right hand against double rhythm with the left. And the public favor for jazz was proved by the eagerness with which *Kitten on the Keys* was received by the early Twenties; "probably no other piano solo ever leaped into such widespread popularity in so short a time."[42] Similarly expressive was the title of another widely popular jazz creation, *Crazy Rhythm*, some words of which

[41] 1923. Introduced in "The Singing Fool." Reproduced by permission of the copyright owner, David Edson Silverman, Chicago.
[42] The quotation is from Henry O. Osgood, "So This Is Jazz."

described the insidious and conquering pervasiveness of the bizarre cacophony:

> Every Greek, each Turk and each Latin,
> The Russians and Prussians as well;
> When they seek the lure of Manhattan,
> Are sure to come under your spell.
> Their native folk songs they soon throw away . . .

The fantastic syncopation of jazz was neither the

A drawing by Leonard Dove in the "New Yorker."

"Let's have the Schubert Serenade and get some dirt into it."

To "Jazz up" the classics meant, in many cases, to play them with a touch of salaciousness.

accident of a kitten on the piano keys nor the haphazard aberrations of the mad. Jazz never made the apology of the reproved member of an orchestra who explained that he had "played the fly-specks." The unusualness of notation was deliberately sought, and attainment of the most outré of cacophonic combinations was the jazz composer's triumph. Erratic syncopation, eccentricity deliberately planned, was only one of the characteristics of jazz. It was rapid, feverish, excited, and exciting.

To write fully and adequately about jazz would be to

write the history of much of the generation. The word passed into common use; to "jazz" or "jazz up" became a transitive verb, used to describe the introduction of speed and excitement into any activity of life, the operation usually being regarded as praiseworthy. To "jazz it up a bit" was the common recommendation for anything whose tempo had failed to keep up to the times.[43]

Some composers and purveyors of jazz took it seri-

"Jazz Sounds Death-Knell Of Opera," Says Mascagni

Famed Italian Composer Sees Little Hope for Higher Music Filling Satiated Public's Demand for Something New

A prediction which, like that of Mark Twain's death, turned out to be premature.

ously, seriously in the sense of approving it, creating it, and performing it. A composer of high standing, George Gershwin, defended it:[44] "Music should be a product of the time in which it was produced. . . . The old masters reflected in their music the spirit of their ages: isn't it up to us to do the same?" A successful orchestra-leader, Paul Whiteman, said, "I sincerely believe that jazz is the folk-music of the machine age."

Some others took it seriously in the sense in which they took pestilence seriously, or as the hind takes the wolf seriously. An English musical critic addressing the National Union of Organists' Associations condemned "that cursed American form of music," and the *Lon-*

---

[43] Jazz had begun before the Twenties, there is some account of it in Volume IV of "Our Times"; it was in the Twenties that it came to apotheosis.

About jazz a small literature grew up: "So This Is Jazz," by Henry O. Osgood, 1926; "Jazz," by Paul Whiteman, 1926; "All About Jazz," by Stanley R. Nelson, 1934. And many others.

[44] In the New York *Times,* January 20, 1929.

don Times solemnly repeated the malediction. Another English critic, Ernest Newman, called it "musical insanity," a product of "brainlessness and boredom." The most eminent of modern Italian composers, Mascagni, composer of *Cavalleria Rusticana*, made a statement which a headline writer[45] epitomized as "'Jazz Sounds Death-Knell of Opera,' Says Mascagni."

But it turned out that an American composer, at the time wise and old, was at once more calm and more accurate than the Italian and English ones. "Jazz," said John Philip Sousa in 1928, "does not truly represent America. . . . It will, I am positive, some day disappear." Just about the time Mascagni made his doleful prediction and capitulation, a good-bye to jazz was sung in the chorus of *Crazy Rhythm*[46]; the farewell was mockingly affected, but turned out nevertheless to be at least partially prophetic:

Cra - zy Rhy - thm, here's the door - way, I'll go my way,

Crazy Rhythm from now on we're through.
Here is where we have a showdown,
I'm too high-hat, you're too low-down,
Crazy Rhythm, here's good-bye to you.

XV

Essential to jazz was the saxophone — "it was the heart, soul, mind, body and spirit of the jazz orchestra."[47] It was not new, it had been invented some eighty years before by a Belgian instrument-maker named Saxe. But it was in the 1920's that extraordinary use,

---

45 In the Philadelphia *Public Ledger,* August, 1929.
46 1928. Reprinted by permission of the copyright owner, Harms, Inc.
47 Quoted from Henry O. Osgood, "So This Is Jazz." From Mr. Osgood's book are taken some of the facts here told about jazz.

leading to widespread vogue, came to this curious hybrid. (The saxophone is the only reed instrument made of brass, the other reeds, the clarinet, the oboe and the bassoon, are of wood; the saxophone player could be at one and the same time both string band and wood wind.) Like all virile invaders the saxophone was ruthless, roughly it elbowed the gentle violin out of its dominance in orchestras.

The very shape and appearance of the saxophone was striking; a player standing up with one to his lips could by dipping and swinging its long length, by sudden starts and rigidities and tremors, by swoops and swerves, give to the instrument an effect of sentience; could create, by the motions he gave it, expressions which supplemented the music, the union of music to the ear and motion to the eye having an extraordinary capacity to create effects of comedy, surprise, dismay, satisfaction, or whatever other emotion the music was designated to convey.

As for the sounds that a skilled saxophone-player could achieve, there was almost no limit to them. The saxophone could be onomatopoetic as no other instrument could. Even an amateur, a boy — as many a parent discovered during the Twenties — could evoke sounds which the household would have preferred to be absent. The saxophone could imitate the yowl of a cat, the moo of a cow, the baa of a calf, the whinney of a horse. Parents imprudent enough to yield to a boy's begging for a saxophone as a Christmas present found by New Year's that their home was housing the entire animal kingdom, a menagerie of wild animals and a barnyard of tame ones, a lunatic asylum in which were segregated victims given especially to maniacal laughter, together with a wide variety of other sources of noise, chiefly unwanted ones, banging doors, howling winds, honking automobiles.

The saxophone could, and in the hands of prankish boys did, reproduce, with rather greater effectiveness than the actual thing, human sounds whose reproduction is not

Cartoonist J. N. Darling (Ding) in the *N. Y. Herald Tribune,* illustrates the contrast between Secretary of the Interior Wilbur reproving the social diversions of some of his Indian charges, and the Caucasian diversions that were current at the same time.

universally desired, a yawn, a grunt, a belch. A skilful player with an acrobatic tongue slapping against the reed, his fingers fluttering over the score of keys, could achieve titillating arpeggios, glissandos, every sort of musical coruscation; he could toot and he could tootle, he could blare and blast, could bleat and blat, he could chatter, he could coo. Especially could he coo; there was wide complaint, where there was not approval, that the saxophone was sensuous, that it was "music in the nude." It was the instrument of the Twenties — and it was a long way from the pipes of Pan.

XVI

The decade was cordial to change, at times seemed to prefer strangers to old friends. Many innovations rushed to take advantage of the period's zest for the new. One of the novelties was "crooning." It was developed by a young man who had been born in Vermont, reared in Maine and educated at Yale — that New England background, especially the Maine and Vermont part of it, seemed somehow incongruous with the art the young man practised, for crooning was on the verge of being regarded as soft, as almost effeminate. Born Hubert Prior Vallee, he came to be called "Rudy"; that abbreviation seemed also a transition in the direction of the sentimental. Crooning heard directly, by one in the same room, made somewhat the slightly disconcerting impression of a male human being making sounds like those a mother makes to a very young child. The microphone, however, and the ether waves seemed to transmute sounds of mother-love into sounds having seductive appeal and gave to crooning over the radio some sort of magic. "A voice that starts its strange journey at the microphone hardly more than banal, fills the air at its destination with some sort of beauty, uniqueness, novelty." [48]

By his art, Vallée,[49] with other crooners, revived some

[48] The quotation is from William Bolitho.

[49] Other songs crooned by Rudy Vallée or others included *Deep Night, Beside an Open Fireplace, The Vagabond Lover* (1929), *Love Made a Gypsy Out of Me* (1929), *I'm a Dreamer—Aren't We All? Life Is Just a Bowl of Cherries, If I Had You* (1928), *Rain* (1927).

old songs, made many new ones familiar: Among the latter, *Good-Night, Sweetheart:*[50]

Good night, sweetheart, till we meet tomorrow,
Good night, sweetheart, sleep will banish sorrow.

And *When It's Springtime in the Rockies:*[51]

When it's springtime in the Rockies,
I'll be coming back to you,
Little sweetheart of the mountains
With your bonny eyes of blue.

Another innovation was called, for whatever reason, "torch singing." The woman most identified with it was Libby Holman, a professional singer, who happened to have a voice with a wide range and an agreeably husky, throaty quality. The general effect, both of the manner of singing, and of the songs, was lament about life, self-pity. The titles of the songs suggested the spirit of them: *Moanin' Low,*[52] *Body and Soul,*[53] *Am I Blue?*[54] Another torch singer, Helen Morgan, asked, with husky dolefulness, *Why Was I Born?*[55] Her manner implied that there wasn't any good reason. Another ditty that lent itself to the throaty self-pity of torch singing was *Ten Cents a Dance,*[56] plaint of a girl who made her living by

[50] 1931. Reproduced by permission of copyright owner, Robbins Music Corp.
[51] 1929. Reproduced by permission of the copyright owner, Marks (Villa March Co.).
[52] 1929.
[53] 1930.
[54] 1929.
[55] 1929.
[56] 1930.

dancing on a commercial basis with the customers of dance halls.

Hardly an innovation, not much more than a mannerism associated with one personality was the "boop-a-

From a photograph by Hal Phyfe.

Libby Holman, whose deep-throated husky voice made her popular as a torch singer.

doop" singing of Helen Kane, a cute, pert little vaudeville performer who discovered she could achieve fame by inserting irrelevant and meaningless syllables,[57] such as "boop-a-doop," here and there in the words of

---

[57] A poetical person who has read the proof of this chapter thinks I am unnecessarily superior about "meaningless syllables," and wrong in the implication that they are modern. He cites Shakespeare, Act IV, Scene II:

It was a lover and his lass
With a hey, and a ho, and a hey no-ni-no . . .
When birds do sing hey ding-a-ding-ding.

her songs. Sigmund Spaeth called it, with some lack of respect, "sillysyllabic singing." Miss Kane's ditties included a satirically solicitous ditty called *Button Up Your Overcoat*,[58] and *Thank Your Father, Thank Your Mother*,[59] *I Wanna Be Loved by You*,[60] *That's My Weakness Now*.[61]

XVII

Another feature of the Twenties, a kind of gargoyle on the cathedral of American music, negro in origin, was the "blues" (not to be confused with "spirituals" which were religious). A "blue" — though the word was never used in the singular — was originally a lament rhythmically wailed by a negro who felt badly; he had the blues and chanted a "blue":

Gwine to de river, take a rope an' a rock,
Gwine to de river, take a rope an' a rock,
Gwine to tie rope roun' my neck and jump right over de dock.

Originally the laments were spontaneous, a gloomy emotion put into moaning, rhythmic words with the facility in musical expression that is native to the negro. An early one, and one that became best known, was the *St. Louis Blues*,[62] in which a colored woman mourned the loss of her lover and considered how to get him back:

I hate to see de ev'nin' sun go down,
Hate to see de eve-nin' sun go down,
'Cause my baby he done lef' dis town.
Feelin' tomorrow lak Ah feel today,
Feel tomorrow lak Ah feel today,
I'll pack my trunk, make ma getaway.

[58] 1928.
[59] 1929.
[60] 1928.
[61] 1928.
[62] In the interest of easier understanding, the cane-brake pronunciations of some of the words are here made to conform more nearly to standard.

St. Louis woman wid her diamon' rings
Pulls dat man 'roun' by her apron strings.
'Twant for powder an' for store bought hair,
De man I love would not gone nowhere.

Got de St. Lou-is Blues jes as blue as— Ah— can be ———
I— loves dat man lak a school boy— loves- his pie ———
A— black head-ed gal make a freight train— jump— the track ———
Lawd a blonde head-ed wom-an makes a good— man— leave the town ———
Oh ash-es to ash-es and dust to dust ———

Got de St. Louis Blues, jes blue as Ah can be!
Dat man got a heart like a rock cast in the sea,
Or else he wouldn't gone so far from me.
(Spoken) "Doggone it!"

Been to de gypsy to get ma fortune tole;
Been to de gypsy to get ma fortune tole;
'Cause I's wild about ma jelly-roll.[63]
Gypsy done tole me, "Don't you wear no black!"
Gypsy done tole me, "Don't you wear no black!
Go to St. Louis, you can win him back."
Help me to Cairo, make St. Louis myse'f;
Git to Cairo, fine ma old friend Jeff,
Gwine to pin myse'f close to his side;
If I flag his train I sho can ride.[64]

The *St. Louis Blues* was genuine, truly negroid in origin; so also was the *Memphis Blues*. While imitation or adaptation came forward in the *Limehouse Blues* and *Birth of the Blues*. Apotheosis, a long distance from the Mississippi canebrakes, came when George Gershwin composed *Rhapsody in Blue*,[65] played by the New York Symphony Orchestra under Walter Damrosch. It was not a "blue," but was about blues, a composition written with high symphonic dignity.

A negro innovation in dancing was the *Charleston*, followed, and made more ultra in the *Black Bottom*. Both

[63] Evidently a cane-brake negro term of endearment, luscious in its implications, equivalent of the Caucasian "honey," "honey bun," "sugar pie."
[64] 1914. Reproduced by permission of the copyright owner, Handy Bros. Music Co., Inc.
[65] 1927.

were violently acrobatic, the dancing equivalent of the
frenzy of a negro jazz orchestra. They were the extreme
manifestation of the negro influence on American ball-
room dancing, the farthest distance that the jazz period

Two of the steps of "The Charleston" as illustrated by Arthur Murray, New
York instructor in the modern dance.

went from the stately waltzes and decorous polkas of the
older generation. Nice people did them only as an occasional stunt under special circumstances; they were a
means by which the younger set at the country club
would have shocked the chaperones — only, by the
Twenties, there were no chaperones. The status of the
Charleston was suggested in a stanza from a popular
song of 1925, *Don't Bring Lulu*:

> We all went to the party, a real high-toned affair
> And then along came Lulu, as wild as any Zulu.
> She started in to "Charleston,"
> And how the boys did stare.[66] . . .

[66] Reproduced by permission of copyright owner, Jerome H. Remick & Co.

XVIII

No account of popular songs during the 1920's, and such fragile relation as they have to history, could pretend to be adequate — it would not be even a skipping

174 South Street, New York City. Birthplace of ex-Governor Alfred E. Smith, and locale of the song *Sidewalks of New York*.

from high note to high note — if it failed to mention the conspicuous revival of an old song of three decades before. The renascence came about through the political prominence of a three times, and each time excellent, Governor of New York, upon whom his parents, and the Catholic priest who baptized him, had conferred the names Alfred Emanuel, but whom America preferred to call by an affectionate abbreviation, "Al." Al Smith had been born on the East Side of New York. About the time he reached the age in which interest in girls goes hand in hand with, and partly accounts for, interest in song, it happened that the popular song of the period — it was during the early 1890's — was one called *The Sidewalks of New York*,[67] in which the most familiar lines were,

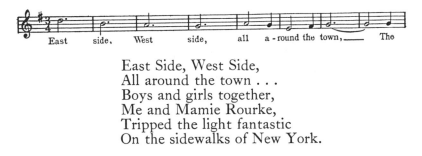

East Side, West Side,
All around the town . . .
Boys and girls together,
Me and Mamie Rourke,
Tripped the light fantastic
On the sidewalks of New York.

The fortuitous conjunction of the name of the song, its locale, and the fact that Smith had been born and brought up in the same section of New York, brought it about that when Smith ran for President in 1928, this song, more than thirty years old, was played more often, and heard by more people than any of the current songs of the day. In vain did the harried artisans of ephemeral hits pound the drum and blow the saxophone of jazz against the greater appeal of a thoroughly old-fashioned song, one that was utterly sentimental, and because of that, in the judgment of the sophisticated, out-moded and banal.

The Sidewalks of New York was more closely associated with Al Smith than any other song had ever been with any candidate or President. Some instinctive sense that Smith in his personality had qualities of homeliness, simplicity, and directness similar to those of the old-fashioned, sentimental waltz caused the combination of

[67] Reproduced by permission of the copyright owner, Leo Feist, Inc.

song and candidate to appeal strongly to the country; it made friends for both man and song.

Four years later, in 1932, when Franklin D. Roosevelt was a Presidential nominee, some of those interested in his candidacy, perhaps remembering the happy association of Smith with *The Sidewalks of New York*, and carrying on the old tradition that every candidate should have a campaign song, put forward for Franklin Roosevelt *Happy Days Are Here Again.*[68]

> So long, sad times!
> Go along, bad times!
> We're rid of you at last . . .
> Happy days are here again,
> The skies above are clear again, clear again,
> Let's sing a song of cheer again,
> Happy days are here again.

In *Happy Days Are Here Again* as the Franklin Roosevelt campaign song of 1932, there was logical aptness, for the country was in the depth of depression, and the implication was that Roosevelt, if elected, would bring good times. But just because in this case the association between candidate and song was artificial and forced, it was less successful than in the case of Smith and *The Sidewalks of New York*, in which the association was natural and honestly sentimental.

XIX

In the Twenties, the new popular songs, like almost everything else, experienced an accelerated ephemeralness. After the radio came, a new air might be sung the first time at some New York night-club at 3 A.M., or in a new musical play, and, if recognized as a "hit," might by seven o'clock the ensuing evening be flying on the

[68] 1929. Reproduced by permission of copyright owner, Ager, Yellen & Bornstein.

ether waves to practically every home in the country, pushed on its feverish way by a hundred instrumentalities of high pressure business organization. And if, the following morning in another night-club, a hit was made by some still newer song, the later favorite might, by the same process of practically instantaneous diffusion, crowd into beginning obsolescence the favorite of twenty-four hours before.

One thought of how the songs of an earlier time had made their way: *The Last Rose of Summer*, sung in a London drawing-room, heard by some one who after days of slow travel carried it to Liverpool, picked up and memorized by a ship-captain or sailor who brought it a six weeks' journey across the Atlantic, sung in a Philadelphia tavern, heard and memorized by a Conestoga wagoner who carried it with him as he travelled westward toward the Alleghanies, singing it in each tavern where he stopped over-night, and repeating it for the benefit of listeners who learned it and in turn carried it upon their various ways. Between the first singing of a song by Thomas Moore or Robert Burns or Stephen Foster, and the complete familiarity of all America with it, years must have elapsed. In that earlier time, a person heard a song and, if he liked it, learned it, committed it to memory, made it a part of his personality, had for it the affection that goes out to that which is at once dear and familiar.

But in the 1920's "the thing," the vogue, was to know not the old songs but the new ones — to know the latest "hit" was one mark of the sophistication that was universally desired. And since new was so soon displaced by newer, hardly any one tried to learn a song. Little more of it was known than a line or two of the chorus, a phrase or two of the music. The musical possessions of the average person became not four or five songs well-learned and permanently remembered, but a mere jumble of melody lines.

XX

Under the spell of recalling the tunes of the Twenties, one might summon up a fantasy: imagine that all the radio waves, which during the 1920's were carrying tunes and melodies up and down America, went on and on and on, up through the ether, through the stratosphere and past the stars, to come together in some Valhalla of tune. Upon the listening gods, the resulting jumble might make one impression or another, depending upon whatever are the gods' standards of taste about music. But to Americans who lived through the 1920's, especially young ones, who were in love, once or more often — to these the medley would be like the mingled scents of lavender, rosemary, and forget-me-not:

Lonesome in the Moonlight (1928) . . . *You Forgot to Remember* (1925) . . . *You've Got Me Picking Petals Off o' Daisies* (1929), a picture of love-madness; its appeal depended on a familiar bit of folk-lore, the swain who, seeking oracular judgment about the fortunes of his passion, consults the gods by plucking alternate petals from the daisy, saying "she loves me, she loves me not" . . . *Margie* (1920) . . . *I Never Knew* (1921) . . . *Linger a While* (1923) — it was a sentimental waltz . . . *Where'd You Get Those Eyes* (1926) . . . *You've Got That Thing* (1929), sung comic-sentimentally, by Maurice Chevalier . . . *Betty Co-Ed* (1930), often sung by Rudy Vallée:

There were variations in the words and colleges to which Betty Co-ed was loyal.

Betty Co-ed has lips as red as rosebuds, Betty Co-ed has eyes of navy blue,

Betty Co-ed's a head of golden sunshine, her voice is like a
   songbird calling you.
Betty Co-ed's a smile for everybody, her heart's a perfect
   treasure so 'tis said.
Betty Co-ed is lov'd by every college boy, but I'm the one
   who's lov'd by Betty Co-ed.[69]

I Won't Say I Will But I Won't Say I Won't (1923)
. . . *Rose of the Rio Grande* (1922) . . . *I Found a
Million Dollar Baby* in a five-and-ten-cent store (1926)
. . . *Let's Talk About My Sweetie* (1926) . . . *Let a
Smile Be Your Umbrella* (1927):[70]

Let a smile be your umbrella on a rainy, rainy day . . .
Whenever skies are gray don't worry or fret,
A smile will bring the sunshine and you'll never get wet . . .

Don't Forget Me in Your Dreams (1930) . . . *Please
Don't Talk About Me When I'm Gone* (1929) — the
song was not about death, but merely lovers' parting attended by some acrimonious feeling. . . . *Yes, Sir,
That's My Baby* (1924) — not an acknowledgment of
paternity; "baby" was tough slang for sweetheart:

Yes, Sir, That's my Ba - by, No, Sir,
Yes, Sir, That's my Ba - by, No, Sir,

   Yes, sir, that's my baby;
   No, sir, I don't mean maybe . . .
   Yes, ma'am, we've decided;
   No, ma'am, we won't hide it.[71]

Ain't We Got Fun (1921) . . . *The Pagan Love
Song* (1929) sung by Ramon Novarro — he was the
talking-picture equivalent of what in a previous generation had been the matinée idol of the stage. . . . *Cut
Yourself a Piece of Cake* and make yourself at home
(1923) . . . *I'm the Sheik of Araby* (1921) — inspired by a novel of desert passion, "The Sheik," and

[69] Reproduced by permission of copyright owner, Carl Fischer.
[70] Reproduced by permission of the copyright owner, Mills, Inc.
[71] Quoted by permission of the copyright owner, Leo Feist, Inc.

associated with a motion-picture hero outstanding in cinematic torridity, Rudolf Valentino:

> I'm the Sheik of Araby, your love belongs to me.
> At night when you're asleep, into your tent I'll creep.
> The stars that shine above, will light our way to love.
> You'll rule this land with me, the Sheik of Araby.[72]

Wedding of the Painted Doll (1926) . . . *Last Night I Dreamed You Kissed Me* (1928) . . . *My Man* (1928), a French importation, originally *Mon Homme*, sung by Fannie Brice with a gusto that shocked the elders but was vastly entertaining to the more sophisticated. . . . *Kiss in the Dark* (1922) by Victor Herbert:

> A kiss in the dark was to him just a lark
> But to me was a thrill supreme.[73]

Follow the Swallow Back Home (1924) was such a hit the song-writers bestirred themselves to produce other bird songs, the results including "*When the Red Red Robin* comes bob bob bobbin' along" (1926), *Bye Bye Blackbird* (1926), *Hello Bluebird* (1926) and, finally, *My Blackbirds Are Bluebirds Now.*

Thinking of You (1926) . . . *Where Did You Get Those Eyes?* (1926) . . . *If You Should Care* (1920) . . . *Jeanine I Dream of Lilac Time* (1928), a waltz-song, sung in connection with the motion picture "Lilac Time," in which Colleen Moore took the leading part. . . . *Roses of Yesterday* (1928) . . . "*You've Got to See Mamma* every night or you can't see mamma at all" (1923) — "mamma," in the slang of the Twenties, was not necessarily a parent, often it meant sweetheart. . . . *Just an Ivy Covered Shack* (1926) . . . *Laugh, Clown, Laugh* (1928) . . . *Tip Toe Through the Tulips with Me* (1929) . . . *Doo Wacka Doo* (1924) and *Doodle Doo Doo* (1924) — these and *Dig Diga Doo* (1928)

[72] Quoted by permission of the copyright owner, Mills, Inc.
[73] By permission of Harms, Inc.

were examples of wordless syncopation that had a brief vogue. . . . *Carolina in the Morning* (1922) . . . *Just a Gigolo* (1929) — self-pity expressed by a male hired dancer. . . . *She Was Just a Sailor's Sweetheart* (1925):

> She was just a sailor's sweetheart,
> And she loved her sailor lad,
> But he left her broke in Hartford,
> He was all she ever had.[74]

"*You'll Get Pie in the Sky* when you die" (1930) . . . *Yoo Hoo* (1921 . . . *Bees' Knees* (1922) — a slang phrase meaning "the very best." . . . *All Alone* by the telephone (1924) . . . *Thanks for the Buggy Ride* (1925):

> Thanks for the buggy ride, thanks for the buggy ride,
> I've had a wonderful time.[75]

Say It While You're Dancing (1922) . . . *When Lights Are Low* (1923) . . . "*Three O'Clock in the Morning*, I've danced the whole night through" (1921) — an example of the virile ability of the waltz to keep a foothold in the jazz age.

Don't Bring Lulu (1925), a suggestion which accompanied an invitation to a party; a thousand party-givers varied it to make facetious and not unfriendly discrimination against Mary or Jenny or Mabel or Lizzie, and in favor of Beth or Sue or Jane or Clare; the verses would also be adapted to ask a guest to bring gin or beer — an occasional postscript to invitations during the dry decade was "b. y. o.," "bring your own":

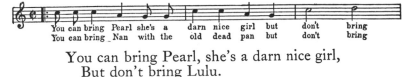

> You can bring Pearl, she's a darn nice girl,
> But don't bring Lulu.

74 Reproduced by permission of copyright owner.
75 By permission of Jules Bufano, Hollywood, Calif.

You can bring Rose with the turned-up nose,
  But don't bring Lulu.
You can bring cake or porterhouse steak,
  But don't bring Lulu.
You can bring peas and crullers and cheese,
  But don't bring Lulu.[76]

I Kiss Your Hand, Madame (1928) . . . "*California, Here I Come,* right back where I started from" (1924) — it was sung satirically about a Californian in politics, William G. McAdoo, when he failed to get the Democratic Presidential nomination . . . *O Katarina* (1924) . . . *Angel Child* (1922) . . . *Peoria* (1925) . . . *Rose Marie* (1924)

Oh, Rose Marie, I love you,
I'm always dreaming of you.
No matter what I do I can't forget you . . .[77]

Blue Moon (1921) . . . *Sweet Georgia Brown* (1924) . . . "*Hard Hearted Hannah,* the belle of Savannah" (1924) — she was a musical cousin of *Louisville Lou* . . . *Avalon* (1920) . . . *Bambalina* (1923) . . . *Out of the Dawn* (1928) . . . *You'll Never Know* (1928) . . . *Someday — Somewhere* (1928) . . . *March of the Vagabonds* (1925) sung by Denis King in the "Vagabond King." . . . *Song of the Flame* (1925) . . . "*In a Little Spanish Town* 'twas on a night like this" (1926) . . . *Just a Cottage Small by a Waterfall* (1925) . . . *Swanee* (1919) . . . *Always* (1926) . . . *Mean to Me* (1929) . . . *Down in Chinatown* (1921) . . . *Blue Skies* (1927) . . . *Whispering* (1920) . . . *Precious Little Thing Called Love* (1928) . . . *Indian Love Call* (1924) . . . *When Day is Done* (1924) . . . *Lover Come Back to*

[76] Reproduced by permission of the copyright owner, Jerome H. Remick & Co.
[77] By permission of Shapiro, Bernstein and Co., Inc.

Me (1928) . . . *The Song of Songs* (1924) written by Irving Berlin:

> Where is the Song of Songs for me?
> Beautiful song of ecstasy!

Irving Berlin's *The Song Is Ended but the Melody Lingers on* (1927) . . . *Among My Souvenirs* (1927):

> There's nothing left for me, of days that used to be.
> Some letters tied with blue, a photograph or two . . .[78]

XXI

Songs That Were Not Written

If "popular songs . . . have a significance in reflecting the times," some of the significance may be found in the songs that are not written. In the Twenties there were no Irish songs, no equivalents of "Down Went McGinty" or "T'row Him Down McCloskey" or "Lanigan's Ball" or "Has Anybody Here Seen Kelly?" or "Harrigan, Proud of all the Irish Blood That's in Me." Nor were there any German songs, no, "Oh, where, oh

---

[78] Some who knew the tunes of the Twenties well, and who have read the proof of this chapter, call grieved attention to some omissions: *Blame It on the Moon* (1929) . . . *Girl of My Dreams* (1927) . . . *Brown Eyes, Why Are You Blue* (1925) . . . *Sleepy Time Gal* (1925) . . . *You're a Real Sweetheart* (1928) . . . *Song of the Flame* (1925) . . . *Singing in the Rain* (1929) . . . *That's My Weakness Now* (1928) . . . *Carolina in the Morning* (1922) . . . *Second Hand Rose* (1921) . . . *Last Night on the Back Porch* (1923) . . . *Me and My Shadow* (1927) . . . *Charmaine* (1926) . . . *Here In My Arms* (1925) . . . *Just a Memory* (1926) . . . *Would You Like to Take a Walk* (1929) . . . *Reaching for the Moon* (1926) . . . *You Forgot to Remember* (1925) . . . *Wonderful One* (1922) . . . *High Diddle Diddle* (1926) . . . *Runnin' Wild* (1922) . . . *Remember?* (1926) . . . *I Never Knew* (1921) . . . *Just for Tonight* (1923) . . . *Mamma Love Papa, Papa Love Mamma* (1923) . . . *Watching the World Go By* (1927) . . . *Alabama Bound* (1925) . . . *So This Is Love* (1923) . . . *I Love You* (1923) . . . *Girl of My Dreams* (1927) . . . *What Is This Thing Called Love* (1929) . . . *Song of Love* (1921) . . . *I'll See You in My Dreams* (1024) . . . *Because I Love You* (1926) . . . *Dirty Hands, Dirty Face* (1923) a "kid song" sung by Al Jolson . . . *Ten Little Fingers and Ten Little Toes* (1921)—a "kid song" which recalled the *Rosary* of a quarter-century before . . . *Pal of My Cradle Days* (1925). . . .

Even so, no doubt readers of this volume will still have cause to complain of incompleteness.

where, has dot leedle dog gone," or "Dot Leedle German Band." The Irishman and the German had ceased to be an immigrant, a greenhorn; they had been merged into America, and with the merging had lost the racy flavor that had caused half the songs of the 1880's to be written about them.

Conspicuously also, there were no post-war songs. America had passed through an adventure of the kind which in former periods had been regarded as glorious, glamorous, romantic, song-inciting.. But we wrote no songs of nostalgic sentiment about the Great War, there was nothing of the mood which, after the Civil War, had led the country to sing, in a reverie of old pleasures recalled, "Tenting Tonight, Tenting on the old Camp Ground."

And there were no ballads; the tempo of the Twenties was too hurried for them — or so the song-writers thought.

XXII

The Cessation of Ballad-Writing During the Twenties — Which Left a Musical Desire Unsatisfied, and Led to the Searching Out, Collecting and Widespread Singing of Ballads of an Older Generation.

In the newer way of things, the ballad, the narrative song, the song that told a story, disappeared utterly — I doubt if any important new one emerged during the 1920's.[79] More and more, popular songs tended to be the mere repetition of a phrase, not pretending to tell a story, hardly even to make sense. They were abbreviated almost to a series of vocal ejaculations, depending, for the

---

[79] Attempts were made at ballads about some spectacular events of the Twenties; there was one about Floyd Collins, who was buried alive in a cave in Kentucky, and one called *The Wreck of the Shenandoah,* about a Navy dirigible that crashed tragically in Ohio. But these efforts at balladry, and all others in the Twenties, achieved no great popularity.

attraction of the words, almost wholly upon reiteration of such simple consonances as June with moon, love with dove, heart with part. The appeal of the ultra-modern songs was to emotion almost wholly. Ignoring the mind, their purpose was mainly to evoke a mood, which can be achieved by mere sound, regardless of the intellectual content of the words; indeed, a state of mere revery in the listener is the more easily evoked if his mind is not called upon to be active or even to pay attention.

This almost exclusive emphasis on the evoking of a mood left a need unmet; man is more completely pleased when both his emotions and his mind are stirred, as is done by a combination of agreeable music with words that move toward some kind of destination.

Man's primitive and age-long liking for a story, a ballad, was unsatisfied. Groping to satisfy this desire, many old-time American ballads were revived. The Southern Appalachians and the Ozarks were combed for "hill-billy" tales in simple verse and music. Cowboy ballads, tales of derring-do on the Western prairies, became a vogue in the drawing-rooms of Eastern cities; a collection of them, which pleased the tuneful and also won the esteem of scholars, was made by a teacher in the University of Texas, John A. Lomax — who thus enabled many a smartly Tuxedo-ed and ultra sophisticated representative of jeunesse dorée to make a hit in Park Avenue pent-houses by singing *The Cowboy's Lament*:

As I walked out in the streets of Laredo,
As I walked out in Laredo one day,
I spied a poor cowboy wrapped up in white linen,
Wrapped up in white linen as cold as the clay . . .

"Go gather around you a crowd of young cowboys,
And tell them the story of this my sad fate;
Tell one and the other before they go further
To stop their wild roving before 'tis too late.". . .

We beat the drum slowly and played the fife lowly,
And bitterly wept as we bore him along;
For we all loved our comrade, so brave, young, and handsome,
We all loved our comrade, although he'd done wrong.[80]

A thesaurus of tales of legendary American heroes
was assembled by Frank Shay in "Audacious Giants."
The same compiler collected sailor songs and chanties

From a drawing by E. M. Ashe in "Scribner's Magazine."

As the evening progressed it was the ballads that could be counted on
to prolong the party.

in "Iron Men and Wooden Ships." Shay, with John
Held, Jr., assembled and illustrated two volumes of
"Ballads From the Dear, Dead Days," which were put
out under the engaging titles of "My Pious Friends and
Drunken Companions," and "More Pious Friends and
Drunken Companions." A similar compilation made by
John J. Niles and Douglass S. Moore, was "Songs My
Mother Never Taught Me."

The old ballads thus or otherwise made available may
have given the 1920's as much pleasure, and a pleasure
with rather more substance, than did the current hits. It

[80] From "Cowboy Ballads," Macmillan and Company, New York.

is quite possible that those who composed the younger
generation, when they will have become the older one,
will recall the time-tested old ballads they sang, as
vividly as the hits of the day.

In convivial gatherings during the Twenties, after the
songs of the moment had had their precedence, some one
would turn to the old-time ballads; and it was to be observed that though the current songs might hold the
guests together until ten or eleven o'clock, it was the
ballads that kept the party going until two or three in
the morning. After a party had reached the point at
which normally it would break up, some one would step
to the piano and begin one of the old ballads. In parties
at Washington during the 1920's, the rescuer from im-
pending dissolution of the gathering was in many instances Speaker of the House Nicholas Longworth; and
his favored ballad, when he was in his less Rabelaisian
mood, was *Abdul A-Bul-Bul Amir:*

Oh the sons of the prophet were valiant and brave,
And quite unaccustomed to fear,
But the bravest by far in the ranks of the shah,
Was Abdul A-Bul-Bul Amir.

When they needed a man to encourage the van
Or harass the foe from the rear,
Or storm a redoubt, they had only to shout
For Abdul A-Bul-Bul Amir.

There are men of renown and well-known to fame
In the army that's led by the czar,
But the best known of all was a man by the name
Of Ivan Petrovsky Skivar.

He could imitate Irving, play poker and pool,
And strum on the Spanish guitar;
In fact quite the cream of the Muscovite team,
Was Ivan Petrovsky Skivar.

One day this bold Russian he shouldered his gun
And with his most truculent sneer,
Was looking for fun when he happened to run
Upon Abdul A-Bul-Bul Amir.

"Young man," said Bul-Bul, "is existence so dull
That you're anxious to end your career?
For, infidel, know you have trod on the toe
Of Abdul A-Bul-Bul Amir."

Said Ivan, "My friend, your remarks in the end
Will avail you but little, I fear,
For you never will survive to repeat them alive,
Mr. Abdul A-Bul-Bul Amir."

"O, take one last look at this cool shady nook,
And send your regrets to the czar.
By which I imply you are going to die,
Mr. Ivan Petrovsky Skivar." . . .

On a stone by the banks where the Danube doth roll,
Engraved in characters clear,
Is "Stranger, remember to pray for the soul
Of Abdul A-Bul-Bul Amir."

A Muscovite maid her long vigil doth keep,
Alone 'neath the cold northern star,
And the name that she murmurs in vain as she weeps
Is Ivan Petrovsky Skivar.

Young folks of the Twenties, when they turned to
ballads, often liked those that had the added attraction of
low-life:

ev - er heard the sto - ry folks of Wil-lie the Weep-er? Wil-lie's oc-cu-pa-tion was a
went to Lon-don town and bought the Pic - ca - dil - ly, Told the peo-ple that it now be-

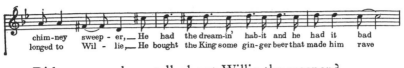

chim-ney sweep - er,— He had the dream-in' hab-it and he had it bad
longed to Wil - lie,— He bought the King some gin-ger beer that made him rave

Did you ever hear tell about Willie the weeper?
Willie the weeper was a chimney sweeper,
Had the dope habit and had it bad,
Listen while I'll tell you 'bout the dream he had. . . .[81]

The ballad that the younger generation liked best and

Published by Macauley — reproduced by permission of the artist.

Johnny and Frankie.

John Held's drawing from "My Pious Friends and Drunken Companions,"
by Frank Shay.

sang oftenest was *Johnny and Frankie*, a raw tale of life
in the underworld which any time before the Twenties
would have been strictly confined to stag parties, but
which, under the changed standard of manners, was sung

[81] The complete text of *Willie the Weeper* may be found in the volume called
"More Pious Friends and Drunken Companions."

freely and frequently in what the older folks used to describe as "mixed company":

> Frankie and Johnnie were lovers.
> O my gawd how they could love,
> They swore to be true to each other,
> Just as true as the stars up above,
> He was her man, but he done her wrong.

Frankie's station in life was made plain by the vernacular candor of the designation of the place in which she carried on her occupation:

> Frankie lived down at the crib-house.

The relation Johnny had to her was made clear:

> Frankie she was a good woman,
> And Johnnie he was her man.
> And every dollar Frankie made
> Went right into Johnnie's hand.
> He was her man, but he done her wrong!

Johnny was faithless; the money Frankie gave him he spent upon the ladies of a rival establishment:

> He spent it all on those call-house girls,
> He was her man, but he done her wrong.

Frankie, naturally, was resentful:

> Frankie went down to the call-house,
> She leaned on that call-house bell,
> "Get out of the way, all chippies and fools,
> Or I'll blow you straight to hell;
> I want my man who is doing me wrong."

> After she shot him she was sorry,
> And it wrang her poor heart sore,
> To see her loving Johnnie
> Stretched across that hotel floor.
> But he was her man and he done her wrong! . . .[82]

[82] The complete text of *Johnny and Frankie* — at least one complete text — may be found in the volume called, appropriately, "My Pious Friends and Drunken Companions." Another version, adapted to tell an army tale, is in the volume whose standard of selection, and exclusion, is expressed by its title, "Songs My Mother Never Taught Me." There are yet other variations, indeed the versions of *Johnny and Frankie* are as numerous as the humor of man is in-

In the springtime of 1927, observers of the come-and-go of street phenomena, noticed that in New York and other cities hawkers were selling great numbers of a ditty called *Hallelujah, I'm a Bum*. Since the song was not new, there arose discussion about the reason for its apparently spontaneous re-emergence — the New York *World* printed a learned editorial speculation about it, without, however, being able to come to a conclusion. The song had been well-known in the West about 1915 as the "hymn of the Wobblies" — Wobblies being a corruption, derisively intended, of "I. W. W.," the "Industrial Workers of the World." (By another exercise in derision, the initials "I. W. W." were amplified into the "I Won't Works.")

In its earlier existence, *Hallelujah, I'm a Bum*, as sung by the I. W. W.'s, had been defiant, threatening, almost sinister; the I. W. W.'s were perhaps the most radical labor organization America had ever known, the most nearly committed to violence as a policy and method — one of their leaders, William D. Haywood, "Big Bill," became later an important leader in the Russian revolution. In choosing the tune for their song of defiance, they had turned, with deliberate irreverence undoubtedly, to one of the most venerated hymns of the evangelical churches, *Hallelujah, Thine the Glory; Hallelujah, Amen*, and to that solemn music had written words of contempt and scorn for capitalism and the accessory institutions of American society.

Subsequently, the I. W. W. had ebbed, and with it

---

genious; 110 separate variations were identified by a patient investigator of American folk-songs, R. W. Gordon. But only in books published in the Twenties, I think, is the ditty to be found in print; it may have appeared earlier in pamphlets designed for furtive circulation; it had had word-of-mouth existence for some seventy years before. The incident described in the song is said to have had authentic origin, an episode of love accompanied by jealousy and followed by murder which occurred in Kansas City or St. Louis about the middle of the nineteenth century.

their hymn. *Hallelujah, I'm a Bum* had been forgotten for years. Then, in the spring of 1927, it turned up in Eastern cities, with, however, new words, words that implied no great truculence toward society, but pictured, rather, the freedom and pleasure of a vagabond life. It was in this incarnation that the song became popular during the late Twenties. Could it have been that the popularity was a sign of reaction from the conditions of intense economic activity of the boom days? That singing *Hallelujah, I'm a Bum* gave a sense of vicarious release to men who felt themselves bound tighter and tighter into the meshes of business at high speed? One could imagine that a business man, especially one still young, riding in the Pullman from care in New York to care in Chicago, could look with some longing at a group of carefree hoboes about a pot of stew beside the railroad track:

Hal-le - lu-jah, I'm a bum   Hal-le - lu-jah, bum a - gain,   Hal-le -

Rejoice and be glad, for the springtime has come,
We can throw down our shovels and go on the bum.
 Hallelujah, I'm a bum,
 Halleljuh, bum again,
 Hallelujah, give us a hand-out to revive us again.

I went to a house and I rapped on the door,
And the lady said, "Bum, bum, you've been here before."
 Halleljuah, I'm a bum,
 Hallelujah, bum again,
 Hallelujah, give us a hand-out to revive us again.

I like Jim Hill[83], he's a good friend of mine,
That is why I am hiking down Jim Hill's main line.
 Hallelujah, I'm a bum . . .

[83] James J. Hill built the Great Northern Railroad, from St. Paul and Minneapolis west to the Pacific Coast; throughout the Northwest "Jim Hill's road" was a more frequent colloquial designation than "Great Northern."

I went to a house and I asked for some bread,
And the lady says, "Bum, bum, the baker is dead."
  Hallelujah, I'm a bum . . .

Why don't you save all the money you earn?
If I didn't eat I'd have money to burn.
  Hallelujah, I'm a bum . . .

I don't like work and work don't like me,
And that is the reason I am so hungry.
  Hallelujah, I'm a bum . . .

Among the older ballads and fragments of ballads that scholars and others collected and published during the Twenties, and which the generation sang with a kind of robust gusto that the ephemeral songs did not incite were:

The Ballad of Captain Kidd . . . The Dying Hobo . . . I've Been Workin' on the Railroad . . . Jesse James, song of an outlaw whose fame endured half a century after his death . . . *Oh, Susanna!:*

Oh, Susanna, don't you cry for me . . .
I'm gwine to Louisiana, my true love for to see.

The Face on the Bar-room Floor . . . The Charming Young Widow I Met on the Train . . . Home on the Range — Oh, Give Me a Home Where the Buffalo Roam . . . Casey Jones — probably the best song of an occupation ever written in any tongue, and undoubtedly the best ballad ever composed in America:

Come all you rounders, [84] if you want to hear
A story about a brave engineer;
Casey Jones was the rounder's name,
On a six-eight wheeler he won his fame.
The caller called Casey at half-past four,
Kissed his wife at the station door,
Mounted to the cabin with his orders in his hand,
And he took his farewell trip to that promised land.

[84] Generic term for railroad men of all degrees, from "roundhouse." The "caller" is similarly a railroad institution.

Casey Jones mounted to the cabin,
    Casey Jones, with his orders in his hand;
Casey Jones mounted to the cabin,
    And took his farewell trip to that promised land.

*The Wreck of the Old 97 . . . Springfield Mountain
. . .* the dreadful maledictions of *Samuel Hall:*

My name is Samuel Hall, Samuel Hall,
My name is Samuel Hall and I hate you one and all —
    Damn your eyes . . .
O, I killed a man 'tis said, so 'tis said,
O, I killed a man 'tis said, and I smashed his bleeding head
And I left him lying dead,
    Damn his eyes . . .
So, a-swinging up I'll go, up I'll go,
So a-swinging up I'll go,
    Damn your eyes.

*Shanahan's Ould Shabeen . . . Rollicking Bill the
Sailor* — he was known also as *Barnacle Bill . . . I
Was a Bachelor, I Lived by Myself . . . Old Noah
. . . The Dying Ranger . . . Minnie the Moocher
. . . Christofo Columbo . . . Wal, I Swan,* express-
ing the naïveté of a New England farmer who thought
he was sophisticated:

I run the old mill over here in Reubensville,
My name's Joshua Ebenezer Frye;
I know a thing or two, you bet your boots I do,
Can't fool me 'cause I'm too darn spry.
I've met your bunco men, always get the best of them;
Once I met a couple on a Boston train.
They says "How be you?" I says, "That'll do —
Travel right along with your darn skin game."
Wal, I swan, I must be getting on;
Git up, Napoleon, it looks like rain;
Wal, I'll be switched, the hay ain't pitched —
Come in when you're over to the farm again.

1919

January 6. Colonel Theodore Roosevelt, former President, died at his home, Sagamore Hill, Oyster Bay, N. Y.[1] At the funeral, two days later, in the Oyster Bay cemetery, Roosevelt's one-time intimate friend, from whom he had been estranged in 1912, William Howard Taft, was a mourner. Also the ever-faithful General Leonard Wood, who had shared with Roosevelt command of the Rough Riders in Cuba in 1898. At the moment of interment bells tolled throughout the country and business ceased for one minute. Hundreds of poems were written in commemoration of Roosevelt's passing, among them a Poe-esque dirge by Grace D. Vanamee:

> Toll the bells, toll the bells,
>   Solemn and slow;
> Let the world know
>   A whole nation's woe.
> Toll the bells, toll the bells,
>   Solemn and slow.

January 29. The State Department at Washington proclaimed the Prohibition Amendment ratified, and set January 16, 1920, as the date when it would become operative.

February 21. Doctor Mary E. Walker, 87 years old, for more than half a century a famous woman eccentric and proponent of greater liberty for women, died near her birthplace, at Bunker Hill, Oswego, N. Y. As a girl in her teens she became interested in her father's work as physician, and when she grew up boldly decided to follow in his footsteps in defiance of the preju-

---

[1] An account of Roosevelt's last years is in "Our Times," Vol. V.

dices of the day against women in professional careers. She managed to gain entrance to the Syracuse Medical College, successfully overcame the instructors' stubborn conviction that woman's place is in the home, and at the age of 26, in 1858, was awarded her physician's certificate. With the outbreak of the Civil War she en-

From a photograph by International News Photos, Inc.

A mock burial of John Barleycorn shortly after prohibition was inaugurated.

listed as a nurse in the Union Army and in 1864 was put at surgical work and given the rank of First Lieutenant.

Years before entering the army Doctor Walker had discarded women's clothes for men's. For this practice she was many times arrested, and almost daily, when walking along the streets, was jeered at by women and small boys. During her many years of residence in Washington, Doctor Walker lobbied in Congress for social and political reforms to better woman's place in the world. She had an original mind and made a number of worth-while inventions, among them the inside neck-band on men's shirts which protects the skin from the collar-button.

March 15–17.   One thousand delegates representing all units of the American Expeditionary Force, and including both enlisted men and officers, met at Paris and formed the American Legion.   May 8–10, at St. Louis, Mo., the Legion's first convention was held, at which officers were elected and a constitution adopted. The constitution, in its preamble, set forth the Legion's purposes:

> For God and Country we associate ourselves together for the following purposes: To uphold and defend the Constitution of the United States of America; to maintain law and order; to foster and perpetuate a one hundred per cent Americanism; to preserve the memories and incidents of our association in the Great War; to inculcate a sense of individual obligation to the community, State, and nation; to make right the master of might; to promote peace and good will on earth; to safeguard and transmit to posterity the principles of justice, freedom, and democracy; to consecrate and sanctify our comradeship by our devotion to mutual helpfulness.

April 17.   The *Kaiserin Augusta Victoria*, first German merchant ship to come to the United States since the first year of the war, docked at Hoboken with 2,319 returning American soldiers aboard.

May 12.   Henry Ford's $1,000,000 libel suit against the Chicago *Tribune* for having called him, in an editorial, "an anarchist," began at Mt. Clemens, Mich.

Ford himself, much to his dislike and despite the strong objections of his counsel, was put on the witness stand and questioned by the lawyers for the *Tribune*. Some of Ford's replies, revealing gaps in his knowledge of contemporary affairs and history, constituted a generous addition to the nation's fund of humor — "History is bunk!," an impatient rejoinder which Ford made to a question by one of his inquisitors, was destined to live long in association with Ford's name. Some years later he became a generous patron of history through his purchase and restoration of Wayside Inn in Massachusetts and his founding of a museum of transportation in his factory at Detroit.

The happenings at the trial, observed by a host of newspaper writers, were described *in extenso* in the pages of daily newspapers. With Ford occupying the witness stand ———

The nation awoke one morning to find that Ford had described Benedict Arnold as "a writer." Asked to define his theory of "government" Ford declared, "It's a long subject." Asked whether he was a student of history he replied that he "didn't know much about it." "I live in the present," he suggested; and he was willing to confess that he could neither recall the causes of the War of 1812 nor remember what had precipitated the war with Spain nor define the relations of the United States with Porto Rico any more precisely than to suggest, "We keep some of the army there, I guess." Where the rest of the army was kept he admitted that he did not know; "I haven't been very much interested in armies." Other matters interested him more. He kept abreast of affairs from day to day in the pages of the daily newspapers, but confessed that he "rarely read anything else except the headlines."[2]

The trial ran from May to August, produced two million words of testimony, took the jury over such jumps as Bakunin and Erasmus, and in the end (August 14), after nine ballots by the jury, gave Ford nominal victory by awarding him six cents damages and costs.

May 22.   Sergt. Alvin C. York, Co. G, 328 Infantry, of Pall Mall, Tenn., who at the beginning of the war had objected to fighting on the ground of conscientious scruples, and who as a soldier in France had performed the greatest individual feat of the war, in capturing 132

[2] "And Then Came Ford," Charles Merz.

Germans, after killing 25 and cleaning out 35 machine gun nests, arrived on the transport *Ohioan*.

June 4. The United States Senate, by a vote of 56 to 25 (36 Republicans and 20 Democrats for; 8 Republicans and 17 Democrats against) adopted a Joint Resolution submitting to the States the Women's Suffrage

From a photograph by U. S. Signal Corps.

Sergeant Alvin C. York.

Amendment. The Resolution had previously passed the House.

June 15. A somnolent peat-bog in Ireland, just back of the white headlands at Clifden. Insects buzz in the quiet air and the sun shines clear and bright and cool on the lush swamp grass. Since the days of the Irish kings, and for long centuries before, this field has looked about as it does to-day, untouched by the hand of man, as unchanging as the nearby chalk cliffs which for millennia have been breasting the combined assault of wind and wave. Ignored by History, this morning it wakes to History. In the western sky, close down to the horizon, appears a tiny black speck, accompanied by a strange thin droning. A minute, two, three, pass. Then the first airplane to cross the Atlantic on a non-stop flight makes a wheeling circuit of the bog and, slanting down, plows its wheels deep into the soft loam. The landing is safe, no damage done to craft or fliers; but for two days the machine — it had no name, unlike such later record-makers as the "Spirit of St. Louis" — remains ingloriously stuck in the Irish mud before it can free itself and renew its flight to London.

The plane making this historic flight was a British Vickers-Vimy; pilot, Captain John Alcock, an Englishman; navigator, Lieutenant Arthur W. Browne, an American. To them went the prize of $50,000 offered by the London *Daily Mail* for the first non-stop Atlantic crossing. The 1960 miles between the take-off at St. John's, Newfoundland, and Clifden had been covered in the surprisingly fast time of 16 hours and 12 minutes. Perils beyond the power of words to describe had beset the fliers; every agency of nature seemingly had been enlisted against them. Said Captain Alcock:[3]

We had a terrible journey and the wonder is that we are here at all. We scarcely saw the sun or moon or stars. The fog was very dense and at times we had to descend within 300 feet of the sea. For four hours our machine was covered by a sheet of ice, caused by frozen sleet. At another time the fog was so dense that the speed indicator did not work and for a few minutes it was very alarming. We looped the loop, I do believe, and did a very steep spiral. We did some very comic stunts, for I had no sense of horizon. An hour and a half before we saw land we had no certain idea where we were. We did not suffer from cold or exhaustion, except when looking over the side; then the sleet chewed bits out of our faces.

[3] Alcock was fated to but brief enjoyment of his laurels. December 18 he died, from injuries sustained when a hydroplane in which he was flying crashed near Collevrard, Normandy.

Achievements in the Air during 1919

1919 garnered the harvest of the progress that had been made in aeronautics under the stress of four years of war. 1914 to 1918 had been a hot-house period during which every department of mechanical flight grew as it couldn't have grown in a decade of peace. During the war few records of endurance or altitude were made and, alas, none for safety. Every effort of designer, builder, and flier had been devoted to the furtherance of the aims of war. The great names of aviation were those of war-birds, or the builders of military aircraft: Baron Richthofen, Fokker, de Haviland, Captain Bishop, Sikorsky, America's own Eddie Rickenbacker. Now, beginning in 1919, the vast progress that had been made was soon to become spectacularly apparent.

Of the several air exploits of 1919 Alcock's flight was the most sensational, but there were others almost as remarkable. May 18, two planes attempted to take off from St. John's, N. F. One, a Martinsyde biplane, crashed before it had got into the air. The other, a Sopwith biplane powered with Rolls-Royce engines and piloted by Harry G. Hawker and Lieutenant Commander M. Grieve, made a successful ascent and managed to keep in the air 14 hours and 31 minutes, covering a distance of 1100 miles out over the Atlantic, before a choked circulation system compelled a turn southward to the steamship lanes, where a landing was made beside a small Danish vessel, the *Mary*. For six days nothing was heard of the fliers — the *Mary* had no wireless — and they had been given up for lost when the rescue ship arrived off Scotland and signalled that they were aboard. May 27, when they reached London, they were given a great ovation. The London *Daily Mail*, in recognition of their valiant if unsuccessful effort to win the *Mail's* prize for a transatlantic crossing, awarded them $25,000.

1919 witnessed a notable flight by American Naval seaplanes. Leaving Rockaway, N. Y., May 8, three planes, NC–1, NC–3, and NC–4, under command of Lieutenant Commander A. C. Read, and each manned

The NC–4, at Rockaway, L. I., just before leaving on the first round-the-world flight.

by a crew of five, started a flight which was to be by way of Halifax, Nova Scotia, Trepassey Bay, N. F., the Azores, and Lisbon, Portugal. Only the NC–4 won through, the other two being disabled on the way. For the 3925 miles between Rockaway and the flight's end at Plymouth, England, the flying time of the NC–4 was 57 hours and 16 minutes.

Twice during the year the Atlantic was crossed by a dirigible, the British R–34, which had been built for war service. The R–34 was 643 feet long, 71 feet wide.

Her suspension bags had a capacity of 2,000,000 cubic feet of hydrogen; and her five Sunbeam Maori engines, of 275 horse-power, gave her a cruising speed of 40 to 60 miles an hour. She was manned by a crew of 31 and had a wireless capable of transmitting 800 miles. Leaving East Fortune, Scotland, July 2, she arrived at Mineola, N. Y., July 9. Distance, 3130 miles; time 108 hours

The British R–34, the first dirigible to fly across the Atlantic.

12 minutes (world endurance record). To direct landing operations one of the ship's officers dropped 2000 feet by parachute. On the return she left Mineola July 9, reaching Pulham, England, July 12. Distance 3200 miles (world distance record for lighter-than-air type); time, 74 hours 56 minutes. On her westward trip the R–34 brought a letter of greeting from the Lord Mayor of London to Mayor Hylan of New York. Over a quarter of a million people visited the giant airship while she was at Mineola. No such sight had ever before been seen in the United States.

July 3. By order of the Judge Advocate of the

American army of occupation on the Rhine, marriages of American soldiers with German women, which had been taking place with such frequency as to alarm the martial-minded heads of the American forces, were forbidden.

July 16. The Pullman Trust and Savings Bank at Chicago, Ill., as a measure of self-defense against a crime wave which, coincident with the war's ending, had begun to sweep over the city, installed a steel compartment in which was stationed a police officer with a rifle. As 1919 wore on, crime in Chicago increased. By November 25, three hundred murders had been recorded for the year, and during one week there had been two hundred and fifty hold-ups.

July 23. At Chicago hogs brought $23.50 a hundredweight on the foot in the stockyards, the highest price ever known.

July 30. A "first" which may in time be historic for having inaugurated a new arena for controversy, legislation, and litigation, of the sort which growth and change and mechanical progress are forever creating: Frederick Hoenemann, Missouri farmer, appealed to the courts at Kansas City and obtained a temporary injunction against the operation of airplanes over his farm.

August 11. Andrew Carnegie, philanthropist, retired ironmaster, died.[4] His will, made public August 28, left to his widow the Fifth Avenue, New York, home, country homes in Bar Harbor and Lenox, and the castle and lands at Skibo, Scotland. It provided annuities of $10,000 for Lloyd George and William Howard Taft; of $5,000 for the widows of Grover Cleveland and Colonel Theodore Roosevelt; and of smaller amounts for John Burns, John Morley, Walter Damrosch, George W. Cable, and many others. An appraisal of his

[4] Chapter 8, Vol. IV, of "Our Times" has a biographical sketch of Carnegie.

estate, made public October 23, 1920, assigned a total value to it of $23,247,161, of which $11,338,847 went to his widow.

September 17. British scientist Sir Oliver Lodge, in a summary of what science had learned about the atom delivered before the James Watt Centenary celebration in London, made the statement, widely quoted at the time and for years after, that if the atomic energy of an ounce of matter could be utilized it would be sufficient to raise the German ships sunk at Scapa Flow and pile them on top of the mountains of Scotland.

October 8. The first German to come to the United States on a passport since the war, Erich Hecht, arrived at New York.

October 18. A personal and political quarrel between Governor Alfred E. Smith of New York and William Randolph Hearst, newspaper publisher, reached its climax in a challenge by Smith to a debate on their political careers and private lives. Hearst refusing, Governor Smith, on October 29, before an overflow audience at Carnegie Hall, New York, denounced Hearst and his papers.

November 11. Call money in the New York Stock Exchange, as a result of speculation, ranged from 14 to 25 per cent. To deal with the situation a conference was called by Federal Reserve banks. Next day, the beginnings of a panic manifested themselves, with call money rising to 30 per cent and speculative securities suffering sharp declines. 2,700,000 shares were traded in, an unprecedented figure up to that time.[5]

November 29. Truman H. Newberry, Republican, who had defeated Henry Ford, running as a Democrat, in 1918, for Senator from Michigan, was indicted by a

[5] But small compared to the 16,000,000-share day in October, 1929, which ushered in the great depression of the 1930's.

Federal grand jury at Grand Rapids, Mich., on charges of corruption, fraud, and conspiracy in the conduct of his campaign. Indicted with him on the same charges were 133 friends of Newberry who had worked for his election. In the trial that ensued Newberry and 16 others were found guilty and given jail sentences or fines.[6]

The case against Newberry was brought under the Michigan Corrupt Practices Act, which limited the amount a candidate could spend to elect himself to $3750. How much had been spent in Newberry's campaign was a matter of speculation, with guesses running as high as a million dollars. The money had not come from Newberry, nor had it been spent by him; he himself had lived up to the letter of the law. But large sums had been spent for advertising and hiring speakers by wealthy friends of Newberry and also by wealthy enemies of Henry Ford who saw in the election an opportunity to strike a blow at the automobile manufacturer. No evidence was presented at the trial that Newberry had solicited this help or even that he was aware of the great sums being spent in his behalf.

Following the judge's pronouncement of sentence, Martin W. Littleton, chief counsel for the defendants, declared that "no man will serve one day in jail or pay a dollar fine." He was right. An appeal carried to the Supreme Court of the United States resulted in the act's being declared unconstitutional.

Newberry's tenure of the Senatorship was short and not very happy. A contest was brought against him by Ford and before the Senate voted to admit him,[7] hearings before the Senate Committee on Elections and speeches by Senators on the floor had given him an undeserved national character as a symbol of money in

---

[6] March 20, 1920.   [7] January 12, 1922. The vote was 46 to 41.

politics. After ten months he resigned his seat[8] and retired to private life.

The Books of 1919

Three books by Joseph Hergesheimer: "Java Head,"
a story of Salem in the 40's, in the days of the clipper
ships, "with scents of poppies and waving of fans in the
old garden," "The Happy End," and "Linda Condon,"
the latter called by Carl Van Doren "nearly the most
beautiful American novel since Hawthorne and Henry
James." . . . "Peter Kindred," by Robert Nathan.
. . . "Twelve Men," by Theodore Dreiser. . . .
"Winesburg, Ohio," by Sherwood Anderson. . . .
"Free Air," by Sinclair Lewis. . . . "Peace in Friendship Village," by Zona Gale. . . . "The Brass Check,"
by Upton Sinclair. . . . "The Moon and Sixpence," by
W. Somerset Maugham, a "psychological study of a
perverted nature," of which *The Booklist* warned it was
"not for open shelves." . . . "Jurgen," by James
Branch Cabell. . . . "The Day of Glory," by Dorothy
Canfield Fisher. . . . "The Life of John Marshall," by
Albert J. Beveridge, winner of the Pulitzer prize for the
best American biography teaching patriotic and unsel-
fish service. . . . "The Portygee," by Joseph C. Lincoln. . . . "Mince Pie," by Christopher Morley. . . .
"Michael Forth," by Mary Johnston. . . . "A Man
for the Ages," by Irving Bacheller. . . . "The Avalanche," by Gertrude Atherton. . . . "Nomads of the
North," by James Oliver Curwood. . . . "The Village," by Ernest Poole. . . . "Belgium: A Personal
Narrative," by Brand Whitlock. . . . "The Sea Bride"
and "All the Brothers Were Valiant," by Ben Ames Williams. . . . "Stardust," by Fannie Hurst. . . . "The
Raincoat Girl," by Jennette Lee. . . . "The Tin Sol-

[8] November 19, 1922.

dier," by Temple Bailey. . . . "The Builders," by Ellen Glasgow. . . . "The Promises of Alice," by Margaret Deland. . . . "Dangerous Days," by Mary Roberts Rinehart. . . . "Ramsay Milholland," by Booth

Photograph from White Studio.

Ina Claire in "The Gold Diggers."

Tarkington. . . . "Mr. Britling Sees It Through," by H. G. Wells.

The Theatre in 1919

Bertha Kalich played in "The Riddle: Woman." . . . Chauncey Olcott in a George M. Cohan play, "The Voice of McConnell." . . . William Gillette in "Dear Brutus," by J. M. Barrie. . . . Lillian Lorraine in "The Little Blue Devil." . . . Ina Claire in "The Gold Diggers." . . . James K. Hackett in "The Rise of Silas Lapham," gave a notable American character

study. . . . Laurette Taylor in "A Night in Rome."
. . . "Abraham Lincoln," a play written by an Englishman, John Drinkwater, about the greater incidents of Lincoln's life; the dramatic critic of *Life* said that though the author was English, the play gave to Americans a clearer picture of Lincoln than the countless articles and books written about him; Burns Mantle said it "is easily the most inspiring dramatic success of our time"; the impersonation of Lincoln by Frank McGlynn was one to be "always remembered." . . . Blanche Bates and Henry Miller in "The Famous Mrs. Fair." . . . Ethel Barrymore in "Declassee," an international society drama. . . . "The Royal Vagabond." . . . "A Voice in the Dark." . . . "Scandal." . . . "The Ziegfeld Follies of 1919." . . . "Clarence," a remarkably attractive light comedy by Booth Tarkington. . . . "The Five Million." . . . The Winter Garden's "Passing Show of 1919." . . . "Too Many Husbands." . . . E. H. Sothern and Julia Marlowe began another season's tour in "Hamlet," "Twelfth Night" and "The Shrew." . . . "The Son-Daughter," a play of New China. . . . Billie Burke, after a year in moving pictures, returned in "Caesar's Wife." . . . "Lightnin'," which began its run in August 1918, was still a great attraction. . . . "East is West," which began in December, 1918, was still running. . . . "Friendly Enemies" and "The Better 'Ole" also were held over from the previous season.

1920

January 4.   The French Government granted permission for the removal to the United States of the bodies of 20,000 American soldiers buried in France. April 28, 353 bodies taken from cemeteries in France and England, arrived in New York.

January 7.   Officials of the Brotherhood of Maintenance of Way Employees and Railway Shop Laborers, to reduce the cost of living to their members, purchased knitting and underwear companies in Ypsilanti, Mich., a glove factory at Williamston, Mich., and a tubing factory in New York State.

January 16.   The Peace Conference at Paris summoned Holland to yield the ex-Kaiser of Germany for trial.

During the last year of the Great War there had been in Allied countries discussion as to what should be done about the Kaiser and other German war leaders after Germany had been defeated. During a political campaign in England, Lloyd George made an appeal for votes with the promise to hang the Kaiser in the Tower of London. With the collapse of Germany in November, 1918, the Kaiser had fled to Holland and now if any punitive action were to be taken against him the Allies must first secure his person from the Dutch. This the Peace Conference on January 16 sought to do.

In its reply, issued January 23, Holland refused. The Allies then, February 16, asked Holland to intern the Kaiser, which request, on March 5, was acceded to. (At the time this chapter is written, 1935, the one-time Monarch of Imperial Germany was still a resident of Doorn, Holland, where he lived in comfortable retirement in an estate companioned by his second wife, the former German Princess Herminie of Reuss.)

The Allied plans for the punishment of other Germans turned out equally infructuous. February 3, a demand was made in a note to the German Ambassador at Paris (who refused to transmit it to his Government) for the surrender of 890 persons to the Allies for trial, among them: Von Bethmann-Hollweg, Enver Pasha, Admiral von Tirpitz, Von Hindenburg, Ludendorff, von Mackensen, Crown Prince Rupprecht of Bavaria, the Duke of Württemburg, and other Princes and titled officers. With the Germans stubbornly set in opposition, an impasse was reached, which, however, caused few regrets among the Allied statesmen, long since weary of violence. They realized the possibilities that a programme of reprisal and punishment might restimulate international hatreds, and it was with relief that they gave up thought of going through with it. They were in the mood to smile when on February 13 the ex-Crown Prince of Germany, in a gesture of martyrdom, cabled President Wilson offering to surrender himself for trial in place of the 890. The offer was ignored.

The First Year of National Prohibition

January 16. The Prohibition Amendment took effect at midnight. Since June 30, 1919, the country had been dry under the war-time prohibition act, and consequently the going into effect of the Eighteenth Amendment was not accompanied by the closing of saloons or by any other happenings connected with the physical disappearance of liquor from American life. There were, however, on this day and at different times throughout 1920, developments of other sorts, some of them echoing the repercussions of the new law on busi-

ness, social customs, public health, and the like; and
others the pains of adjustment on the part of communities and individuals to a situation they did not approve
and were not disposed to accept.

The prophesied disastrous fall in property values se-
quential to the closing of saloons did not materialize,
though some businesses were seriously hurt. The management of the long famous Holland House in New
York, anticipating a diminution in hotel revenues, an-
announced on January 4 the permanent closing of the
hotel. Prohibitionists were elated at the final success
that had capped their struggle and were in a mood of
satisfied complacency. William Jennings Bryan, who
had been a late convert to constitutional prohibition but
a zealous worker after being converted, held dry was-
sail at a dinner on his sixtieth birthday (March 19) with
600 friends at the Aldine Club in New York. "The
liquor issue," Mr. Bryan somewhat pontifically told the
company, "is as dead as slavery." Others besides Bryan
— multitudes of them — uttered predictions which time
was to make ridiculous. Daniel C. Roper, Commissioner
of Internal Revenue,[1] in an interview in the New York
Sun, said: "The Prohibition law will be violated — extensively at first, slightly later on; but it will, broadly
speaking, be enforced and will result in a nation that
knows not alcohol." Reporter William Riis printed in
the Kansas City *Star* a statement made to him by Doctor
A. B. Adams, Chief Chemist of the Treasury bureau
which tested beverages to see that none surpassed in alcoholic percentage the .5 per cent permitted by the Volstead Act. "How about this home-brewing business,
Doctor?" asked the reporter. Doctor Adams replied:
"Nothing to that. It's too much trouble for uncertain

[1] Secretary of Commerce in the Cabinet of President F. D. Roosevelt,
1933–

One of New York City's best-known speak-easies; it flourished all during prohibition. At the right is shown part of the secret door and revolving partition in which the liquor stock was concealed, and which successfully eluded agents during many raids.

results. They may try it once or twice, but not more." Eight years later many a home — millions perhaps; it was naturally a thing that would elude exact statistics — had its home-brew equipment, and a large seller on the shelves of grocery stores were the malt preparations wherewith amateur brewers made the beer which Doctor Adams thought would never be a problem for the enforcement agencies.

A condition of aridness in the South which if it really existed in 1920 was destined to swift change, was pictured figuratively by Doctor Adams: "I don't believe there's enough liquor in the Southern mountains to stock the District of Columbia overnight." Federal Prohibition Commissioner John F. Cramer agreed in substance with Commissioner of Internal Revenue Roper. November 7, he said that "Prohibition will not entirely stop the manufacture and sale of intoxicants for a generation." The Commissioner believed that the liquor traffic would cease only with the advent of a new generation that did not know the appetite or the desire for liquor.

The wets were not happy, and they expressed their feelings in brave last-minute attempts to save what they could. Congress, however, was thoroughly "dry" — it remained so for 13 years. A few States held out. The Wisconsin legislature passed an act permitting the manufacture and sale of beer containing 2.5 per cent of alcohol. The drys declared the act a violation of the National Prohibition Enforcement Law and took it to the courts where they met a minor and temporary defeat on March 1 when the United States Court at Milwaukee upheld the Wisconsin statute. In Massachusetts, one of wettest of the States, the legislature on May 3 passed a 2.75 per cent beer bill, which Governor Coolidge promptly vetoed. The wetness of Massachusetts was again attested on February 29 when wet candidates triumphed over drys in State-wide municipal elections. In Colorado it was the wets who sought the aid of the courts. Their hopes were dashed when the State Supreme Court decided that ratification of the Eighteenth Amendment by the legislature, without a previous popular referendum, had been legal. In New York, wettest State in the Union, there was much angry opposition to prohibition — all of it futile. February 26, an unofficial Democratic convention at Albany declared against the

Eighteenth Amendment. March 1, the Assembly, 61 to
52, voted to investigate Anti-Saloon League lobbying.
April 24, the legislature passed a 2.75 per cent beer bill
— Governor Smith signed it May 24 — which drew
the comment from United States Senator Morris Shep-
pard, ardent dry Democrat from Texas, that New York

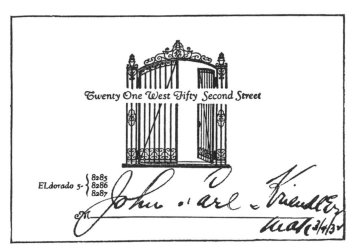

Twenty One West Fifty Second Street

ELdorado 5- { 8285 8286 8287

To protect themselves, the managers and owners of speakeasies issued cards,
which they endorsed, and which had to be presented at the door before
a guest could gain admittance.

was a revolutionary and anarchistic State (May 14).
March 18, the Maryland House of Delegates, 62 to 39,
refused to concur with the Federal Government in the
enforcement of the Volstead Act, and later passed the
Jones 3.5 per cent beer bill, to be operative in case the
Supreme Court should rule that "concurrent action" by
States meant that each State might fix the alcoholic content of beverages manufactured and sold within its borders. February 24, in New Jersey, the House, 37 to 21,
by a combination of wet Republicans and Democrats,
forced through a 3.5 per cent beer bill, which was later
approved by the upper house and signed by Governor

Edwards. New Jersey also, on March 4, through its Attorney-General, Thomas F. McCran, filed in the United States Supreme Court a suit seeking to have the Eighteenth Amendment declared null and void and to prevent enforcement of the Volstead Act.

Such hopes as the wets had that the Supreme Court of the United States might come to their aid were dashed by decision after decision. January 5, the Court, by a 5 to 4 count, upheld the right of Congress in the Volstead Act to limit to one-half of one per cent the alcoholic content of beer. (The minority held that the law invaded the rights of the States.) January 12, in an action brought by the New Jersey Retail Liquor Dealers' Association to test the constitutionality of the Eighteenth Amendment and enjoins its enforcement in that State, the Court held that it had no jurisdiction. Chief Justice White, who handed down the opinion, said a citizen could not sue the State in the Supreme Court without the consent of the State, and this New Jersey had refused. June 1, the Court held unanimously that amendments to the United States Constitution are subject to ratification only by State legislatures, and not by referendums by the people. June 7, the Court in a group of decisions sustained the Eighteenth Amendment, held the Volstead Act to be constitutional, dismissed the petition of Rhode Island and New Jersey to prohibit enforcement, dissolved the Wisconsin beer injunction, sustained an injunction obtained by the drys in St. Louis, upheld the dismissal of an injunction secured in Louisville in a case brought by the Kentucky Distilleries and Warehouse Company, and denied an injunction sought by George C. Dempsey of Boston to restrain enforcement of the Volstead Act.

An attempt to carry prohibition abroad, made by a picturesque figure among the professional drys, W. E

("Pussyfoot") Johnson, met with small enthusiasm in the Scandinavian countries and actually aroused such antagonism in England that the evangelist was roughly handled by a crowd at Reading and lost an eye.

With the prohibition law finally in effect several

A drawing by Wortman in the "World."

A scene, poignant to travellers, frequently enacted during prohibition : liquor being found in the baggage of returning travellers by customs inspectors.

problems promptly thrust themselves forward. One was, how were people who wanted to drink to be prevented from doing so? Though the liquor traffic was no longer legal liquor was still available for those who wished it. Bootlegging of foreign liquor into the country began at once with the closing down of domestic distilleries and wineries, and the manufacture of "moonshine" continued at a steadily accelerating pace. Also beer and wine could be made in the home and grain alcohol became a staple of illegal commerce. Since the liquor industry was now an outlaw there was no check on the purity of the clandestine beverages sold to the public and substances deleterious to health found their way into America's stomach. Denatured alcohol containing wood alcohol and other poisons, made up from Government formulas, was worked over, some of the poison removed, and sold at extravagant prices. A product made from ginger, called "jake," widely sold in Oklahoma and other States in the middle South noted for their political dryness, caused hundreds of deaths and inflicted partial or complete paralysis on thousands.

In their drive for National Prohibition the drys had rested comfortably on the assumption that the Eighteenth Amendment and the Volstead Act would of themselves as by magic cause the disappearance of intoxicating liquors. Promptly it became clear that people who wanted to drink would obtain liquor, in spite of the law. This was a challenge to the authority of the United States Government and Washington set about the task, egged on by the drys, of imposing prohibition by force on the country. This required the building up of an enforcement agency, and for this purpose the House of Representatives on March 4, and the Senate later, appropriated $4,500,000, a little more than the amount Wayne B. Wheeler, dry czar, estimated would be needed.

Promptly came disquieting reports of killings, seizings of properties, violence, and these continued for thirteen years to occupy a conspicuous place in the newspapers. January 17, a liquor-law offender was arrested in New York and on the same day $500,000 of liquor awaiting export on the city's wharves was seized. January 28, 180 Federal agents began a dry round-up of the city. March 4, at Hartford, Conn., four purveyors of poison whiskey which had caused thirteen deaths were sentenced to prison terms. February 23, what the press imaginatively called a "rum rebellion" in the neighborhood of Iron River in upper Michigan caused the despatch of armed prohibition officers from Detroit. Two days later Major A. V. Dalrymple, prohibition chief for Michigan, against the heated protests of the local county prosecutor of Iron River, emptied nine barrels of homemade red wine in the snow, and the "rebellion" ended. September 9, at Camden, N. J., 300 saloon keepers were arrested on 1000 indictments for unlawful selling. October 13, brewers and saloon keepers of Bridgeport, Conn., were fined $750,000 for violations of the Volstead Act. October 20, at New York, a prohibition agent, who had killed Harry Carlton, chauffeur, was acquitted by a jury in the United States Court. December 24, at Bayonne, N. J., a prohibition agent was found shot to death.

On the other side of the ledger was the report published late in January of the New York Commissioner of Public Charities: "There are so few patients in the alcoholic ward of Bellevue Hospital . . . that the Hospital Committee has just approved its abandonment." The action was premature. Long before prohibition was ended Bellevue again had need for an alcoholic ward.

January 17.   William Snowden Sims, sinewy, spare-framed Rear-Admiral of the United States Navy, appearing before a Senate committee, touched off a broadside against his war-time chief, Secretary of the Navy Josephus Daniels, which shattered the calm of official Washington and for a week was echoed in excited headlines in the country's newspapers. Sims related that on being sent abroad as a special representative of the Navy Department before America entered the war he had been given the admonition: "Don't let the British pull the wool over your eyes; it is none of our business pulling their chestnuts out of the fire; we would as soon fight the British as the Germans." He then read a long letter written by him to Secretary Daniels in 1919, making eleven specific complaints against what he termed "grave

From a photograph by Underwood & Underwood.

Rear-Admiral William S. Sims.

errors in violation of fundamental military principles" committed by the Navy Department during the War. These in their sum charged that because of incompetency in the Department, the Great War had been prolonged four months beyond when it should have ended, with a consequent unnecessary loss of 400,000 lives.

Following America's entrance into the War, Admiral Sims had been placed in command of American naval operations in European waters, co-operating with his old friend, Sir David Beatty, Commander-in-Chief of the British Grand Fleet. The post was much to Sims's liking, although his content failed of completeness because of the steady control over him exercised by Washington. He wanted freedom to use his own judgment in meeting situations and he wanted to make his own policies.

To Secretary Daniels the Sims charges constituted a challenge which he seemed only too eager to accept. "We are so well fortified," he said in a statement to the press, "not with perfect wisdom but in things accomplished by the Navy, that the more people learn about the work of the Navy in the war the more satisfied they will be that we did a good job. We are proud of our record." He denied that he had told Sims not to let the British "pull the wool over your eyes," but admitted that he had cautioned him to be discreet.

January 26. Fourteen months after the Armistice, New York saw its last parade of returned soldiers — 600 of them.

February 13. At President Wilson's demand, Robert Lansing resigned as Secretary of State.[2] He had incurred his chief's displeasure by calling meetings of the Cabinet during Wilson's illness, a function which Wilson considered as belonging solely to the President, and by other acts. March 23, he was succeeded by Bainbridge Colby.

February 28. President Wilson signed the Esch-Cummins Railroad bill, returning the roads to private control at 12:01 A.M., March 1, 1920. The bill, about which much controversy had raged during its passage through Congress, provided for competitive private operation, under control of the Interstate Commerce Commission, with a guaranteed net income in each rate-making group equivalent to $5\frac{1}{2}$ per cent on the value

2 See "Our Times," Vol. V, p. 564.

of the roads in the group; the creation of a Railroad Labor Board to settle labor disputes; permissive consolidation of railroad lines; and certain financial arrangements enabling the railroads to tide over the transition period. Existing rates, wages, and government rental guaranty were to continue until September 1. After September 1 the Interstate Commerce Commission was to fix rates which for two years must allow 5½ per cent profits. The roads were given ten years in which to refund their indebtedness to the Government.

March 1. The United States Steel Corporation was declared not to be a trust in restraint of trade within the meaning of the Sherman Act, in a decision handed down by the United States Supreme Court, the judges participating in the decision dividing 4 to 3. The case now disposed of had a long history in the courts. The United States Steel Corporation was formed in 1901. In 1907 it took over the Tennessee Coal and Iron Company, after President Roosevelt had been consulted. On October 26, 1911, the Department of Justice filed a petition in the United States Circuit Court in Trenton charging the corporation and its subsidiaries with being an unlawful combination in restraint of trade. The next year the Steel Corporation filed an answer stating that it had cheapened steel, had extended the home market, had increased its foreign business in steel from $8,000,000 to $60,000,000 in ten years, that it had not suppressed competition or restrained trade or effected a monopoly in any steel products or attempted to do so. On June 3, 1915, the Federal Court unanimously decided against the dissolution of the corporation. The case then went to the Supreme Court, was argued in March, 1917, and was put over from time to time, and then suspended until 1920 because of war conditions. Justice Brandeis and McReynolds, because of their previous connections with the litigation, took no part in the decision. The prevailing decision was written by Mr. Justice McKenna, who was joined by Chief Justice White and Justices Holmes and Van Devanter. The majority opinion stated that since 1911 no act in violation of law could be established against the Steel Corporation "except its existence be such an act." Continuing, the decision settled a point around which much discussion had revolved:

> The corporation is undoubtedly of impressive size, and it takes an effort of resolution not to be affected by it or to exaggerate its influence. But we must adhere to the law, and the law does not make mere size an offense or the existence of unexerted power an offense. It, we repeat, requires overt acts and trusts to its prohibition of them and its power to repress or punish them.

The substance of the dissenting opinion, read by Mr. Justice Day, was contained in this paragraph:

> I know of no public policy which sanctions a violation of the law, nor of any inconvenience to trade, domestic or foreign, which should have the effect of placing combinations, which have been able thus to organize one of the greatest industries of the country in defiance of the law, in an impregnable position above the law forbidding such combinations. Such a conclusion does violence to the policy which the law was intended to enforce, runs counter to decisions of this Court, and necessarily results in a practical nullification of the act.

March 9. Memories of the Filipino Insurrection of the years about the turn of the century were evoked by the action of the Philippine Legislature granting an annual pension of $6000 to General Emilio Aguinaldo, who had led an insurrection against the Spaniards in the Philippines in 1896 and another against the forces of the United States after the islands had been taken over from Spain.[3]

March 28. Mary Pickford and Douglas Fairbanks,

---

[3] See "Our Times," Vol. I.

moving picture stars, were married at Los Angeles.

March 30. Herbert Hoover, in a telegram to the Hoover Republican Club of California, avowed his willingness to receive the Republican nomination for the

From a photograph by International News, Inc.

Mary Pickford and Douglas Fairbanks, moving picture stars, at the time of their marriage in 1920.

Presidency. Mr. Hoover based his decision to throw in his lot with the Republican Party instead of the Democratic one with which he had been closely associated during the War, on "stagnation" in adjusting our economic problems, developments with respect to the Peace Treaty, and the "urgent representations" of his Republican friends — "to confirm the action that my Republican friends have already taken without consulting me."

He stipulated that if the nomination be offered him he would accept it only on certain conditions:

If the Republican party, with the independent element of which I am naturally affiliated, adopts a forward-looking, liberal, constructive platform on the Treaty [of Versailles] and on our economic issues, and if the party purposes measures for sound business administration of the country, and is neither reactionary nor radical in its approach to our great domestic questions, and is backed by men who undoubtedly assure the consummation of these policies and measures, I will give it my entire support. While I do not, and will not myself, seek the nomination, if it is felt that the issues necessitate it and it is demanded of me, I cannot refuse service."[4]

May 24. President Wilson, acting on the suggestion of the Allied powers, asked the Senate to authorize an American mandate over Armenia. May 27, the proposal was rejected, 11 to 4, by the Senate Foreign Relations Committee; and on June 1, the Senate itself, 52 to 23, "respectfully declined" to give its consent.

June 15. At San Francisco, William Harrison (Jack) Dempsey, world's heavyweight champion, was found not guilty after being tried for evading the draft during the war. Dempsey had passed the war years as a worker in shipyards.

July 26. Agents from the office of the Boston District Attorney started an investigation of Charles Ponzi's "Securities Exchange Company." Ponzi, who for months had been carrying on a mysterious financial business which brought him, for "investment," millions of dollars of the savings of Boston immigrants and working people, maintained a calm pose in the face of the investigation, and, to allay the nervousness of the many who had entrusted their money to him, announced that he would redeem on demand every claim that should be presented. He was as good as his word. In one day he paid out over $300,000. Confidence in him on

[4] *Literary Digest*, April 10, 1920.

the part of his investors was restored. Thousands believed his statement that he was an innocent victim of the savings banks, which resented the withdrawal of deposits from them for investment with Ponzi.

Because of many strange and dramatic happenings Ponzi became first-page news, not only in Boston but throughout the country. Groups divided over whether he was a fraud or a genius. Nobody understood very clearly how Ponzi operated, how he earned the large sums he claimed he did, which enabled him to pay his investors 50 per cent interest for three months' use of their money, and make a large profit for himself besides.

As time went on, reporters and the police unearthed details of Ponzi's past which failed to harmonize with his claims to financial astuteness. Coming to America from Italy seventeen years before, he had never taken out citizenship papers. Mainly he had worked as cook and waiter in restaurants and at unskilled tasks in factories, but had never been able to hold any job for long. Twice he had served terms in jail.

The denouement came August 11, when the authorities closed the Hanover Trust Co., of which Ponzi was a director and large depositor. The following day he was arrested and charged with larceny and unlawful use of the mails. The "international reply coupons" turned out to have no existence in fact. He had paid the large interest increments to people who had early turned over their money to him by taking the money from later deposits. On October 1, a Federal Grand Jury indicted him, and on November 30 he pleaded guilty. The long prison term to which he was sentenced probably saved his life. Hundreds among those he had fleeced were angry enough to risk death themselves if they could but be revenged on him. He was released in 1934, and sent back to his native Italy.

August 18. The Tennessee Legislature passed the Woman's Suffrage Amendment to the Federal Constitution. Tennessee was the thirty-sixth State to approve the Amendment. Following a proclamation by Secretary of State Colby on August 26, the law went into effect.

After woman became a voter, cartoonist Harry Westerman of the *Ohio State Journal* scandalously pictured the G. O. P. as having a "girl friend."

It was estimated that by the Amendment 9,500,000 women voters were added to the 17,500,000 who already, by State enactment, had the suffrage.

September 28. At Chicago, a grand jury brought in indictments for "throwing" the 1919 world series baseball games between the Chicago "White Sox" and the Cincinnati "Reds," against eight players of the Chicago team.

The indictments plunged professional baseball, which up to then had been regarded as the most honest of professional sports, into the worst scandal of its history. There was doubt whether with public confidence in the honesty of the game shaken the sport could survive. To owners of the major league teams the situation seemed so serious that they decided, as an earnest of their determina-

From a photograph © by Edmonston.

This photograph has some historic importance; it pictures one of the first voice amplifiers ever used — by 1935 it had long been obsolete. Forty horns enlarged the voice of Warren G. Harding for an audience of 40,000 at the Minnesota State Fair, September, 1920, when Harding was campaigning for the Presidency.

tion to prevent crookedness in the future, to employ a "czar" whose specific function would be to prevent the recurrence of such happenings. For this post they chose a picturesque individual, Federal Judge Kennesaw Mountain Landis, whose renown as a national character rested in large part on his having levied a $29,000,000 fine against the Standard Oil Company.

The trial of the indicted players was held in Chicago in late July, 1920, and ended in a verdict of acquittal.

When the verdict was announced spectators in the court-room applauded vociferously and the twelve jurymen, gleefully leaping from the jury box, hoisted the players to their shoulders and carried them outside. Despite this legal and popular vindication none of the players ever received Judge Landis's consent to his returning to big league baseball.

October 26. Terence MacSwiney, Lord Mayor of Cork, Ireland, died following a voluntary fast — one of the first "hunger strikes" — for a period of seventy-five days. He was serving a two-year prison term for conspiring against British military authority in Ireland. In America Mayor MacSwiney's fast aroused widespread interest and much sympathy on the part of Americans of Irish blood.

Beginning of the Ku-Klux Klan

October 30. (Saturday night.) Sheeted and hooded members of the Ku-Klux Klan paraded through Jacksonville, Fla. Bulking large among the sidewalk crowds were many negroes whose interested absorption in the spectacle showed that they had as yet no suspicion of the trouble the Klan was to bring them, as well as Catholics, Jews and the alien-born.

The appearance of local klans in many communities in the South, which began in 1920 and continued for years, brought reporters of large city newspapers to Atlanta, Ga., where the Klan had its birthplace and headquarters. An account of an interview with the head of the Klan, by a New York *Herald* reporter, said:

The Klan is organized along military lines and the leader is surrounded by his chief of staff and staff officers. The executive offices occupy the third floor of a downtown office-building (in Atlanta) and spread over into half a dozen rooms

in another building. As you approach the offices there appear
in large black letters on the door "Kuklux Klan," and below
the name "Col. William J. Simmons, Imperial Wizard." Inside is a big force of clerks, stenographers, and assistants.
Colonel Simmons sits at a desk in an inner room with a large
American flag draped at his back.

The Imperial Wizard is a powerful man, something over
forty years of age, smooth-shaven, clear-eyed, deep-voiced,
more than six feet tall. When he grasps your hand you feel
that he has to hold himself back to keep from crushing it. He
was for many years a circuit-rider of the Methodist Episcopal
Church. Later he became a professor of history at Lanier University, Atlanta. He is a veteran of the Spanish-American
War. His title of Colonel is a complimentary one.

In a talk with Angus Perkerson of the Atlanta *Journal*, Simmons explained that he alone had brought the
Klan into being. All his life, he related, he had been
fascinated by stories about the old Ku Klux Klan of post-
Civil War days. "From a child in dresses," he told the
reporter, "I can remember how old Aunt Viney, my
black mammy, used to pacify us children late in the
evening by telling us about the Ku Klux." Fearsome
and calculated to scare little boys though some of those
old tales were, they never made shivers run down
William's back. He listened with open mouth and was
always ready for more. Late one night a vision came to
him. On the wall of his room appeared the Ku Klux
as they had been accustomed to appear so many years before. "On horseback in their white robes they rode
across the wall in front of me, and as the picture faded
out I got down on my knees and swore I would found a
fraternal organization which would be a memorial to
the Ku Klux Klan." For years he pondered his project;
then "finally the thought got so heavy on me that I mentioned it to one or two friends," and they joined with
him in taking the oath of fealty. That was on October
26, 1915. The new Klan, Simmons said, resembled the

old one in having "the same spiritual purpose but a different material form; the same soul in a new body." However, not until five years after its organization did Simmons's klan make progress. Then in 1920 it found an environment favorable to its growth in a mood of national and racial exaltation that swept over America

Picture of a night scene when the Ku Klux Klan was spreading through the country. Similar scenes were common.

following the war. Once again, after a hiatus of fifty years, white-robed, masked figures assembled in midnight conclaves under flaming crosses on lonely mountain tops and in deep woodlands.

November 2. Warren G. Harding and Calvin Coolidge, Republican nominees for President and Vice-President, were elected by a popular vote of 16,152,200 to 9,147,353 for James M. Cox and Franklin D. Roosevelt, Democratic nominees. The Republican candidates carried 37 of the country's 48 States and in the Electoral College won 404 out of 531 votes. A historic note of the day was the broadcasting, for the first time, by the pioneer radio station KDKA at Pittsburgh, of the election returns.

November 4.   William Jennings Bryan, in an interview, suggested that President Wilson should resign so that newly elected Senator Harding could become President and carry out with the greatest possible despatch the policies approved by the voters. (This same proposal was advanced during the panic years of the thirties, following the defeat at the polls of President Herbert Hoover by the Democratic candidate, Franklin D. Roosevelt. On neither occasion was it carried out.) Mr. Bryan explained that President Wilson's resignation would make Vice-President Marshall President and that after appointing Mr. Harding Secretary of State, Marshall should resign. This would make the Secretary of State the next in succession to the Presidency.

The Books of 1920

"The Age of Innocence," by Edith Wharton, which won the Pulitzer prize, a story of New York society during the 1870's. . . . "Tutt and Mr. Tutt," by Arthur Train. . . . "Main Street," by Sinclair Lewis, described by the *Publishers' Weekly* as the most popular book in America in the post-war period. . . . "Miss Lulu Bett," by Zona Gale. . . . "Mooncalf," by Floyd Dell. . . . "Poor White," by Sherwood Anderson. . . . "The Outline of History," by H. G. Wells; in the referendum conducted by the *International Book Review* to determine the ten best books of the twentieth century, it received more votes than any other. . . . "The Valley of Silent Men," a romance of the Canadian Northwest, by James Oliver Curwood, popular author in America during the post-war period. . . .

Two books by Joseph Hergesheimer, "Steel," and "San Cristobal de la Habana." . . . "This Side of Paradise," by F. Scott Fitzgerald. . . . "The Americanization of Edward Bok," by Edward Bok, winner of the Pulitzer prize for biography. . . .

Richard Bennett and Helen MacKellar in "Beyond the Horizon." A Pulitzer Prize Play.

The Theatre in 1920

"Smilin' Through" with Jane Cowl, having a strong appeal to the believers in spiritualism, which was strong in the years following the war. . . . Richard Bennett in "For the Defense," a thrilling crime-and-sex melodrama. . . . John and Lionel Barrymore in "The Jest," a drama of Florence in the Middle Ages, "an outstanding dramatic success." . . . "The Light of the

World," a religious drama. . . . . "The Purple Mask,"
with Leo Ditrichstein and Matheson Lang. . . . Tol-
stoy's "The Power of Darkness," a gloomy tragedy of
Russian peasant life. . . . . "Beyond the Horizon," by

From a photograph by Underwood & Underwood.

Theda Bara, who gave rise to the motion-picture term "vamp."

Eugene O'Neill, a tragedy of American farm life which
won the Pulitzer prize. . . . . "Sacred and Profane
Love," with Elsie Ferguson. . . . . "The Gold Diggers," with Ina Claire. . . . . "The Passion Flower,"
with Nance O'Neil. . . . . "Mary," a musical comedy
by George M. Cohan, which featured the song hit,
"The Love Nest," which *Life* called the "Unofficial
national anthem." . . . . "The Woman of Bronze,"
with Margaret Anglin. . . . . "The Acquittal," prob-

ably the best performance of melodrama of the season. . . . "Mamma's Affair," Harvard prize play, by Rachel Barton Butler. . . . "The Wonderful Thing," with Jeanne Eagles. . . . "Shavings," made from a study of Cape Cod life, by Joseph C. Lincoln; the dramatic critic of *Life* said it "sends the person who sees it away with a kindlier feeling toward humanity. . . . The Scotch musical comedy "Lassie," with kilts and hoop skirts. . . . "The Piper," with Mabel Taliaferro as "a frail and appealing heroine." . . . "Ed Wynne Carnival," with dialog and songs; the dramatic critic of *Life* said "Mr. Wynne is funny, very funny . . . with a minimum of effort"; the entertainment was "chaste and free from vulgarity." . . . John Barrymore, in his first Shakespearean rôle, "Richard III." . . . Theda Bara, the "vamp" of motion pictures appeared in "The Blue Flame," the story of a young agnostic who thought he could create life and who tried it on the body of his fiancée after she had been killed by lightning; the curiosity to see it in certain eastern cities was so great that frequently riots were threatened. . . . At the close of the season 1919–1920, Burns Mantle said: "The fact that there have been more long runs than ever before is not particularly significant, being traceable directly to the prosperity prevailing." There were produced in New York approximately 150 new plays, dramatic and musical. Of these there were 6 with more than 300 performances each, 14 with over 200, and 26 that passed 100.

1921

January 22.   Hog Island, improvised during the war as the world's greatest shipyard, sent its last vessel, the Army transport *Aisne* on a trial run off the Delaware Capes; with delivery of the *Aisne* to the Government, January 27, ship-building at the big plant ceased.

February 13.   A mile-stone in wireless telephony. By combining land lines with wireless, a telephone conversation was carried on between Catalina Island, off California, and a ship 90 miles east of New York — a total distance of more than 3000 miles.

February 22.   Senate and House conferees agreed upon a bill limiting the admission of aliens during 15 months following April 1, 1921, to 3 per cent of the number of natives of each of the respective countries in the United States at the time of the 1910 census.

March 1.   An echo of the 1920 Presidential elections. Expenditures of the two great political parties in the 1920 campaign were more than $10,250,000, according to Senator Kenyon of Iowa. Of this amount the Republicans, he said, spent $8,100,739 and the Democrats $2,237,770.

March 2.   Champ Clark, of Missouri, former Democratic Speaker of the House of Representatives, died, aged 71. For more than a quarter of a century he had been an important figure in national politics; in 1912, he failed by a narrow margin of getting the Democratic nomination for President.

March 4.   Warren Gamaliel Harding and Calvin Coolidge were inaugurated President and Vice-President. President Wilson rode with Harding to the Capitol; on his doctor's orders he did not remain for the inauguration but went to the home he had provided for his retirement, on S Street, Washington. Wilson's continuing to live in Washington occasioned comment, for an ex-President of an opposing party, living in the capi-

From a photograph by Brown Brothers.

Champ Clark of Missouri, former Democratic Speaker of the House; contender for the Democratic Presidential nomination against Woodrow Wilson in 1912.

tal city, is supposed to be an embarrassment to the President in office. Wilson, however, was too ill to be active; besides, he said he was "going to show Harding how an ex-President ought to behave."

March 24. James Cardinal Gibbons, Archbishop of Baltimore and Dean of the American Hierarchy of the

Catholic Church, died in his 87th year. Born in Baltimore, July 23, 1834, he received part of his early education in Ireland, returning to the United States at the
age of 10. He entered business in New Orleans, but

From a photograph by Underwood & Underwood.
Cardinal Gibbons.

later attended St. Charles College, near Ellicott City,
Md., and in 1861 was ordained priest. He was secretary
and chancellor to Archbishop Spalding from 1861 to
1868, when he was appointed first Vicar Apostolic of
North Carolina, where he served a sparse Catholic population until 1872. Bishop Gibbons was appointed to the
see of Richmond, Va., in 1872, and five years later succeeded Archbishop Bayley as Archbishop of Baltimore.
In 1886, he was elevated to the Cardinalate.

Cardinal Gibbons did much, said a writer in the San Francisco *Monitor* (Catholic) "to dispel prejudice against Catholics as citizens and to inspire respect for the Church as an institution in harmony with American ideals, and to place Catholic principles of religion and patriotism in their true light." *Life* said of him: "His study was the soul of man and he seemed to have become highly proficient in it. He was full of knowledge and wisdom and grace. He was gentle, he was urbane, but strong in the faith and constant to his conclusions about it. He lived to be the leading clergyman of the United States. Thousands not of his communion thought of him as a great Christian leader — thought of him with respect and affection and with confidence in his character and his spiritual leadings. His life was happy. He was very cheerful. He feared nothing. One thought of him as a man on whom vanity had no claim, who cared nothing for power except as the means of service, nor for applause except as it helped his work."

March 25.   Soviet Russia was rebuffed by Secretary of State Charles E. Hughes; in a reply to overtures from the Russian Government, he said, "This Government is unable to perceive that there is any proper basis for considering trade relations."

March 29.   John Burroughs, naturalist, died while on a New York Central train on his way to his home in West Park, N. Y., in his 84th year.

April 1.   The White House announced the appointment of Colonel George Harvey to be Ambassador to the Court of St. James.

April 11.   Sale of cigarettes to adults in Iowa became legal.

April 25.   Congressman Andrew Volstead, who wrote the Prohibition enforcement statute, in an effort to make Prohibition more effective, introduced a bill in the House prohibiting the sale of beer to the sick on a physician's prescription.

April 30.　An increase in assets from $306,695,109 as of the year previous, to $345,140,557, marked the

From a photograph by Underwood & Underwood.

John Burroughs, naturalist and nature writer.

successful outcome of a serious crisis in the business of the Ford Motor Co. Six months previously, due to a let-up in buying by the public, the Ford Co. had on hand 125,000 finished cars and, according to rumors, was in urgent need of a loan of $75,000,000. Henry Ford met the problem by closing his plants and forcing the surplus of cars on his Company's 17,000 dealers, against the protests of many. A revival of buying by the public, coming opportunely, made it easy for the dealers to sell the cars.

May 11.　The Senate passed the Emergency Tariff

Act, 63 to 28. It had already passed the House and on May 27, when signed by President Harding, went into effect. The act increased tariff rates on a number of agricultural commodities.

May 20.   Mme. Curie, co-discoverer with her husband of the metal radium, was presented by President Harding with a capsule of radium worth $100,000, the gift of American women.

May.   A questionnaire prepared by the inventor Thomas A. Edison and submitted to young men seeking employment in Edison factories, was published in the newspapers and aroused nation-wide interest. Some of the questions, with answers prepared by the staff of the New York *Times*, were:[1]

2. What city and country produce the finest china?
   Some say Limoges, France; some say Sèvres, France; some say Dresden, Germany.
6. What city in the United States leads in making laundry machines?   Chicago.
12. In what country other than Australia are kangaroos found? In New Guinea.
23. Who was Francis Marion?
    General Marion was a principal leader of the American forces in the Southern States during the Revolutionary War.
34. Who invented logarithms?
    John Napier.
43. How far is it from New York to Buffalo?
    396 miles by the shortest route.
49. What State has the largest amethyst mines?
    Virginia.
54. How is leather tanned?
    By immersion in an infusion of oak or hemlock bark, or other material strong in tannic acid.
55. What is shellac?
    A base for varnish made from lac, which is a resinous incrustation formed on certain trees in the East Indies by an insect resembling the cochineal.

[1] "College men are amazingly ignorant" — a remark said to have been made by Edison after studying the examination papers, elicited caustic rejoinders from college professors and educators generally.

56. What is the longest railroad in the world?
    The Trans-Siberian.
80. What cereal is used in all parts of the world?
    No cereal is used in all parts of the world. Wheat is used
    most extensively, with rice and corn next.

June. With a unanimity rarely displayed by the press of America, editorial writers forgot their political ties and joined in a denunciation of George Harvey, recently appointed Ambassador to Great Britain, for saying in an address to the Pilgrim Society of London:

We sent them [American soldiers] solely to save the United States of America, and most reluctantly and laggardly at that. We were not too proud to fight, whatever that may mean. We were afraid not to fight. That is the real truth of the matter. So we came along towards the end and helped you and your Allies shorten the war. That is all we did and that is all we claim to have done.

June 30. President Harding appointed William Howard Taft Chief Justice of the United States Supreme Court to succeed Edward D. White. The appointment was approved by the Senate, 61 to 4.

July 2. President Harding signed the joint Congressional Resolution declaring peace with Germany and Austria.

July 2. Jack Dempsey knocked out Georges Carpentier, French heavyweight boxer, in four rounds at Jersey City.

August 2. Enrico Caruso, famous Italian tenor, died in Naples, Italy, in his 49th year. A tribute to him as an artist, written a year before during the early stage of his illness by the critic James G. Huneker (who himself died before Caruso) and published in the New York *World*, said:

Enrico Caruso is dead. There have been and will be other tenors, yet for this generation his memory is something sacred and apart. It is doubtful if the Metropolitan Opera House will again echo such golden music as made by his throat —

Buying liquor on board a Rum Row boat 20 miles off shore.

From a photograph by Brown Brothers.

Five hundred cases of scotch worth $40,000, found in the hold of fishing boat, being removed from the hold where it was concealed under a pile of decaying fish. The crew of the boat could not be found after the inspection.

that is, doubtful in our time. Always the word golden comes to the lips; golden, with a thrilling human fiber.

August 16.   Secretary of Labor James J. Davis estimated unemployment in industry at 5,735,000 persons. This month the extreme low point was reached in the business depression which had set in in the Fall of 1920. A turn came for the better in November, when a million men were taken from the ranks of the unemployed and given jobs. After November recovery was rapid.

August 24.   The giant British-built dirigible R–38, near the end of a 35-hour test flight, after which it was to have been turned over to the American Navy as the ZR–2, collapsed and burned near Hull, England, with a loss of 42 killed, including 16 Americans.

August 30.   Rumors that had been in circulation about mysterious ships off the New Jersey coast — said variously to be pirates, "phantoms," and even Bolshevist vessels — were dispelled by the seizure by the Coast Guard of the schooner *Marshall* and several other vessels, which were found to be loaded with liquor intended to be smuggled into the United States. This was an early example of liquor-smuggling vessels hanging off the coast; a strip some twenty or more miles off the Atlantic seaboard came to be known as "Rum Row."

August.   Newspapers in all parts of the country gave increasing attention to a wave of lawlessness in Texas, Florida, and other parts of the South, for which it was claimed the newly organized Ku Klux Klan was responsible. In Texas, during the first six months of the year, forty-three persons, one of them a white woman, were tarred and feathered. The initials "KKK" were branded on the forehead of a negro bellboy. In Missouri, a sixty-eight-year-old farmer was whipped by a mob, and in Florida an archdeacon of the English Episcopal Church was both whipped and tarred and feathered. Indignant, the Dallas, Texas, *Journal* asserted that "anarchy is terrifying the State with a bucket of tar and a sack of feathers." The Houston *Chronicle* denounced the terrorism and gave the Klan this advice:

Boys, you'd better disband. You'd better take your sheets, your banners, your masks, your regalia, and make one big bonfire. Without pausing to argue over the objects you have in mind, it is sufficient to say that your methods are hopelessly wrong. Every tradition of social progress is against them. They are opposed to every principle on which this Government is founded.

October 21. Senator Philander C. Knox of Pennsylvania died suddenly in his home in Washington in his 69th year. He had been Attorney-General under Theodore Roosevelt and Secretary of State under William Howard Taft.

November 11. (Armistice Day.) The nation thrilled to the wonder of a demonstration of progress in the new art called "Radio." The voice of President Harding, heard over loud-speakers by a vast gathering of 100,000 people, covering acres of ground at the Arlington National Cemetery near Washington, where the President spoke, was carried by wires to New York and San Francisco and heard by 35,000 people in Madison Square Garden and 20,000 in the Plaza in San Francisco. The three groups sang hymns in unison. Editorial comment about the event, of which there was much, was on the note "Will wonders never cease!"

November 12. The Conference for the Limitation of Armament was opened at Washington.[2]

December 22. Colonel Henry Watterson, long-time newspaper editor, known affectionately by a wide public as "Marse Henry," died at Jacksonville, Fla., in his 82nd year. At the end of the Civil War he became editor of a newspaper in Louisville, Ky., and afterward

[2] See Chapter 10.

edited and published *The Courier-Journal*, which he built into one of the foremost newspapers of the South. Always a forceful writer, always picturesque, both in literary style and personal appearance, he was famous in his later years for his reiteration, during the war, of "To hell with the Hohenzollerns and Hapsburgs."

December 30. A monoplane piloted by Edward Stinson and Lloyd Bertaud finished a continuous flight of 26 hours, 19 minutes, 35 seconds, at Roosevelt Field, Mineola, L. I., eclipsing the former record for sustained flight by 2 hours, 33 seconds.

During the year another world record was broken by an American pilot, when on September 28, J. A. Mc-Cready, of the Army Air Corps, reached an altitude of 37,000 feet above sea level at Dayton, Ohio, eclipsing the existing mark of 33,114 feet.

December 31. Boies Penrose, Senator from Pennsylvania and long Republican boss of the Keystone State, died at Washington following a long illness, aged 61.

December. The style of knee-high skirts, which had achieved a universal vogue in 1921, was taken as a theme by rhymsters and jokesmiths. "We object," said the Wheeling *Intelligencer*, "to hearing a woman referred to as a 'skirt.' There is very little reason for such a name." A joke first appearing in *Opinion* of London was widely reprinted:

Policeman: "Lost yer mammy, 'ave yer? Why didn't yer keep hold of her skirt?"
Little Alfred: "I cou-cou-couldn't reach it."

A student at Cornell University, writing for the *Cornell Widow*, put shrewd comment on short skirts and other innovations in feminine styles and social customs in rhyme:

They used to wrap their hair in knobs fantastic, high, and queer; but now they cut it short in bobs or curl it round their

"Ladies Home Journal," 1894.

"Vogue," 1926.

A cycle in women's styles.

"McCall's," 1935.

Starting at floor length, they rose to the knee, only to descend to the floor again.

ear. The skirts they wore would scrape the street, and catch the dust and germs; they're now so far above their feet, they're not on speaking terms. The things they do and wear today, and never bat an eye, would make their fogy forebears gray, they'd curl right up and die.

Times have waxed and waned a lot, as old-timers can recall, and the dancing now is not what it used to be at all; only awkward rubes and hicks execute the bows and kicks that were clever parlor tricks when our paters threw a ball. Our progenitors took pleasure in a slow and solemn way; they would tread a stately measure that was anything but gay, and the orchestra would render sentimental stuff and tender which the folks of either gender wouldn't listen to today. With a flock of flutes and 'cellos, plus a harp and silver horn, these accomplished music fellows would play on till early morn; they could keep "Blue Danube" flowing without letting up or slowing, till the bantams started crowing and they'd leave to hoe the corn. But your strictly modern dancers don't go in so much for grace, and the minuet and lancers have been boosted from the place; for the "poetry of motion" has been backed into the ocean, and a sort of "free-verse" notion has possest our jaded race. Now the orchestra that's snappy and a hit with all the boys, aims to keep the rabble happy with a slew of fancy noise; and the syncopated stammer of a cow-bell and a hammer add the sort of blare and glamour that contain a thousand joys. With a saxophone complaining, and a banjo chirping in; a fiddle that is straining to be heard above the din; and a handy man and drummer, who I think should be a plumber tho he's mentioned as a comer — how they make the flappers grin. It is said they play with feeling, yet somehow it misses me; they are experts at concealing all the tune and melody; but for present ways of tripping, cheek to cheek and closely gripping, I admit they're simply ripping, and they suit it to a T !

Books of 1921

"A Daughter of the Middle Border," by Hamlin Garland, awarded the Pulitzer prize for biography. . . . "Autumn," by Robert Nathan. . . . "Alice Adams," by Booth Tarkington, a pathetic story of a small-town social climber. . . . "The Brimming Cup," by Dorothy Canfield Fisher, a best-seller. . . . "Beggar's Gold," by Ernest Poole. . . . "Erik Dorn," by

Ben Hecht. . . . "The Girls," by Edna Ferber. . . .
"The Briary Bush," by Floyd Dell. . . . "The Day of
Faith," by Arthur Somers Roche. . . . "Brass," by
Charles G. Norris. . . . Among the books of this year,

Courtesy of "Life."

When dancing was done cheek-to-cheek.

"The Sheik" by E. M. Hull became a best-seller; "any
writer [said *Life*] who can pull off the same old sex
stuff, and make it look new, is always rewarded by the
public." . . . "Three Soldiers," by John Dos Passos,
was rated "the first important novel that the A.E.F. has
produced." . . . *The Dial's* first annual award of
$2000 to advance the work of the most promising Amer-
ican author was bestowed on Sherwood Anderson, whose
greatest quality, said John Farrar, is "a curious ability
to give voice to the tragedies of starved lives"; in the
same year appeared Anderson's "Triumph of the Egg,"

of which *The Nation* declared that "in these episodes and stories there are pages as memorable as have been written by any contemporary American." . . . "Scaramouche," by Rafael Sabatini. . . . "Messer Marco Polo," by Donn Byrne. . . . "Joanna Godden," by Sheila Kaye-Smith. . . . "If Winter Comes," by A. S. M. Hutchinson, a "literary photograph of a lovable personality" which became a best-seller. . . . "The Beautiful and Damned," by F. Scott Fitzgerald. . . .

The Theatre in 1921

Plays of 1921

Lionel Atwill playing the rôle of pantomimist in "Deburau." . . . William Faversham in "The Prince and the Pauper." . . . George Arliss and Winthrop Ames in "The Green Goddess." . . . Fred Stone in "Tip-Top." . . . Miss Genevieve Tobin in "Little Old New York." . . . Zona Gale's dramatization of her own novel, "Miss Lulu Bett." . . . Nora Bayes in "Her Family Tree." . . . John Drew and Mrs. Leslie Carter in Somerset Maugham's "The Circle." . . . The Irish Players brought "The White Headed Boy" to New York. . . . Lynn Fontanne and Frank Bacon in "Dulcy." . . . Marilyn Miller in "Sally." . . . Ina Claire in a comedy of chorus girl life, "The Gold Diggers." . . . Mrs. Fiske "thrown away on a copy-book play, 'Wake Up Jonathan.'" . . . Madge Kennedy in an old-fashioned crook play, "Cornered." . . . Laura Hope Crews, very pleasing in "Mr. Pim Passes By." . . . Willard Mack in "Smooth as Silk." . . . Pauline Lord in Eugene O'Neill's Pulitzer Prize play, "Anna Christie." . . . William Courtenay in "Honors Are Even." . . . Katharine Cornell in "A Bill of Divorcement." . . .

"Goat Alley," a drama of primitive love and life, with an all-negro cast. . . . "Blossom Time," musical comedy operetta founded on the life of Franz Schubert. . . . Irving Berlin's "Music Box Revue," "a beautiful thing

Photograph from International News Photos, Inc.

Charles Spencer Chaplin performed hilarious slapstick pantomime with a wistfulness that belied his comic antics, and this touch of seriousness reached a climax when Chaplin appeared in "The Kid" in which he helped to skyrocket Jackie Coogan to movie fame in 1920. Above is a scene from the now famous picture "The Kid."

to watch." . . . Billie Burke and Alfred Lunt in "The Intimate Strangers." . . . Leonore Ulric in David Belasco's production, "Kiki," "the outstanding comedy success of the year." . . . Ed Wynn in "The Perfect Fool," of which he himself wrote the book, lyrics, and music. . . . Among the revivals were "Alias Jimmy Valentine" and "Bought and Paid For."

1922

January 23.   William Jennings Bryan spoke before the Kentucky Legislature in support of a bill prohibiting the teaching of the theory of evolution in State-supported schools.   The bill was defeated in the House of Representatives March 9 by a margin of 1 vote, 42 to 41.   This was the beginning of a controversy into which almost everybody was dragged sooner or later, which reached an explosive climax in 1925 in a trial at Dayton, Tenn., of a young high school teacher, John Thomas Scopes, on the charge of teaching evolution in violation of a Tennessee law.[1]

February 6.   Achille Ratti, following election by the House of Cardinals, became the 261st Pope, taking the name Pius XI.   The New York *Evening Mail*, commenting on the training and character of the new Pontiff, said, with a prescience which was to be borne out by Pius' career, that while some Popes were "political" and others "religious," Pius XI would probably be "sociological."

February 21.   The *Roma*, a semi-dirigible purchased by the United States Government from Italy, crashed to earth and exploded at the Hampton Roads Army base when the rudder failed to work; 34 out of its crew of 45 were killed.

Prohibition Notes

February.   A change wrought by prohibition in Broadway night life — the introduction of the "night club" — was described in the New York *Times:*

Broadway had lost its thrill — had become a mere Main Street of motion-picture emporiums and synthetic orange-juice

[1] See page 641 for an account of the Scopes trial.

568

booths. Dissipation ran in ugly subterranean channels, unlit by glamour or the romance of beauty. Out of such ruins a night life was to be reconstructed — a night life that would hold out an appeal alike to the hardened old rounder, and to the unsatiated flapper, tingling with curiosity.

The answer has been a group of cafés that call themselves clubs — although technically they have no more right to the name than has the Waldorf-Astoria. But the very name "club" is a part of the general scheme of surrounding patrons with the psychology of privacy and intimacy — which psychology has been no small factor in ousting the clammy dread of the law that had placed its damper on Broadway's spirits since July 1919.

The very architecture of the new places is part of the propaganda. The successful "club" is full of booths and alcoves and cozy wall benches, which somehow contribute to the atmosphere of "just us members." . . .

A club this season is not considered a real success unless there is a care-free tendency among the guests to toss remarks to each other from table to table.

April. By the early Spring of 1922, after two years of existence, the Prohibition Bureau of the Treasury Department became famous for some of its methods of enforcement. Two of its agents, Izzy Einstein and Moe Smith, were a new type of detective, evolved by the dry age; in their hands the ancient and highly ingenious art of sleuthing showed new and dazzling developments. They stood forth, in the words of a journalistic appreciator, "as the master hooch-hounds, alongside whom all the rest of the pack are but pups." Though chary of talking about their work, they consented on one occasion to be interviewed by a reporter of the New York *Times*, who wrote about them:

Izzy, on giving up his job as a postal clerk and joining the rum squad, decided upon a category of true-to-life disguises that would fit him for all the avenues, highways, and alleyways in the labyrinth he was entering, and, like the true actor rehearsing for a long run, he not only learned his parts but grew into them. He became a man of parts. He prepared himself to move in high, low, and medium circles — on the excellent theory that the taste for liquor and the desire to sell it are no respecters of persons — and in all those circles he has since been whirling with rapidity and a quick-change adeptness. "Dress clothes for Broadway and overalls for the waterfront," Izzy says in partial explanation of his methods. . . .

One of Einstein's earliest exploits, in which he took great pride even though the haul was slight, occurred on a Fourth

FEDERAL ENFORCEMENT AGENTS

Courtesy of The Evening World
From the "Evening World."

A satire by Clive Weed on prohibition enforcement, showing prohibition agents in a speakeasy — "Less have 'nother round o' evidence."

of July parade of wets in 1921. Not only did Izzy march with the wets —

He followed some of them into the by-paths, with devastating effect on the unsuspecting dealers in the very article for which the demonstrators were perspiringly parading. . . .

So crowded with seizures and confiscations has his career been that he remembers only some of the notable ones. Two thousand cases of whisky and 367 barrels of wine constituted one little haul. A 700-case seizure of whisky he mentioned as another trifle. . . .

Once he and his pal, Moe Smith, became hostlers for a few days. They had a tip about a certain stable. There was a still in the back of it, they were told. The two forlorn-looking stablemen, as horsy as the thorough Izzy could make them, applied for jobs. There was nothing just then, but there might be later. They hung around. They dropped in from day to day, got acquainted with the boss and gradually nosed their way about. They found the still before they got their jobs. . . .

Street-car conducting seems remote from bootlegging, yet the tip that saloons near certain car barns were doing rush business took Izzy there. He appeared bright and early one morning dressed in all the regalia of a B. R. T. employee. He entered a saloon and laid a $5 bill on the bar.

"Can you give me a lot of change for this?" he asked. "I need it for my run."

The bartender also had use for small change.

"Why don't you buy a drink?" he asked. "That's the way to get change."

Izzy ordered a glass of beer.

"Why don't you take a good drink?"

Izzy ordered whisky. He got $4.25 in change. The bartender got arrested. . . .

May 15. The United States Supreme Court (6 to 3) ruled that alcoholic liquors could not be transported through the country in bond, nor transferred from one foreign ship to another in an American port. . . . *June* 19. A mob of "wets" stormed and partly demolished the jail at Ocean City, Md., and released two men committed for intoxication. . . .

September 4. In Red Hook, Brooklyn, twelve people died from drinking whiskey made from wood alcohol. . . . *September.* Results of a poll on prohibition conducted by *The Literary Digest:*

For Enforcement. . . . . .356,193 — (38.6%)
For Modification. . . . . .376,334 — (40.8%)
For Repeal. . . . . .189,856 — (20.6%)

October 6. Attorney-General Daugherty ruled that the selling of liquor on American ships, Government owned or privately owned, anywhere in the world, was contrary to law, and also that no foreign ship could bring liquors within the three-mile limit, sealed or unsealed, whether the liquors were or were not intended for consumption in this country; the President had already instructed Chairman Lasker of the Shipping Board to discontinue the transport and sale of alcoholic beverages on Government-owned boats and had directed Secretary

Courtesy of The Evening World

"Watcha Got in that Bag?"

A satire by Clive Weed on prohibition enforcement which appeared in the "wet" New York *Evening World*.

of the Treasury Mellon to deliver equivalent instructions to privately owned American ships. . . . *October* 6. Prohibition raiders seized $500,000 of liquors secreted in cellar on East 44th Street, New York City. . . . *October* 16. The United States was notified that Great Britain would not consent to the search of vessels flying the British flag outside the three-mile limit of the American coast by customs officers seeking liquor smugglers. . . . *November* 18. 105 doctors of New York brought suit in the United States Supreme Court to annul the provisions of the prohibition law restricting physicians to a limited amount of whiskey or other alcoholic beverages in the treatment of patients.

The Ku Klux Klan

March 11. At Wisner, La., a band of masked and hooded Ku Kluxers killed a man; Governor Parker (March 23) appealed to law officers of Louisiana to suppress "with an iron hand the evil of Ku Kluxism wherever it raises its head." . . . *May* 8, a national congress of the Klan began at Atlanta, Ga. . . . *June* 3, 3000 men were initiated into the Klan at Plainfield, Ill. . . . *June* 17, Masonic officials in Connecticut issued a warning to Masons against the Klan. . . . *July* 22, Ku Klux Klan headquarters in Atlanta, Ga., banned the use of masks except in lodge rooms. . . . *July* 22, candidates for State and National offices indorsed by the Klan won in the Texas primaries. . . . *November* 21, suit was begun by the State of Kansas in the State Supreme Court to oust the Klan. . . . *November* 23, charges were made against the Ku Klux Klan of attempting to interfere with the mails in Louisiana and Texas. . . . *November* 23, the Police Commissioner of New York was ordered by Mayor Hylan to drive the Klan out of the city; two weeks later, in defiance of the Mayor, a white-robed and hooded Klansman spoke from the pulpit of a church in Brooklyn. . . . *June* 24, a mass initiation of Klansmen at Tulsa, Okla., was reported by *The Tribune:*

One thousand and twenty men pledged allegiance to the Ku Klux Klan at a giant ceremonial, which lasted for hours last night, on a pasture range about nine miles southeast of the city on the Broken Arrow Road. They were inducted into Tulsa Klan No. 2 before a fiery 70-by-20-foot cross at one end of the immense pasture. A smaller cross lighted up the other end of the initiation grounds. More than 30,000 motorists from Tulsa and surrounding towns tried to reach the scene of the spectacle, but only a few thousand succeeded. The huge crowd was in 10,000 automobiles. Several small boys were able to view the entire spectacle. "Every one knelt before the flag and seemed to kiss it," one of the boys said. "It was awful solemn and spooky. White figures were every place."

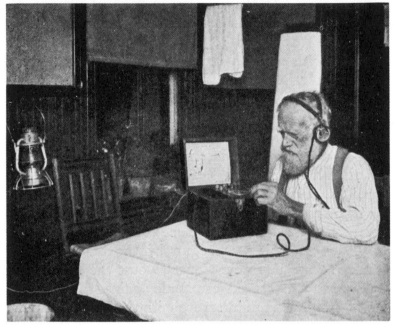

From a photograph by Ewing-Galloway.

An early form of the radio, about 1924.

March 29. The Naval armament limitation treaty and the treaty restricting the use of submarines and poison gas in warfare were ratified by the United States Senate.[2]

March. Radio broadcasting of news, Sunday sermons, music was put on a daily basis in New York City. Receiving sets, of the crystal-head phones type, were selling rapidly.

[2] See Chapter 10.

April 12. At San Francisco, a verdict of acquittal was returned by a jury in the third trial of Roscoe C. ("Fatty") Arbuckle, moving-picture comedian, on a manslaughter charge growing out of the death of a young woman at a party given by Arbuckle. Though acquitted, Arbuckle continued in the bad graces of the

From a photograph by Acme.

A posed photograph showing the preparations of armored door, etc. made by a Chicago labor official to resist racketeers.

public and was never again permitted to act in the films.

May 10. Labor racketeering in Chicago. Following the slaying of two policemen by gunmen alleged to be employed by labor racketeers, 200 suspects were arrested, including many labor leaders, as the first step towards repressing an apparently organized campaign of terror.

"For several years past[3] a gang of professional thugs have gradually gained control of a number of Chicago labor unions. Through intimidation and violence they

[3] Telegram from the Chief of Police of Chicago to the New York *World*.

have worked their way into the inner councils of certain unions until they have become absolute dictators of the terms on which a man may work, for whom he may work, when and where. This grip is so tight that by systematic blackmail of workers and their employers alike they have accumulated large sums of money, which they have used in bribery and corruption on a scale so enormous that they have been almost immune from successful prosecution. . . ."

May 11. President Harding signed a bill extending for two years from June 30, the 3 per cent immigration restriction act.

May 13. Otto L. Wiedfeldt, first German Ambassador to the United States since the War, reached New York from Bremen.

May 15. The United States Supreme Court declared the Child Labor law enacted by Congress in 1919 to be unconstitutional, on the ground that it attempted to regulate an exclusively State function.

A Landmark in American Art

May 30. At Washington, in a great open space at the end of the Mall and in the presence of 100,000 people, the Lincoln Memorial was dedicated. Chief Justice Taft, presenting the Memorial to the nation, said that the fifty-seven years which had passed since Lincoln's death had "faded the figures of Lincoln's contemporaries," leaving him to stand "grandly alone." President Harding accepted the monument on behalf of the nation.

Artists and critics spoke of the Memorial as the "most beautiful edifice in America"; a "flawless monument"; it had "not an unnecessary line, not a fault in proportion; line and mass combine to make that for which idealists strive — the unity of perfection." They likened its beauty to that of the earth's other superlative architectural gem, the Taj Mahal in India. It stood "on a mound built of a series of terraces rising to a height of 122 feet. A colonnade of great Doric columns of white

From a photograph © by Harris & Ewing.

The Lincoln Memorial, Washington, D. C.

marble surrounds the walls, within which, in the centre space, is the colossal statue of Lincoln. Each column, thirty-six in all, represents a State, one for each State existing at the time of Lincoln's death. On the walls above the colonnade, supported at intervals by eagles, are forty-eight memorial festoons, one for each State existing at the present time. The setting of the Memorial is magnificent. Behind it flows the Potomac and beyond rise the hills of Virginia. . . . To the East, a third of a

mile away, stands in its austere dignity Washington's
Monument, which is to be connected with the Lincoln
Memorial by a great lagoon that will reflect both monu-
ments. A mile beyond the Washington Monument is
the Capitol. These three — the Capitol, Washington's
Monument, and the Lincoln Memorial — form the
three great features of the Mall, the plan of which provides for walks and drives and rows of elms for the
entire distance. It is a composition without parallel in
any other city in the world."

The success of the architect, Henry Bacon, in bringing into being so surpassingly lovely a product of the
builder's art, was equalled in the great figure of Lincoln
sculptored by Daniel Chester French which the monument enshrines. Sitting in a great chair with its back to
the west, it gives a startling simulation of life as it gazes
placidly out through the always open eastern portal facing the Washington Monument and the Capitol.

June 21. Twenty-one strikebreakers employed by a
coal company near Herrin, Ill., after surrendering to
strikers following a fight, were shot, beaten to death, or
hanged. "Nothing we have ever read of the Russian
pogroms," said the Knoxville *Sentinel*, "of the Turkish
massacres of Christians, nor of the midnight descents
of the Red Indians on settlements of the American
pioneers surpasses this Illinois horror in unfeeling ferocity and gloating cruelty." Five union miners charged
with the murders, following a trial attended by violence,
were acquitted January 19, 1923.

June. The morals of America's young people engaged the worried attention of the religious press. Samuel Byrne, editor of the Pittsburgh *Observer* (Catholic)
wrote:

There has been a change for the worse during the past year
in feminine dress, dancing, manners, and general moral stand-

ards. The causes are the lack of an adequate sense of responsibility in the parents or guardians of girls, a decline in personal religion, a failure to realize the serious ethical consequences of immodesty in girls' dress, a dulling of moral sus-

© N. E. A. Service, Inc.

There was endless discussion pro and con about the flapper and her short skirts. One of her defenders, in the *Outlook*, pictured the young lady on the right as an example of the real flapper as opposed to the exaggerated type shown on the left.

ceptibilities, an inability to grasp the significance of the higher things in human life, and, last, but not least, the absence of sufficient courage and determination to resist the dictates of what is known as Fashion when these are opposed to decency.

The Southern Baptist *Review and Expositor* held similar views:

There is a great deal of frank talk among young people that

in many cases smacks of boldness. One hears it said that the girls are actually tempting the boys more than the boys do the girls, by their dress and their conversation. Not all the boys and girls are bad but evil is more open and defiant of

"Evangeline! That is not the way to try on a coat."

From a drawing by Helen Hokinson in the "New Yorker."

"Evangeline! That is not the way to try on a coat."

Shock of the older generation when the younger adopted the pose that was a vogue during the '20's.

public opinion and restraint. The situation causes grave concern on the part of all who have the ideals at heart of purity and home life and the stability of our American civilization.

The Wilkerson Injunction

July 1. 400,000 shopmen employed on railroads throughout the country went on strike in protest against a $60,000,000 wage-cut ordered by the Railroad Labor Board. During the first week schedules were disarranged, many passenger trains were withdrawn from service, disorders occurred in a number of places and numerous accidents were reported, some the result of the incompetency of strikebreakers, others brought about by sabotage. After two weeks, and with no prospect of a settlement in sight, President Harding issued a proclamation "directing all persons to refrain from all interference with the lawful effort to maintain interstate transportation and the carrying of the United States mails." The proclamation was ignored by the strikers.

The strike continued without abatement until September 1, when on motion by Attorney-General Harry Daugherty a temporary injunction restraining the strikers from interfering in any manner whatever with the operation of the railroads was granted by United States District Judge James H. Wilkerson in Chicago. By the terms of this injunction, the striking shopmen and certain of their union officials were enjoined from combining to interfere with railroad transportation or to interfere with any person employed by the roads or desirous of such employment. They could not aid any one "by letters, telegrams, telephones, word of mouth, or otherwise" to do any of the forbidden acts. They were warned to keep off railroad property and not to try "to induce by the use of threats, violent or abusive language, opprobious epithets, physical violence, or threats thereof, intimidation, display of numbers or force, jeers, entreaties, arguments, persuasion, rewards or otherwise," anybody to stop work in railroad shops. Picketing was forbidden. Union officials were restrained from issuing any strike directions or saying anything which might keep any strikebreaker from work. They were enjoined from using any union funds to do any of the things forbidden in the injunction writ.

The strikers' union countered September 7, by petitioning the District of Columbia Supreme Court for an injunction restraining local authorities from carrying out the provision of Judge Wilkerson's injunction. The Court refused, September 9. September 11, Judge Wil-

kerson extended his injunction ten days more. By this
time the back of the strike had been broken; it came to
an end September 15, when the Pennsylvania Railroad
made an arrangement with its men, and striking workers
for the Chicago and Northwestern, St. Paul, and Baltimore and Ohio Railroads returned to work.

August 2. Alexander Graham Bell, inventor of the
telephone, died in his 76th year at his estate near Bad-
dack, N. S.

September 16. Reverend Edward Wheeler Hall,
rector for ten years of the Church of St. John the Evangelist, New Brunswick, N. J., and Mrs. James Mills,
choir leader and wife of the sexton were found shot to
death on an abandoned farm two miles west of New
Brunswick. Suspicion pointed at the family of the widow of the male victim, but a grand jury held in November decided the evidence was not sufficient for an indictment. Four years later, in 1926, a New York tabloid
newspaper on the hunt for scandal dug up what purported to be important new evidence. Mrs. Hall and her
two brothers were arrested, tried, and acquitted. The
trial was one of the most sensational in American history.

September 22. The Government's wooden fleet of
226 vessels, built during the war at a cost of $300,000,-
000, was sold by the Shipping Board to a business man
of San Francisco for $750,000.

September 12. The Protestant Episcopal House of
Bishops voted 36 to 27 to take the word "obey" out of
the marriage ceremony.

September. "From now on," read a notice newly
posted on the walls of Henry Ford's automobile factory
in Detroit, "it will cost a man his job, without any excuse or appeal being considered, to have the odor of
beer, wine or liquor on his breath, or to have any of these

intoxicants on his person or in his home. The Eighteenth Amendment is a part of the fundamental laws of this country. It was meant to be enforced. Politics has interfered with enforcement of this law, but so far as our organization is concerned it is going to be enforced to the letter."

This ultimatum to Ford workmen to live up to the Volstead Act, like much else done by Henry Ford, provoked discussion. Drys were elated and in their comments said that Ford was a "patriot" and that his action "was a fine example to other manufacturers and business men in these days when there is a tendency to treat the 18th Amendment and the Volstead Law with contempt." [4] Dissent was voiced on several grounds, among them that Ford had "no right to peer into his workmen's homes to see whether they had liquor there."

November 21.   Mrs. Rebecca L. Felton, of Georgia, appointed to fill the vacancy caused by the death of Senator Watson, was sworn in as the first woman Senator of the United States. She held the office only a few hours and was succeeded by Senator-elect Walter F. George.

October 14.   New York's first telephone machine switching central office, "Pennsylvania," was placed in operation.

October 26.   Work was begun on the Holland vehicular tunnel under the Hudson River between Manhattan and Jersey City.

October 29.   Beginning of the Fascist régime in Italy. King Emmanuel called on Benito Mussolini, Fascist leader, to form a new Cabinet.

November 1.   The flow of American capital to Europe from 1914 onward was pictured in a statement by Comptroller of the Currency Crissinger. *Wallace's Farmer*, commenting, predicted that within twenty

[4] Anti-Saloon League, Westerville, Ohio.

years America would be the "most hated nation" in the world.

American securities purchased from abroad....	$3,000,000,000
American Government loans (War loans)......	10,000,000,000
Interest on Government loans...............	2,000,000,000
Commercial credits extended abroad..........	3,000,000,000
Dollar securities bought from other countries:	
1919...............................	713,000,000
1920...............................	571,000,000
1921...............................	596,000,000
1922 (eight months)....................	751,000,000
Foreign money securities sold here 1919 to 1922.	620,000,000
Foreign currencies bought by America........	500,000,000
	$21,751,000,000

November 7. "A peremptory warning to the party in power to do better," was the interpretation one newspaper put on the heavy losses sustained by the Republicans in the November elections to the United States Senate and House of Representatives. Republican membership in the House dropped from 296 to 227, a loss of 70 seats, and in the Senate from 60 to 53. Even the slim majorities which the Republicans retained were more apparent than real, for in both houses there was an increase of Progressive strength. Balance of power in the Senate, it was correctly predicted, would rest with the Progressives or "farm bloc" Senators — Borah, LaFollette, Johnson, Brookhart, Norris, Howell, Norbeck, Capper, Ladd, Frazier, and Shipstead.

November 11 (Armistice Day). Ex-President Woodrow Wilson made his first public address in three years, a brief talk exhorting America to join the League of Nations, to 7000 persons assembled in the street before his residence in Washington.[5]

November 13. The United States Supreme Court ruled that Japanese are not eligible for United States citizenship. Its ruling was based on Section 2169 of the

[5] See "Our Times," Vol. V.

Revised Statutes, which restricts naturalization to "free white persons" and those of African descent.

November 15. An important advance in medical knowledge. Announcement was made in New York that Doctor Alexis Carrel, surgeon of the Research Staff of the Rockefeller Institute, had found that "leucocytes," the white corpuscles of the blood, are the agency which prevents the spread of infection in animal tissues and brings to those tissues substances which they need for re-building themselves.

December 1. Heartened by gains made in their numbers in the November elections, thirteen Senators and Senators-elect and twenty-three Representatives and Representatives-elect, belonging to the "farm bloc" or

New York Tribune

First to Last—the Truth: News—Editorials—Advertisements

Vol. LXXXII No. 27,751   WEDNESDAY, NOVEMBER 8, 1922

Smith Elected by 400,000; Copeland Wins; Republicans Hold Congress and Legislature

The New York *Tribune's* announcement of the result of the election.

Progressive faction of the Republican Party, met behind closed doors in Washington and adopted a programme of "progressive" legislation. Senator LaFollette in a statement following the conference said the group would work for the abolition of the Electoral College, direct primaries for all elective offices including the Presidency, the prompt convening of newly elected Congresses, and the driving of "special privilege out of control of Government." "Regular" Republicans denounced the group. Republican Governor Henry Allen of Kansas, in his newspaper, the Wichita *Beacon*, attacked LaFollette:

Special privilege, as used by Senator LaFollette, is the high sounding phrase used by political demogogs. So-called "Progressivism" is merely another name for radicalism. These Progressives are organizing for a raid on wealth. There are some in this group who are undoubtedly sincere and honestly believe that the country's welfare is at stake, but if they tie up with demagogs of the LaFollette stripe they will defeat their own aims and will bring much distress upon the country.

December 1. "The greatest archeological discovery of all time," as the newspapers characterized it, was the

From a photograph by Harry Burton, © *New York Times Co.*

The inner door of the tomb of Tutankhamen, as it looked when it was unsealed in February, 1924. It is guarded by the statues of two servants.

finding of the tomb of the Egyptian King Tutankhamen (fourteenth century before Christ) in the Valley of the Kings near Luxor, by Lord Carnarvon and his American assistant, Howard Carter. An account by Lord Carnarvon in the London *Times* told what met the eyes of the excavators when the tomb was opened:

We began clearing the passage. . . . We reached a sealed door or wall. We wondered if we should find another staircase, probably blocked behind this wall, or whether we should get into a chamber. I asked Mr. Carter to take out a few stones and have a look in. This was done. He pushed his head partly into the aperture. With the help of a candle, he could dimly discern what was inside. A long silence followed, until I said, I fear in somewhat trembling tones, "Well, what is it?" "There are some marvelous objects here," was the welcome reply. . . . I myself went to the hole, and I could with difficulty restrain my excitement. At the first sight, with the inadequate light, all that one could see was what appeared to be gold bars. On getting a little more accustomed to the light, it became apparent that there were colossal gilt couches with extraordinary heads, boxes here and boxes there. We enlarged the hole and Mr. Carter managed to scramble in — the chamber is sunk two feet below the bottom passage — and then, as he moved around with a candle, we knew we had found something absolutely unique.

Even with the poor light of the candle one could see a marvelous collection of furniture and other objects. There were two life-sized statues of the king, beds, chariots, boxes of all sizes and shapes — some with every sort of inlay while others were painted — walking-sticks, marvelous alabaster vases. After slightly enlarging the hole we went in; this time we realized the extent of the discovery, for we had managed to tap the electric light from the tomb above, which gave us better illumination.

One of the finest objects is the chair or throne of the King. It is in wood. The back panel is of surpassing beauty, and portrays the King and his Queen protected by Aton rays. All the figures in this scene are built up by means of semi-precious carved stones, inlaid into wood. The delicacy and grace of this work of art are indescribable, and it is, indeed, fortunate that we have struck a period when Egyptian art reached one of its culminating points. A few minutes later, beneath one of the beds of state, we came on a small opening, giving into another chamber. There the confusion was beyond conception. It was utterly impossible to enter, as the room was packed with chairs, beds, boxes, statuettes, alabasters, and every other conceivable object.

December 7. Twelve to fourteen years have been added to the average human life in the last half century by progress in medical science, Dr. John M. Dodson, Dean of Rush Medical College, said in an address before the University of Chicago forum. Infant mortality, he said, had been cut in half, tuberculosis largely robbed of its terror, and epidemics brought under control. He said that 600,000 still die in the United States annually from preventable diseases.

December 30. Benedict Crowell, Assistant Secretary of War in the Wilson Administration, and six other

From a photograph by Underwood & Underwood.

The famous Four Horsemen of Notre Dame:

Miller,	Stuhldreher,	Crowley,	Layden.

members of the Emergency Construction Committee of the Council of National Defense of the War Department, were indicted by a special grand jury in Washington on charges of committing fraud in connection with contracts for the erection of cantonments, port terminals, warehouses, and fortifications during the Great War. In the ensuing proceedings it was demonstrated beyond any shadow of doubt that Crowell was blameless of any wrong doing and that in his war service he had been exceptionally able and conscientious.[6]

[6] See Chapter 10.

December. Sports went increasingly "big business." During the football season all attendance records were broken. Despite three defeats which put it well down on the winning list, Yale played to greater crowds than ever before. Twice the immense Yale Bowl was filled to capacity — 77,000 seats — at games with Harvard and West Point. 55,000 attended the Iowa game and the same number watched the Yale-Princeton game at Princeton. Total receipts reached $500,000. Yale's performance was exceeded by that of the University of Pennsylvania, which had built a great new stadium. An aggregate of 385,000 persons, paying approximately $700,000 attended the ten games played at Pennsylvania's Franklin Field.

In baseball, payments for ball players sold by major to minor leagues and vice versa amounted to $2,056,-246, another new record.

Race-track attendance and receipts exceeded anything in track history, and the purses and prizes paid in 1922 set a new financial record. Three American winning horses alone took away $261,576 in stakes. "Pillory" topped all the horses with $95,654.

Tennis drew its largest crowds in history in 1922. At the National Championships at Manheim early in September the crowds numbered 15,000 and were limited to that number only by the capacity of the stands.

Books of 1922

"Cytherea" and "The Bright Shawl," by Joseph Hergesheimer. . . . "Gentle Julia," by Booth Tarkington. . . . "One Man in His Time," by Ellen Glasgow. . . . "The Vehement Flame," by Margaret Deland. . . . "Hungry Hearts," by Anzia Yezierska, depicting the lives of immigrants in New York's ghetto, later successfully filmed. . . . "Stella Dallas," by Olive

Higgins Prouty, which became a film success. . . .
"Babbitt," by Sinclair Lewis, a satire on American
small-town life. . . . "One of Ours," by Willa Cather,
a war novel which won the Pulitzer prize. . . . "Where
the Blue Begins," by Christopher Morley, called "a little

By courtesy of Paramount Pictures.

"Going West," from the motion picture, "The Covered Wagon."

masterpiece." . . . "Captain Blood," by Rafael Sabatini, a stirring tale of the Spanish main. . . . "The Forsyte Saga," by John Galsworthy. . . . "Command," by
William McFee, a romance with a salty flavor. . . .
"The Covered Wagon," by Emerson Hough, a tale of
the pioneer days in America, which became a very successful film. . . . "Vandemark's Folly," by Herbert
Quick, a story of canal-boat days before the Civil War.
. . . "Gargoyles," by Ben Hecht. . . . "Glimpses of
the Moon," by Edith Wharton. . . . "The Life and
Letters of Walter Hines Page," by Burton J. Hendrick.

. . . "The Great Adventure at Washington: The Story of the Arms Conference," by Mark Sullivan.

The Theatre in 1922

Frances Starr in a light comedy, "Shore Leave." . . . Glenn Hunter in "Merton of the Movies," a big comedy

From a photograph by Vandamm Studios.

Pauline Lord in "Anna Christie."

success. . . . Ina Claire and Bruce McRae in "The Awful Truth." . . . George Bernard Shaw's philosophic fantasy "Back to Methuselah," which the Theatre Guild had to divide into three parts, playing each part one week and then repeating each part for a second week. . . . Barney Bernard and Alexander Carr in "Partners Again." . . . John Barrymore's "Hamlet," which started an interesting revival of Shakespearean plays, among them David Warfield in "The Merchant of Venice" and Ethel Barrymore in "Romeo and Juliet." . . . A charming play was A. A. Milne's "Truth About Blayds," which was a distinct success. . . . Miss Billie Burke in a Booth Tarkington play "Rose Briar." . . . "Why Not?" a divorce comedy by Jesse Lynch Williams. . . . Don Marquis's "The Old Soak." . . . Wallace Eddinger in "Captain Applejack." . . . "Abie's Irish Rose," described by reviewers as "something awful," and "just about as low as good clean fun can get"; however, it remained five years and five months, playing 2327 performances. . . . Balieff's "Chauve-Souris," a "rollicking Russian vaudeville." . . . "Six Characters in Search of an Author," translated from the Italian of Luigi Pirandello. . . . James Kirkwood and Lowell Sherman in "The Fool." . . . The Theatre Guild's "R. U. R." which added the word "robot" to our speech. . . . Olga Petrova in "The White Peacock," written by herself. . . . Jeanne Eagels in "Rain," adapted from Somerset Maugham's "Miss Thompson." . . . Pauline Lord in Eugene O'Neill's play "Anna Christie."

The Motion Pictures in 1922

The ten best pictures of the year, as determined by a vote of critics and editors conducted by *The Film Daily:* "Orphans of the Storm," "Prisoner of Zenda," "Nanook of the North," "Robin Hood," "Grandma's Boy," "When Knighthood Was in Flower," "Smilin' Through," "Oliver Twist," "Blood and Sand," "Tol'-able David."

1923

January 4.   Emile Coué, originator of a system of autosuggestion for the curing of mental and physical ills, arrived in New York City. A great crowd at the steamship pier cheered him as he landed. In New York M.

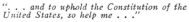
". . . and to uphold the Constitution of the United States, so help me . . ."

Violation of the prohibition law by those high in Governmental office, as well as the use of containers resembling books is hinted at in cartoon shown here by Frueh. One of the most familiar developments was the use of "book" containers, which gave rise to infinite punning about "best cellars."

Courtesy of the "New Yorker."

Coué organized a clinic, which he staffed with men and women familiar with his methods, and then he left for a lecture trip to the large cities of the Mid-West. Everywhere he was received with enthusiasm and even the largest halls were too small to contain the multitudes who wished to hear him. Part of his treatment consisted of having his patients repeat over and over the phrase, "Every day in every way I am getting better and better."

January 6. William D. Upshaw, ardent "dry" Congressman from Georgia, introduced in the House of Representatives a bill making the buyer of alcoholic beverages equally subject to penalties with the seller. Zealous "drys" were pleased; they wished strongly that the prohibition law should succeed; they felt that from the moral standpoint the buying of liquor was no better than the selling; and from the start they had maintained that the difficulties of enforcement would be multiplied by the practical immunity which the law gave to the purchaser. The bill did not pass. Both houses of Congress had "dry" majorities at this time, but the "wets," who were resourceful and energetic, were able to give to this and to other similar measures advocated by "drys" the color of "fanatical" and "extremist" legislation, thereby alienating from them the support of moderate "drys" and middle-of-the-roaders.

The British Debt Refunding

January 17. The British Debt-Funding Commission, unable to agree with the American negotiators as to the rate of interest to be paid on the approximately four billions of dollars owed by Britain to the United States, decided to return to England for further discussion with the home government. Of the two sides of the debt settlement question, that of Great Britain was set forth by Chancellor Stanley Baldwin on January 8 at the first meeting of the two commissions:

We have come with the express intention of repaying our debt, and it is owing to the practical difficulties of making international payments that we are about to consult with you in order to accomplish the end which we both have in view.

This debt is not a debt for dollars sent to Europe. The money was all expended here, most of it for cotton, wheat, food products and munitions of war. Every cent used for the purchase of these goods was spent in America; American labor received the wages; American capitalists the profits; the United States Treasury the taxation imposed on these profits.

The payment of our debt to you involves much more than the transfer of huge sums from London to Washington. It must affect the future wellbeing of both countries, and on their prosperity depends to a large extent that of the entire world. The payment of our debt to you will impose upon us the necessity of levying heavy taxes to meet these payments. From the beginning of the war we were the heaviest taxed nation in the world. The total annual per capita taxation in Great Britain is today still greater than that of any other people. It amounts to more than $100 per head of the population.

Further taxation would decrease the purchasing power of the British working men and reduce our consumption of American products. If we are unable to purchase from you, if we are forced by stern necessity to economize still further, to buy from you only those things we must have, the American farmer, as well as the American workingman, will feel the pinch.

We are not here to ask for favors or to impose on generosity. We want, on such terms as will produce the least possible disturbance in the trade relations of the two countries, a fair business settlement — a square deal — a settlement that will secure for America the repayment to the last cent of those credits which the United States Government established for us.

The other side of the question — at least, the view held by many Americans — was given by the Providence *News*:

Under the Treaty, the United States received no reparations; England took hers until she was gorged. She got nearly all the merchant shipping of Germany. She scrapped the German Navy, thereby eliminating her only great naval rival in European waters — and saving herself in naval expenditure two hundred millions a year, or enough to take care of the interest on the debt. She then killed Germany as a trade rival in manufactured steel and iron, as well as soft coal and lumber, by handing over to France and Poland some of the most fruitful mineral and forest territory of the former German monarchy. Finally the British statesmen took from Germany an entire empire in Africa, abounding in mineral wealth. England got all that and further reparations in gold that are to come from Germany. We got nothing except a big national debt, a pension list that will grow as the years roll by, 100,000 graves, and disabled soldiers that are costing us $450,000,000 a year.

Why we should concede anything on this debt question cannot be successfully answered. We borrowed this money from the people of the United States, and we pay interest semiannually at the average rate of four and one-quarter per cent. In order to meet the interest charges we have to collect from our own taxpayers more than two hundred millions a year. Everybody who pays a Federal tax pays some proportion of this sum, has done so for several years, and will continue to do so until Great Britain meets the annual interest rate.[1]

January. The introduction, several months previously, of a bill in the Kentucky Legislature forbidding the teaching of evolution in State-supported schools — which failed of passage by one vote — marked the beginning of a controversy over evolution which was to hold the attention of the country for years. Discussion gained new impetus in January, 1923, when a body of ministers at St. Paul, Minn., encouraged by William Jennings Bryan, denounced the theory of evolution as a "program of infidelity masquerading under the name of science," and called upon "Christians throughout the State to appeal to the Legislature to eliminate from all tax-supported schools this anti-scientific and anti-scriptural theory of man and the universe." In the newspapers people who thought as these ministers did came to be called "Fundamentalists"; those who took the opposite stand, "Modernists."

Quickly following the St. Paul meeting, the Modernists took up the debate. The Reverend J. G. Duling of Minneapolis said that the Fundamentalist leader, William Jennings Bryan, was "doing more harm to the cause of Christianity than any man before the public today; his ability as a speaker and his large following

[1] See Chapter 10.

among the masses make people think him an authority on the subject [whereas] the facts are that Mr. Bryan has never been an authority on any subject. [The effect of his oratory is to arouse] prejudice against educated people [and to engender the belief that if you want to be a true Christian] remain ignorant."

February 21. Secretary of the Treasury Mellon declined to accede to the formal demand of the House of Representatives to make public figures regarding importations of liquor into the United States by foreign diplomats.

March 31. The "Marathon Dance," by which is meant, as the name suggests, continuous dancing by couples day and night as long as the participants can keep awake and moving, had its start in America in a contest won by Miss Alma Cummings, who established a world's record of 27 hours. The idea seemingly originated in England and Scotland on the same day, March 6, when dances were held in Sunderland and Edinburgh, lasting respectively nine and one-half hours and fourteen hours thirty-six minutes. Following the first dance in New York the idea spread and soon Marathons were being held in half a dozen cities. Miss Cummings' performance was quickly surpassed. April 19, a record of 90 hours and 10 minutes was set at Cleveland.

A reporter of the New York *World*, covering a Marathon dance, wrote:

The dingy hall, littered with worn slippers, cigaret stubs, newspapers and soup cans; reeking with the mingled odors of stale coffee, tobacco smoke, cold broth, chewing-gum and smelling-salts, was the scene of one of the most drab and grueling endurance contests ever witnessed. There is nothing inspiring in seeing an extremely tired pretty girl in a worn bathrobe, dingy white stockings in rolls about scuffling felt slippers, her eyes half shut, her arms hung over her partner's shoulders, drag aching feet that seemed glued to the floor in one short, agonizing step after another. . . .

The sun sifted in, reporters and substitute dancers washed up, after a fashion, outsiders stopped to glance inside, and still the phonograph continued grinding out its slow, level jazz — until one never wanted to hear jazz again. Breakfast was served at 7:30. After that the dancing was more like dancing.

The first of a number of deaths attributed to over-

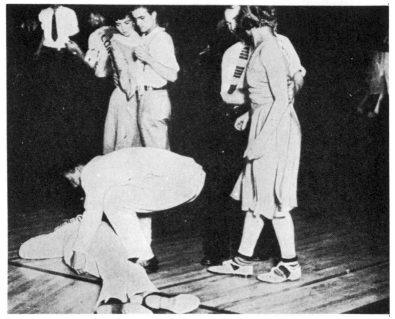

From a photograph by International News Photos, Inc.

Physical collapse of a dancer was a not uncommon incident of Marathon dances.

exertion caused by Marathon dancing was that of Homer Morehouse, twenty-seven, who in a dance at North Tonawanda, N. Y., dropped dead as he walked off the dance floor with his partner, after completing eighty-seven hours of continuous dancing.

April 30. The United States Supreme Court decided that American ships could carry and sell intoxicating liquors outside of the three-mile limit, but that both American and foreign ships were prohibited from bringing them into port.

May 9.   Judge John C. Knox of the United States District Court in New York held that under the prohibition law prescriptions of whiskey by physicians may not be limited.

May 25.   "Abolition of the 12-hour day in the steel industry is not now feasible, as it would add 15 per cent to the cost of making steel and would require 60,000 additional workers," stated Elbert H. Gary, head of the United States Steel Corporation, in presenting the report of a special committee which had made a study of the matter for President Harding.

June 13.   Secretary of State Hughes made public a letter to the British Ambassador, suggesting an extension of the 3-mile limit from its shores over which a nation exercises sovereignty to 12 miles, as a means of combating rum-running into the United States. The reply of Sir Auckland Geddes, published at the same time, expressed objection.

July 1.   Edward W. Bok of Philadelphia offered a prize of $100,000 to the American who should devise the best practical plan for co-operation of the United States with other nations in attaining and preserving world peace.

July 4.   Jack Dempsey won the decision in a 15-round fight with Tommy Gibbons at Shelby, Mont.

July 16.   Magnus Johnson, a farmer, was elected United States Senator from Minnesota to fill the vacancy caused by the death of Knute Nelson.

August 2.   President Warren G. Harding died.

August 3.   Vice-President Calvin Coolidge took the oath of office as President at 2:30 A.M.

August 17.   Following ratification by the French Chamber of Deputies and the French Senate, the Five-Power Naval Disarmament Treaty (concerted by the Disarmament Conference called at Washington by

President Harding in 1921) was signed in Washington.

September 1. A catastrophe combined of earthquake, tidal waves, and fire laid waste almost the whole of Tokyo and Yokohama, as well as several other cities

From a photograph by International News Photos, Inc.

The Dempsey-Gibbons fight.

on the eastern seaboard of Japan, where the mortality list was estimated at 150,000 to 300,000. The disaster was said to be the greatest of its kind in history.

September 9. While steaming through dense fog, seven United States destroyers were wrecked on the California coast off Arguello Light, seventy-five miles north of Santa Barbara. Twenty-two sailors were reported missing.

September 14.   At the Polo Grounds in New York
City, Jack Dempsey, heavyweight champion, defeated
Luis Angel Firpo of Argentina in the second round of
what was said to have been the greatest heavyweight bat-

From a photograph by Underwood & Underwood.

A bizarre Senator from Minnesota, Magnus Johnson, who was one of the early
manifestations of farm discontent, taking part in a milking contest.

tle of modern times.   In the first round Firpo, after being
floored seven times by Dempsey, knocked the champion
out of the ring.   The gate receipts totalled $1,082,600.

September 18.   Twenty-five hundred web pressmen
went on an "outlaw" strike in New York, and all but one
of the large metropolitan newspapers failed to appear.
The strike lasted a week, during which the large dailies
joined in issuing an eight-page sheet containing news
but no advertising except theatre advertisements.

October 6. A tall man "with white teeth flashing from a grease-blackened face" climbed out of the cockpit of a tiny Curtiss plane at St. Louis, and immediately word went out by telephone and telegraph to the far corners of the country that Naval Lieutenant A. L. Wil-

The Combined New York Morning Newspapers

New York American
THE NEW YORK HERALD
The Journal of Commerce
DAILY NEWS
The Morning Telegraph

The New York Times.
New York Tribune
The World.
New-Yorker Staats-Zeitung
IL PROGRESSO ITALO-AMERICANO

Vol. LXXXIII No. 28,066		Wednesday, September 19, 1923				
Peters Not in Gunman Car, Ward Admits	Visit by Lloyd George Expected by Coolidge	Oklahoma's Legislators Defy Walton	White Star and Cunard Merge Winter Service	Wilson Ready ToRunAgain, Say Friends	Pressmen's Chief Orders End to Walk-Out at Once	Press Strike Is Denounced As 'Outlaw'

When the New York morning newspapers, on account of a printers' strike, September 19, 1923, united in one issue for all.

liams, formerly a baseball pitcher for the New York Giants, had broken the world's speed record for airplanes, flying at the rate of 243.67 miles per hour over a 125-mile triangular course marked off for the Pulitzer Trophy contest. This was 38 miles an hour faster than the mark set by Army Lieutenant Maughan in the previous year's Pulitzer contest.

October 8. Monday. Frenzied inflation of the German currency reached a point where one United States cent would buy six and a quarter million paper marks. Tuesday, the same coin would buy fourteen million marks. Wednesday morning it could buy twenty-five million marks; and Wednesday afternoon sixty-five million marks.[2]

[2] The Berlin humorous paper *Ulk* used the collapse of the mark as the subject for a somewhat labored joke:

Housewife: "What! 20,000 marks? I only paid 10,000 last time."
Shopkeeper: "Ah, that was in the good old times of half an hour ago."

October 26.   Charles P. Steinmetz, renowned as a mathematician and experimenter in electricity, died suddently at his home in Schenectady, N. Y. Born a hunchback at Breslau, Germany, April 9, 1865, son of a government railroad official, he studied at the Universities of Breslau and Berlin and later at the Polytechnic in Zurich, Switzerland. Becoming embroiled with the German police because of his association with Socialists, he travelled steerage to America, accompanied by an American with whom he had struck up a friendship while a student. At New York, immigration inspectors, viewing his stunted body, feared he might become a public charge and were loath to grant him entrance. Released from Ellis Island he set about finding a job and eventually secured one as draftsman at $2 per day with Rudolph Eickemeyer, an inventor, manufacturer, and pioneer in electrical research. Here his extraordinary genius quickly manifested itself. When Eickemeyer's business was purchased by the General Electric Company, Steinmetz went with it. He was transferred from New York to Schenectady and given a great laboratory where he could make whatever experiments he chose. At his request no salary was paid him, but he was given an open account on which he could draw at will and in any amount. He lived frugally and on his death left an estate consisting of a $1500 insurance policy and a ten-year-old automobile.

Steinmetz[3] was the outstanding example in America of the close relationship between modern science and modern industry. His work did not consist merely of applying the results of scientific inventions to business. On the contrary, he was the exponent both of pure science and applied science, devoting himself to research and inventions which, with his farseeing eye, he counted

[3] From an obituary account in the New York *Times*.

on to result in ultimate benefit to industry and through it to society as a whole, as well as dealing with problems of immediate importance to the company which employed him.

An example of Steinmetz's devotion to pure science

Charles P. Steinmetz.

was his invention of a lightning generator, which was given wide publicity in 1922. For producing in his laboratory at Schenectady an "indoor thunderstorm," hurling a bolt of artificial lightning with the energy of 1,000,000 horse-power, and getting the shattering effect of real lightning, he was likened to Jove.

Steinmetz was greatly interested in efforts to produce "cold light," which would be much more efficient and economical than ordinary electric light. He frequently said that steam locomotives were doomed to be supplanted by electric ones and that the change would not be long delayed.

Steinmetz spoke often on the relation of science and religion, denying that they are necessarily incompatible. He declared that science had not disproved the beliefs on which religion is founded, and that the question was "still open."

November 10. In an Armistice Day address to the nation, Woodrow Wilson declared that the attitude of the United States in withdrawing "into a sullen and selfish isolation" from our associates in the World War was "cowardly and dishonorable."

November 14. A scene enacted on the crowded ticket platform at 55th Street, Brooklyn, where the subway runs on elevated tracks, typifies the boldness and ruthlessness of city bandits during the 1920's. Two employees of the West End Bank, Barlow and McLaughlin, carrying $43,607, left a train and approached the stairs leading to the street. Barlow, a retired police detective-sergeant, marched ahead with one hand on a gun in his overcoat pocket and carrying in the other a decoy satchel stuffed with newspapers. Behind him, McLaughlin, a younger man who had served in the Great War, assistant teller of the bank, carried the actual money wrapped in old newspapers and oilcloth, like a kit of tools. As Barlow appeared in the door leading to the stairway, a tall man who had been standing in full view of the street pointed a revolver carefully at his head and fired twice. Barlow, trying to pull his gun, went down, stone dead. The bandit grabbed his bag and bolted for the stairs. At the same time a short stocky man beside him opened up a fusillade at McLaughlin, who was rushing forward. Spun half-way around by the impact of a steel-jacketed bullet through his chest, the ex-soldier staggered half-way across the landing, still headed toward the bandits. Two other shots finished him. The stocky bandit grabbed his money bundle and thundered down the stairs after the other. On the crowded corner

CROOKS ADMIT ROBBING TO PAY LAWYERS' FEES

THE SACRAMENTO BEE

VOL. 130

Chicago Bandits Usher In 1922 With Many Crimes

Kill Storekeeper, Kidnap Two Couples in Auto and Rob Them of $10,000 in Gems

2 Chinese Slain; White Wife of One Missing

Orientals Found Hacked to Death With Cleaver in West Side Rooms Where Girl Often Was a Visitor

BANK BANDIT SUSPECT DIES, TWO OFFICERS SHOT IN FIGHT

Robber Kills Gem Dealer; Shoots Wife

Wounded Woman Fights Slayer of Aged Husband in Home; Gives Alarm That Leads to Capture

Guard Kills Look-Out as Bandits Flee

Negro Marksman Halts 6 Who Rob Woman Attache of San Juan Hill TenementOffice of $800

THE CHICAGO

352 MURDERS IN YEAR

Two Killings In City-Wide Bandit Raids

2 Slain and 2 Shot in Battle Of Thugs and Bank Helpers

Bullets Fly When Pearl River Cashier Resists Gunmen and Bandits Flee Without a Dollar

Wounds Robber as He Falls and Dies

ʝe Boston

STON, WEDNESDAY MORNING, DECE

THIRD MARANGI BROTHER IS SHOT

Leo Attacked in Crowded Poolroom Near Station 1

The *Literary Digest* assembles some current headlines to illustrate the most conspicuous news of the Christmas period.

below an automobile with motor running had been waiting for an hour. At the sound of the first shot, its doors were thrown open by a dark-faced man who bent forward watching the stairway. The two bandits jumped into this car, which roared away at seventy miles an hour, in a cloud of smoke. The car was later found abandoned — it had been stolen. The bandits never were caught.

November 21. Doctor Frederick A. Cook, one-time Arctic explorer, who in 1909 claimed that he was the discoverer of the North Pole, was convicted at Fort Worth, Texas, of using the mails to conduct oil swindles and sentenced to fourteen years and nine months of imprisonment and fined $12,000. Twelve of his associates were also fined and sentenced to prison.

During and after the trial Doctor Cook insisted that he had not been guilty of wrongdoing — "I wouldn't swindle anybody." He said he would not be able to appeal his case because he had lost all his own money, $14,000, in the promotions.

The Books of 1923

"The Rover," by Joseph Conrad, a romance of the Napoleonic wars. . . . "Deirdre," by James Stephens, a retelling of the tragic story of an Irish queen. . . . "The Enchanted April," by "Elizabeth." . . . "Black Oxen," by Gertrude Atherton, a "caricature of gland rejuvenation." . . . "Jennifer Lorn," by Elinor Wylie, "a sedate extravaganza." . . . "His Children's Children," by Arthur Train. . . . "J. Hardin and Son," by Brand Whitlock. . . . "Lummox," by Fannie Hurst. . . . "The Quare Woman," by Lucy Furman. . . . "A Lost Lady," by Willa Cather. . . . "Bread," by Charles G. Norris. . . . "Doctor Nye," by Joseph C. Lincoln. . . . "Wheels Within Wheels," by Carolyn Wells. . . . Margaret Wilson's "The Able McLaughlins," Pulitzer prize winner and Harper prize novel. . . . "Faint Perfume," by Zona Gale. . . . "The Florentine Dagger," by Ben Hecht. . . . "Through the Wheat," by Thomas Boyd. . . . "From Immigrant to Inventor," by Michael Pupin, winner of the Pulitzer prize for biography.

The Theatre in 1923

In January the Moscow Art Theatre troupe arrived, under the chaperonage of Morris Gest; the performances of the first week were "jammed with the elite." . . . Genevieve Tobin in "Polly Preferred." . . .

Left: Lon Chaney in "The Hunchback of Notre Dame." *Right:* A scene from the motion picture "Scaramouche."

Louis Mann and George Sidney in "Give and Take." . . . "Icebound," by Owen Davis. . . . Philip Barry's "You and I." . . . Rachel Crothers's "Mary the 3d." . . . Henry Miller in "The Changelings," a comedy by Lee Wilson Dodd. . . . Ethel Barrymore in "The Laughing Lady." . . . Laurette Taylor in Fanny Hurst's "Humoresque." . . . Cyril Maude in "If Winter Comes" was not very successful; it ran for five weeks at the end of which time Mr. Maude produced a new comedy "Aren't We All?" which scored a big success. . . . Alice Brady in "Zander the Great." . . . Lynn Fontanne and Ralph Morgan in "In Love with Love." . . . Madge Kennedy and W. C. Fields in "Poppy." . . . Emily Stevens and William Faversham in "A Lesson in Love," an English importation. . . . Lowell Sherman and Katharine Cornell in "Casanova." . . . Eva LeGallienne, Basil Rathbone, and Philip Merivale in a comedy by Ferenc Molnar, "The Swan." . . . Lionel Barrymore and Ian Keith in "Laugh, Clown, Laugh!" . . . Fred Stone introduced his daughter Dorothy in "Stepping Stones." . . . Donald Meek in "The Potters." . . . Earl Carroll's "Vanities," with a cast headed by Peggy Hopkins Joyce and Joe Cook. . . . In October Eleanor Duse paid her last visit to America. . . . Walter Hampden revived "Cyrano de Bergerac."

The Motion Pictures in 1923

The ten best pictures of the year, as determined by a vote of critics and editors conducted by the *Film Daily*: "Covered Wagon," "Robin Hood," "Safety Last," "Little Old New York," "Merry-Go-Round," "Green Goddess," "Rosita," "Hunchback of Notre Dame," "Scaramouche," "Down to the Sea in Ships."

1924

January 1.   A picturesque and erratic soldier, Brigadier-General Smedley D. Butler, on leave from the Marine Corps of which he was the head, began his duties as "Director of Public Safety" of the City of Philadelphia. He had been appointed because of pressure from Philadelphians desirous of better enforcement of the liquor laws. Philadelphia had a foretaste of the bizarre and spectacular methods Butler was to pursue when on taking office he called the city's police force before him for a harangue:

The Lieutenants know their districts and the bad spots in them. Let them go out and clean them up. We won't want any help from reformers. We don't want any help from the Marines, or the Constabulary, or anybody else. Good God Almighty, men, let's do the damned thing ourselves! Hell! We don't want any pussyfooting squads around. Put on your uniforms and go after 'em. . . .

At first the people of Philadelphia accorded generous support to Butler, but in time came to feel distaste for what they regarded as undignified showmanship on his part. Opposition to him became so general by the Fall of 1925 that President Coolidge was forced to take account of it; on November 3, he rescinded Butler's leave and ordered him to return to duty with the Marine Corps.

January 21.   Nikolai Lenin (V. I. Ulianov), 54, leader of the Russian Revolution of 1917 and organizer of the Communist Government of Russia, died in a village near Moscow, of apoplexy.

February 4.   Charles Herbert Levermore, of New York, Secretary of the New York Peace Society, student of international relations, writer, and former college President, was announced as the winner of the Bok Peace Prize for the best plan by which America might help to preserve world peace. He received half of the $100,000

From a photograph by Brown Brothers.

President and Mrs. Coolidge on the grounds of the White House.

prize, the remainder to be given if his proposals should be accepted by Congress or endorsed by the American people. His plan advocated adherence by the United States to the Permanent Court of International Justice and close co-operation with the League of Nations.

February 15. Senator Frank L. Greene of Vermont was accidentally shot and seriously wounded, as an innocent bystander, during a pistol fight between prohibition agents and bootleggers on the streets of down-town Washington.

February 18. Secretary of the Navy Edwin L. Denby resigned.[1]

March 1. By a vote of 66 to 1, the Senate passed a resolution introduced by Senator Wheeler of Montana providing for an investigation of Attorney-General Daugherty and the Department of Justice.[2]

March 8. The value of the French franc fell to 3.4 cents American money on the Paris Exchange. Prior to the Great War the franc had been worth 19.3 cents. During the War and until 1920 it had been held at between nine and ten cents. Its fluctuations thereafter, until its drop in March, 1924, are shown below:

Jan. 2, 1920	9.30c	Jan. 2, 1924	5.00c
Jan. 2, 1921	5.91	Feb. 1, 1924	4.70
Jan. 2, 1922	8.00	Mar. 1, 1924	4.19
Jan. 2, 1923	7.20	Mar. 8, 1924	3.42

In 1928, it was fixed by law at 3.92.

Uneasiness created in world financial centres by the fall of the franc was dispelled in large part on March 12 when it was announced in New York that the banking firm of J. P. Morgan and Company had placed at the disposal of the Bank of France a credit of "not less than $100,000,000."

March 18. The Soldiers' Bonus bill, involving a cost to the Treasury of more than $2,000,000,000, was passed by the House of Representatives by a vote of 355 to 54. The bill provided twenty-year paid-up endowment insurance policies for the majority of ex-service men. Only those entitled to adjusted compensation of $50 or less were to be paid cash. April 23, the bill passed the Senate, 67 to 17. May 15, President Coolidge vetoed it. May 17, the House, and May 19, the Senate, repassed it over the Executive veto.

[1] See page 342.   [2] See Chapter II.

March 31. Oregon's compulsory school law, which prohibited children of grammar-school age from attending any but public schools, was declared unconstitutional in an opinion handed down by the Federal Court in Portland. The law, adopted by initiative at the general election in 1922 by a vote of 115,506 to 103,685, had been opposed chiefly by Catholics and Lutherans.

Challenge of the constitutionality of the law had been begun by the Society of the Sisters of the Holy Name of Jesus and Mary, in behalf of parochial schools, and by the Hill Military Academy, in behalf of non-sectarian private schools. Aligned with these were the Protestant Episcopal Church, the Seventh Day Adventists, and the American Jewish Committee, all of whom filed briefs with the court supporting the position of the petitioners.

Following the decision of the Portland court the Governor of Oregon carried the case to the Supreme Court of the United States. The Supreme Court, January 1, 1925, held the law unconstitutional.

April 2. Harlan Fiske Stone, dean of Columbia University Law School, was appointed Attorney-General to succeed Harry M. Daugherty, resigned. The Senate concurred in the appointment April 6.

April 5. Two men were killed and thirteen injured in a battle between residents of the small Pennsylvania town of Lilly and a mob of about 500 men from a near-by city wearing the regalia of the Ku Klux Klan. Twenty-six of the invaders were put in jail.

April 8. Senator Burton K. Wheeler, prosecutor of the Senate Daugherty investigating committee, was indicted in Great Falls, Mont., on a charge of unlawfully receiving money as a retainer fee to influence the issuance of oil and gas prospecting permits by the Secretary of the Interior and the Commissioner of the General

Land Office. Wheeler declared the charges were groundless and had been brought against him in retaliation for his investigation of Attorney-General Daugherty. In the ensuing trial Wheeler was exonerated.

April 11. Japanese Ambassador Hanihara lodged with the State Department a protest against proposals being discussed in Congress to further restrict Japanese immigration to the United States. He protested that the "gentleman's agreement" between the two countries was adequate to the wants of the United States, and that discriminatory legislation against Japanese would wound the national susceptibilities of the Japanese people and be attended by the "gravest consequences." Use of this phrase by the Ambassador was unfortunate; it provoked an overwhelming rejection by the Senate (76 to 2) of a resolution calling for a continuance of the "gentleman's agreement" arrangement, and paved the way for adoption of a resolution barring all Japanese immigration. By the "gentleman's agreement," Japan had herself exercised restraint on emigration of her citizens to the United States.

April 15. Governor Alfred E. Smith of New York announced his candidacy for the Democratic Presidential nomination before the Democratic New York State Convention, which unanimously endorsed him.

May 15. Both Houses of Congress, after conference, passed the Johnson Immigration bill. (President Coolidge signed it May 26.) This put restriction of immigration into the United States on a permanent basis. It reduced the total of aliens to be permitted to enter the country from roughly 350,000, as provided in the law of 1921, to roughly 150,000. Admissions were to be on a quota basis, 2 per cent of the number of persons of foreign birth residing in the United States in 1890.

Passage of the Johnson bill through Congress had

been watched with interest and approval by the public. Opposition to it came chiefly from liberals and radicals and the newer American stock. Objection to the bill on sentimental grounds was voiced by the Baltimore *Sun* (Democratic):

The United States abandons definitely and perhaps finally that old and admirable tradition that this land was to serve as a refuge for the oppressed of all nations. No longer is the foreigner, to American eyes, a welcome fugitive from the political, economic and religious oppression of the Old World.

The good effects which advocates of immigration restriction believed the Johnson law would bring were stated by Senator Reed of Pennsylvania:

No law passed by Congress within the last half century compares with this one in its importance upon the future development of our nation. Its adoption means that America of our grandchildren will be a vastly better place to live in. It will mean a more homogeneous nation, more self-reliant, more independent, and more closely knit by common purpose and common ideas.

Among the strongest supporters of the Johnson bill was organized labor.

May 26. Victor Herbert, one of America's most popular music composers, died suddenly on the way to his physician. He was born in Dublin on February 1, 1859, the son of Edward and Fannie Lover Herbert. His grandfather, Samuel Lover, was the Irish novelist.

Herbert was regarded as the American equivalent of the British composer, Sir Arthur Sullivan. He wrote the catchy airs for "The Serenade," "The Singing Girl," "Babes in Toyland," "Mlle. Modiste," "Princess Pat," "Orange Blossoms," and dozens of other musical comedies. It was upon these, and not his more serious works — operas, oratorios, and symphonic overtures — that his fame rested.

May 27. The Methodist Episcopal General Conference at Springfield, Mass., lifted the ban on dancing and theatre attendance, leaving it to the individual conscience to decide what amusements one might indulge in.

June 9. A unanimous decision of the United States Supreme Court upheld the Willis-Campbell Act of November, 1921, which provided that not beer but "only spirituous and vinous liquors may be prescribed for medicinal purposes." This decision closed a leak in the prohibition dam caused by Attorney-General Palmer's ruling, just before the end of the Wilson Administration, that beer is a medicine within the meaning of the Prohibition Enforcement Act.

June 12. Calvin Coolidge and Charles Gates Dawes were nominated for President and Vice-President respectively by the Republican National Convention.

June 15. It was announced that during the preceding week the Ford Motor Company had made its 10-millionth automobile. It took Ford seven years to make his first million; the tenth million were made in 132 working days.

June 24. Lieut. Russell L. Maughan, Army Air Service, set a new transcontinental air flight record, flying from New York to San Francisco, 2680 miles, in 18 hours and 26 minutes.

July 2. Gaston B. Means, convicted of accepting bribes to obtain whiskey withdrawal permits, was sentenced to two years in the Atlanta penitentiary and fined $10,000.

July 9. John W. Davis, a native of West Virginia and formerly Ambassador to Great Britain, and Charles W. Bryan, Governor of Nebraska and brother of William Jennings Bryan, were nominated for the Presidency and Vice-Presidency by the Democratic National Convention at New York. Selection of Davis, on the 103d ballot, had been a compromise. The convention, one of the longest of record, had been deadlocked by the rival candidacies of William G. McAdoo, son-in-law of

From a photograph by Underwood & Underwood.

Gaston B. Means as a witness at one of the innumerable investigations to which he contributed picturesque testimony. He figured as defendant in several criminal trials and had, perhaps, the distinction of being the most miscellaneous and colossal liar of his time. If any excelled him their superiority did not emerge in public life.

Woodrow Wilson and war-time Secretary of the Treasury, and Alfred E. Smith, Governor of New York.

July 13. At Paris, for the eighth consecutive time since the modern revival of the Olympic games, American athletes won first place, with a total of 255 points. Finland was second with 166, and Great Britain third with 85½.

August 16. Germany and the Allies signed an agreement putting into effect the "Dawes Plan" for untangling the snarl of German reparations payments. The Dawes

Plan, which had been prepared by three Americans—Charles Gates Dawes and Henry M. Robinson, bankers, and Owen D. Young, industrialist — provided in substance that Germany should pay the Allies the first year $250,000,000 (and thereafter increasing amounts) obtained from railroads, loans, and industry; that a bank should be set up in Germany to act as the depository and fiscal agent of the German government; that the Allies and the United States should loan Germany $200,000,000; that the French troops occupying the Ruhr should be withdrawn.

July 18.   Senator Burton K. Wheeler, Democrat of Montana, was chosen to run on the Progressive ticket with Senator Robert M. LaFollette for the Presidency and Vice-Presidency, by the National Committee of the "Conference for Progressive Political Action."

August 21.   It was announced from Jerusalem that an American automobile had travelled in four hours the route of the Exodus, across the Sinai Desert, a distance of 130 miles. The exodus of the Israelites had lasted 40 years.

August.   In the Summer of 1924 talk about war-born power development at Muscle Shoals, Ala., reached the peak of what was to be a 15-year debate over what disposition should be made of the properties, into which the National Government had put more than $100,000,000. Senator George Norris of Nebraska advocated Government ownership and operation. At this time Congress had under consideration four offers from private interests — a fifth, from Henry Ford, had been withdrawn shortly before. Ultimately all the proposals for private operation were rejected and the dams and power houses (in 1933) were placed under the management of a Government corporation, the Tennessee Valley Authority.

August 23. Mrs. Miriam A. Ferguson, known as "Ma" Ferguson, won the Democratic nomination for Governor of Texas by more than 80,000 votes. She was

From a photograph by International News Photos, Inc.

The Prince of Wales during his visit in 1919 reviews the "middies" at Annapolis. The man with high hat and cane on the left is Franklin D. Roosevelt, then Assistant Secretary of the Navy. The other man in a high hat is Josephus Daniels, then Secretary of the Navy.

elected and became the first woman Governor of a State.

August 28. The Prince of Wales arrived on a visit to the United States.

September 3. Edward F. ("Pop") Geers, called the "Grand Old Man of the Turf," was killed in a fall while racing at Wheeling, W. Va.

September 27. Robert Tyre Jones, of Atlanta, Ga.,

won the national amateur golf championship, when in the final round of the twenty-eighth tournament of the United States Golfers Association, played at the Merion Cricket Club, Ardmore, Pa., he defeated George Von Elm, nine up and eight to play.

October 15. The dirigible airship *ZR–3* ended a

"Pop" Geers.

flight from Friedrichshafen, Germany, to Lakehurst, N. J., covering 5066 miles in 81 hours and 17 minutes. After being taken over by the U. S. Navy it was renamed the *Los Angeles*.

October 23. Records of the Internal Revenue Bureau giving the names of income-tax payers of 1923 and the amounts paid were opened to the public. Among those whose payments were smaller than the public had anticipated were John D. Rockefeller, Sr., whose $124,266 was in striking contrast to his son's tax of $7,435,169; J. P. Morgan, whose income tax of $98,643 was less than that paid by some other members of his firm; and Harry F. Sinclair, of Teapot Dome fame, whose 1923 income yielded a Federal income tax of only $213. Henry Ford paid $2,467,946; Edsel Ford $1,984,254;

Lew Dockstader.

Secretary of the Treasury Mellon $1,173,987; Clarence H. Mackay $488,353. Mary Roberts Rinehart, novelist, led the list of writers with a payment of $42,612. Douglas Fairbanks, moving picture actor, paid $225,679.

October 25. Laura Jean Libbey, novelist, died in Brooklyn, N. Y., aged 62.

October 26. Lew Dockstader, famous American minstrel of the early years of the century, died in New York, at the age of 68.

October 27. Percy D. Haughton, football coach, died suddenly of acute indigestion, at the age of 48. When Haughton became coach at Harvard in the Fall of 1908, the Harvard team was reaching the end of a ten-year period during which no games had been won against Harvard's rival, Yale, and few against other

One of Reginald Birch's illustrations for Mrs. Burnett's "Little Lord Fauntleroy."

strong teams. In Haughton's first year, Harvard won from Yale, 4 to 0, and thereafter victories by Harvard became frequent. "Haughton's passing [wrote Grantland Rice] was much after the manner of a brilliant flame that suddenly dies out to leave the field in darkness. He was something more than a great coach. He was an inspiration such as few may ever chance to know."

October 29. Mrs. Frances Hodgson Burnett, author of "Little Lord Fauntleroy," and famous as a novelist and playwright for nearly half a century, died. She was born in Manchester, England, in 1849.

November 4.   Calvin Coolidge and Charles G. Dawes, Republicans, were elected President and Vice-President.

November 9.   Henry Cabot Lodge, United States Senator from Massachusetts, died, aged 74.

November 21.   Mrs. Florence Kling Harding, widow of President Harding, died at Marion, Ohio.

November 25.   For the first time since the beginning of radio broadcasting, people in New York, New Jersey, and Connecticut heard programs broadcast from the British Isles and continental Europe, as an incident of "International Radio Week."

December 1.   Photographs, of President Coolidge and the Prince of Wales, were successfully transmitted by radio from London to New York.

December 13.   Samuel Gompers, President of the American Federation of Labor and for a generation the dominating force in organized labor in America, died at San Antonio, Texas, aged 74, after a short illness starting when he was in Mexico City attending a labor congress. Gompers' creed for labor, which he had never changed in all the years from his beginning as a leader, was brief and simple. He believed in conciliation and negotiation in disputes between worker and employer and resort to strikes and other methods of violence only after peaceful efforts had failed. Always he opposed alliances of labor with political parties and also the formation of a political labor party.

May 21.   At 4 o'clock in the afternoon[3] (Wednesday) thirteen-year-old Bobby Franks, son of Jacob Franks, millionaire retired pawnbroker and real estate investor, left the exclusive Harvard School, in the Hyde Park section of Chicago, to walk a few blocks to his home. He stopped for a ball-game with some school-

[3] Paraphrased from a story by Rowland Thomas in the New York *World*.

mates, then went on. An automobile, described at first as a gray touring car, was standing near the curb. Little Irving Hartmann, nine, saw Robert beside this vehicle. Irving turned to look at a tulip. When he looked ahead again, Robert was not in sight. The car was gathering headway down the street.

That night, in the Franks home, there was increasing uneasiness over Bobby's failure to appear. Finally alarmed, the father sent for his friend and attorney, Samuel A. Ettelson. At 10 P.M., while they were talking, the telephone rang. Mrs. Franks answered; after listening for a few moments she screamed and fell to the floor in a faint. Revived, she turned her husband's anxiety into panic. On the phone a man who said his name was Johnson had told her that Robert had been kidnaped and was being held for ransom. "Don't try to trace this call to find me," he had warned. "It will be no use. We must have money. We will let you know to-morrow what we want, and if you don't give us what we ask for we will kill the boy."

Lawyer Ettelson called the telephone superintendent and asked that a watch be made of any other incoming calls. None came and Mr. Franks, after waiting in suspense till 2 A.M., went with the lawyer to Police Headquarters and told what had happened, insisting on secrecy for the time being.

Thursday at 9 A.M. a special delivery letter arrived at the Franks home. It had been written on a typewriter and bore the typed signature "George Johnson":

"Your boy is safe and you need not worry. But if you let the police know, we will kill him. If you have already informed them, go no further. We want $10,000 ransom."

Then followed instructions to make up the sum in worn bills of specified denominations and place it in a cigar-box. Mr. Franks was told he would receive a telephone call at 1 P.M. giving "all necessary information as to how you are to put the money in our possession."

The father had promised to go to City Hall that forenoon and report the kidnaping to Chief of Police Collins, but instead he got $10,000 from his bank and waited for word from the kidnapers. At 1 o'clock, the telephone rang. Answering, he received a message from "Mr. Johnson" giving him instructions about delivering the money.

Mr. Franks set out alone in a car with his cigar-box of currency, but in his excitement he had forgotten where "Mr. Johnson" had told him to go. He returned home. Now came a startling development. About 9:30 that morning a laborer had been tramping a marshy ditch alongside the Pennsylvania Railroad right-of-way on the outskirts of Chicago. In a culvert connecting two small ponds near the track he saw something white. It was the nude body of a boy. The police were called. They found several wounds on the head of the corpse, and brown stains on the face and lips. Search of the vicinity yielded only two clues — a single woollen stocking and a pair of shell-rimmed spectacles, which an undertaker's assistant stuck upon the face of the dead boy before he was taken to the morgue.

The afternoon papers printed the story, and Lawyer Ettelson read it just after Jacob Franks had set out with the ransom money. At the morgue identification was made of the corpse as Bobby Franks. All this Mr. Franks learned on returning home, still with the cigar-box of money in his possession.

On Friday, the second day after the abduction, the horn-rimmed spectacles began to come in for attention and the mistake made by the undertaker's assistant was rectified. Robert Franks had never worn glasses. Aside from the one stocking, the glasses afforded the only clue found near the culvert.

But another forward step had been taken through examination of the typewritten note received by Mr. Franks. An expert was sure it had been written on a portable machine of a certain make, built prior to April 1914, when the manufacturers had changed the arrangement of their keyboard.

The spectacles had been the object of a thorough inquiry. They were unusual. Their thick lenses betrayed their wearer as squinty-eyed and myopic. The frame, only six inches wide at the temples, indicated an extremely narrow head. It was even possible the wearer had been a woman.

After days of investigation, the manufacturer of the spectacles was found — an optical company in Brooklyn. Then the Chicago distributor, an optical supply house, was discovered. In the files of this supply house were thousands of prescriptions, which had to be gone over patiently, one by one, till the right one was unearthed.

The oculist was found. His office records in turn disclosed the name and address of a patient. Promptly followed two arrests which at first made all Chicago reel with incredulous amazement.

Nathan Leopold, Jr., and Richard Loeb, both about nineteen, were accused of the murder. Both were counted the youngest, most brilliant and most promising graduates of their respective universities, Chicago and Michigan. Both were post-graduate students at the University of Chicago. Both had attended the Harvard School. Both were sons of leading Jewish families of the city. Leopold's father had been for years a commanding figure in Lake transportation, and was rated many times a millionaire. Albert H. Loeb, Richard's father, was vice-president of the great mail-order house of Sears, Roebuck & Co.

Leopold, identified as the owner of the glasses, accepted his predicament with equanimity. First he denied ownership of the glasses; he had a pair like them,

From a photograph by International News Photos, Inc.

Nathan Leopold, Jr., and Richard Loeb, sons of wealthy Chicago families who confessed killing and kidnapping fourteen-year-old Bobby Franks for the "thrill of it." Clarence Darrow, seated between them, saved them from the gallows. They were sentenced to life imprisonment and 99 years.

but they were at his home. Confronted then by the empty case which had been found in his father's residence, he wondered if he had lost the spectacles the Saturday before the murder. He had that day been, as it happened, close to the culvert in the marshy prairie — a locality he often visited to study bird life, being an ornithologist. Yes, he mused aloud, he must have dropped them in the grass there.

His composure was disconcerting. But his questioners knew one thing he had overlooked — a very small thing. For four days previous to the night Robert Frank's body was shoved into the culvert there had been almost constant rain. The weather had cleared late on Wednesday afternoon. A pair of glasses lying in the marsh through those four rainy days would have been spotted with mud. Leopold's, when found, were clean and shining. The inquisition continued. Leopold was asked to give an account of his movements on Wednesday. He gave it in convincing fashion. Loeb, questioned separately, told essentially the same story. As an alibi, it was perfect. But as a defense it was pathetic, had the culprits realized that the police following custom would check back on all their statements. Doing so, they pried out the brick that brought the wall down. Sven Englund, the Leopold family's head chauffeur, told them young Nathan's car had been in the garage all Wednesday — the day the crime was committed — for repair of defective brakes. The two boys had said that on Wednesday afternoon they had toured about for several hours in Nathan's machine.

After a trial in which the two youthful murderers were defended by Clarence Darrow, famous radical and criminal lawyer, Judge Caverly on September 10 imposed sentence of life imprisonment on the murder count and ninety-nine years each on the kidnaping charge. So universal had been the expectation that the youths would be given the death penalty that Judge Caverly's decision came as a surprise. In the year this volume was published, 1935, the two youths were still in prison.

Books in 1924

"Blind Raftery," by Donn Byrne. . . . "The White Monkey," by John Galsworthy, a continuation of the Forsyte family chronicle. . . . "The Little French Girl," by Anne Douglas Sedgwick. . . . "The Green Hat," by Michael Arlen. . . . "The Glory Hole," by

Stewart Edward White. ,... "Balisand," by Joseph Hergesheimer, the tragic love story of a Virginia aristocrat of 1800.... "The Avalanche," by Ernest Poole. ... "So Big," by Edna Ferber, won the Pulitzer prize. "The Green Bay Tree," by Louis Bromfield, the story of the growth of an Ohio city through fifty years.... "The Tattooed Countess," by Carl Van Vechten.... "Rugged Water," by Joseph C. Lincoln.... "Are Parents People?" by Alice Duer Miller.... "The Constant Nymph," by Margaret Kennedy.... "Beggars of Life," by Jim Tully, being a realistic account of the author's life as a hobo — a best seller.... "Barrett Wendell and His Letters," by M. A. DeWolf Howe, winner of the Pulitzer prize for biography.

The Theatre in 1924

"The Miracle," a German pantomime, with Lady Diana Manners as the Madonna, and Rosamond Pinchot as the Nun.... "Outward Bound," by Sutton Vane, with Alfred Lunt, Leslie Howard and Margalo Gilmore.... "Charlot's Revue," imported from London.... "The Goose Hangs High."... George Kelly's "The Show-Off."... "Beggar on Horseback."... Jane Cowl in "Antony and Cleopatra." ... "The Outsider," with Lionel Atwill and Katharine Cornell.... Mrs. Fiske in "Helena's Boys." ... An all-star revival of "Leah Kleschna."... Judith Anderson, Ralph Morgan and Louis Calhern in "Cobra."... The Four Marx Brothers in "I'll Say She Is."... Mistinguett, the French soubrette, in "Innocent Eyes."... Two of William Congreve's comedies of the Restoration, "Love for Love" and "The Way of the World."... Bernard Shaw's "Cæsar and Cleopatra" was the opening attraction for the new Guild Theatre.... Elizabeth Hines in "Marjorie."...

"Dancing Mothers." . . . "Lady, Be Good." . . .
"Ladies of the Evening." . . . "Quarantine," a ro-
mantic comedy with Sidney Blackmer and Helen Hayes.
. . . George Arliss in "Old English." . . . Henry

Photograph by White Studio.

Beatrice Lillie, Jack Buchannan and Gertrude Lawrence in the "First Charlot's Review."

Miller in "The Man in Evening Clothes." . . .
"What Price Glory," by Maxwell Anderson and Lau-
rence Stallings, the outstanding dramatic success of the
season. . . .

The Motion Pictures in 1924

The ten best pictures of the year, as determined by a
vote of critics and editors conducted by the *Film Daily:*
"Thief of Bagdad," "Beau Brummel," "Ten Command-
ments," "America," "Sea Hawk," "Secrets," "Girl
Shy," "Monsieur Beaucaire," "Marriage Circle,"
"Abraham Lincoln."

1925

January 10. Secretary of State Charles Evans Hughes resigned, to take effect March 4. President Coolidge chose Frank B. Kellogg, at the time Ambassador to Great Britain, to succeed him.

January 10. Charles B. Warren of Michigan was appointed Attorney-General of the United States to succeed Harlan F. Stone. On March 10, when Warren's name came before the Senate for action, strong opposition developed and the appointment failed of ratification. March 17, the President sent to the Senate the name of John Garibaldi Sargent, of Ludlow, Vt.; he was approved, the Senate suspending its rules to expedite the appointment.

January 31. A short, thin, wiry young man working as a reporter for a Louisville, Ky., newspaper, after hours of search in the subterranean labyrinth beneath Cave City, Ky., heard a faint call. Following it, he came upon his friend, Floyd Collins, lying on his back in a slanting passage where roof and floor were so close together that Collins's body, lying flat, just filled the space. Early the previous day, Collins, for whom the caves held a morbid allure, had gone underground on an exploring expedition — his last of many. Calmly, Collins told the reporter: "I was crawling out of Sand Cave, which is the most beautiful I have ever seen, when, soon after ascending a steep wall, I dislodged a huge rock. It caught my foot." For 24 hours he had lain there, shouting from time to time to attract the hunting party he was sure would be looking for him.

The reporter tried to drag Collins clear, but all his efforts were fruitless. Leaving Collins, he squirmed his way back out of the vault, and on reaching daylight notified the police.

Had the rock dislodged by Collins killed him outright instead of imprisoning him alive, the event would have received at most only a paragraph or two in the local newspapers. As it was, within a day or two Collins's name was on the first page of every newspaper in the country and bulletins about him were broadcast by radio; within a week the whole nation was absorbedly following the efforts at rescue. So great was the nationwide sympathy for the trapped man that it seemed almost a force capable by itself of dragging him out of his underground prison.

To several of those who at risk of their lives worked their way to Collins's side, bringing him food and the cheer of their company, he said he realized that "a lot of people" were trying to help him and that he was grateful. He himself, as long as his strength lasted, continued trying to extricate his mangled foot. As time wore on and attempts at his rescue were not successful, he became convinced that he was going to die, and his mind turned to prayer. Over and over again he would cry: "O Lord, dear Lord, gracious Lord, Jesus all powerful, get me out if it is thy will, but thy will be done."

As happens always, tragedy was accompanied by its twin, farce. With the beginning of rescue operations, crowds assembled at the entrance to the cave created disturbances and got in the way of the rescuers. Troops had to be called to keep them back. Then queer rumors started. One was, that the whole story was a hoax; another, that natives of the region were trying to obstruct the rescue attempts. A military court was set up and for three days spectators watched as a parade of witnesses gave testimony, while a short distance away frantic efforts were being made to save Collins.

The first plan put in effect by rescuers was to heat the boulder with gasoline torches so that it could be broken up. That proved unsuccessful. Collins himself pleaded that he be pulled out at the cost of his foot; that was tried, unsuccessfully. Meanwhile, a pair of insulated copper wires were strung through to where Collins was lying and an electric light bulb placed at his side. With light and food the horror of his situation was to a degree mitigated. However, the line had no sooner been strung when a cave-in occurred, shutting off the doomed man from his rescuers and preventing a surgeon, brought from Chicago to amputate his leg, from reaching him. From behind the slide workers heard him call out that he had freed his foot but was unable to move. That was the last time his voice was heard. An effort was now made to get to him through a shaft and tunnel started from outside. Sweating crews worked day and night. Finally, on February 16, the report was given out that Collins had been reached — he was dead. He was left there, because to remove the corpse would be dangerous to the rescuers. Funeral services were held on the hill above the cave.

February 2.   Into Nome, Alaska, at 5:36 on a black, howling winter morning limped a blinded half-frozen giant, Gunnar Kasson, clinging for support to the up-rights of a sled drawn by a half-frozen team of Alaskan huskies and malamutes. In a little twenty-pound box swathed in wrappings on the sled were 300,000 units of anti-diphtheria serum, carried by relays of dog-teams from the rail head at Nenana, 655 miles away, to combat an epidemic of the "black death" of the Northland — diphtheria — that had broken out at Nome. The trip was another epic of the Yukon, perhaps the greatest in the spectacular history of that adventurous region. From beginning to end it was a story of heroism, great skill, almost incredible endurance on the part of the men and dogs who took part in it. For five and a half days the relays struggled onward through the screaming blast of a 50-below-zero, 80-mile-an-hour blizzard, in blinding clouds of scourging snow, through waist-deep drifts over mountainous crags of pack-ice. To save precious time one of the drivers crossed the perilous mouth of Norton Bay on ice cracked and fissured by the heavy ground-swell of Bering Sea. The serum arrived in time and the one physician at Nome, Doctor Curtis Welch of the United States Public Health Service, aided by a handful of nurses, was able to stop the epidemic.

February 14. A daughter, Paulina, was born to Congressman and Mrs. Nicholas Longworth — Mrs. Longworth was the daughter of Theodore Roosevelt, President of the United States 1901–1909.

February 17. The Senate voted to increase the pay of members of the Senate and House from $7,500 to $10,000 a year, and the pay of the Vice-President, Speaker of the House, and Cabinet members from $12,-000 to $15,000. Previously the increases had been voted by the House. In neither Chamber was there a roll-call.

February 25. Senator Medill McCormick of Illinois died suddenly in Washington, aged 47.

March 4. For the first time in its existence of 135 ʻyears, the Senate of the United States was compelled to listen to an oral castigation from its presiding officer, the Vice-President of the United States. Washington had expected General Charles Gates Dawes to do the unconventional, and he lived up to expectations by vigorously denouncing the rules of the Senate, over which he was to preside for the next four years. Not only did General Dawes by his tirade stir up a tempest in a teapot, but also he stole the spotlight from the man who

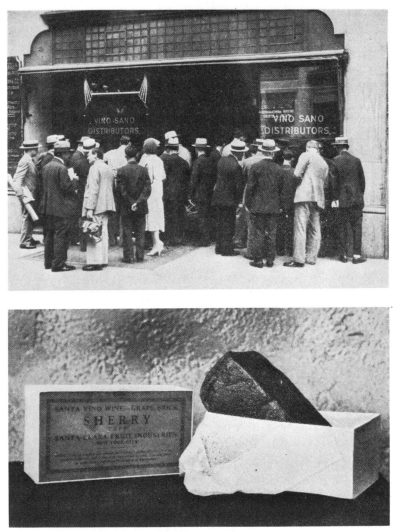

Photographs by Underwood & Underwood.

Top—A "wine brick" store with customers crowding the doorway.
Bottom—One of the "wine bricks," an invention of the later years of prohibition, from which fairly palatable wine of high alcoholic content could be made.

should have been the hero of the day, President Coolidge. The grounds for General Dawes's spectacular scolding of the Senate were shrewdly chosen — there was little the Senate could say in self-defense. "That rule," said the Vice-President, "which at times enables Senators to consume in oratory those last precious minutes of a session needed for momentous decisions, places in the hands of one or of a minority of Senators a greater power than the veto power exercised under the Constitution by the President of the United States." After the address, Senators of all parties in statements to the press denounced Dawes. The public, on the other hand, was delighted. Dawes was a hero. He had made a dent, as one observer put it, "in that fine old encrusted Senatorial tradition, buttressed by antique rules and practices, and solemnly defended by conservative and radical Senators alike."

March 6. While participating in a military manœuvre over Kelly Field, Texas, Cadet Charles A. Lindbergh collided with an airplane piloted by another student aviator and was forced to abandon his plane and descend to earth by parachute, thus becoming automatically a member of the select "Caterpillar Club" composed of aviators forced to "bail out" while in flight. Cadet Lindbergh, in his report on the accident, gave one of the most lucid and interesting descriptions ever written about such an adventure:[1]

A nine-ship SE-5 formation, commanded by Lieutenant Blackburn, was attacking a De Haviland 4B, flown by Lieutenant Russell Maughan at about a 5,000-foot altitude and several hundred feet above the clouds. I was flying on the left of the top unit, Lieutenant McAllister from the right. After Cadet Love pulled up, I continued to dive on the DH for a short time before pulling up to the left. I saw no other ship near by. I passed above the DH and a moment later felt a slight jolt, followed by a crash. My head was thrown forward against the cowling and my plane seemed to turn around and hang nearly motionless for an instant. I closed the throttle and saw an SE-5 with Lieutenant McAllister in the cockpit,

[1] Two years later, in 1927, he became world famous for making the first flight from New York to Paris.

a few feet on my left. He was apparently unhurt and getting ready to jump.

Our ships were locked together with the fuselages approximately parallel. My right wing was damaged and had folded back slightly, covering the forward right-hand corner of the cockpit. The ships started to mill around and the wires began whistling. The right wing commenced vibrating and striking my head at the bottom of each oscillation. I removed the rubber band safe tying the belt, unbuckled it, climbed out past the trailing edge of the damaged wing, and with my feet on the cowling on the right side of the cockpit, which was then in a nearly vertical position, I jumped backward as far from the ship as possible.

I had no difficulty in locating the pull-string and experienced no sensation of falling. The wreckage was falling nearly straight down, and for some time I fell in line with its path. Fearing the wreckage might fall on me, I did not pull the rip-cord until I had dropped several hundred feet and into the clouds. During this time I had turned one-half revolution and was falling flat and face downward. The parachute functioned perfectly; almost as soon as I pulled the rip-cord, the risers jerked on my shoulders, the leg straps tightened, my head went down and the chute was fully opened.

I saw Lieutenant McAllister floating above me and the wrecked ships pass about 100 yards to one side, continuing to spin to the right and leaving a trail of lighter fragments along their path. I watched them until, still locked together, they crashed in the mesquite about 2,000 feet below, and burst into flames several seconds after impact.

Next I turned my attention to locating a landing-place. I was over mesquite and drifting in the general direction of a plowed field, which I reached by slipping the 'chute. Shortly before striking the ground I was drifting backward, but was able to swing around in the harness just as I landed on the side of a ditch less than a hundred feet from the edge of the mesquite. Although the impact of the landing was too great for me to remain standing, I was not injured in any way. The parachute was still held open by the wind and did not collapse until I pulled in one group of the shroud lines.

March 23. By a vote of 63 to 14, the Senate ratified the Isle of Pines treaty, which vests ownership of that island in the Republic of Cuba. The treaty had been pending before the Senate since March 3, 1904.

April 1. Announcement was made by the New York banking house of Dillon, Read & Co., that it had purchased the Dodge Brothers automobile company for $146,000,000, the largest single cash transaction in America's industrial history. Eight days later, a banking syndicate organized under the leadership of Dillon, Read & Company, began to pass out to the public the securities of the new Dodge Company. These securities consisted of bonds, preferred stock, and two classes of common stock , A and B. The first issue was $85,000,-000 worth of 7 per cent preferred stock, each share carrying as a bonus a share of common stock, Class A. This issue was oversubscribed, as was also the second issue, an offering of $75,000,000 of 6 per cent bonds.

The Dodge Company had been started in 1914 by two brothers, Horace E. and John F. Dodge, who had been in the manufacturing business in Detroit since before the turn of the century. Their first big order had come from Henry Ford, for whom they continued to supply parts until their own automobile company was formed. In part payment for the materials supplied Ford they had taken stock in the Ford Company, which they sold in 1920 for an estimated $25,000,000. In 1920, both brothers died, and thereafter management of the business was in the competent hands of the trustees of their estates. The trustees, however, felt that "the continual change in industrial activities" menaced the security of the estates and put upon them personally a burden which they did not believe they should be made to bear. Their representations to the Dodge widows was the reason for the Company's sale.

April 13. Making a round trip, from Detroit to Chicago and back again, the "Maiden Dearborn," two-engined, all-metal Stout monoplane, inaugurated a private air transport system for the Ford Motor Company.

April 15. John Singer Sargent, American artist, died in London, at the age of 69.

April 29. The Indiana State Legislature passed the Wright Prohibition law which imposed a jail sentence and fine for the purchase or possession of liquor, for carrying it on the person, or for selling or giving it away, and made the smell of liquor in containers prima facie evidence of the operation of a "blind tiger."

April 30. Orville Wright announced that the origi-

The Wright airplane that made the first flight in history, December 17, 1903.

nal Wright airplane invented by himself and his brother, Wilbur, which made its first flight on December 17, 1903, would be sent to the Times Museum, South Kensington, England.

May 12. Miss Amy Lowell, poet, essayist and critic, died at her home in Brookline, Mass., aged 52. "A principality and a power" was the apt phrase used by the *Herald-Tribune* to describe her. Her principality was modern poetry, mainly in the realm of "free verse," though her title for it was "cadenced" verse; and the influence she had was almost autocratic in that field. Her last work, upon which she labored for five years, was a life of John Keats; upon this, in the opinion of critics, her fame would rest secure.

May 13.   By a vote of 76 to 2, the Florida House of Representatives passed the Senate bill requiring daily reading from the Bible in public schools.

May 15.   Lieut.-General Nelson A. Miles, retired, commander of the American forces in the war with

When cross-word puzzles were very much to the fore. From a drawing by Herb Roth in the New York *World*.

Spain, veteran officer of the Civil War and famous for his subjugation of the last warring tribes of Indians, died suddenly in Washington while attending a circus. He was eighty-six years old.

May.   A new vogue in the field of diversion, the cross-word puzzle, had outré philological consequences which a writer in *The Bookman* illustrated with a dialogue between two housewives:

Mrs. W.   What is that you are working at, my dear?

Mrs. F.   I'm tatting Joe's initials on his moreen vest. Are you making that ebon garment for yourself?

Mrs. W.   Yea. Just a black dress for every day. Henry says I look rather naif in black.

Mrs. F.   Well, perhaps; but it's a bit too anile for me. Give me something in indigo or, say, ecru.

Mrs. W.   Quite right. There is really no neb in such solemn vestments.

Mrs. F.   Stet.

Mrs. W.   By the way, didn't I hear that your little Junior met with an accident?

Mrs. F.   Yes. The little oaf fell from an apse and fractured his artus.

Mrs. W.   Egad.

June 18.   Senator Robert M. LaFollette of Wisconsin, leader of the progressive element in American politics, and candidate of the Progressive party for President in 1924, died in Washington. He was born June 14, 1855.

The Scopes Trial

July 21.   John Thomas Scopes, Tennessee high school teacher, was found guilty by a jury of teaching the theory of evolution in the Dayton, Tenn., high school.

Tennessee was the first of several States to enact laws prohibiting the teaching of evolution in State-supported schools. The Tennessee statute, which went into effect March 21, 1925, read: "Be it enacted — that it shall be unlawful for any teacher in any of the universities, normals, and all other public schools of the State which are supported in whole or in part by the public school funds of the State, to teach any theory that denies the story of the Divine Creation of man as taught in the Bible, and to teach instead that man has descended from a lower order of animals." Much acrid debate had attended the passage of the law through the Legislature, with Fundamentalists solidly for it, Modernists against it.

With the law in effect, no attempt was made at its enforcement by the State authorities and doubtless in time it would have become a dead letter had it not been for the bitter fight to keep the bill from being enacted. One of those who had fought the bill's passage was a jocose, free-thinking mining engineer, George Rappelyea. In sympathy with Rappelyea's views was the 24-year-old high school teacher Scopes, who, in his classes used a biology text-book, approved by the State Board of Education, which taught the theory of evolution. To Rappelyea's half-serious suggestion that he bring a court action against Scopes for violating the law, Scopes gave enthusiastic consent. Thereupon Rappelyea swore out a warrant for his arrest and Scopes gave himself into custody, being released on a bond provided by the American Civil Liberties Union.

In the strange drama that followed, the attention of the country, and indeed of all the civilized world, was fixed on the normally humdrum little town of Dayton. Not only were people everywhere deeply interested in the issue at stake — dissension between Fundamentalists and Modernists was raging in almost every community — they were interested even more in the event as a spectacle, a battle between giants. Chief aid to Attorney-General Stewart of the prosecution was William Jennings Bryan, long a political leader and for some years prior to 1925 a zealous and indefatigable champion of the Bible against some of the teachings of biological 'science. Opposing Bryan, as defense counsel, was Clarence Darrow, agnostic, famous liberal, criminal lawyer, who a year before had defended Richard Loeb and Nathan Leopold in the trial for the "thrill killing" of little Robert Franks. An added fillip of dramatic bizarrerie was given by photographs widely published in the newspapers showing the two leading adversaries, Bryan and Darrow, chatting amiably together or posing with their arms around each other's shoulders. Once the trial got under way, the long-standing personal friendship between the two was forgotten; each fought ruthlessly, with every resource at his command. Bryan charged Darrow with "slurring the Bible" and being an enemy of Christianity; Darrow did his best to make Bryan out a bigot and a fool.

Into Dayton on the day the trial opened trekked hundreds of Tennesseans from the surrounding mountains, Fundamentalists in viewpoint but curious too as to what was behind all the talk of monkeys and amœbas, the origin of the species, Darwin and Huxley, survival of the fittest. Rubbing elbows with them on the crowded sidewalks were well-dressed folk from nearby cities, drawn to Dayton by the prospect of a Roman holiday. Lodged about town, in such cramped accommodations as they were able to find, were more than a hundred newspaper men, among them Henry Mencken, "sage of Baltimore," long-time caustic critic of things American. To handle the reporters' despatches, telegraphic facilities sufficient for a large city were set up in lofts over stores, but even these proved less than adequate for the two million words of press matter filed for transmission during the twelve days the trial lasted.

Coincident with the trial's beginning, July 10, a heat wave struck Dayton, making the atmosphere of the tiny crowded courtroom almost unendurably hot. Bryan, Darrow, and even austere Judge Raulston, sans coats, shirts open at the neck, mopped perspiring brows and stirred the stifling air with palm-leaf fans.

The highest point of the trial came on July 20, when Defense Attorney Arthur Garfield Hays proposed that Bryan be put on the stand as an expert on the Bible, and Bryan consented. Because of the heat and the crowd, Judge Raulston mercifully moved his court out of doors to the shady lawn before the courthouse, and there the inquisition of Bryan, which turned out to be the greatest humiliation of his life, took place.

Darrow asked Bryan about Jonah and the whale, Joshua and the sun, where Cain got his wife, the date of the Flood, the significance of the Tower of Babel. Bryan affirmed his belief that the world was created in 4004 B.C. and the Flood occurred in or about 2348 B.C.; that Eve was literally made out of Adam's rib; that the Tower of Babel was responsible for the diversity of languages in the world; and that a "big fish" had swallowed Jonah. When Darrow asked him if he had ever discovered where Cain got his wife, Bryan answered: "No, sir; I leave the agnostics to hunt for her." When Darrow inquired, "Do you say you do not believe that there were any civilizations on this earth that reach back beyond five thousand years?" Bryan stoutly replied, "I am not satisfied by any evidence I have seen." Tempers were getting frazzled by the strain and the heat; once Darrow declared that his purpose in examining Bryan was "to show up Fundamentalism . . . to prevent bigots and ignoramuses from controlling the educational system of the United States," and Bryan jumped up, his face purple, and shook his fist at Darrow, crying, "To protect the word of God against the greatest atheist and agnostic in the United States!"[2]

Next day, with the refusal of Judge Raulston to admit the testimony of scientists, as demanded by the defense, the trial ended, with Scopes losing. An appeal was taken but the Tennessee Supreme Court, wisely deciding that the peace of the State was more to be desired than the judicial settlement of a question that could not be settled, made short shrift of the appeal, declared the law constitutional, and freed Scopes on a technicality.

[2] "Only Yesterday," Frederick L. Allen.

A regretted aftermath to the trial was the death of Bryan on July 26, undoubtedly hastened if not caused by the strain and fatigue of defending the religious beliefs which had become the central interest of the later years of his life.

September 3. The *Shenandoah*, one of America's two great dirigibles of the Zeppelin type, while flying during a storm near Cambridge, Ohio, collapsed and fell to the ground, with the loss of fourteen of its officers and crew.

September 10. The missing naval seaplane *PN-9* No. 1, with its crew of five men, under Commander John Rodgers, was picked up fifteen miles east of Kauai, of the Hawaiian Islands, by the submarine *R-4*, after the plane had been adrift nine days.

September 15. Robert M. LaFollette, Jr., won the primary elections of the Republican party in Wisconsin to determine the party nominee to fill the vacancy in the United States Senate left by the death of his father, Robert M. LaFollette, Sr.

October 7. "Christy" Mathewson, so-called "Big Six" of baseball pitchers, died of tubercular pneumonia at Saranac Lake, N. Y., after an illness lasting several years. "The best-loved of all the baseball players and the most popular of all American athletes of all time" — was Mathewson, according to a despatch from Pittsburgh, where the first game of the 1925 world series had just been played, by W. O. McGeehan, sports writer for the New York *Herald-Tribune*. Continuing his tribute to "Matty," McGeehan, who ranked among sports writers about as Mathewson did in baseball, said:

Always a cheerful and fair fighter, he lost a most unfair fight. Mathewson in his prime had sinews of steel in his right arm, he had speed, he had everything, they said, but his greatest asset was his calm courage. This held him up, cheerful and calm, to meet the end. . . .

In the old days it was a Polo Grounds tragedy when Matty was batted out of the box. When Matty failed, the Giants failed, and everything was wrong. The bulletin, "Mathewson out of the game," always saddened the fans while Mathewson was young Christy Mathewson with the strength still in that right arm and the vitality to come back. Toward the last

"Christy" Mathewson.

this began to happen more frequently, and those who loved the game for the game's sake became sadder.

Then there came the day when Mathewson himself decided that his pitching days were over, and announced that he would stand in the box no more. To thousands the game never could be the same without Matty. But after he gave up active playing his influence remained with the sport to which he had given all of his splendid, vital youth.

October 14. Harvey S. Firestone, tire manufacturer, announced the completion of an agreement with the Liberian Government by which the Firestone Plantation Company obtained a ninety-nine-year lease of one million acres of land suitable for rubber-growing.

October. All of America's gold rushes, all her oil booms, and all her free-land stampedes dwindled by comparison with the torrent of migration pouring into Florida during the early fall months of 1925. If Ponce de Leon's Fountain of Youth had just been found, it could hardly have attracted a greater multitude. Motor roads throughout Florida were crowded with cars from every State in the Union, while added streams of humanity arrived by steamship, by train, and afoot. Roadsides were dotted with tent colonies of tourists and fortune-seekers. It was such a development as was never before seen, in America or anywhere else. Miami, a city of 10,000 at the turn of the century, had become a metropolis of 150,000 and was planning for a million in another ten years. And what was taking place in Miami was taking place on an equal scale in other parts of the State. "The lots that are platted and staked out for sale," wrote one observer, "and the acreage that has been sold to be subdivided, amounted to approximately 20,000,000 lots." Thousands of orange groves on the ridge country were destroyed to make way for town sites. The road from Jacksonville to Miami, more than 300 miles long, was practically a city street, with mushroom settlements along practically its entire length. In Miami especially, but also on the West Coast and indeed almost everywhere in the State, the buying and selling of land was the paramount industry, organized on mass production lines. Methods of the most ingenious sort were evolved for drawing prospective buyers to land developments and there getting their signatures to contracts. Free bus rides and free luncheons lured buyers by the thousand to subdivisions where they were worked on by high pressure salesmen. Any and every device that would assemble a crowd was resorted to. Day after day for months during the winter of 1924–25 William

Jennings Bryan had delivered a daily oration as part of the crowd-attracting ballyhoo of a real-estate firm at Coral Gables.

November 3. James J. Walker, Democrat, formerly State Senator, was elected Mayor of New York City by a majority of approximately 400,000 over his Republican opponent, Frank D. Waterman.

November 19. In a widely commented-on speech before the Chamber of Commerce of New York State, President Coolidge called for co-operation between the Government and business, each in its own sphere. He warned American bankers to see that money loaned abroad was not used for military or unproductive purposes, and plead that the United States join the World Court. Business, he said, in a passage which provoked much discussion, "rests squarely on the law of service. It has for its main reliance truth and faith and justice. In its larger sense it is one of the greatest contributing forces to the moral and spiritual advancement of the race."

November 29. Publication of a report on waste elimination in industry by Secretary of Commerce Herbert Hoover led to widespread discussion, of which the following editorial from the Detroit *News* was typical:

Mr. Hoover has been in office a little more than four years. In that time he has elevated a relatively unimportant Cabinet position to one of major rank, by creating opportunities for endeavor and following them up with all the resources at his disposal. Other Secretaries in times past have had the same resources, but they lacked Mr. Hoover's vision, his organizing ability, and his passion for obtaining results.

It was freely predicted after the war ended that the United States was threatened by an industrial slump. Europe, with its cheap labor, would undersell American goods all over the world, and might penetrate America herself, regardless of her tariff wall. The American foreign market, built up during the war, would be lost; America would produce for herself alone; there would be hard times, and a vast contraction of industry.

But there has been nothing of the sort, for the simple reason that Hoover saw the threat to our prosperity. Instead, however, of giving up to pessimism and fear, he worked out the answer. That answer lay in elimination of waste; in greater efficiency; not in cutting wages, but in raising them, so that contented labor would do better work.

An estimate of the annual saving to American business resulting from Mr. Hoover's labors put the sum at the immense total of $500,000,000. In comment on this, the writer of this history, in a newspaper despatch, stated:

If all this were the news of a sensational gold discovery it would go on the first page, and recall to older readers the streaming headlines of the Klondike gold rush. Yet all the gold taken from the Klondike during the seven years its richness lasted was less than $100,000,000, whereas the "astonishing economic transformation" recorded in the Commerce Department report constitutes an enrichment of America amounting probably to at least $500,000,000 in a single year.

November. Harold "Red" Grange, whose exploits as a football player on the team of the University of Illinois brought him a nation-wide renown so great as to set a new norm for fame in college athletics, abandoned his college career and became a member of a professional team, at a salary which, together with the other financial returns accruing from his status as a professional celebrity, was said to place him in the higher brackets of income-tax payers. Grange's decision came shortly after the Illinois-Pennsylvania football game of October 31, on which occasion the young man reached the peak of his prowess and afforded so spectacular a spectacle that George Trevor, hardy sports writer for the Brooklyn *Eagle*, confessed himself so moved that he could not collect his faculties to write his despatch until an hour after the game was over. Mr. Trevor's description of the game, written after his nerves had quieted, gives an eloquent picture of Grange at his more than best, and answers the query sure to be asked by later generations of sports lovers, what it was about Grange's playing that caused scores of thousands of people to flock to games in which he played and other millions to listen to Graham McNamee's radio broadcasts of the plays:

Picture to yourself a cadaverous face, deeply etched with the grooves that bespeak ascetic self-denial and years of rigorous training. A sad face, radiating grim determination, the corners of the mouth drawn down to heighten the forbidding aspect. Grange looks as though he means business. His bearing, his walk, his postures are impressively dramatic. He is the all-time all-American halfback in flesh and blood.

In action, Grange is a composite moving picture of the great backs we have seen in the past, with an added something that sets him in a class apart. Calmly, with exasperating deliberation, he takes his station behind the rangy Illinois line, the last man in a triple tandem. There is no lost motion, no wasted effort. Every move has a meaning. Red plays football with his brains as well as his body. Like a baseball shortstop, body thrust forward, legs spread apart, hands resting on knees, Grange awaits the ball. As stealthily as a shadow he dogs his interference, only to split away from it at the psychological moment.

With infinite care — like a slow-motion picture — he picks his way through the line. Then, with the zip of a skyrocket leaving its shell, he is off· once in the open he throws in high gear.

As a tackler dives for him Red twists his torso like a contortionist and sidles sideways like a fiddler-crab. Out goes that straight arm, down goes the tackler, off goes Grange.

He has the knack of shortening or lengthening his stride instantaneously; he has the speed to outsprint the fastest defensive back, the guile to sidestep the adroitest tackler, the strength to straight arm the most powerful adversary.

December 29. The Board of Trustees of Trinity College, North Carolina, decided to change the name to Duke University in order to meet the terms of the $40,-000,000-trust fund established by James B. Duke.

December. Bryn Mawr, a leader among America's colleges for women, revoked a twenty-eight-year rule against smoking by students within the confines of the college. Echoing interest which this action everywhere aroused were hundreds of editorials, for the most part expressing approval though some were uncompromising in dissent — the whole constituting a significant foot-note in the history of the feminist movement in America and in the evolution of American social customs. The Indianapolis *News*, in thoughtful and representative comment, said:

This part of the country still looks askance at the girl who indulges the habit in public, although privately the cigaret has long since lost the element of novelty. Young girls think it smart; some women think it bohemian. Others enjoy smoking and see no reason why they should be criticized. Their argument does not readily admit an answer.

The head of Bryn Mawr has realized that she is dealing with a condition and not a theory. The girls at the college, perhaps 50 per cent of them at least, have been smoking clandestinely, and in addition to the sport of puffing away at their cigarets probably have derived more pleasure from the fact that they were doing something forbidden by the college rules. If the institution officially sanctions smoking and provides a place where the girls may indulge the habit, it may be spiking the guns of those who clamored for the right partly because it was denied. With a special smoking-room set aside for the smokers, the ban on the use of cigarets elsewhere on the campus likely will be strictly enforced. This plan of handling the situation in that type of college should offer the best way out of a puzzling situation.

Books in 1925

"Life of Abraham Lincoln," by W. E. Barton. . . . "Beau Geste," by Percival Christopher Wren, mystery story of life and adventure in the French Foreign Legion. . . . "The Constant Nymph," by Margaret Kennedy. . . . "Drums," a novel of the American

Revolution, by James Boyd. . . . "Wild Geese," by Martha Ostenso, tale of the Scandinavian Northwest. . . . "The Perennial Bachelor," by Anne Parrish; it won the Harper Prize. . . . "An American Tragedy," by Theodore Dreiser, called by *The Nation* "the greatest American novel of our generation." . . . "Arrowsmith," by Sinclair Lewis; Lewis declined the Pulitzer prize for this novel in 1926. . . . "Sorrell and Son," by Warwick Deeping, "one of the magnetic creations of modern fiction." . . . "Carry On, Jeeves," by P. G. Wodehouse. . . . "Father Abraham," by Irving Bacheller. . . . "Private Life of Helen of Troy," by John Erskine. . . . "The Red Lamp," by Mary Roberts Rinehart. . . . "Barren Ground," by Ellen Glasgow. . . . "The Professor's House," by Willa Cather, which "depicts mechanized standards of social life." . . . "Pig Iron," by Charles G. Norris. . . . "Manhattan Transfer," by John Dos Passos. . . . "Thunder on the Left," by Christopher Morley. . . . "Twice Thirty," by Edward Bok. . . . "Virgin Flame," by Ernest Pascal. . . . "He Was a Man," by Rose Wilder Lane. . . . "God's Stepchildren," by Sarah G. Millin, moving record of miscegenation in South Africa. . . . "Jungle Days," by William Beebe. . . . "The Mother's Recompense," by Edith Wharton. . . . "The Great Gatsby," by F. Scott Fitzgerald. . . . "Points of Honor," by Thomas Boyd, a war book. . . . "Sea Horses," by Frances Brett Young. . . . "The Crazy Fool," by Donald Ogden Stewart. . . . "St. Mawr," by D. H. Lawrence. . . . "Dark Laughter," by Sherwood Anderson. . . . "The Venetian Glass Nephew," by Elinor Wylie. . . . "Possession," by Louis Bromfield. . . . "The Crystal Cup," by Gertrude Atherton. . . . "The Life of Sir William Osler," by Dr. Harvey Cushing, winner of the Pulitzer prize for biography.

The Theatre in 1925

Helen MacKellar in "The Mud Turtle." . . . "The Kiss in the Taxi," a French farce with Arthur Byron. . . . Eugene O'Neill's "Desire Under the Elms," which *Life* characterized "the stirrings of sex in the rock-ribbed Massachusetts farmlands." . . . "They Knew What They Wanted." . . . "White Cargo." . . . George White's "Scandals." . . . "What Price Glory." . . . Earl Carroll's "Vanities." . . . Charles Bickford and James Cagney in "Outside Looking In," a dramatization of Jim Tully's "Beggars of Life." . . . Holbrook Blinn and Judith Anderson in "The Dove." . . . Noel Coward in his own play "The Vortex." . . . Lynn Fontanne and Alfred Lunt in "Arms and the Man." . . . Katharine Cornell, magnificent in "The Green Hat." . . . Marilyn Miller in "Sunny." . . . E. H. Sothern in Brieux's dialectic drama "Accused." . . . Lionel Atwill and Helen Hayes in "Cæsar and Cleopatra." . . . Chrystal Herne in "Craig's Wife." . . . "Hamlet," in modern dress, with Basil Sidney as the Prince in tuxedo. . . . "Hamlet," in regulation costumes, with Walter Hampden and Ethel Barrymore. . . . Madge Kennedy in "Beware of Widows."

The Motion Pictures in 1925

The ten best pictures of the year, as determined by a vote of critics and editors conducted by the *Film Daily*: "Gold Rush," "Merry Widow," "Phantom of the Opera," "Miss Me Again," "Unholy Three," "Last Laugh," "Lost World," "Don Q. Son of Zorro," "The Freshman," "Big Parade."

INDEX

INDEX

657

COMPLETE INDEX

COVERING

OUR TIMES

VOLUMES I–VI

COMPLETE INDEX

Abbey, Edwin A., IV, 580.
Abbott, Lawrence F., II, 445; IV, 312
    (*f.n.*), 322 (*f.n.*), 428 (*f.n.*), 430
    (*f.n.*).
Abbott, Dr. Lyman, IV, 411 (*f.n.*);
    V, 467.
ABC countries, V, 584.
Abruzzi, Duke of, I, 526.
Acheson, Samuel Houston, III, 276
    (*f.n.*).
Actors and Actresses—
    Adams, Maude, I, 567, 602; II, 624,
        646, 648; III, 463, 559; IV, 583;
        V, 593.
    Allen, Viola, I, 567; II, 647; III, 468.
    Ames, Winthrop, VI, 566.
    Anderson, Judith, VI, 629, 653.
    Anglin, Margaret, I, 567; II, 625;
        III, 461; IV, 584; V, 659; VI, 550.
    Arliss, George, III, 559; IV, 584;
        V, 641; VI, 566, 630.
    Atwill, Lionel, VI, 566, 629, 653.
    Bacon, Frank, VI, 566.
    Bainter, Fay, V, 641.
    Bara, Theda, VI, 551.
    Barrymore, Ethel, I, 567, 581; II,
        624, 634; III, 527, 559; IV, 572,
        602, 609; V, 629, 659; VI, 525, 591,
        608, 653.
    Barrymore, John, II, 634; III, 468;
        IV, 555, 572; V, 614, 659; VI, 549,
        551, 591.
    Barrymore, Lionel, II, 634; III, 468;
        VI, 549, 609.
    Barrymore, Maurice, II, 634.
    Bates, Blanche, I, 229, 581; II, 646,
        649; III, 559; V, 593; VI, 525.
    Bayes, Nora, III, 364 (*f.n.*), 526; V,
        641; VI, 566.
    Bellew, Kyrle, I, 567, 602; III, 528.
    Ben Greet Players, I, 601; II, 649;
        IV, 571.
    Bennett, Richard, VI, 549.
    Bernard, Barney, VI, 591.
    Bernhardt, Sarah, II, 648; III, 463;
        V, 629.
    Bickford, Charles, VI, 653.
    Bigelow, Charles A., III, 467.
    Bingham, Amelia, I, 567; II, 625.
    Blackmer, Sidney, VI, 630.
    Blinn, Holbrook, VI, 653.
    Brady, Alice, IV, 584; V, 593, 661;
        VI, 608, 609.

Brian, Donald, V, 593.
Burke, Billie, III, 527; IV, 585, 602,
    610; V, 593; VI, 525, 567, 591.
Byron, Arthur, VI, 653.
Cagney, James, VI, 653.
Cahill, Marie, IV, 584.
Calhearn, Louis, VI, 629.
Calvé, Emma, I, 263.
Campbell, Mrs. Patrick, I, 582; II,
    626; IV, 186; V, 593.
Cantor, Eddie, VI, 448 (*f.n.*).
Carr, Alexander, VI, 591.
Carter, Mrs. Leslie, I, 229, 567, 581;
    II, 647; VI, 566.
Caruso, Enrico, II, 628.
Castle, Vernon, III, 467; IV, 49, 258.
Cawthorn, Joseph, V, 641.
Chapin, Benjamin, III, 469.
Chatterton, Ruth, IV, 602.
Claire, Ina, V, 614, 641; VI, 524, 550,
    566, 591.
Cohan, George M., I, 232, 568; II,
    647; III, 559; IV, 610; V, 593, 613.
Cole and Johnson, III, 383.
Collier, William, IV, 602; V, 593, 614.
Cook, Joe, VI, 609.
Corbett, James J., III, 462.
Cornell, Katherine, VI, 566, 609, 629,
    653.
Courtenay, William, VI, 566.
Coward, Noel, VI, 653.
Cowl, Jane, IV, 609, 610; V, 641;
    VI, 549, 629.
Crane, William H., I, 232; II, 625;
    III, 469, 559.
Craven, Frank, II, 648; V, 593.
Crews, Laura Hope, V, 614; VI, 566.
Crosman, Henrietta, III, 468.
Dailey, Peter F., III, 467.
Daly, Arnold, II, 625, 626, 647, 648;
    III, 462.
Dawn, Hazel, IV, 585; V, 614.
Dean, Julia, IV, 585.
Ditrichstein, Leo, II, 626; V, 614;
    VI, 550.
Deslys, Gaby, IV, 610; V, 627.
Dixey, Henry E., I, 601; II, 648; IV,
    584; V, 629.
Dockstader, Lew, VI, 621.
Doro, Marie, V, 593.
D'Orsay, Lawrence, I, 601; II, 646;
    III, 470.
Dovey, Alice, IV, 585.

677